If yesterday I fought you as an enemy,
today you have become a friend with the
same national interest, loyalty, rights
and duties as myself. If yesterday you
hated me, today you cannot avoid the love
that binds you to me and me to you.

—Prime Minister Robert Mugabe
as Rhodesia became Zimbabwe, 1980.

Reggae

INTERNATIONAL

Stephen Davis
Peter Simon

THAMES AND HUDSON

The countenance of one man
Brighteneth another
Iron sharpen Iron

First published in Great Britain in 1983 by Thames and Hudson Ltd, London, in association with Rogner & Bernhard, München

Stephen Davis is a writer with a special interest in music. **Reggae International** is the second volume of a projected trilogy of books about Jamaica. The first, **Reggae Bloodlines** (also with Peter Simon), was published in 1977. The trilogy will be completed by a forthcoming biography of Bob Marley. Stephen Davis has also written a book about music in Morocco, to be published shortly. He lives in Blue Hills, Massachusetts.

Peter Simon's books include **Holding On / Moving Still** (1971), **Decent Exposures** (1973), **Carly Simon Complete** (1975), **Reggae Bloodlines** (with Stephen Davis — 1977), **Goin' Back to Houston** (1978), **On the Vineyard** (1980). An avid reggae broadcaster, he has hosted reggae shows in stations all over New England, and currently presides over a program called "Reggae Bloodlines" on WGBH-FM, Boston. Peter Simon lives in Gay Head, Massachusetts.

Associate Editors: Adrian Boot, Luke Ehrlich, Roger Steffens and Jon Goodchild.
Book design and production: Jon Goodchild and Type By Design, Fairfax, California. Photo credits appear on page 192. Front cover: Peter Simon and Daniel Lainé.

The Editors extend deep thanks to all our friends who helped on **Reggae International:** Thomas Landshoff, Dominic Sicilia, Coco Pekelis, David Dalton, Donna Herman, Bill Berkson, Sara Schrom, Craig DuMonte, Howard Greenberg, Michael Caccia, Danny Schecter, Al Larkin (**The Boston Globe**), Ed Dwyer, Byron Reimus (Ruder & Finn), Charlie Comer, American Airlines, Michael Thelwell, Billy Glasser, Gordon Rohlehr, Lauren Jones, Chuck Krall, Ted Halperin, Rob Partridge, Chris May, Dan and Rebecca Mortimer, Gene Greene, Graham Dawes, Roy Pace, Christopher Davis, Bay State Dick, Lily Aisha, Ronni Susan Simon, Cosmos Simon, Kate Simon, James Isaacs, Archives, Rob Friedlander and Units 1 and 2, Judith Arons, Jeff Steinberg (RIP), and Mum.

A special note of thanks to associate editors Roger Steffens and Luke Ehrlich, whose generous knowledge and difficult editorial work helped make this project possible, and more fun.

For our friends and colleagues on the island of Jamaica, we give special thanks: Edward Seaga, Neville Gallimore, Byron Henry, Suzanne McManus, Perry Henzell, Robin Farquharson, Andy Bassford, Paul Issa, Trevor Fearon, Valerie Cowan, Dermot Hussey, G. White, Orville, Rick of Rick's Cafe, Negril; John Dread, Hansel Dunn, Pauline Henry, Johny Blacke, and the management and staffs of the following: New Kingston Hotel, Sutton Place Hotel, Royal Caribbean Hotel, Casa Montego, San Souci in Ocho Rios, the Intercontinental Hotels in Ocho Rios and Kingston, St. Andrew's Guest House, and Hedonism II in Negril (formerly Negril Beach Village).

Special thanks to the National Library of Jamaica, Jamaica Information Service and the Jamaica Tourist Board for their kind assistance and access to their picture archives in Kingston.

Reggae dis a reggae
Dis a roots rock reggae
Reggae dis a reggae
Its an African reggae

Reggae gone international
Reggae gone multinational

Me say we mek it down in yard
And export it out abroad
Mix it down on tape
And transfer it to record

Reggae gone international
Reggae gone multinational

Well we make 45s and
We make LPs
Its a little sound
For you and for me

Reggae gone international
Reggae gone multinational

Me seh me hear it on radio
And see it pon television
Hear it in America
And hear it in London

Reggae gone international
Reggae gone multinational

Reggae make you feel
Make you feel alright
Doesn't matter if you're black
If you're brown or if you're white

Reggae gone international
Reggae gone multinational

Well we started with the ska
Then rock steady and now reggae
Ska and the rock steady
Pave the way for the reggae

Reggae gone international
Reggae gone multinational

Me seh me hear it on Venus
And me hear it on Mars
Feel it in the sun
And the moon and stars

Reggae gone international
Reggae gone multinational

"Reggae Gone International"
Michael "Mikey Dread" Campbell

C O N T E N T S

In 1977 Peter Simon and I published *Reggae Bloodlines*, a book about reggae music based on a research visit we had made to Jamaica the previous year. Three years later, in 1980, we saw an astonishing image on television: a million Irish schoolchildren singing "By the Rivers of Babylon" to Pope John Paul II on the occasion of his visit to Dublin.

Not long after that, we discovered that "The Harder They Come" is the fight song at some university in New Mexico. Everywhere we went —Morocco, Paris, Indonesia, Brazil—people were listening to reggae. A whole generation had discovered that, culturally, the reggae life can be *it*, exactly what's been needed, a hip and humane cultural life that really *means* something righteous, optimistic, spiritual, something that's so essentially wholesome that it's almost illegal.

Reggae is dance music and a philosophy that heals. "It's the healing of the nations. It was written from creation." The mini-trance conjured by hard roots reggae is in reality Jamaican psychic hygiene for our very troubled millenial times.

Reggae International is an anthology of essays and interviews connected to the amazing Jamaican cultural diaspora of the last ten years, which has seen a vital immigrant culture take root firmly in North America, Europe, Asia and the whole of Africa. (I'm reminded of the friend who traveled to extreme northwest Nepal and spent the night in the house of a village elder high in the Himalayas, passing the evening passing the chillum and listening to his Nepalese host's collection of bootleg Hong Kong Bob Marley cassettes.) Some of the material in *Reggae International* has been published before, but most has been commissioned especially for this book.

The writers are Jamaican, American and English. We suspect in the next anthology they'll all be Japanese, Nigerian and Dutch. Wherever possible, we use interviews to let the Jamaican and Anglo-Jamaican musicians tell their own stories.

While not posing as a reggae encyclopedia, *Reggae International* aims to be definitive. Michael Manley's introduction is based on his experience as prime minister of Jamaica in the years (1972–80) that both reggae and his country exploded onto the international wavelength.

Garth White's histories of the pre-reggae Jamaican music of the last 500 years, and of the ska and rock steady eras, are born of his work at Kingston's African-Caribbean Institute.

Carl Gayle, whose jeremiad on the deejays is the soul of this particular text, is one of the founders of reggae journalism and the editor of the exalted *Jahugliman* magazine, published in Kingston.

Trevor Fearon, who introduces the chapter on reggae singers, wrote some very important reggae reportage for the *Jamaica Daily News*.

Mervyn Morris, who writes on the dub poets, is himself a major Jamaican poet of especially beautiful sensibility, and teaches poetry at the University of the West Indies.

Wherever possible, we asked musicians to write about reggae. Luke Ehrlich, who writes on the history of dub and on the reggae arrangement, is both a reggae historian and bassist for the I-Tones, based in Cambridge, Massachusetts. Lenny Kaye writes on white reggae with the authority of an early participant in the great white reggae experiment as guitarist with the Patti Smith Group. Crispin Cioe, who interviews Sly & Robbie, is a saxophone player based in Manhattan (his group is called The Uptown Horns) and contributor to *Musician* magazine. Linton Kwesi Johnson does not even claim he is a musician, but his gripping music is ranked very high by most reggae fans nevertheless.

Tim White, who writes on Bob Marley and the Wailers, is one of the most widely read writers in America from his work for *Rolling Stone*. Carol Cooper, who writes here on reggae women, is best known to reggae fans from her important pieces for the *Village Voice*. Randall Grass, who writes on early reggae and harmony trios, is also a *Voice* contributor. Chris May writes on reggae in England from the persepective of the editor's chair at *Black Music & Jazz Review*, London.

Dick Hebdige contributes his essay on the 2 tone movement as a kind of disembodied adjunct to his masterwork, *Subculture—The Meaning of Style* (Methuen). And Rory Sanders' Rastafarian primer is an outgrowth of her research both in Jamaica and at Harvard Divinity School.

Other friends, other voices, other eyes: Roger Steffens, responsible for some of our best interviews and an associate editor of this book, is also a reggae fan of legendary appetite and broadcasts "The Reggae Beat," over KCRW-FM, Santa Monica, California. David Silver, whose "Reggae Epiphanies" describe the soaring life experiences of the hard-core reggae addict, is an Englishman transplanted to the wilds of New York, where he works in films and television.

Among the many photographers whose images grace this project are Adrian Boot (also associate editor) of Surrey, England; Kate Simon, some of whose work was accomplished on assignment for Island Records; David Burnett, a New York-based photographer who has worked extensively in Jamaica; top-ranking Jamaican photographers Robin Farquharson and Johnnie Black; Chuck Krall of Los Angeles; Daniel Lainé of Paris, France; as well as Kwame Braithwaite, Gerard Rancinan, Alan Reininger, Annie Leibowitz, Alan Greenberg, Kim Gottlieb and others. As always, Peter Simon spent two years with his psychic antennae attuned to capture the *pic juste*.

Finally, the authors have been helped immeasurably by dozens of reggae disc jockeys who blast out Jamaican music from the safety of college and public radio stations all over. Particular thanks to Doug Wendt of KTIM-FM, San Rafael, Cal; Lance Linares of KUSP-FM, Santa Cruz, Cal; and Michael Perkins of WERS-FM, Boston, Mass.

We're all rooting for the same cause.

—*Stephen Davis, September 1982*

Opposite: He does not paint/
pictures/of sunsets/colourful
landscapes/meaning/less
abstracts . . . He paints/pictures/
of twisted tortured/bodies
burning/labouring under raging
sun/youths/with stabbing eyes/
that tell tales/abstracts/that
kindle fire/and liberate
—Oku Onuora, "The Painter"

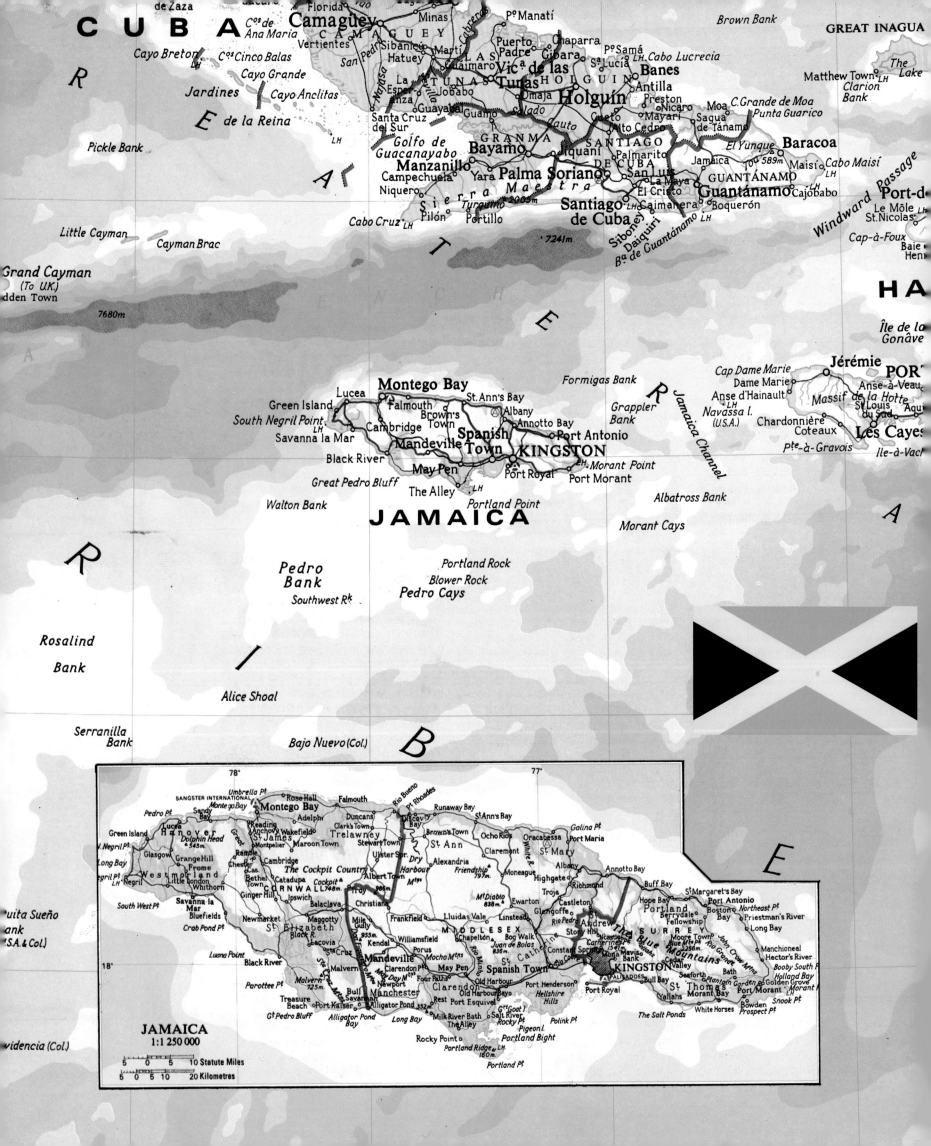

Reggae, the Revolutionary Impulse

It is important to distinguish two things. The first has to do with the process by which folk music takes on the characteristics of a national art form. The second has to do with how music goes beyond national boundaries to become a part of an international culture. Throughout the ages, in Europe, for example, traditional village songs and dances would spread within the boundaries of the nation states that were emerging. A polonaise or a mazurka would attain a national status. In due course, they would form a part of the thematic basis of the music of a Brahms or a Chopin, and by those means would enter the realm of international communication. In this case, the two processes are comparatively easy to identify and understand because of continuity and contiguity. The peoples of Europe, each in their national area, have been in continuous occupation of their territory without significant interruption for a thousand years, sometimes more. The nations involved carried on a curious double existence. They fought and killed each other with monotonous regularity. At the same time their upper classes were evolving a culture that spread amongst and between aristocracies who were really neighbours.

European civilization has no new folk statement to make because its people have all long since been homogenized by the interaction between the industrial revolution and modern communications. Folk culture reflects the individuality of communal life which expresses itself in a distinctive way because it is itself distinct.

Consequently, one must look to the Third World to discover a surviving folk culture, because they are not yet fully homogenized; although the lumps, grits and sinews of individuality are probably disappearing more rapidly than is realised.

Within the Third World, there is a unique social phenomenon. It was created by one of the terrible diasporas of history. The slave trade, stretching in the main from the 17th to the 18th centuries, uprooted millions of black Africans, depositing them throughout the Caribbean, the United States and the more northerly regions of Latin America. There our ancestors were subjected to the most systematic and sustained act of deculturisation in modern history. Here was no oppression of a people on their native soil. The

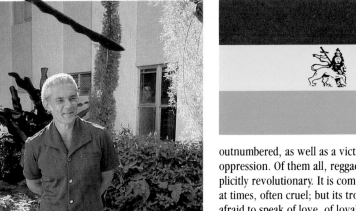

slave had no familiar ancestral earth into which to plant his feet and dig his toes while waiting for the tide of oppression to recede or the opportunity for rebellion to present itself. The slaves were uprooted, detribalised, de-named, de-humanised. The only thing the oppressor could not take away was their humanity. Any discussion of the blues, calypso, or reggae begins at this point. Like all folk music, it is all essentially commentary; but what is unique about this commentary is that it reflects in every thought, in every musical pulse, something to do with survival and accommodation. The children of the diaspora struggle for a place in society to this day. Worse, they struggle for their identities, mislaid as the slave ships made their way to the New World through the Middle Passage. Therefore, their commentaries must deal with these realities.

The calypso, exclusively Trinidadian, is cynical, satirical, amoral and often savage. The Trinidadian masses survived at least until the 1960s

by a collective disregard of both the laws and the values of the oppressor. The individual spirit endured its degradation and transcended its hopelessness by laughing at everything including itself. But this was not the laughter of gentle good nature, illuminating a comfortable companionship. This was laughter like a weapon, like a rapier or a razor honed in centuries of surviving.

The blues have some of this, but are more reflective of the consciousness of oppression. Perhaps the American black has always known his situation to be closer to the hopeless. He is

outnumbered, as well as a victim of systematic oppression. Of them all, reggae is the most explicitly revolutionary. It is commentary: satirical at times, often cruel; but its troubadours are not afraid to speak of love, of loyalty, of hope, of ideals, of justice, of new things and new forms. It is this assertion of revolutionary possibility that sets reggae apart.

Of the distinguished writers who have contributed to this book, there are many who are eminently qualified to speak of reggae in musical terms. I am not so qualified, though there have been aspects of the music that interest me. As others will explain, reggae evolved from the original folk form of the mento. From this there sprang ska, which began a sort of marriage between American rhythm and blues, gospel and the indigenous mento form. Then mento itself often was driven on the strong beat of the digging song which helped the workers to survive the monotony of long hours with the pick-axe. It was unlikely, therefore, that the beat of Jamaican music would be more than lightly influenced by rhythm and blues and would certainly never entirely succumb to it. In due course, ska yielded to rock steady, with the entire period of transition providing its heroes, like the late great trombonist Don Drummond. But we were still in transition. Then it all came together with reggae.

When one listens to everything from mento to reggae, one hears upon reflection the dilemma of identity. The strong African root is there, particularly in the rhythm and the use of drums. But so great was the act of cultural destruction that all of the infinite subtlety and sophistication,

Michael Manley, prime minister of Jamaica, 1972-1980; the national bird of Jamaica, the swallowtail hummingbird; and the tricolor banner of Rastafari.

11

which sets African drumming apart, is missing. I can remember the first time I heard an authentic African drummer. I was astonished and for a while had difficulty in understanding what was going on, so intricate were the variations, so complex the rhythmic embroidery around the central driving beat. In Jamaica, only the central beat has survived. Even this survival is a miracle in the circumstances.

The most fundamental question that arises about reggae is: how did it become explicitly and positively political? The greatest of the calypsonians, the Mighty Sparrow, has journeyed into political commentary; but even he, quintessentially a part of the Trinidadian environment (although born in Grenada), has stopped short of the assertion of rights, has not essayed a positively revolutionary call. By contrast, the greater part of Bob Marley is the language of revolution.

Middle-class intellectuals had claimed a future for the Caribbean. But this was not reflected in the spontaneous music of the ghetto. What gave Marley the courage to go beyond mockery to

Bob Marley and Michael Manley discussing plans for the "peace concert" that tried to unite warring Jamaican political factions in April 1978.

the diaspora are enmeshed that their traditional, Christian faith is visualised in white terms. Inevitably and obviously, a religion that was spawned at the very centre of white civilization expresses its faith through familiar symbols. If the servants and children of God are white, they will think of both God and Christ in terms of self-image. Therefore, the God that emerges will be imagined to be white. Every church has its sculpture and its painting expressed in white terms. So the children of the slaves begin with a visual contradiction. To compound the problem, the particular expression of Christianity was first the creation of the oppressor. Yet, the children of the slaves need faith and have faith. They are sure there is a God and they are sure that somewhere that God is their God, rooted in the land of the past and visualised in terms of their self-image.

Rastafarianism is a true faith in the sense that its believers have taken that step beyond mere rationality into the acceptance of a view of the unknown, unknowable and unprovable, which is faith. To them Haile Selassie is the symbol of God on

tion that made him a kind of spontaneous, uncompromising revolutionary, untouched by wealth, unfailingly generous, eternally unspoilt.

I first knew Bob Marley in 1971, in the days of "Trench Town Rock." At this stage his music was still visceral protest carried on the wings of a relatively uncomplicated commentary on the ghetto. Throughout that year, he performed as part of a group of artists who travelled all over Jamaica with me while the Party which I led prepared for the General Elections of 1972. Until that time, my own political perceptions had reflected a mutually reinforcing marriage. On the one hand, there was the political theory which I had absorbed from my father as a youth and had developed into explicit Socialist doctrine as a student in University. On the other hand were some twenty years as an organiser and negotiator with the Jamaican trade union movement. To this was now added a vital and new ingredient. I could never pretend that the lyrics of the protest music which were the driving motivation of reggae taught me things that I did not know.

hope; to transcend comment and assert right? To find the answer to this you must enquire: did Bob Marley redeem this identity by recrossing the Middle Passage and reentering the Kingdom of his past? He who knows his past can believe that the future is the territory of hope. He who knows not his past finds that in spite of himself, his future is, in his mind, a burial ground. Faith begins with an acceptance of the possibility of continuity. If you cannot survey a continuity into your own past, you cannot believe in a continuity into your own future. Marley had that faith.

How did Bob Marley successfully undertake this journey into his past which released him to a belief in his people's future? Rastafarianism. I enter into no controversy about people and their faith. To each his own. But it is inextricably a part of the psychodrama in which the blacks of

Earth and God Himself is as revealed in the Holy Scriptures. The true Rastafarian, therefore, has traced his identity beyond mere history and geography to the ultimate source of all things, for the believer, the Creator Himself. But he has arrived at his Creator through the images and the soil of Africa. By that act he has rediscovered the self that was mislaid in the Middle Passage.

Robert Nesta Marley, Order of Merit (O.M.), superstar, father and definitive exponent of reggae, was a Rastafarian. He had taken that journey. By that act he had solved his identity crisis. He had become a complete human being. In his completeness he could sing songs of compassion: "No Woman, Nuh Cry;" he could spit revolutionary defiance: "War;" he could embrace proletarian internationalism: "Zimbabwe." And he could do it all with an unselfconscious convic-

From an intellectual point of view, they were confirmatory of all that I believed as a Socialist, and have struggled against as a Trade Unionist. But I had not myself been born in the ghetto and was not personally a part of that experience. Reggae music influenced me profoundly by deepening the element of emotional comprehension.

I suppose a rough equivalent might be found by considering the influence of a writer like Dickens upon the sensibilities of English readers in the 19th century. In highly literate societies, the pen is a mighty instrument. It cannot change the structure of classes, nor the relations between classes, because it cannot, of itself, change the nature and organisation of production. But it can pry loose from traditional class attitudes those extraordinary individuals who become a part of the processes of political

12

change in a society. Jamaica had produced a handful of great writers like George Campbell, Roger Mais and Vic Reid, who had spoken to the issues of suffering and oppression. Their works helped create an awareness of the imperatives of change. But how many people read them? Everybody listened to Marley and his school of reggae protestors. Certainly, I listened and was reinforced in the conviction that we had to struggle for change.

cannot, and is not going to, compete with escape music; but unlike calypso, it has already carved a significant niche for itself. I can only hazard a guess that this owes much to two factors. There is Marley himself: an authentic innovator, a genuine original in the sense that is true, say, of a Stevie Wonder. Reggae has gone international, therefore, partly on the back of Marley's gifts. But it must also be true that the protest of reggae, the positive assertion of moral categories,

goes beyond parochial boundaries. Among other things reggae is the spontaneous sound of a local revolutionary impulse. But revolution itself is a universal category. It is this, possibly, which sets reggae apart, even to the international ear.

Michael Manley
October 1981

In the second question distinguished at the start of these comments, the real issue to be examined is why reggae established an audience for itself among the myriad of competing musical forms which jostle for space in the communication apparatus. Pride of place is held by synthetic escape music. The bromides and anodynes of everything from the Bee Gees to the Jackson Five are there to pour balm on the souls that are either damaged by their failure to beat the economic system, or bored because they have. At the other end of the spectrum is the biting but parochial satire of the calypso, which makes no impression on the international system whatsoever. Blues hold a significant place because sadness is a recognisable part of the human condition. In any case, America has produced most of the great technical virtuosos who have come out of the non-classical tradition. Clearly, reggae

DE TALKIN PICTURE

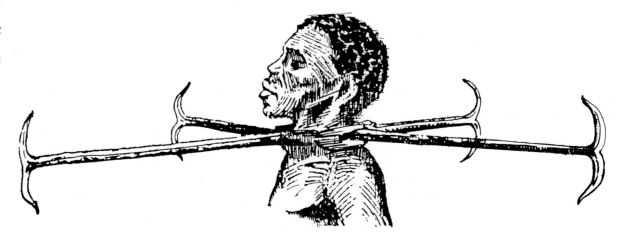

Tracin' de Riddim

CARTA DELL' ISOLA
GIAMMAICA
Di M.r Bellin Ing.re della Marina.

Scala di Leghe Marine di Francia.

1

Jamaica: The Stone that the Builder Refused

Over the past ten years we have seen reggae music, the primary cultural artifact of the Jamaican people, re-energize the popular culture of most of our world, providing musicians, writers, artists and civilians with a fast-flowing, new river of revolutionary ideas and relentlessly compelling rhythms. But the music that the island nation exports to the rest of the world is not the first commodity that Jamaica has used to inspire Western civilization.

It was Europe's insatiable lust for sugar that developed the Caribbean island from a buccaneer's haven to an agricultural factory during the late 17th century, and in this chapter we trace the cruel history of Jamaica, from the time of the Arawaks to today's amazing human polyglot culture—black, white, Indian, Syrian and Chinese. Jamaica never amounted to much after the sugar industry died; the island was the stone that the builder refused. But, culturally, Jamaica has become the head cornerstone.

Notes on the History of Jamaica

I will praise thee: for thou hast heard me, and art become my salvation.

The stone which the builder refused is become the head stone of the corner.

This is the Lord's doing; it is marvelous in our eyes.

Psalm 118: 21–23

But the stone that the builder refuse
Shall be the head cornerstone
And no matter what games they play
There is something they could never take away
Something they could never take away

Bob Marley, "Ride Natty Ride"

A people without the knowledge of their past history, origin and culture is like a tree without roots. Marcus Garvey

It was West Indian sugar, extracted from the vast canebrakes of 17th- and 18th-century Jamaica, that literally energized early modern Europe's inexorable drive to imperial domination over the rest of the world. Until the early planters in Jamaica, Barbados and Cuba began to send their sugar back to Europe in large quantities, the European diet was very bland; salt was scarce, and black pepper to flavor ill-kept meat was an expensive luxury. There had never before been an addition like sugar to the European diet, and there would be none again until canning and refrigeration brought cheap protein to the masses in the 19th century.

But in Europe, there wasn't only a lust to eat sugar. Given the extraordinary profits to be made, there was also a lust to grow it, a lust that drove men to extremes of competition in the West Indian sugar colonies themselves; a lust

Opposite: **1781** Italian map of "Giammaica" by Master Bellin, with Columbus' flagship, the Santa Maria.

An Arawak hunter and his trademark pipe.

that caused the kings of England, Spain, France and Holland to wage war and dreadful human sacrifice for 300 years for their possession, as well as a hateful, inhuman conspiracy of planters, sea captains, and African kings to trade in slaves.

Genocide

The Arawak
The Arawak
The Arawak
Were here first!

—Culture, "Pirate Days"

The aborigines, or at least the earliest inhabitants of Jamaica for whom there are historical records, were the Arawak indians, also called Tainans. Originating in the region of the Guianas and Venezuela, these people sailed northward in dugout canoes to settle the islands of the Antilles from Trinidad to Cuba, possibly arriving in Jamaica around 700 AD.

By the time Christopher Columbus "discovered" Jamaica in 1494, the island appears to have been one of the most thickly populated in the Antilles. The Arawaks were a peaceful people who cultivated maize, sweet potato and arrowroot, and brewed an intoxicating drink from fermented cassava. Above all, the Arawak loved to smoke; the word tobacco comes from their term for their pipes, which were made of Y-shaped tubes inserted into the nostrils. Smoking in this style eventually produced intoxication and unconsciousness.

Just before the European discovery of the West Indies, the Arawaks' generally peaceful existence was shattered by the invasions of migrating Carib indians in the late 15th century. The Caribs were fierce and warlike, and were much feared by the Awarak for their nasty habit of eating their victims.

As for the name Jamaica, its origin is obscure. The early Spanish chroniclers tended to substitute X for J, and in the earliest accounts the name appeared as Xaymaca. But the name appears in its present form as early as 1511. Columbus called the island St. Jago (Santiago), but over time the Arawak name prevailed. Conventional wisdom has the name Xaymaca meaning "Land of Springs" in the Arawak language.

Put bluntly, the Arawaks were exterminated by the Spaniards. When Columbus landed at Discovery Bay on his second voyage in 1494, his party was attacked by the suspicious tribes. Nine years later, on his fourth voyage, he was stranded in St. Ann's Bay for a year while his ships rotted out from under him.

Spanish colonists gradually began to settle

Caribbean Migrations

Ciboney
Proto Arawak & Arawak
Yucatan
Carib
Columbus' 2nd voyage, 1494

Cuba

Jamaica (Santiago)

Hispaniola

The Caribbean Antilles were settled by a series of migrations over five millenia. First came stone-chipping people from the Yucatan, followed by the Ciboney, proto-Arawak and Arawak peoples from the area of Venezuela. The war-like Carib indians and small bands of Amerindians from the Yucatan had arrived in smaller numbers by the time Christopher Columbus showed up in the late 15th century.

A romantic depiction of Columbus claiming the Indies for Spain, "400 years and it's the same philosophy."

An Arawak cacique, or chieftan, receives Columbus.

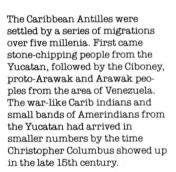

Jamaica, prodded by vast royal land grants providing for the enslavement of the native population. The accounts of the Spaniards' treatment of the Arawak are truly horrifying, almost pornographic in their description of the violence and genocide visited upon this population.

To satisfy the Spanish greed for gold, Indians were forced into mines that proved worthless. Countless thousands were worked to death, and thousands more committed suicide by hanging

de la Vega, better known as St. Jago de la Vega, now known as Spanish Town.

The Spaniards established settlements all over Jamaica, but soon fell to quarrelling among themselves over land, power and religion. Local governors were often killed in riots and factional scuffles in Spanish Town. After the Spanish Crown annexed Portugal in 1580, a large number of Sephardic Jewish families emigrated to Jamaica to escape the Inquisition, further in-

creasing tension among a Spanish colony already incensed that Jamaica's only wealth was purely agricultural. Add to this increasing attacks by French and English pirates who successfully plundered the Spanish Main, and the days of the Spaniards in Jamaica were numbered.

Until 1600, Spain was the only colonizer of the West Indies. Other nations only raided and smuggled. The first English colonial experiments began after 1600 in Virginia, Bermuda (by accident of shipwreck), and Guiana. It wasn't until St. Kitts was settled in 1624 that England gained a foothold in the Caribbean. Three years later Barbados was colonised. In 1643, English seadog William Jackson plundered Spanish Town with a thousand soldiers, many of whom liked the island so much they deserted and stayed behind.

By 1655 the Spaniards were through. Lord Protector Oliver Cromwell sent a 38-ship fleet and 8,000 soldiers (under Admiral William Penn) against Jamaica. The entire Spanish population numbered about 1,500, and there was little resistance. But before they fled Jamaica, embarking at Runaway Bay, the Spaniards freed their African slaves and left them behind in the mountains to harry the English under the command of a black chief named Juan de Bolas. These freed slaves settled into the hills of St. Catherine with the remnants of the Arawak and eventually formed the nucleus of the Maroon nation that would later fight a bloody 80-year guerrilla war against the British.

The English and Spanish, sensing the vast wealth that lay in these islands, continued to fight over them. One of their wars ended with the Treaty of Madrid in 1670, which formally ceded Jamaica to England.

The extermination of the Arawak was ruthlessly administered by Columbus and his successors. Many Indians chose suicide rather than be murdered or worked to death by the Spaniards.

themselves or drinking poisonous cassava juice. Also, the Spanish and the animals they brought with them carried new strains of disease, and a general pestilence among the Indians in 1520 wiped out a large number.

In 1598, the Spanish governor took notice that the Arawak were dying off, and proposed setting up a reservation where they could live and cultivate in peace. The colonists objected, saying this plan would deprive them of the Indian labor they needed to survive.

By 1655, when the English captured the island, the Arawak had been destroyed.

The Spanish

Spain's Jamaican colony was a failure from the start. The Spanish crown lost interest in the island after it became clear that there was no gold to be found, and as early as 1512 there was a move to withdraw the colonists and send them to Cuba.

However, the Spaniards did leave their mark on Jamaica. They introduced to the island the banana, the plantain, and all forms of citrus except the grapefruit. They grew sugar for local consumption and cultivated cotton, cocoa, and tobacco. The original Spanish settlement was at St. Ann's Bay, and was called New Seville; but the marshy climate was unhealthy, and within a few years the colony moved to the south side of the island and settled on the site known as Villa

These freed slaves settled in the hills of St. Catherine with the remnants of the Arawak, and eventually formed the nucleus of the Maroon nation . . .

The Brethren of the Coast

The English ascendency in Jamaica brought with it the heyday of the buccaneers. During much of the later 17th Century, Jamaica was the pirate capital of the world.

The original buccaneers were the dregs of the

By 1540 Spanish settlers had laid the foundations for the sugar industry in Jamaica, with the technical assistance of Canary Islanders and the physical labor of the first generation of African slaves in the New World, imported from Angola by Portuguese traders. Here, an early sugar factory.

By 1675 and the English ascendency in Jamaica, the harbour town at Port Royal was the pirate capitol of the Caribbean, from which Henry Morgan and his Brethren of the Coast plundered the Spanish Main. In 1692, Port Royal was dumped into the sea by an earthquake and many of its inhabitants killed. The city of Kingston was laid out across the bay to replace "the wickedest city in the world."

Arab slave hunters off the west coast of Africa. European merchants and sea-captains, African chieftains and Arab slavers all participated in the lucrative trade in human flesh. Millions of Africans were transported to the New World in the largest forced migration in recorded history.

European settlement of the New World. They were mostly English, Dutch and French and consisted of runaway white bondsmen, castaways, escaped criminals, and political and religious refugees. They were united only in their opposition to the Spanish and lived off the land in Hispaniola, slaughtering the wild cattle and hogs the Spaniards had introduced. The original buccaneers supplied meat, hides and tallow to ships that occasionally put in at ports and coves along the coast.

The buccaneers were famous for working in pairs, each partner taking a share of the game they got with their dogs and the long-barrelled muskets known as "buccaneering pieces." (The term buccaneer is said to come from the French *boucan*, adopted from a Carib term referring to the frame used for curing beef.)

After a Spanish incursion drove buccaneers to Tortuga around 1630, the loose gangs banded together for survival into the "Confederacy of the Brethren of the Coast." At first, they used Indian war canoes and light ships to prey upon Spanish convoys. Early successes brought them ships and more recruits, and their raids grew increasingly bolder.

With the British in Jamaica, the buccaneers soon moved to Port Royal, where merchants offered a ready market for the pirated Spanish loot. At first they were welcomed by the British, but an untimely treaty with Spain caused an early governor, Sir Thomas Modyford, to try to suppress them. But by November 1664, the Second Dutch War had broken out and a fleet could not be spared for the protection of the West Indies. In an abrupt change of policy, the Jamaican governor began commissioning buccaneer ships with "letters of marque" that granted them authority to war on the ships of nations hostile to the Crown. The buccaneers, suddenly legitimized, turned into slightly more respectable "privateers."

The greatest of the buccaneers was Sir Henry Morgan (born 1635), who commanded the Brethren from a ship's deck in Port Royal, at that time one of the richest and most licentious cities in the world. Port Royal as a pirate capital was the Las Vegas of the 17th century. Morgan's greatest feats were the sacking and pillaging of the Spanish empire of the Caribbean, including the 1671 burning of the ancient city of Panama, for which he was made Lieutenant Governor of Jamaica by a grateful Charles II and granted vast tracts of good land in Clarendon and St. Mary parishes.

By the time Morgan died in 1688, the glory days of the buccaneers were drawing to a close. To Jamaica's great planters and merchants, buccaneering had brought some wealth; but to the small landholder, it had brought disaster. The large planters could replace indentured white laborers who had run off to the pirates with African slaves, but the small planters could not. Jamaica began to be an island of vast estates run exclusively by slave labor.

In 1692, Port Royal was a city of 8,000 people and many homes of finely cut stone. Wharves and warehouses fetched higher rents than if they had been in London. In June of that year, an incredibly violent earthquake dropped half the city into the ocean, killing most of the inhabitants. The new city of Kingston was laid out in a grid pattern across the harbor, so the survivors of Port Royal might have some place to live.

Slavery and Sugar

Jamaica never was a major British colony, in that the island was never extensively settled by the English. Rather, it was used more as a huge agricultural factory island worked by an army of slaves taken from Africa for the purpose of growing sugar.

Sugar cane originated in the South Pacific and reached Europe via trade with India. The Spanish introduced sugar into the West Indies, with Columbus himself carrying cane to Hispaniola on his second voyage in 1494. The English first began large-scale cultivation on Barbados in 1640. The demand for sugar in Europe was so high, and the profits made by a few planters in

Sugar was the cocaine of its time. Arcane historians feel it energised the white race to enslave the black.

Barbados so astronomical, that when Jamaica was captured—with a land area 26 times that of Barbados—the island's national destiny was fixed from the beginning.

The rise of sugar production in Jamaica was incredible. In 1673 there were 57 sugar estates. Sixty-six years later, in 1740, there were 430 separate plantations. Sugar was the cocaine of its time. Arcane historians feel it energised the white race to enslave the black.

Agriculture was primitive, and a crop like cane was manpower-intensive, to say the least. Huge gangs of workers were required, and the resultant slave trade with West Africa resulted in one of the largest forced migrations in human history. The slave trade was three-sided: captured Africans were exchanged in Jamaica for sugar, rum and molasses, which were then taken back to England, whereupon trade goods would be sent to Africa to exchange for slaves. The dreaded Middle Passage carried the anguished captives to the New World on ships outfitted with shelves on which the slaves were chained together without even room to sit up. From the millions of slaves landed in the West Indies (and Jamaica was the central Caribbean trans-shipment port in this time), one can only wonder and despair at the agonies of those who didn't survive the brutality of this voyage.

By the year 1700, the expression "as rich as a Jamaican planter" became a standard description of an extremely wealthy person in Europe. Most of the major planters were absent most of the

time, and Jamaica itself was run by a paid bureaucracy of overseers and attorneys.

The sugar estates themselves were run according to an extremely brutal slave code. Punishment for disobedience could be severe flogging, the loss of a limb, or death.

But in spite of the various draconian measures against the slaves, their desire for freedom refused to die. Runaway slaves from the beginning of the Jamaican sugar empire could find

refuge in the deep hills with the Maroons, the descendents of the slaves the Spanish freed to fight the English (the word comes from the Spanish *marrano*, meaning wild). In 1690, there was a big slave revolt in Clarendon, during which a large number of slaves escaped to the Cockpits, a series of impassable forested pits and glens in west-central Jamaica.

One of the slaves who escaped that year was a Coromanti named Cujo, who would become one of the greatest guerilla warriors in history. From

strongholds near the present-day Maroon Town and the village of Accompong, Cujo and his warriors held off for nearly eighty years repeated sorties by British Redcoats, at the time the best troops in the world.

It wasn't until 1738 that terms were sought by the British, and a peace treaty signed with the Maroons at Petty River Bottom. Unfortunately, the terms called for the Maroons to act as bounty hunters for the British, capturing and returning

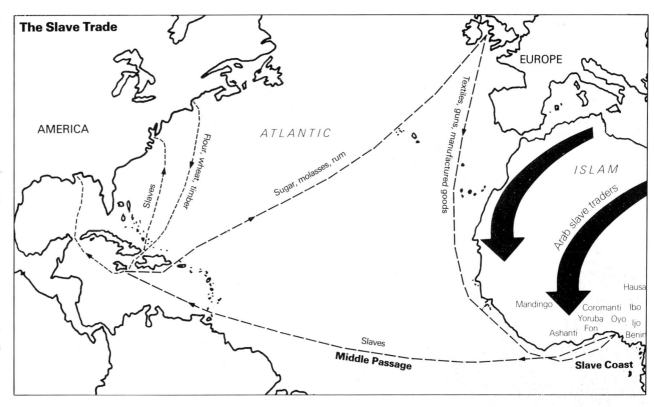

The Slave Trade

all future runaway slaves. This task was faithfully performed by the Maroons for another hundred years. It was the Maroons who suppressed the extremely serious 1760 slave revolt in St. Mary known as Tacky's Rebellion after its leader, a brave Coromanti who had been a village chief before his capture in Africa.

The planters and the Maroons managed to live in peace for almost fifty years, but a second Maroon War broke out in 1796, and this time the Maroon combatants were defeated. A large group

The three-sided slave trade sent European goods, mostly guns and trinkets, to Africa where they were exchanged for slaves, who were shipped to the west in the inhuman, immensely profitable "middle passage." In Jamaica, the human cargo was exchanged for sugar, rum and molasses, which were traded in the British colonies in North America or then sent back to Europe.

The average working life of an African slave in Jamaica was fourteen years. Thousands perished from cruelty and overwork.

Planting surgar, backbreaking work in virgin soil.

was deported to Nova Scotia; the survivors were later sent to the new territory of Sierra Leone, on the west coast of Africa, where their descendents live to this day.

In Jamaica, sugar was still king throughout the 18th century, and the demands for more slaves to work the plantations—Coromantis from the Gold Coast, Ibos from Benin, Mandingos—continued unabated until a 1795 census of the island showed 200,000 slaves and 13,000 white settlers. To feed the slaves, the mango and ackee plants were introduced from Africa, while the breadfruit tree was brought in from the South Pacific by the notorious William Bligh (of "Mutiny on the Bounty" fame) in 1793.

The last major slave rebellion broke out in 1831 in western Jamaica, led by a remarkable man named Samuel Sharpe. The Quakers and other religious groups had been agitating for the abolition of slavery, and in that year a rumor spread that slavery had indeed been abolished in London, but that the slaves were being kept on the sugar estates by their Jamaican masters. Sharpe's Rebellion was quickly suppressed, but the final seed of Jamaican freedom had been sown. In 1838, slavery was formally abolished, and more than 300,000 people found themselves nominally free.

The British slave ship "Brookes." Thirty percent of African slaves did not survive the appalling conditions of the Middle Passage. By 1788 regulations began to limit the number of people who could be crammed into the holds of the slavers, not for humanitarian reasons, but to insure the "cargo" arrived in better condition. The Brookes was allowed 454 slaves by the 1788 Regulation Act (each person stacked in a space measuring 5' 10" by 1' 4"), but the Act was never enforced and the ship's captain later confessed to transporting as many as 620 slaves.

Below: A Maroon bounty hunter. After fighting the British redcoats to a draw in an 80-year guerilla war, the Maroons became hunters of runaway slaves under the terms of a peace treaty signed in 1739 at Petty River Bottom.

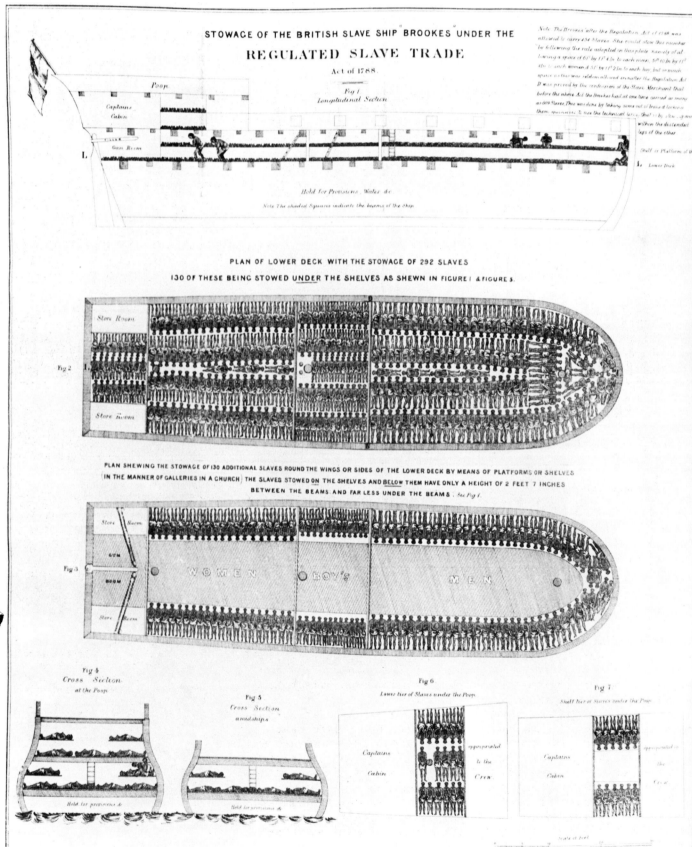

Poverty

Abolition meant the end of the legendary riches of the West Indian planter. Freed slaves left the countryside for life in the towns, and the cane-brakes stood mostly idle despite the influx of Chinese and East Indian laborers to work them. (Some scholars believe it was these indentured East Indians who introduced marijuana to Jamaica. The Jamaican term for marijuana is the

Hindi word *ganja,* which has long been institutionalized by the Jamaican courts and legal system.)

By 1865, conditions had grown very bad for the Jamaican peasantry. Work was almost non-existent, wages were very low, and a series of droughts had ruined most gardens and provision crops. In addition, the price of imported food like salt fish, upon which the common people heavily depended) had risen steeply because of the civil war raging in the United States. It was these conditions, compounded by a corrupt colonial governor, that led to the Morant Bay Rebellion under the philosophical leadership of George William Gordon of Kingston. The "rebellion" consisted mostly of small riots in Morant

Bay in eastern Jamaica led by a Baptist deacon named Paul Bogle; the disturbances were quickly put down, Gordon was tried and hung under martial law, and Bogle was captured by Maroons and executed.

With the decline of sugar in Jamaica (from 500 estates in 1850, to 70 in 1910) the island's economy foundered until the banana became a major trade crop in the 1880s. From then until intense labor unrest developed almost fifty years later, Jamaica was a relatively peaceful backwater of the Caribbean. But the amazing human polyglot of Jamaican culture—black, white, Indian, Syrian, and Chinese—was in place.

—Editors

Samuel Sharpe (bottom left) led the slaves of St. James parish in a bloody but futile 1831 revolt (above). Eight years later slavery was abolished in Jamaica. In 1865 the moral and political agitation of George William Gordon (top) inspired the Morant Bay Rebellion under Paul Bogle, here commemorated on a Jamaican banknote.

Important Dates in Reggae History

1494.—Columbus "discovers" Jamaica, landing May 4 at Dry Harbour, now Discovery Bay.

1509.—Juan de Esquivel becomes first Spanish governor of Jamaica, under the authority of Columbus's son Diego.

1534.—Spanish Town (Villa de la Vega) founded.

1655.—English fleet under Adm. William Penn invades Jamaica.

1670.—Jamaica ceded to England by Treaty of Madrid. The buccaneers begin their era of legitimacy at Port Royal, "the wickedest city in the world."

1692.—Port Royal destroyed by earthquake, June 7. Kingston founded.

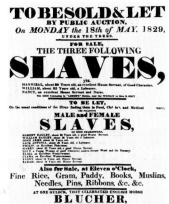

1738.—Eighty-year Maroon rebellion ended by Treaty of Peace signed at Petty River Bottom by Cudjoe the Mountain Lion and Redcoat Col. Guthrie.

1760.—Tacky's Rebellion, slave revolt in St. Mary.

1795.—Second Maroon War.

1807.—African slave trade abolished in British colonies.

1831.—Sam Sharpe's Rebellion, slave revolt in St. James.

1838.—Abolition of slavery in Jamaica.

1865.—Morant Bay Rebellion.

1916.—Marcus Garvey's farewell address to the Jamaican people.

Continued on page 71

2

Voices Crying in the Wilderness

Jamaica has two sets of traditions. The Great Tradition comprises the island's cultural heritage from Africa, Europe and the rest of the Caribbean. It includes Afro-Jamaican religious and witchcraft sects, the established churches and popular music of Europe in the colonial era, and every manner of rhythm and song from all over the central Americas and the United States. The Little Tradition consists of new beliefs—Rastafari and the reggae way of life.

Garth White, of Kingston's African-Caribbean Institute, believes that today Jamaica is experiencing the relative eclipse of the Great Tradition by the Little Tradition. In this first part of his history of Jamaican music from the Arawak to the Skatalites, he takes us through the Great Tradition, from African music to Jamaican spirit cults.

Music in Jamaica— 1494–1957

The earliest inhabitants of the island, the Arawak Indians had peopled Xaymaca, as they called it, by about 700 A.D. The first recorded descriptions of these people by the Spanish invader speak of a simple folk only partially emerged from the Stone Age.

Christopher Columbus, some months after his initial arrival in May 1494, reportedly had an audience with a "cacique" (Arawak chieftain) who "came in state," not only with ordinary attendants and standard-bearers but with a band of musicians as well. One of the Spanish historians recording the event described the band as consisting of two Indians with ". . . caps or helmets of feathers of uniform shape and colour and their faces painted in similar manner . . ." who "beat upon tabors." Two others ". . . with hats curiously wrought of green feathers, held trumpets of a fine black wood ingeniously carved."

This organised and uniformed quartet is the earliest musical ensemble in the West Indies recorded by the Spanish historians, our earliest informants.

From these reports, it is safe to speak of the Arawaks using at least six instruments. For percussion they used small drums—the "tabors" mentioned above—and large drums fashioned from hardwood logs covered by Manatee skin, plus tambourines called "maguey" or "maguei," made from the trumpet tree indigenous to Jamaica and covered with shells. The large drums, we are told, had a deep sound audible over "immense" distances. The use of the tambourine was restricted to the cacique or next most senior person of the village, and could only be played on certain occasions to accompany sacred songs.

The Arawaks also possessed wind instruments in the form of trumpets and flutes. The trumpets were usually made from stems of the trumpet tree which are naturally divided into hollow sections.

Opposite: **A kumina** performance in 1981, by a dancer named Queenie.

25

Smaller sections of the trumpet tree were used to make flutes, as were the stems of papaw trees. The Spanish also wrote of flutes made of bone. In Astley Clark's view some flutes were very probably made from the wild cane which grew in abundance and whose stems were also hollow.[1]

Aboriginal musicians also used a kind of Aeolian harp fashioned from the Aeta Palm. It has been suggested that this tree also provided material for the making of other stringed instruments. As to the musical contents of the ordinary songs of the Indians, the Spanish historians say nothing, but undoubtedly the Arawak would have had their secular festive songs and their war chants celebrating victory over aggressors. Later historians like Bryan Edwards have suggested that included in the Indian repertory were also lamentations in time of public calamity and the language of love. Dancing, an essential part of performance, was "grave or gay as the occasion required."

The early Spanish writers do mention types of traditional sacred songs. These were cast in a historical vein and had to do with the great actions and accomplishments of the cacique. Dancing accompanied the performance. The recital signified ancestral traditions and was a lesson in oral history particularly instructive to the younger generations.

The brutal sway of the Spanish virtually wiped out all traces of the Arawak past. Some few of these relatively peaceful villagers managed to join the Maroons at the time of the British invasion, after African slaves had long been introduced to take the Indians' place as chattels

Ras Michael and the Sons of Negus, legatees of the ancient **burru** drumming tradition, rehearsing in 1976.

[1]Astley Clark. Extract from a lecture given in 1913 "Arawak Musical Instruments." In **Jamaica Journal**, Vol 11, Nos 3 & 4.

to the Spanish overlords. Musically almost nothing remains. Scant evidence exists only in the form of a fragment of a tune, or the use of a few words among the Maroons acknowledged by them as being from an Arawak source.

African Foundation

To speak of this foundation and the development of neo-African music is not, as Trinidadian journalist Eric Roach asks, ". . . to tie the drum of Africa to our tails and bay like mad dogs at the Nordic world to which our geography and history tie us."[2] Instead, we give history its due and correctly approach the problem of "building creatively on what we have because of who we are." The history shows that up until fairly recently this was not a view commonly put into practice.

Because Africa and "Africaness" were negatively valued, it was often assumed that no vestiges of his original culture could be left after the African was forcibly transported to the New World, but that the nonmaterial aspects of his culture managed to survive. In this regard those slaves shipped to the Caribbean fared better than their mainland cousins. Herskovits submits that,

The contact between Negroes and whites in the continental United States as compared to the West Indies and South America goes far to explain the greater incidence of Africanisms in the Caribbean. In the earliest days, the number of slaves in proportion to their masters was extremely small and though as time went on thousands and tens of thousands of slaves were brought to satisfy the demands of the Southern plantations, nonetheless the Negroes lived in constant association with whites to a degree not found elsewhere in the world.[3]

[2]**Trinidadian Guardian**, 14 July, 1971.
[3]Melville J. Herskovits. **The Myth of the Negro Past.** Boston: Beacon Press, 1941.

When speaking of African music, one has in mind the music of over three-quarters of the population who live in the country. It is to be distinguished from the popular or dance music heard in the cities which resembles neo-African forms in the urban centers of the western hemisphere. There are several readily recognisable elements of African music present in the music of the masses in Jamaica, whether rural or urban, traditional or popular.

An important feature of African music is that, in Africa, it is a communal, functional expression. Of course it can be shown that music anywhere has a function—pleasing God or gods, or as an aid to work or simply to give pleasure. Even so, there is no doubt that music in Africa is more bound up with the details of daily living than it is in Europe.

Another readily identifiable aspect of African music that has carried over the water is that it constitutes only part of a greater artistic whole. Despite the huge array of instruments in Africa, virtually all its music is conceived vocally; the human voice is of overriding importance. Even ordinary speech has a relationship to African music—there is often a "sing-talk" style of rendering which is reminiscent of the deejays in Jamaica—and many instruments are used to imitate the human voice, the well-known "talking drum" being but one of many. Similarly, hoarse, raspy singing, a characteristic of African singers, contrasts to the usual European insistence on conservatory standards of purity of tone. Some songs in Africa are actually shouted rather than sung. The use of "slide and slur," the bending of notes, a particular use of vibrato and falsetto, "blue tonality" (the flattening of the 3rd, 5th and 7th notes in the European scale into various quarter tones, the so-called notes between the keys)—all are distinguishably African musical traits.

Another feature of the African musical legacy is the common use of "call and answer" as a group vocal technique. This, for Leroi Jones, is the "most salient characteristic of African, or at least West African music."[4] This form features a leader singing the leading lines with a chorus alternating a refrain. These answers or responses are "usually comments on the leader's theme."[5] Group singing of this sort was probably more

[4]Leroi Jones. **Blues People.** New York: William Morrow and Co., 1963.
[5]Jones. Ibid.

popular in an earlier Europe than it has been of late. By the time of the meeting of the African and European traditions in the New World it had survived in Europe only as church litanies and ballad refrains.

When drums are used, and they figure greatly in most forms of African music, there is usually a lead drum which improvises along with one or two others repeating accompanying sequences. This lead or "male" drum in the most common West African percussion family is the smallest and highest-pitched drum. In the West Indies and South America, drums are often similarly grouped in families of three. Today's Rastafarian trio of drums—the "repeater" as lead, the "funde" as mid-range and the bass drum—resembles the Ashanti "atumpan" (lead), "apentemma" (alto-drum), and "petia" (bass).

And all this in spite of the fact that in Jamaica, there was a time when drumming was proscribed to the extent that if any of the slaves "dared to beat a drum, and the attention of the government was called to it, his owner was condemned to pay a fine of nearly £ 10."[6]

An early form of **Jonkonnu** dancing, which has existed for hundreds of years in Jamaica and which may be a survival of West African harvest rites.

European Incursion

Language is the main means by which a culture is transmitted. It is the "bearer of the social genes." For these reasons alone, the British component in Jamaica's culture has to be acknowledged. Nettleford puts it this way:

. . . Africa is indeed tolerated in spurts of syncretised or reinterpreted folk-lore—a little bit of dance, a little bit of music, a little bit of storytelling, and a few words here and there lacing the Anglo-Saxon tongue with exotic tone and colour. But everything which matters or is said to matter draws heavily on Europe. Our formal educational system, our accepted belief system, our art, law and morals, the legitimate customs and so many of our habits and perceived capabilities—all indices of a so-called cultural sense are dominated by the European heritage.[7]

Early on, many melodies and certain harmonic structures were taken over from the British by the blacks. In addition to the unison singing or "parallelism" of Africa, the "triad" of Europe, for example, was also utilised. The first contact was probably provided by sailors attempting to make their job of transporting the slaves to the New World easier by singing ditties and chanties. When pitting themselves against other "waters" in the drinking-houses and taverns on land, these songs would again be heard. Snatches of these airs and even complete songs, however transmuted, would be used by the slaves. The English verse form in songs was thus early on the scene.

In the early period of slavery, musical recreation was restricted to the slave group and was largely sporadic. This of course is to be distinguished from music made in the fields which, while showing traces of European influence, was largely worksongs or "digging-songs" done in the African antiphonal style. Mainly on weekends but sometimes on week-nights, the slaves would gather and dance and sing. By the latter half of the 18th century and the eventual demise of slavery, the seasonal holidays that had come to be celebrated by the slaves had acquired the form of national festivals with the entire population participating.

Besides the sailors' songs, blacks would by then have been acquainted with the planters' balls and the dances of high society like the Scotch reel and the French quadrille,[8] the quick waltz, the polka, the mazurka and the Alpine country waltz. While the black secret cults may have used music and dances almost purely African, the population as a whole was developing a cultural blend, the browns and free people of colour being the main carriers among the black population of the white styles.

[8]The quadrille can provide an example of how difficult it is sometimes to affirm ultimate origin and thus be enabled to ascribe influence. It was in origin an ". . . English country dance

The "camp style" of quadrille dancing, the confluence of European melodies and Jamaican rhythms.

[6]Astley Clark. "The Music and Musical Instruments of Jamaica." Extract in **Jamaica Journal**, Vol 9, Nos 2 & 3, 1975.

[7]Rex M. Nettleford. "Caribbean Perspectives: The Creative Potential and the Quality of Life." In **Caribbean Rhythms—The Emerging English Literature of the West Indies**. Ed. Jones T. Livingston. New York: Washington Square Press, 1974.

Jamaican black music also developed during the seasonal holidays of Christmas, Easter or "Picaninny Christmas," Crop-over or harvest-home, and the yam festival. The yam festival was generally celebrated by blacks only. *Jonkonnu* dancing had been largely African in the beginning, derived from dances used in the yam festivals and other cult activities in West Africa. The central dancer was almost always a fertility dancer celebrating the glorious bond of man and nature. Early Jonkonnu made use of drums and rattles and probably flutes. The fife and fiddle and the military side-drum also came into use.[9]

By the end of slavery, the *Gumbay* music and dances of the blacks were stigmatised, and even Johkonnu with its range of styles went into decline. In 1825, De la Beche could write that the

which the French transformed into the cotillion at the beginning of the 18th century. This dance spread to England and, one would imagine, to planter society (such as it was) in Jamaica." (Sylvia Wynter – "Jonkonnu in Jamaica . . ." in **Jamaica Journal**, Vol 4, No 2.) From here, it was watched by servants situated near the great house who soon learnt it. But the story doesn't end there. As seen in the more public forms nowadays there seem to have developed at least four styles.

Around Kingston and St. Andrew, dancers who still practice the quadrille, "attempt a version of the Ballroom type of quadrille with all its smoothness and finesse." (Ivy Baxter – **Arts of an Island**. Metuchen, New Jersey: The Scarecrow Press, 1970.) The rural areas of St. Andrew and Portland support a more ". . . lively type of quadrille with intricate footwork." These often perform in what has come to be known as the "camp style." "This style is often frowned upon by the purists of the classic Jamaica Ballroom Quadrille, but it makes for some joyous dancing in the rustic manner and for exciting Jamaican movement." The "camp style," at the same time seems ". . . to have been derived from the older form of quadrille as it was danced in France in the early days." (Baxter, ibid). There are, not surprisingly, groups in the area (St. Andrew and Portland) who can to good effect combine the classic ballroom style with the robust Jamaican one.

Clarendon, Manchester and Trelawny "seem to have developed a different tradition in quadrille movement. The men, even more than elsewhere, insist on virtuosity, moving away from their partners with reels and jigs, their bodies making low bobs, feints and dips, and beautiful wheels. In addition, they specialize in the mento figure." (Baxter, ibid). Yet another variant has been seen in the western part of the island. "These people very clearly demonstrate the influence of Scottish dancing in that area. Their quadrille dance includes a remnant of the figure of Scottish folk dancing known as the pousette . . . Other figures are circular join-handed figures, reminiscent of Scottish reels." (Baxter, ibid) John Storm Roberts speaks of recording some quadrilles which ". . . still preserved recognisable Scots tunes and rhythms."

Dances ". . . which originally were correct, even-measured European airs have become impregnated with the dynamic characteristic of Jamaican music . . . It is very curious to hear, even today, in the hills of St. Andrew, the intriguing Jamaican rhythmic versions of such tunes as "The Blue Bells of Scotland," "God Save the Queen" or "Rule Britannia" played for an exciting fourth figure. The quadrille is thus an involved mixture of European traditional then popular dance steps and a Jamaican quality in music and movement.

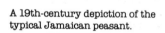

A 19th-century depiction of the typical Jamaican peasant.

"new school" among the Negroes much preferred the fiddle reels and dances of the whites. Those of that mind found it very easy to adapt to the playing of fife, fiddle and banjo. Again, against any premature assumptions that blacks uncritically borrowed must be placed the fact that instruments like the guitar and fiddle were introduced to Europe from the Islamic North African world. As time went by, the instruments of military bands and visiting orchestras were in their turn mastered by local blacks.

In addition to the influence of sailors and soldiers and planters, there was also the culture contact that arose between the blacks and the poor whites, the bookkeepers and the indentured servants who came from Ireland and Scotland as well as England. It seems likely that the British folk music and dance like the Morris and Merry-Andrew dances were seen by the slaves. Elements of these were incorporated by the slaves in their developing body of folk tradition. So Jonkonnu, for example, could also feature dancers in a "doctor-play" or "sword-dance."

Toward the end of slavery, the slavemaster underplayed his earlier antipathy for the work of the missionaries. He was able to foist his religion and its rituals on his hapless subjects with such success that even today, after his proven and generally recognised "wickedness," his church denominations still have a fair amount of credibility among Jamaicans and a continuing use is made of his hymns, psalmodies and litanies.[10]

But even here there is evidence of the musical continuum. Although the "church of state"—the Anglican—and its near associates conform very strictly to a European model, the revivalist churches and those descended from the secret cults rework their European material. Use was, and still is, made of call-and-response, increased rhythmic flexibility, hand-clapping and foot-stomping. There is still an emphasis on possession-states.

The slaves and their descendants after Jamaican Abolition in 1838 no doubt danced with more purpose, but white "backra mass" had his "sessions" too. So much so that Anthony Trollope, writing about the planter's belles in the 1850s, could offer that "the soul of a Jamaican lady revels in dance. Dancing is popular in England, is popular everywhere in Jamaica, it is the elixir of life, the Mede's cauldron which makes old people young, the cup of Circe which neither

[9]I.M. Belisario. **Sketches . . . of the Negro Population in the Island of Jamaica.** Kingston 1837. Writers on Jonkonnu like Sloane, Long, Leslie, Chambre, Stewart and Lady Nugent, saw the Jonkonnu procession at varying stages of its development and thus give varying descriptions. Sloane's description of dancers who "tie Cows' Tails to their Rumps" refers to the more African form. By the time of Long's description, "John Connu" also has a sword in his hand. Lady Nugent sees the dance when "Johnny Canoe" figures "dance, leap and play a thousand anticks." "Monk" Lewis happens to see the dance when the "set-girls" are dominant.

[10]cf. C.L.R. James' "Black Jacobins" for an account of the slaver captain composing "How sweet the name of Jesus sounds" while awaiting his human cargo in a harbour off the West Coast of Africa.

man nor woman can withstand."[11]

The African Spirit in Jamaica

It is highly improbable that tribespeople captured in Africa were allowed to carry any musical instruments with them. On the horrendous Middle Passage across the Atlantic, the tightly packed slaves can hardly be imagined producing tones from "below the diaphragm." Low, fearful moans and groans, a melodic-rhythmic humming was more the order of the day. Sad, melancholy songs as the realisation seeped in that there was never to be a return home. Wails and screams as the possibility dawned that they might be eaten by the white devils. Occasionally, probably a shout of defiance as help was sought from ancient gods. No joyous key here, only the laments of the bewildered. The only joy was with the coming of death and return to the land of the ancestral spirits.

Landed, they would remember the songs of home and fashion rude instruments out of the limited materials at hand. There could be a renewal of spirit even though up against impossible odds. Drums and dances became part of the whole ritual of revolt. The planters soon came to know of this relation and banned the drum, enacting laws proscribing the private gathering of slaves from more than one plantation as well.

For some time to come, besides the smaller-scale provision ground festivities, funerals were the only events where the slaves could associate with any degree of privacy. For this reason, the rites for the dead, already central to the African world-view, gained added significance. Furthermore, as the mortality rate among the slaves was high, funerals were turned into occasions for cementing loyalties and plotting revolts. It was out of this that the *Myal* cult grew.

As the sacred and the secular were not rigidly separated by the Africans, the more war-like movements of the Myal leader would bear resemblance to those of a dancer exulting on the plantation provision grounds of a weekend night when he gave thanks or asked for success in his planting. The planters would tolerate this last, the Jonkonnu masquerade procession and the more creolised forms even being actively encouraged.

Not so Myal. While framed in a religious or quasi-religious mould, its purpose became political, serving to unify the various tribal groups. The Myal "medicine man" would infuse enthusiasm and give out potions and charms that steeled the beleaguered chattels in their near hopeless struggle. He was doctor-psychologist, priest and ritual warrior-chief, all in one. The cult was driven underground, Wynter suggests, "because the planters realised the danger of such a unifying dance, ritual and religion." Laws enacted in 1774 prescribed the sentence of death for anyone attending these ceremonies.

However, both Myalism and Jonkonnu contained elements of each other. Both transmitted aspects of their rituals, beliefs and dances to the surviving dances and versions of folk religion

[11]A. Trollope. **The West Indies and the Spanish Main.** 1859

that exist today. On the more African side of the Afro-Christian continuum, Convince, Kumina; in the middle of the continuum, Pukkumina; and on the more Christian end, Zion Revival.

Kumina, readily recognisable as the most African of the early cults, still reflects the influence of other cultures and there will probably always be some difficulty in apportioning the input of at least three nations. Kumina developed in isolated areas which have had relics of Spanish-Indian tradition, and it was later reinforced directly by African or Haitian elements. Some researchers, however, point to an African origin while allowing for influences from other countries and groups. Barrett, for example, states that "Kumina is from the Twi *akom* (to be possessed) and *ana* (an ancestor). The word Kumina is from Akom-ana, an ancestor possession cult of the Ashanti people."[12] Other researchers inform us that "Linguistic evidence cites the Kongo as a specific ethnic source for the 'language' and probably the music of Kumina."[13] Yet still others speak of Angola as a likely source of the word. Slaves would have come from all of these regions and it is likely that they all had fairly similar forms of ancestral worship. In Jamaica, they lost their specific tribal significance, becoming more generally "African" and less specifically Ashanti, Congolese, Yoruba or Ibo.

Drums are central to the practice of Kumina. They are the mechanism of control that prepares a ceremonial person physiologically and psychologically. The usual "family" consists of the "bandu"—two lower pitched drums providing basic rhythm—and the "playing cas" (pronounced *cyas*) on which the more complicated and specific spirit rhythms are played. The drums are used to summon ancestral spirits. Singing at ceremonies most often takes on an

antiphonal verse and chorus structure, whether between one man and a chorus provided by the drummers and other singers, or between the "King/Captain" and the "Queen."

The basic dance posture displays an almost erect back accompanied by propelling actions of the hips as the feet inch along the ground. As the dance progresses, the feet, arms, shoulders, ribcage and hips are employed, offering the dancers ample opportunity for variations and interpretations of the counterbeats and polyrhythms. Dancing is taken seriously.

Spirits invoked are said to travel down the centrepole of the dancing booth into the ground; from thence through the open head of the drum to the playing surface, at which point both the drummer and the Queen must salute them. The spirits then re-enter the ground and ravel up the feet of persons selected to be possessed. The

spirit passes along the entire length and breadth of the person, reaching the head when the possessed are said to "ketch myal." The initiated can recognise the spirit involved by the particular dance style used by the possessed and the song and drum rhythms to which it responds.

Not all participants at Kumina ceremonies are musicians or dancers, but most are at least involved in the handclapping that is woven polyrhythmically and contrapuntally with the drumming and singing. Kumina ceremonies, while usually associated with burials or memorial services, are not restricted to the religious. They can be performed at more secular occasions such as births, thanksgiving, marriages, anniversaries and the calling of spirits to work good or ill.

Also related to Myal were two other cults, less supported and rarely found today, *Convince* and *Gumbay*. Convince makes use of handclapping only, while Gumbay also uses drums: the term "Gumbay" or "Gumba" itself is used not only to refer to a special one-headed square goatskin drum but also to a specific dance and generically to refer to the more African dances and music of the blacks. Both cults recognise Christian deities but are primarily concerned with invoking and exercising spirits. They can also be called to "pull" or "set" obeah.

In Jamaica, Christianity became the dominant religion. Nearly all Christian churches and sects came to be represented, and these shade into the African. Historically, for a number of reasons "many elements of Christianity, both doctrinal and ritual, have overflowed the bounds of any of the Christian churches and become mingled quite inextricably with the remains of African cultist practices brought over by the slaves . . . Obeah and Myal were once distinct; now they are not. Christianity and paganism were once separate; now the Bible is read at ceremonies otherwise largely devoted to the worship of ancestral spirits. The former enthusiasm of Protestant sects has become interfused with possession by zombies and Catholic medallions are valued as good guards (amulets) against obeah."[14]

Pocomania and Zionism both deal with the summoning and use of spirits, although the fondness of Pocomania for use of "groundspirits" and "fallen angels" makes it readily distinguishable from Zion. Pocomania is the more African and ancestor-oriented of the two, while Zion makes use of Jesus and the Holy Trinity and often resembles the evangelical Christian, Pentecostal and Native Baptist forms. Both employ rhythmic groaning—known as "trumping" or "labouring"—and spiritual dancing to achieve possession. In Zion Revival, the moaning is polyrhythmic and drums are often played.

For "Pukkermerians," as one writer has called them, the forced inhalation-exhalation of breath accompanied by bowing motions sets a one-two beat that governs the rhythm of the attendant music. Pocomania uses drums also, especially when East Indian spirits are involved.

Beside the singing of hymns and similar airs, both cults also practise "cimballing," which is vocal and usually led by a person within the group who "has the spirit." Rhythmically, the

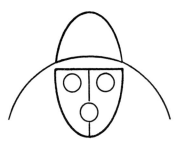

Above: The emblem of reviving Jonkonnu awareness in the Bahamas. The magazine **Junkanoo** is dedicated to the indigenous Caribbean cultures and the annual Jonkonnu festival in particular.

An obeah man outside of Kingston. Obeah is Jamaica's powerful folk magic, and its wizards and practitioners are feared for their ability to cast spells and manipulate duppies, the wandering spirits of the dead whose graves have been violated.

A kumina queen goes into spirit in a recent ceremony.

Above, left: A more recent Jonkonnu (John Canoe) troupe juking through the streets of Port Antonio at Christmas time.

[12]Leonard Barrett. The Sun and the Drum: African Roots in Jamaican Folk Tradition. London: Heinemann, 1976.

[13]Jamaica Journal, Vol 10, No 1.

[14]F.G. Cassidy. Jamaica Talk. 1961.

Pocomania sectarians in spirit. Their ritual rhythm and breath pattern produces a deep trance among the faithful.

voice cuts across the prevailing beat that is being carried by the worshippers in the form of "trumpets." The musical phrase is short, is repeated with variation and ornamentation and may be doubled or harmonised spontaneously by other worshippers.[15]

In Jamaica, the music is often based on orthodox religious hymns and sankeys, along with the occasional spiritual. The tendency to flatten the third and the fifth, the particular relation between the "leader" and the "chorus" and the

joyous approach to the occasion are all identifiably African.

There are groups, found in the rural areas, who have special "plays" for these festive, solemn occasions. Two, the *Etu* and the *Nago* people, use kerosene pans as part of the rhythm section. Other forms like *Tambu* and *Dinkieminnie* are passing out of usage, losing their specific identity.

Even though rituals for the dead like "ninenight" and "forty-night" and the whole range of

cult activity are still observable in the urban areas, albeit on a much reduced scale, the social needs of the growing depressed areas of Kingston and St. Andrew and other major townships saw the spread of *Burru*, which came, as Gumbay had done, to refer generically to all social activities practised by the underclasses where drumming, dancing and singing was involved.

Recent research[16] seems to indicate that *burru* drumming had existed from slavery times and is one of the underground African streams that managed to survive, although it is reported that *burru* drummers were sometimes employed to play while the slaves worked. After Emancipation, the *burru* players acquired the reputation of criminals; their dancing was described by whites as wild and indecent. *Burru* flourished in the later period only around Christmas time when the drummers would be allowed to play in public. In their own communities they were not restricted to official holidays, and many informants tell of the occasions when *burru* players would welcome home prisoners who had served their time. In the ghettos *burru* drummers were the exemplars of the "other tradition"—the urban, spiritual descendants of Myal.

Burru drums are similar to the Rastafarian basic family. Some say that Rasta really inherited the *burru* music form. A complete line-up of *burru* musicians would also include a rhumba-box player and assorted scrapers and shakers and "saxas," the name by which the bottle saxophone is known.

In addition to entertainment music, burru musicians sang "topical songs about current events and songs about individuals in the community who during the year may have been guilty of some misconduct."[17] This is a well-known practice of musicians in some West African groups. What is notable here is the maintenance of the defiant mood. Until they passed the baton, so to speak, to the Rastafarians, the *burru* people kept alive a conscious creative awareness of the suppressed African heritage.

The Maroons, descendants of the runaway slaves, also managed to sustain a consciousness of African traditions. The Maroons have an interesting variety of drums. Probably the most well-known is the *gumbe* (gumbay), the square, singleheaded drum mentioned earlier. In some of the Maroon communities are to be found "rolling" drums and "cutting" drums. The *grandi* and the rolling drums are deeper-toned than the cutting drums, which are usually cast in a lead role, playing complicated rhythmic patterns. Maroon musicians devised a wide range of other instruments. Among them are the various shakers and gourd rattles. The most well-known instrument of the Maroons is the *Abeng*, a replica of the Akan *abertia*. Made of cow's horn, the abeng is still used to send messages.

Among these proud, reserved people, a distinction is made between "business" or "country" songs and dancers and the *salo* or

Rastafarian drummers lay out the throbbing pulse of the groundation prayer meeting, where chanting, meditation and prayer are dedicated to JAH, Rastafari.

---

[15] **Jamaica Journal**, Vol 10, No 1.

[16] cf. Verena Reckord. "Rastafarian Music— An Introductory Study." In **Jamaica Journal**, Vol 11, Nos 1 & 2.

[17] Verena Reckord. Ibid.

ententainment forms used for recreation. "Business" sessions are held on the occasions where the intercession and mediation of the ancestors is required. One of the most important of these sessions is called the Koromanti Play or Koromanti Dance, which no outsider can attend. The purpose of the play is to summon Maroon ancestral spirits. "Dancer-man," the principal celebrant at these rituals, becomes possessed and is used by the spirits to relay information to the living.

Salo songs and dances are of a more secular nature and range from sad lamentations sung after the injury or death of a loved one to the declamatory "Ambush" war dances commemorating the guerrilla tactics of the early Maroon warriors who fought the British redcoats to a draw in 1738.

The Maroons were conscious of their separateness and managed to maintain their own villages. As time went on, however, links between their villages and the outside world were inevitably strengthened. For some of their recreational sessions, Maroons relied on popular musicians from outside village communities. They also developed a style called *Tambu* music, said to be a Maroon version of a Kumina style played on Maroon drums. Even while insisting on their distinctiveness, Maroons willingly acknowledge that cults and sects like Kumina or Convince belong to kindred "nations."

For all the forced, official, European dominance, an indigenous culture, with strong African roots, has always flourished, at times underground, at others more overt and confident.

And so it is that today we are paradoxically experiencing the relative eclipse of the "Great Tradition" by the "Little Tradition," at least as far as the performing arts in Jamaica are concerned. The traditions of the established churches, and their neo-African forms are experiencing the "return to roots." The group that has steadily gained ascendency in the cultural life of the island is the Rastafarians, who have become the philosophical interpreters of the Little Tradition.

Cuba, Calypso & Carnival

Musical interconnection and exchange have been most noticeable among the islands in the Caribbean speaking the same language, but inter-island migration has led to a great degree of contact across language barriers. Jamaican agricultural workers travelled to Cuba, Panama and Costa Rica in the early and middle years of this century. Within the English-speaking islands, Trinidadian calypso, up until fairly recently, was the most popular sound. This position has now been captured by Jamaican reggae.

Each island has its own particular blend of African and European music. In Cuba, the influence is Spanish. Since the cha-cha and the revolution of 1959, Cuba has had a more quietly pervasive influence than that which accompanied the brassy volume of former years. Think of the durable Latin jazz stream that sprang from the Afro-Cuban jazz of the '40s. The use of particular brass arrangements, the Spanish guitar sound as used in many guitar solos, the popularity of the conga drums and the bongos and the linked timbales and maraccas in many Caribbean

Cuban-style **habanera** dancing during an inter-Caribbean dance festival in 1955.

A mento/calypso unit performing at the Upper Deck Hotel near Montego Bay. Some mento musicians scratch out marginal livings playing at country dances and fairs in the Jamaican interior, but most serve the tourist trade along the island's north coast.

bands testifies to the power of Cuban soul.

In the '20s and '30s, the Cuban rhumba swept the cities of North America and Europe. In Jamaica, the radio eventually provided this "gringo latino" kind of music, but contact was not to be limited to Xavier Cugat, Edmundo Ross and Perez Prado,[18] the highly successful bands of the '50s. The more authentic rhumba and mambo versions still managed to filter through.

In spite of the circuitous route much island music took to reach Jamaica, it would still be true to say that a fairly large number of Jamaicans, especially the patrons of urban nightclubs, were familiar with the Cuban *habanera*, the Argentinian *tango*, the Dominican *merengue*, and many Trinidadian calypsos.

While it is possible that calypso is an interisland style, the nod must be given to Port-of-Spain in Trinidad as the place where calypso matured. It is a much older form than is commonly known; by the middle of the 19th century something similar to the popular form known today had already developed. As in Jamaica, we can speak of an African foundation as evidenced in Trinidad by the widespread reliance on choral refrain, call-and-response song structure and the dancing chorus. These provide ". . . striking parallels in form between the calypso and indigenous songs of the old Guinea Coast. Even the word calypso (ka'iso) has been traced to a West African source."[19]

The annual Carnival festivities in Trinidad which preceded Lent actually began as a white affair patterned on the French Mardi Gras, until it was taken over by the blacks soon after Emancipation. The earliest reports make mention of the "wild Guinea songs" sung by the blacks when they practised "Cannes Brulées," or *Canboulay* as it was popularly pronounced. The majority of

these *kalinda* songs were composed in patois or French creole, the language of the majority. By the 1870s, calypsos were being sung in English and the music had become highly eclectic.

Carnival festivities provided the main stimulus for calypso, but the form, even while being festive, drew heavily from other sources within Trinidad. The African people of Trinidad and Tobago had, as elsewhere in the Americas, a literal fight to be free. In the face of official antagonism, the developing forms often went underground or developed alternative strategies. For example, when official society forced the stick-fighters underground the "tamboo-bamboo" and "croix-croix" emerged. When these in turn were beset by official condemnation, the steel-band was created. And even this, which may yet prove to be one of Trinidad's

---

[18]Prado's 1955 hit "Cherry Pink and Apple Blossom White" outsold even "Rock Around the Clock" in the US.

[19]Hill. "Calypso." In **Jamaica Journal** Vol 5, No 1, 1971.

most valuable and enduring contributions to the stream of human culture, was at first disdained by officialdom.

For whatever reasons, not the least of which was the resourcefulness of the black Trinidadian, calypso refused to be suppressed. In Jamaica the satirical wit of most calypsonians, the Afro-Spanish rhythm and strong percussion were readily appreciated. As we have noted, calypso even came to be confused with Jamaican mento music in the minds of some people. The international record companies at this time were bent on promoting "Island Music" and calypso came to be the generic term for all the music of the English-speaking territories. As a boy, Bob Marley sang calypso.

Mento

Musically, the strongest early influence on Jamaican mento, the great-great grandparent of reggae, was probably Jonkonnu in its use of flute, fife and side drum (with the snares removed), recalling the early *kalinda* influence on calypso. To the atonal rhythms were added a

Hotel mento musicians, 1981.

chord structure taken from European music. From Cuba, the claves and congo drums were borrowed and a basic mento bass-drum rhythm was adapted from the rhumba original. One can say that mento's Latin flavour was more that of the Cuban rhumba, while calypso reflected its practitioners' exposure to the Venezuelan *paseo* and Brazilian *samba*. Both come off the same four-beat timing, a common rhythm with a different syncopation.

A typical band of the early mento years might have consisted of instruments fashioned almost entirely from materials close at hand. Later on, when mento musicians adopted modern instruments, it didn't mean that their style of playing changed; they were only doing what had been done many times before by the black folk, selectively choosing useful elements of the new and blending it with the traditional.

The mento audience was largely rural because the majority of bands were located in the countryside, but for some time after its appearance in the late 19th century, mento was nearly as popular in the growing cities. Mento bands could be heard at village dances, fairs and concerts and on occasion at the "tea-meetings" put on by community organisations. At the "coney-island," a local term for amusement parks, they provided background music and accompaniment for maypole and quadrille dancing.

In the urban areas, mento musicians were employed in nightclubs and did service also at bars, town fairs, and the homes of music-loving people who would employ them for house-parties and community gatherings.

By the '20s and '30s of this century, some observers noted that Jamaicans, particularly those living in urban areas, were showing less affection for traditional styles of music. Mento was relegated to the occasional rural festivity and the growing tourist industry for a number of reasons. Many young Jamaicans, increasingly migrant, were not happy with the association of mento and country-style forms with the harsh

deprivations of rural life. Also, changed patterns of migration exposed Jamaicans to a wider variety of music. Until 1900, migration was largely a redistribution of the rural population, a flight from plantation life to small villages and independent settlements. In later times, with the development of transport and communications and the "push" of land security, Jamaicans poured into the cities and towns. Additionally there was a demand for labour in the US and Panama which attracted the restless Jamaican folk in search of something better.

During the late '50s, Jamaican mento began to evolve into ska, and the mento musicians valiantly applied their skills to smaller audiences. Sections of the folk still belonged to the various traditional religious groups, and a relative newcomer, Rastafari, was gathering strength. Musically, a most creative surge would occur, as once again, Jamaicans borrowed from the outside to develop a new popular music—a music that was to gain international appeal.

—Garth White

Talking Drums Sound Systems and Reggae

The Jamaican mobile disco, or sound system, is in many ways the most vital element in the development of reggae. Often downplayed and misunderstood outside of Jamaica, the dances serviced by these sound systems are the most significant outlet for reggae music in Jamaica itself and have deeply influenced the music. The recordings and stage performances of reggae musicians, by which reggae is best known outside Jamaica, are

tems first appeared in Jamaica in the late 1940s, but really emerged as a cultural force with independence from Britain in 1962. This coincided with a decline in quality of music imported from the US and the subsequent invention of Jamaican pop and dance music in the eras of ska and rock steady. At sound-system dances the deejay was always the center of attention. His rapping intros and interjections derived from the styles of the southern US rock & roll disc jockeys of the '50s. The deejay also humanized for Jamaicans the potentially dry experience of dancing to recorded music. With the quasi-accidental development of dub music around 1965, the deejay's importance was greatly increased.

By the late 1960s, all the important elements of modern sound systems had been developed: the

At another point along the perimeter the "control tower" is set up, consisting of power amplifiers, crossovers, turntables, tape recorders, mixers, echo units and microphones. The control tower always attracts a crowd curious to observe its mysterious, high-tech operation; many hold portable cassette recorders to capture their

acts as a literal talking drum. He chants rhythmically along with the record, generally entering on anticipatory beats and keying his phrases to rhythms and syncopations based on sixteenth notes. He rhymes as much as possible, and often repeats a phrase twice before rhyming it, a device which may derive from blues phrasing.

themselves strongly influenced by the requirements of the discos, and many otherwise puzzling facets of reggae make better sense when the role of the dances is better comprehended.

The sound systems also provide a fascinating study of how a developing culture can adapt exterior technological development to its own needs. And in purely social terms, the dances provide a unique and unusually democratic form of personal and class-identified artistic expression through the unique institution of the Jamaican disc jockey, or deejay.

Urban and country sound sys-

custom of dancing to portable recorded music; the development of records specifically tailored to the needs of the disco; and a new role for the deejays as the focus of the music rather than as a mere announcer.

Today a typical Jamaican roots sound-system dance is an extension of all these elements. The sound system sets up its equipment in any available large space near a power line, enabling dances to be held in a variety of locations. On hand are usually at least two, and generally four or more speaker systems set up around the perimeter so that dancers are enveloped in sound.

favorite deejays' live rapping.

The sound system is controlled by two technocrats, the deejay and the selector, whose job is similar to that of a radio station engineer. Working with the deejay, the selector programs the music, cueing up records as crowd response dictates. The deejay introduces each record, as well as endless variations of himself, and fills the awkward gaps between songs with his febrile musings, as well as toasting while the record plays.

The prime function of the deejay is to enhance the rhythm and encourage the customers to dance to it. In a sense, the Jamaican deejay

Deejaying structure also bears resemblance to classic jazz. Like jazz, where hundreds of tunes and solos have been based on the chord structures of "I Got Rhythm" or "Honeysuckle Rose," hundreds of deejays have chanted over the bass lines to such seminal rock steady late-'60s rhythms as "Satta Amassagana" and "Chiang-Kai-Shek." The sound system will usually play the vocal version of a song first, without deejaying, then will immediately repeat the dub side of the record, with deejaying. This corresponds to a jazz group playing the "head" of the tune straight, then continuing to use its harmonic structure as the basis for soloing.

As the dub comes to a close, the deejay will quell his rap and introduce the next deejay while the selector begins the record again. Anywhere from three to five deejays will take turns rapping over the same rhythm. Sometimes two deejays will toast at the same time, just as two jazz soloists might trade "fours" or "eights."

While the deejay is working, the selector uses any number of electronic tricks to goose both deejay and dancers, just as a hot jazz drummer will "drop bombs" behind a soloist. Reggae discos are generally set up so that the bass alone goes through the woofers, and all the other instruments, including the deejay, go through the midrange and tweeters. The selector often cuts out the bass or the high end while the deejay is toasting, and then drops it back in to reduce the tension. He often adds

Skateland in Kingston is one of Jamaica's major dance halls, where sound systems and deejays vie with each other for the ears of the nation. Depending on the night, the sound system at Skateland (or in Montego Bay, center) might be one of the four top-ranking "sounds" that dominate reggae's existence as a dance music—Jah Love, Jack Ruby, Gemini and Virgo. The poster (below) is typical of those advertising dances at Skateland. Ironically, Eek A Mouse was arrested on the Skateland stage that night, just as he was about to take the mike and blast into "A Wa Do Dem." Police accused him of putting a boulder through the windscreen of his producer's BMW.

echo to the treble range, generating a separate set of polyrhythms against the constant throb of the bass line. Sometimes he fools with the volume and tone controls, or sweeps the stereo separation in a rhythmic pattern to enhance the drive of a record. A selector and deejay who work well together can really rock a dance, adding a dra-

Jack Ruby of Ocho Rios, St. Ann, owns a sound system (broken down on the way to a dance), a record store, and has recorded some of Burning Spear's most important music.

Sledge Hammer sound system, London.

Dillinger, a popular deejay on the sound systems, (see page 117).

"THAT'S WHAT I WOULD LIKE TO DO WITH SOME OF THOSE D.J. LOCAL RECORDS.

L. Charlton

is persistent enough can generally pester a disco operator into allowing him a turn at the mike, especially early in the evening when the crowd might be thin.

Deejaying is one of the only public positions in Jamaica actually open to public participation in any direct sense. Thus, the tremendous national popularity of the great

matic, improvised touch to the monotony of recorded music.

The interaction between the deejay and his audience also humanizes the process. Sometimes this interaction is as straightforward as that between preacher and parishioner in a Jamaican church: the deejay exhorts people to answer him, or they cheer as he makes a funny or ribald point. But this interaction has more subtle aspects as well, which arise from the populist origins and leanings of the deejays and their role as spokesmen for the poor Jamaican who must take his entertainment at public gatherings like sound systems.

Who are the Jamaican deejays? Mostly, they are exactly the same people who attend roots dances, the deprived and ignored element of Jamaican society. Being a deejay requires nothing other than a quick tongue and good time, abilities many Jamaicans possess in abundance (see "Long Time I No Deejay Inna Dance," Chapter 9). It's quite common in Jamaica to see people deejaying to themselves in the street, working on catch-phrases, and any person who

as the deejays themselves, but several themes recur consistently. Sex and love (sometimes pornographically elucidated as in the currently popular [1982] "slackness style") are eternally in demand, with the deejay usually relating his amorous adventures and boasting of his staying power. Social commentary, expressed in terms of

Jamaican deejays results from their skintight identification with the public and their ability to speak to the people. The dance halls of Jamaica are the only places where the voices of the poor are clearly, consistently and publicly heard without restraint from church and state. As a result, the Jamaican press and radio often mock the intense roots music of the sound systems and the behavior of their patrons.

What do the deejays talk about? The answers are as varied in style

anecdote and actual event, runs a close second to sex.

Deejays also rap on the prevalence of ghetto violence or on the importance of moral behavior. Marijuana and dancing are heavily celebrated, and of course self-promotion is every deejay's greatest talent. Humorous chants with plenty of local references are always great crowd-pleasers.

Rastafarianism, once the most popular topic of the mid-1970s, has declined in the 1980s as the most faddish aspects of Rasta have re-

ceded. An important deejay staple is commentary on current events. Communications in Jamaica are rudimentary and a large portion of the Jamaican folk are illiterate, so the sound systems are a vital medium for the dissemination of news and gossip.

Any interesting topic is liable to spread like wildfire, since the deejays go to all the dances and rip off each other for ideas and chants. For example, in early 1982 it was reported in the *Gleaner* that two lesbians were discovered locked together in Spanish Town and taken to hospital for relief. Within hours, thousands had gathered at the hospital to gawk and laugh over the incident. For the next two months, no dance in Jamaica was complete without the deejay referring to the two women and the shocking nature of their behavior. The assassination of Anwar Sadat caught the deejays' fancy, and the death of Bob Marley in 1981 was, of course, an obsession for months.

In addition to deejays, sound systems also occasionally feature vocalists who sing over the dubs. Sometimes a popular singer like Dennis Brown might drop by and sing one of his hits over the appropriate rhythm. For some artists, singing with sound systems provides an opportunity to test new material before recording it. For others, it's a way to develop their craft as a prelude to being discovered.

Another popular feature of dances is a showdown between two rival sound systems. The competition among the mobile discos is fierce, and these contests are an important way of making and keeping a reputation. Each system tries to line up the hottest deejays, and tries to score exclusive new rhythms direct from the studios, recorded on acetate "dub plates," which are very expensive but prized for their greater fidelity and increased bass response when compared with commercial pressings.

The sound systems are judged by the amount of "weight" they throw, the clarity and presence of their bass sound, the selection of dance rhythms, the wit and clarity of their deejays, and the response of the dancers. The verdict is rendered on the street the next day and in the gate receipts of the next dance.

—S.D.

3

Ska & Rock Steady

Dozens of essays on the apotheosis of modern Jamaican music—from mento to ska to rude boy to rock steady and finally to reggae and its advanced forms—have been churned out all over the world, but an analysis of this evolution from a Jamaican perspective hasn't been given the attention it deserves. In this section, **Garth White** continues his notes toward an outline of Jamaican music from the early '50s to the present. We also talk to one of the founding fathers of ska, guitarist Ernest Ranglin, and to Alton Ellis, perhaps the one Jamaican singer who most ably personifies the halcyon days of rock steady.

Mento to Ska: The Sound of the City

It isn't surprising that the Jamaican people enjoyed swing music. Popular during and after World War II, swing music derived from black American bands like those of Eckstine, Basie and Duke Ellington. The white bands in the US that came to be identified as the big names in swing (Woody Herman and Benny Goodman) had really taken over a black music and commercialized it for their own large audience. Although the white "Kings of Swing" softened the music considerably, it usually retained its rhythmic "swing" and exhibited a more than casual flirtation with jazz.

These swing tunes were heard in Jamaica on the radio, and through the activity of the big road bands of the era. Some of these bands served a middle-class audience almost exclusively. Other bands played in working-class locations or places to which black people could gain access. They were then given the opportunity of appreciating swing, jazz, rhumba, and the ballads of Tin Pan Alley alongside their mento. The so-called "society bands" played only token mento numbers, but the road bands that catered to the masses would be more liberal in the spicing of their repertory with mento.

The number of practising mento musicians declined notably, particularly in the urban areas. In Kingston, these "Princess Street" (where they could usually be found hanging out in bars) musicians found only occasional employment. Even in the rural areas, demand for their services had lessened. By 1965 the heaviest demand for mento was coming from the growing tourist industry centered on the North Coast.

The mento, however, did not die. With the growth of international interest in calypso, some local entrepreneurs decided to give mento a try on record. While the efforts of producers Ken Khouri, Stanley Motta, and Chin in this regard were admittedly sporadic, they did give birth to

The Dragonaires, performing at ReggaeFest, 1982, one of the early ska bands still working.

Alton Ellis (left), ghetto singer ("Cry Tough") and hero of rock steady, and Tommy McCook, keyboardist of the Skatalites and arranger with producers Clement Dodd and Lee Perry, among others.

the modern Jamaican recording industry. Mento musicians, who formerly had been personally involved with their audience, could now be heard on record.

Paradoxically, just as mento went into decline, it became more national. Performers like Count Lasher, Lord Flea and Lord Fly, among others, made national hits with humourous topical songs that were played on the radio. Their raunchier material was circulated privately in homes or else was heard on the sound systems.

Considering that mento is rurally spawned, it is a most resilient traditional music. But neither mento, nor the swing music of the society bands, was fully adequate to meet the needs of Jamaican city dwellers. They were turning more and more to the rhythm and blues of North American black culture.

The Pull of R&B

The appeal of rhythm and blues to the Jamaican black masses was almost total. Blacks in the US were experiencing, albeit on a much larger scale,

The first radio broadcasts in Jamaica were made from a boat offshore in 1935-36. In 1939, with war on the horizon, on-shore ham operator John Grinan donated his world-class equipment to the Government and ZQI, Jamaica's first national radio station, was born. ZQI was bought by Rediffusion, an English company, in 1950. Its successor was RJR (Radio Jamaica Rediffusion), a cable service for rented receivers and over-the-air commercial broadcasts for those with their

own radios. RJR was staffed by Englishmen and their Jamaican employees, and played little local music. With the advent of the cheap transistor in the late '50s, another station was feasible in Jamaica, and the JBC (Jamaican Broadcast Corp.) went on the air in September 1959. Historically, the two Jamaican stations have served the island's elite, and until recently Jamaican music took a backseat to American popular music. During the early development of Jamaican music, Jamaicans beamed into New Orleans and Miami stations like WINZ and WGBS to get the latest in r&b and soul music.

of mobile discotheque supplying music for dances, house parties, fairs and nightclubs. Their arrival signalled the end of the swing band era.

Despite the disruption in traditional ways brought on by urbanisation and industrialisation, Jamaicans were still grounded in traditional ways. So-called "creole culture" still had its firmly based African reference point. The popularity of r&b was no departure from this inclination. This was not cultural imperialism, but a step in the direction of the unification of all the blacks in the Americas. Elements of r&b would be combined with the mento to form the basis for the development of the *ska*.

Admittedly, much of r&b was concerned with man-woman relations and the vicissitudes of life and love, but it was a music of quite a wide range. The Jamaican audience preferred what they call the "harder" kind of tune. The crisp, sweet bands of New Orleans, with locomotive rhythm sections, were particularly favoured. Probably the most featured artists were Louis Jordan and Fats Domino. Because the r&b artists dealt with black life, they became the symbolic representatives of the black man in the street.

The radio programmed classics and ballads until the advent of rock and roll, and even then only occasionally would one hear an authentic r&b tune. Yet in time the radio was also to have a heavy influence on Jamaicans, and in turn Jamaican music succeeded in gaining increased airplay.

The Birth of Ska

Local musicians were by this time thoroughly familiar with the relatively new instruments that were included in the lineup of the small number of urban professional bands. There now existed a small group of master players. By 1955, both the rhythm of mento and the relatively simple chord progression of American boogie and r&b could be heard strummed on the guitar on many a gully-bank. Budding wind and brass virtuosi were excited by "banana boat" players from Latin America and the US, and by jazzmen more frequently heard on the radio.

There is evidence of formal training in the playing of alumni of the Alpha School for Boys. In other musicians an almost military precision and crispness can be heard, resulting from formative stints with the Jamaica Military Band. There are also many self-taught musicians and, of course, many cases of "Mi father (or similar figure) teach me how to play."

Some local sound operators (including the current Prime Minister, then an anthropologist working in the field), operating independently for the most part, decided to produce *native* music, in quantity, on record. While mento had been recorded, this had been largely the work of a few small entrepreneurs. Now there sprang up many companies.

In varying proportions, a blend of r&b and mento gave rise to the *ska*, a shuffle-rhythm close to mento but even closer to the backbeat of the r&b, with the accent on the second and fourth beats often moving in a 12-bar blues-frame. The afterbeat, strummed by a rhythm guitar or played on the piano (whose sound the

"ska" sought to approximate) came to be characteristic of the form. From ska developed *rock steady* and from rock steady, current reggae.

In ska (known in England as *BlueBeat* following its passage with the hopeful immigrants of the '60s), no one instrument really predominates. Horns and saxes emphasise the guitar chordal beat, the bass often strides in the fashion of the American walking bass, the drum provides the basic 4/4 framework, and the trumpet, saxophone or trombone solo on those ska cuts which feature instruments.

With the development of ska bands, soloists of great skill and talent emerge. On the vocal side, singers feel for styles of expression, with a strong indigenous root in most. The African "call-and-response" pattern is still very much evident. Sometimes even in instrumental tunes, "the soloists make their statements against the background of a continuously answering chorus."[1] Usually the tendency is toward the down-south bluesy style of T-Bone Walker or the urban r&b of Louis Jordan, Fats Domino, or Huey "Piano" Smith.

Many black Jamaicans were proud of the experiments and developments, but the middle classes were somewhat ashamed. They had little desire for African roots to be recognized. They did not like the lyrical form which used almost anything accompanied by the distinctive beat—nursery rhymes, digging songs, Jamaican proverbs, Biblical verses, Rastafarian chants, movie and television themes and revivalist gospel. Above all, they were uneasy with the critical social commentary in some tunes which were increasingly airing social and economic grievances.

The Early Performers

The sound-system operators who sought a means to provide themselves with "hard" tunes for their systems did not really enter the field of music production for the potential sale of records. They wanted tunes to "beat down" opponents. The legendary sound system pioneers like Duke Reid and Clement Dodd (Sir Coxsone's Downbeat) had early tunes which received no radio airplay and were known only to the followers of their systems. Dodd and Reid had sold r&b and the new Jamaican music to avid fans, but the numbers of these copies were in the hundreds.

Chris Blackwell of Island Records and Edward Seaga of West Indies Recording Ltd (WIRL) had an instinct for the commercial viability of Jamaican music, and their attempts to get radio airplay were successful. Their artists (Laurel Aitken, Wilfred Edwards, Owen Grey, Joe Higgs and Roy Wilson) were the first to come to national attention over the radio.

An examination of this late-'50s "proto-ska" period shows that Jamaican music was *not* merely an imitation of r&b. Musical cross-fertilisation was going on apace. Early artists like the Mellowlarks, the Magic Notes, the Maytals

[1] F.G. Rohler. "Some Problems of Assessment: A Look at New Expressions in the Arts of the Contemporary Caribbean." **Caribbean Quarterly**, Vol. 17, nos. 3&4 (Sept.-Dec. 1971).

social changes similar to those being encountered by their Jamaican cousins. Additionally, many of the migrants to Costa Rica, Panama, Cuba and the US were returning to Jamaica armed with new records. The black folk of Jamaica quickly recognised kindred souls in the sounds of their mainland cousins and were readily appreciative. On their newly acquired radio sets, they would pick up US radio stations, particularly southern-based ones like WINZ in Miami that featured r&b and rock and roll.

To tap this demand for r&b, enterprising businessmen attempted to string up small sound systems consisting of radio, turntable and independent speaker boxes. A few of them had their own bars or clubs where they entertained their patrons with recorded music. The sound systems soon took to the road, becoming an early form

and Baba Brooks, a prolific session trumpeter, were clearly in the mento and Afro-Christian stream. Even when the r&b format was used, as in the music of such artists as Simms and Robinson, Alton (Ellis) and Eddie (Perkins), Keith (Stuart) and Enid (Cumberland), Bunny and Scully, Prince Buster, Derrick Morgan, Delroy Wilson, Monty Morris, Theophilus Beckford, Neville Esson, the Jiving Juniors (including Derrick Harriot and Count Prince Miller) and

others, a very strong indigenous ingredient is clearly audible.

Some artists like Laurel Aitken had their feet in both camps. Aitken's middle-'50s "Nightfall" was a "mento off-time" form and is the transitional record of the modern pop music era. Later, in 1957, his tunes like "Boogie in My Bones," "Comeback Jeannie" and "More Whiskey" were heavily influenced by r&b, but couched in Jamaican accents. These accents were brought out more clearly in other early Aitken hits like "Little Sheila" and "Judgement Day," the last a key example of the blend of Afro-Jamaican religious music, mento and r&b.

In the ghettos of Kingston and St. Andrew, and in some rural areas, a new religious movement was making itself heard. The Ras Tafari brethren, hailing Selassie I as God and King and foretelling of African redemption, sought consciously to unite the people of Jamaica in their

struggle against colonial oppression. Maligned and hounded by the police and official society, these latter-day descendants of Garvey developed a brand of African nationalism that appealed strongly to the young people of the depressed areas. Confident, proud and independent, they became the sages of the ghetto.

At the Rasta campsites and meetings, whether the more public "street-meeting" or the more esoteric "nyahbinghi," music and dance were used to "give thanks and praise" (*Satta amassa-gana*) to Jah and to "Chant down Babylon." By the late '30s, the Ras Tafari had virtually merged with the Burru people who still practised their ways in ghetto areas. The alliance was mutually beneficial. Rasta drummers, many of them trained by Burru musicians, adopted the Burru drum family, while the Burru people embraced the religion, ideology and life-style of the Rastafarians. One of the earliest of the Rasta drummers, Count Ossie (Oswald Williams), while experimenting with various rhythms came under the influence of Brother Job, a master

Burru drummer. The relationship was extremely fruitful as Count Ossie and his band of drummers were to wield an influence surpassed only by Don Drummond, the Skatalites, and later by Bob Marley.

The Count carried on his experimentation at the successive campsites he established in Kingston. These sites were visited by many top-flight musicians who, if not obviously of the Rastafarian faith, were at the least very sympathetic to it. Many of them (like Rico Rodriguez, Roland Alphonso, and Dizzy Johnny Moore) were established session musicians. One singer-producer, Prince Buster, decided to try to use some of Ossie's rhythms and "Oh Carolina," probably the most popular ska oldie, was born. The singing was done by the Folkes Brothers, with Ossie and his drummers providing rhythmic

accompaniment and background harmonies.

In this early period, much attention was given to love songs and relations between the sexes. "Oh Carolina" and "Chubby" (sung by Bunny and Scully) were of this type, although backed by a religious ensemble. Not often recognised nowadays is the fact that critical social commentary and protest were in ska almost from its inception. Ossie was responsible for the earliest of these in cuts called "Babylon Gone" and "Another Moses."

Enter the Skatalites

Ska, then, was made up of diverse, related elements. It brought together in one form many of the musics of the blacks in the Americas. Ska had a mento basis and an r&b framework, plus strains of revivalism and pocomania and the rhythms of the Rastafarians. Trinidadian and Latin American influence could also be detected especially in the area of brass arrangements. The structure of some songs gave evidence of exposure to ballads, rock and roll and Tin Pan Alley.

With the coming of the Skatalites the contribution of jazz was increased.

In the swing era and the early '50s, jazz had enjoyed some measure of popularity in Jamaica. Jamaica had been producing jazz musicians for quite some time. Bertie King (alto sax and clarinet), for example, played with "leading British, European and continental musicians in the 1930's."[2] Now Jamaica possessed several impressive musicians with the technical proficiency required to play jazz well. Many of them followed the pattern set by King and migrated, the most famous being Joe Harriot (alto-sax), Dizzy Reece (trumpet), Harold "Little G" McNair (alto and tenor sax), and Wilton Gaynair. Enthusiastic newcomers emerged to take their place in the

Toots and the Maytals, gospel-ska pioneers.

The Skatalites were the major musicians of the ska era. The group's members—led by master trombonist Don Drummond—dominated Jamaican music for ten years.

Roland Alphonso, saxophonist for the Skatalites, a jazz-based reedman whose single "Phoenix City" helped usher in the era of rock steady.

[2]Rohler. Op. cit.

39

ranks of bands that played for dances and experimented with jazz styles.

Typical examples of such bands were those led by Eric Deans, Roy Coburn and Sonny Bradshaw. In contrast to some of their counterparts in American jazz, most of these musicians maintained close contact with mass culture and willingly integrated their professional craftmanship with popular songs. So it was with the legendary Skatalites band that was formed in 1963, nearly all of whose members were stars in their own right with years of training and experience behind them.

The band consisted of Tommy McCook, Roland Alphonso (tenor saxophones), Lester Sterling (alto sax), Johnny Moore, Leonard Dillon (trumpets), Don Drummond (trombone), Jackie Mittoo (piano), Lloyd Brevette (double bass), Lloyd Knibbs (drums) and Jah Jerry (guitar). Most of these musicians were veterans of the local recording industry. Together with session stalwarts like Rico Rodriguez (trombone), Arkland "Drumbago" Parks (drums), Gladstone Anderson

Don Drummond's soulful, wailing trombone established him as Jamaica's premier instrumentalist until his tragic death in 1966. One of the first prominent musicians to espouse the Rasta faith, Drummond touched the island's heartstrings with music like "Addis Ababa" and "Farther East." Nourished by white rum and ganja and maddened by the lack of recognition of his talent, Drummond murdered his girlfriend and died in a Kingston asylum.

The Pioneers, an important vocal group of the 1960s.

also recorded, and one of them, Byron Lee and the Dragonaires, still exists today on the nightclub and hotel circuit.

The list of bands that emerged is quite long, but the most influential or popular excepting the Skatalites and the Dragonaires were Carlos Malcolm and the Afro-Jamaican Rhythms, the Vikings, the Sheiks, and Kes Chin and the Souvenirs. The band of Cluett Johnson (possibly the earliest bassist in the modern era) that had set the pace on recordings in the "proto-ska" era, disbanded in the early '60s.

In a manner of speaking, the Skatalites, successors to Clue J and the Blues Blasters, came to represent the soul of a revitalized cultural movement among the black poor. Moreover, the frontline soloists were excellent instrumentalists, the most celebrated of them, Don Drummond, being rated as one of the better trombonists in the world by respected voices in US jazz. They were able to give an original touch to everything they played, even as they eclectically brought together all of the elements to which they were exposed.

Like Count Ossie, who in some respects was their mentor, they were highly conscious of their African heritage and sought to stress this in their music and in their lives. The Skatalites became culture heroes. Largely of the Rastafarian faith, they made it possible to carry the message musically, confidently and creatively.

Ska into Rock Steady: Voices Crying In The City

Ska is remarkable for its instrumental virtuosity. It is quite ironic in retrospect to recall that the middle class used to see it as "bufbuf," not really listening to the instrumental solos that gave expression to a range of experience. For all its happy, carefree abandon, ska captured a spirit of dread. This quality is examplified in the playing and arranging of Don Drummond.

Drummond, who studied at the Alpha School, became a teacher there, giving classes to people like Rico Rodriguez. He gained practical experience in early road bands like the Eric Deans and Baba Motta aggregations and early jazz bands which encouraged a high degree of technical efficiency. To this he added his enormous talents as a composer, imaginatively weaving local colour and his personal experience into the very fabric of ska.

The slide trombone possessed a particularly Biblical ring in his hands. It mirrored the religiosity of Jamaicans, an African spiritualism that was manifest in Drummond songs like "Addis Ababa" and "Far East." Don became the musical conscience of the Jamaican people. His music "contained the hurt of his people,"[3] and his recurrent bouts of mental illness seemed to reflect the contradictions of his country—scenic and lush, but deformed by extremes of affluence and poverty.

In the midst of great natural beauty and social pathology, a sensitive artist like Don sounded black and blue, so much so that even happy, effervescent tunes such as "Don Cosmic" (the first Don Drummond tune recorded), "Treasure Isle" and "Dick Tracy" have more than a hint of

melancholy—a "brooding melancholy which seems always on the verge of exploding, but which is under some sort of formal control"[4]—well-suited to the developing Rastafarian ethos. Tunes like "Snowboy,"[5] "The Return of Paul Bogle" and the "Reburial of Marcus Garvey" underlined the connection between the leading musicians in the popular field and the Rastafarian faith.

Drummond, and to a lesser extent the other soloists in the Skatalites, employed themes and improvisation that often seemed rhythmically conceived and reminiscent of folk traditions, even when, in jazz-like fashion, they were at their most lyrical. These and other musicians like Ernest Ranglin and Carlos Malcolm were innovative performers at a highly creative level within the context of a simple ska tune.

The rhythmic underpinning provided by Brevette, Knibbs, Mittoo and Jah Jerry was tight, ominous, subtly anticipating forms to come. Brevette, using the common string bass, and Knibbs on the traps are probably the first example of the modern reggae "rhythm pair." In the drum-and-bass playing of today are many echoes of their original approach.

The Skatalites did most of their work for Clement Dodd's Jamaica Recording and Publishing Studio, on the Studio One, Coxsone and Supreme labels. Most of Jamaica's popular singers did their apprenticeship at this studio, where they benefited from the Skatalites' technical competence. The two ends of Kingston's ghettoes were joined symbolically and practically in this union of band and singers: the Skatalites were for the most part from eastern Kingston, while the majority of singers were from the west.

The studios like those of Dodd and Duke Reid were conveniently located in the heart of western Kingston. The centrally located radio stations, RJR in Cross Roads and JBC[6] in Half Way Tree, also made two-track facilities available to the growing music industry.

In the '50s and early '60s, the new Jamaican singers focused on the economic deprivation and social injustice suffered by their people. They

(piano), Mr. Campbell (tenor sax), Ernest Ranglin (guitar) and Cluett Johnson (bass), they provided accompaniment for virtually all of the top vocal performers of the ska era.

A most important effect of this concentration of personnel was that the musicians involved, especially the Skatalites, became intimately acquainted with each other's stylistic idiosyncracies and were thus able to respond to the barest hint, the subtlest nuance contained in their collective playing. Skatalites' recordings that were done using at most only two microphones still sound spontaneously hot, fresh and exciting today.

To remain the vaunted session and dance band that they were, the Skatalites had to maintain a consistently high standard as the general growth in popular entertainment had led to a mushrooming of bands. Some of these bands

[3]Ibid.
[4]Ibid.
[5]It was rumoured that this ship had been transporting herb (marijuana). Drummond's tune was made after the vessel disappeared in the "Bermuda Triangle."
[6]Radio Jamaica Rediffusion, and the Jamaica Broadcasting Corporation.

40

still sang on mostly about man/woman and "romance" relationships, but covered other areas of social life as well. Their music was mostly ignored by middle-class critics who spoke of the simple-mindedness and naiveté involved in the refashioning of nursery rhythms and ghetto talk in tunes like "Humpty Dumpty" by Eric "Monty" Morris and "Easy Snapping" by Theophilus Beckford.

To most of the middle class, who affected a lack of interest in the culture of Trench Town, the new music was just a beat. But even nursery rhymes had their relevance and Monty Morris's reference to the

Old lady who live in a shoe
She had so many children
She didn't know what to do

had its parallel in ghetto life. Artists like Beckford, Derrick Morgan and Clancy Eccles didn't confine themselves to "sweet" songs. They recorded all the elements in the life of the poor. They recounted both personal and collective experience. Beckford sang in "Georgie and the Old Shoes:"

Georgie and the Old Shoes has gone to jail
Georgie and the Old Shoes has gone to jail
Well if you're looking for poor Georgie
He's behind de wall

Derrick Morgan pleaded "We are suffering," and Monty Morris lectured that "Money can't buy life." Justin Hines and the Dominoes brought revival tones and harmonies to bear in "Carry Go Bring Come," a song which spun Biblical imagery with social comment:

Better to seek a home in Mount Zion high
Instead of keeping oppression upon an innocent
*   man*
But time will tell on you
You old Jezebel
How long shall the wicked reign over my
*   people.* [7]

The term "ska" was used for both music and dance. A good dancer, known as a "legsman," one who could execute a wide variety of moves, was also seen as an artist and was given status similar to other heroes of the ghetto, the popular singers. Some dancing involved close bodily contact, especially those of the duos (Keith and Enid, Derrick and Patsy, Roy and Millie) dealing with love themes and relations.

"Rudie Come From Jail Cause Rudie Get Bail"

When in 1964 the Wailers urged the restless urban young to "Simmer Down," they were really warning of the turbulent days of the later '60s that were still to come. In 1964 the Wailers were in the forefront of a movement, counselling through music the need for black unity, the love of God and the brotherhood of a just mankind. Subsequent to their reorgan-

---

[7] The lyrics of "Carry Go Bring Come" were said to refer to Lady Bustamante, the wife of the JLP prime minister.

isation as a trio, they became an archetype of the vocal group that was to dominate the music scene in the '60s.

It was a period marked by the growth of consciousness and increased militancy on the part of black people the world over.

One Love, One Heart
Let's join together
And I'll feel alright

On the international level, of particular importance to the young black adults of the ghetto was the fact that the colonised countries of Africa were regaining their independence. In the nearby United States, militant black spokesmen were questioning the legitimacy of establishment democracy and encouraging an active opposition to the corrupt inequalities of American life. Violent riots were often sparked off in the face of the continued inability or unwillingness of Americans to effectively address the plight of the black poor.

In Jamaica the same picture of black dispos-

session held true. The young black adult became increasingly disenchanted and alienated from a system which seemed to offer no relief from suffering. Many of the young became *rude*.

"Rude boy" (bwoy) applied to anyone against the system. It described the anarchic and revolutionary youth of the poorer classes and the young political "goons" (mercenaries of the two political parties), as well as the Rasta-inspired "cultural" rude boys (like the Wailers) who rejected white standards. Some of the youths became predatory, harassing the very poor, prompting singer Alton Ellis in "Dance Crasher" to ask for better behaviour:

You could be a Champion
You can be a gentleman
Like Mr. Bunny Grant

Prince Buster was more stern. On "Judge Dread," he takes the role of a merciless judge heaping incredible 400-year sentences on criminals.

Most of the singers who entered this topical arena painted the picture of a heroic type. For "Bob Marley and the Wailing Rude Boy Wailers," as the deejays of the time called them, the rebellious young man was a "good, good rudie."

Can't fight against the youth now
Cause its wrong

Chorus: *He's a good, good rudie*

Can't fight against the youth now
For they're strong
He's a good, good rudie.

Desmond Dekker and the Aces ("007," "Rude Boy Train") and other performers like the Clarendonians and Derrick Morgan ("Rudie Don't Fear") dealt heavily with the rude boy theme, describing an urban situation that was tense, violent, and anguished.

In response to the growing militancy of the

Desmond Dekker, one of Jamaica's greatest singers, began his career in 1962 when he recorded "Honor Thy Father" for Leslie Kong's fledgling Beverley's Records. One of the kings of rude boy music ("007—Shanty Town"), Dekker later scored the first international reggae hit in 1968 with "Israelites."

The Clarendonians were a rude, aggressive young vocal trio that recorded some of the hardest social commentary of the rude boy era, 1965-67.

Jamaican delegation promoting ska music at the 1964 Worlds Fair in New York. Prince Buster stands at left, and the young Jimmy Cliff crouches at left.

Singer Ken Boothe reached the height of his career during the rock steady era of the late '60s and the early reggae days of 1970-71.

HIM Haile Selassie I of Ethopia in Kingston, 1966.

Marcia Aitkins, one of the most important female rock steady stars.

urban poor and the observed connections between alienated youth, popular music, Rasta and this new mood, official Jamaica encouraged a policy of increased repression. Although some of this militancy was manipulated by politicians to serve their own ends, the brunt of corrective measures fell squarely on the poor. The police made no distinctions and treated all youth in the ghetto as criminal. This hardening of attitude only served to heighten social tension, and to underline the conflicts and division in the society. Pre-reggae acted as a social barometer, becoming the main means of peaceful protest against intolerable conditions.

Get Ready to Rock Steady

In April 1966, the visit to Jamaica of His Imperial Majesty, Emperor Haile Selassie I of Ethiopia, was ecstatically welcomed by thousands. Few in official circles had grasped the extent of Rasta influence until then. In the field of popular music, most of the top performers pledged allegiance to the movement, or at the very least were sympathetic to it. Although a gaping void had been left by the exit of Don Drummond, committed to a mental asylum for the murder of his woman, his colleagues were developing a new music. Music which in fact Drummond himself had hinted at in prophetic tunes like "Green Island."

The disbanding of the Skatalites in 1965 was accompanied by the demise of many other big road and studio bands. Leading members of the Skatalites formed separate aggregations, Roland Alphonso leading the Soul Brothers and Tommy

McCook guiding the Supersonics. New names like Lynn Taitt (a Trinidadian-born guitarist), trombonist Vin Gordon (called "Don Drummond Jr."), Cedric "Im" Brooks, David Madden and others were emerging to carry on the tradition of instrumental witnessing placed at the service of popular culture. On the vocal side, a younger generation of artists were "facing the make." Always willing to experiment, adopt and refashion, the new rock steady music reflected exposure to resurgent American soul and relatively new sounds from Latin America like the samba and bossa nova.

Typical tunes of the transitional, experimental period between ska and rock steady are provided by songs like "Dancing Mood" by Delroy Wilson in the period closer to ska, and "I've Got to Go Back Home" by Bob Andy, recorded just before the ska slowed down into rock steady. Andy's classic concisely stated the problem:

I've got to go back home
This couldn't be my home
It must be somewhere else
Lord I could kill myself
'Cause I can't
Can't get no food to eat
Can't get no clothes to wear
Can't get a job to get bread
That's why I've got to

Chorus: *I've got to go back home.*

This type of critical social commentary was to characterise the rock steady period. The music became more menacing and laced with dread than the ska had been. The slowing of tempo and the cutting of the rhythm in half seemed a little sinister. The bass line took over the music. The drummer and the bass man were as "solid as a rock, *rocksteady.*"

The call for social justice, for "truth and rights," mirrored the sentiments of the black poor exactly. Political fratricide, economic hardship and social disorientation on the verge of anomy forced ambivalent responses from many of the urban poor and helped to erode the bonds of community that had begun to be developed. In spite of this, their music maintained a kind of cultural solidarity for them. It provided an aesthetic bulwark. In range of content, it was if anything, *more* developed. The qualities of rugged morality, fearless protest and transcendent music so evident in reggae today were already there when rock steady turned to reggae in the late '60s.

—Garth White

Trench Town, Kingston 12.

Ernest Ranglin on Ska

Talking Rock Steady

Guitarist Ernest Ranglin was already a veteran Jamaican musician by the time he played on some of the earliest ska sessions in the early '60s. Ranglin is a particularly diversified player, at home playing bebop solo guitar to a worshipful audience at Montreux or taking deft, floating lead breaks while touring with Jimmy Cliff's bands in the late '70s.

We found him recently in the piano bar of the Casa Montego in Montego Bay. For three or four hours a night, this smiling, greying master musician runs incredible bebop changes on old standards like "Just In Time" and "Strangers in the Night." Ranglin is so adept at his craft that his fingers seem to dissect the fingerboard of his big electric Gibson like a fishmonger expertly filleting a cuttlefish. The effect was something like a Jamaican Charlie Parker on guitar. Incredibly, his bassist was the legendary Cluett Johnson, *the* bass of the ska era.

Q: *Where are you from, and how did you get to be one of the top guitar players in Jamaica?*

Ernest Ranglin: I'm from Harry Watch, Manchester. It's about the middle of the island, yunno? I was born in 1932, and had two uncles who played guitar all the time. While they were off at work I'd tune up their guitar and run down a few things before they got home. They also had a ukelele and I used to play that too because it was more to my size. When they finally found out, they were so proud to hear me play!

When I was 14, I left school and decided to do something with my playing to prove to myself that I had learned something in school. Two years after that I started to play with good-sized bands, Val Bennett and Eric Dean. And then I keep stepping up to better and better bands, like Count Boysie.

What about ska?

I was the first person who did ska. I did it at JBC studio and I did it for Coxsone. The group was comprised of Roland Alphonso, Cluett Johnson on bass, Rico Rodriguez on trombone, Theophilus "Easy Snappin'" Beckford, and some others. Sometimes we were called Clue J and the Blues Blasters, and we did about six recordings of instrumentals and those were some of the first ska records.

I always wanted to be versatile, so sometimes I was doing jazz and sometimes I was doing band or dance music. As a small boy my first influence was Charlie Christian, and then I heard Django Reinhardt years after that. But the first person who really inspired me was a Jamaican guy named Cecil Houdini. After I studied from tutor books, I finally end up with him. To me he was the greatest guitar player who ever lived in this country. Gradually, I got to play a lot of bebop music and got to listen to a little Fats Domino, Otis Redding, Louis Jordan, those were my favorites, yunno?

Eventually we had the ska era, the rock steady era. I was the musical director at Treasure Isle studio, which was owned by Duke Reid. I did the first lead guitar on the first reggae record, although we called it *raggay* then because that was what the rhythm sounded like. I worked for producers like Lee Perry and Clancy Eccles, and I was the musical director for most of them. I wrote parts and arranged songs and put the music together. I arranged Bob Marley's first hit, which was called "It Hurts To Be Alone."

Who were the prominent session musicians from the era?

During the late 1960s, when we first started to do reggae, the personnel was Jackie Jackson on bass, and a guy named Hugh Malcolm, that was one of the best reggae drummers that we had, long before Sly came along. Hugh Malcolm was the best reggae drummer, just like Drumbago was the best ska drummer until Lloyd Nibs came along. Harvey Adams played Hammond organ. On piano we had Winston Wright, and sometimes Gladdy [Gladstone Anderson] was around. We had other guitar players, like Lynn Taitt. Anyway, those were the nucleus of the rhythm sections that invented reggae music.

We had heard you were living in New York, so it's a surprise to find you in Jamaica . . .

I'm satisfied I've done enough in my jazz field, and I've been nearly every place you can think of, especially Europe. I toured with Jimmy Cliff for three and a half years. I played every jazz festival in Europe because I wanted people to get to know who I was. But now it suit me to be home . . .

—Stephen Davis

Alton Ellis was one the heroes of the rock steady era. His hits (some as Alton Ellis and the Flames) include "Rock Steady," "I've Got Love," "Cry Tough" and many more. Today Alton lives in England, but we found him on the road playing a reggae club on Long Island . . .

Q: *How did you first get started in reggae and rock steady?*

Alton Ellis: I started from the days when there was no set pattern of music in Jamaica. We just recorded anything that was good for recording. From then we just progressed a riff onto another riff until we get to where we are, but we usually followed a pattern of the r&b from the States, the boogie-woogie rhythm like Louis Jordan and so forth.

We progress from that to ska, and then we go a little slower and get the rock steady, which is a more relaxed rhythm and more clearly explained itself; from there we progress on and on 'til we are here.

Your biggest period in music was during the rock steady era with your song "Rock Steady." Was that your first big hit?

No, my first big hit was in 1960, a song called "Murial." We used to write like soft tunes, calypso, blue beat, anything. It was in the mid-'60s when I tuned into rock steady. I have that gift of feel that I could create, that I could turn an American song into the reggae beat we call now, that was rock steady then. But I was in complete demand during the rock steady era.

Did you actually make up the term rock steady*?*

Well, it came from my mind because of the feel of the rhythm. If you listen clearly you can feel it rocking, and it was more steadier than the ska. I could feel the rock, and it was more steadier, so I just called it rock steady and then I create this song "Get Ready To Do Rock Steady."

At that point, were you recording under the auspices of Coxsone or some other producer?

Ernest Ranglin, Montego Bay, 1982.

At rock steady point I was recording at Treasure Isle, which was Duke Reid. But after about two years or eighteen months I went back to Coxsone, which was Studio One, and I did a lot of hits on Studio One label likewise.

Was there much popularity or money to be made from recording in those days?

No, there wasn't. There was some money but not enough to satisfy the producer because the studio time was four pounds an hour, and the musicians usually get 15 pounds a song. You have to be god blessed to pick up any royalties from those records, otherwise you keep singing every week for 15 pounds a song. This was the early early stage, before Bob Marley got into the business or Ken Boothe or any of those names; we're talking

The original Heptones in Kingston, circa 1970. Consisting of Leroy Sibbles, Earl Morgan and Barry Llewellyn, the Heptones were founded in 1965 and recorded for Clement Dodd's Studio One Label. Their first hit was the very lewd "Fatty Fatty" in 1966. In the mid-70s, the Heptones recorded two important albums for Island Records and producers Harry Johnson and Lee Perry. In 1978 Leroy Sibbles, prime Heptone and inventor of some of the hardest riddims in reggae, emigrated to Canada and the original Heptones were no more.

about people like Wilfred Edwards, Owen Grey, Laurel Aitkin, very early stage of it.

What about your sister Hortense Ellis? Did you get involved with her singing or did she start her own career?

We all started out together. We begin singing at the Ambassador Theater, Majestic Theater and so forth, at a contest where you get 15 pounds for first prize. I took Hortence one night to this contest and she won like that, first try. She was a winner. The most consistent voice in Jamaica as a female. But it didn't work for her like me, financially. So people said leave, like Jimmy Cliff and Millie Small. Then I decided to leave and spent two years in Canada and then went to England for the final kill. I was in England hoping to be closer to the big recording studios so something might happen.

In your career you've done a lot of duets with people like Larry Marshall. Was this mostly you backing him up, or a real duet?

No, it was just like working at Studio One; it's everyday work, you'd find something to sing, whether by yourself or singing with somebody. But you got to sing to collect some money when the week end. This was it. There were some other people I was involved in, not for this reason but for partnership as an artist; like I used to sing with John Holt for a year, and we did many tunes. Then I went to Alton and the Flames, which was my biggest group activity, involving all, or most, of my hits.

Then there was time when the Flames were not present in my recording, and then anybody who would be there would be a Flame for the moment, like Ken Boothe, Delroy Wilson, anybody. We would work like this if Bob Marley is doing something in the studio and there is no harmony, he come in and say back up this song. We're supposed to be paid for this, but sometimes we didn't do it for the money, because in those days we were singing for recognition in the eyes of the public more than anything else. You want to be a guy from the ghetto, you want to be on the radio, the TV, you want to be on the Christmas morning big concert. It was more recognition than anything.

I know guys who were singing in groups in Jamaica from then over 15 years and never collect a penny from the group because he was working otherwise in a good

job. But he was getting *recognition* as a singer over this period of time.

So who made money on rock steady music?

People like Duke Reid and Coxsone, the producers. The artists didn't know their rights; they didn't know the business; we're all young in it in every way, publishing and so forth we knew nothing about. Every song we did, the Downtown guys did, people like Byron Lee. Every song for the whole year that was a hit tune, he recorded with his band—anthology records— and then he shipped them to Nassau and the whole of the West Indian islands. Then when our records go down there, our records seem to be the version or the copy, because Byron

already spread it down there.

If he hear a song yesterday, he can record it tonight, and by tomorrow it is ready to be ship out. So this was the situation. I didn't know I should ask for publishing rights. I was just proud that Byron Lee would do an Alton Ellis song.

When did that change? Did Bob Marley change it?

No, the violence in Jamaica change a lot of things. Now an artist sends two of his friends with guns and then no reason don't compensate for that; it's just gunshot, gunshot. So this help to change it a bit. Then, what they do now, as money people, they go abroad, and transact their business from abroad, so your arm have be *very* long to get at them.

How does your career coincide with the other rock steady singers like Slim Smith?

Well, Slim was a good friend of mine. I way before Slim. He's about Bob Marley's age now, and I, well, let's leave that out.

You look no older than 40.

Well, I'm 43.

Are you one of the older reggae performers right now?

Yes, right now. I came on very strong over a period of five years, from 1965 to 1969. I was completely way ahead like Bob, but only on a different level financially. Presently I'm one of the oldest still in the business.

How do you feel about the other rock steady bands at the time, like the Heptones, the Cables, Horace Andy, Bob Andy? Was the rock steady movement unto itself, and were you really interested in a rock steady beat, or more in American r&b music at the time?

I was into the beat, very much into the beat. But I could take a song like "Willow Tree" or "Ain't That Loving You" and make it into a Jamaican song. Every young artist do it over today. It's an American song. But I was capable of placing the song *so properly* within rock steady rhythm that you could *hear* the r&b flavor at the same time and *feel* the rock steady rhythm at the same time. See, I put them together properly. And this is one thing I can tell I am proud of.

Who were some of your favorite rock steady musicians?

To be honest, all the names you called did their work and I enjoy them very much, all the singers. I see it as a job we all have to do instead of competing.

—*Peter Simon*

Alton Ellis in New York, 1981.

44

Do the Reggay

To believe the myth, reggae was born one day in 1968 when Toots and the Maytals recorded a driving little number called "Do the Reggay." But, as Toots is quick to point out, he didn't invent the term; "reggae" was just an expression circulating in the streets meaning, roughly, "raggedy, everyday stuff" (which took on different connotations depending on the context). But the popularity of "Do the Reggay" captured the term on vinyl and popularized it. It also associated reggae with the new type of rhythm on "Do the Reggay."

The pulse of Africa, says Philadelphia-based musician/writer **Randall Grass,** had arrived in the city from its countryside haven, and it was the Rasta influence with its biblical imagery, coupled with extreme urban poverty, that made reggae the expressive form for the restless ghetto youth.

Coxsone Dodd, the pioneering record producer of the famous Studio One, talks to Randall about his contribution to the development of the reggae style, and **Luke Ehrlich** explains how reggae is arranged and how it affects our minds and bodies.

Rock Steady into Reggae 1968-1972

"Do the Reggay" still had a lot of rock steady mannerisms, but new aspects of rhythm were emphasized. The bass became stronger, more emphatic, driving the beat and allowing the drummer to play around it a bit more with rim shots and cymbal accents. The guitar was played

In Kingston

in a loose, loping strum, with bright emphasized chords on the head of the upbeat—but the up-beats didn't come as rapidly as in rock steady: the overall pulse of Jamaican music had slowed again, though certain elements were played faster. The drive came from an unvarying two-chord pattern which provided a persistent counterpoint for the call-and-response of Toots' chant-like repetition and the Maytals' answering harmonies.

Coxsone Dodd explains the emergence of a reggae beat as a spontaneous innovation during rehearsals. The piano player and guitarist

45

Clement "Sir Coxsone" Dodd, 1976.

Right: The Melodians' "Rivers of Babylon," written by founding member Brent Dowe, is one of reggae's most famous songs. Originally on the soundtrack album for the film The Harder They Come, "Rivers" was later covered by Boney M and became a planetary smash. The Melodians were founded in 1962, and recorded for Coxsone, Duke Reid, Lesley Kong and Sonia Pottinger. The group disbanded in 1973.

The Maytals, circa 1970.

Bernard Collins of the Abyssinians vocal trio outside his record shop, Kingston 1981. Formed in 1969, the Abyssianians are best known for the classic song "Satta Amassagana," co-written by Bernard and fellow Abyssinian Donald Manning.

suddenly meshed their chording so that the accents took on a more pulse-like character. A recording by Larry & Alvin captured the sound, and a new rhythm was born.

This "random creation" explanation for reggae's genesis makes as much sense as any other. Toots' record still has elements of rock steady and there is no record from the late '60s that can be identified as "purely reggae." Continuous evolution, spontaneous bursts of creation by musicians who were influenced by everything going on in their environment, was in effect. There were a lot of changes in Jamaica by 1968, many of them beautifully portrayed in the film The Harder They Come.

Young Ivan in The Harder They Come was part of a massive migration to the glittering lure of Kingston by country people in search of a better life—a job, more money, or sheer longing for novelty. The country people came to Kingston with the traditional music of the countryside—hymns, folk songs, and drumming patterns—indelibly stamped in their minds. At the same moment, the previously obscure Rastafarians suddenly began appearing in the city, sparking a social fad among the disaffected youth of the city who found the city's glitter to be a mirage when they tried to grab the gold. Suddenly, little groups of drummers and chanters appeared on streetcorners where harmonizers or solitary guitar players had hung out before. The pulse of Africa, preserved in the country, was brought to the city and urban air was leavened by ancient melodies.

The Melodians' "Rivers of Babylon" on The Harder They Come soundtrack captures the Rasta-influenced new mood. The lyrics, based on Psalm 137 of the Bible, reflect the apocalyptic outlook of Rastas. Christian sects may have shared this version but they did not inject it into secular life to the same degree. The psalm's sombre mood, the droning harmonies, and the measured reggae pulse add up to a hypnotic spell that is miles away from the music called rock steady. There's no sense of beginning, middle or

end (nor verse, chorus, bridge) to the song: it seemingly could go on forever, just as the Rasta drummers would play endlessly, obliterating time.

Even more reflective of the Rasta influence is the Abyssinians' "Satta Amassagana," with its minor chords and modal harmonies. What began as a Rasta hymn—chanted and drummed by the hour—evolved into one of the most widely used rhythms in reggae. The Abyssinians' "Declaration of Rights" illustrates the effect of minor keys even better. Over a classic Studio One rhythm, used on countless reggae tunes, the Abyssinians weave a modal melody through minor chords. Traditional drum rhythms, especially *funde* and *repeater* patterns, are voiced by rhythm guitar chucks while the one-drop bass mimics the *akete*. The same rhythm with major chords would give an entirely different feeling: more dynamic, less chant-like.

Besides the apocalyptic metaphors and Biblical

imagery stemming from Rasta influence, reggae became a vehicle for non-Rasta ghetto youth to express themselves. Where rock steady had been overwhelmingly romantic, with the odd message tune or social commentary building on traditional proverbs ("I've got the handle, you've got the blade") or a generalized plea for justice (the Heptones' "Equal Rights"), reggae frontally expressed the ghetto lifestyle.

In the wake of post-Independence euphoria, those who had flocked to the cities were beginning to realize that there was little hope of post-Independence bounty including them. "The pressure" began to build in the overcrowded, scuffling ghettos (c.f. "Pressure Drop" by the Maytals in The Harder They Come). Young people reacted by creating fantasy worlds based on Italian horse operas or gangster films (the spaghetti westerns featuring Clint Eastwood and Lee Van Cleef were incredibly popular). So reggae voiced the rude boy's reality. Though the Wailers, ahead of their time as usual, had done this in the ska days ("Simmer Down," "Rudie") as had the Clarendonians ("Rudie Gone a Jail"),

rude boy music now became mainstream reggae. The Slickers' "Johnny Too Bad" and Desmond Dekker's "Shanty Town" epitomised this music in The Harder They Come.

As the currents flowed together, the proto-reggae of the late '60s and early '70s streamed out of myriad studios which had sprung up. Randy's, Federal, Beverley's, Harry J's and others had joined Dodd's Studio One and Reid's Treasure Isle. New recording equipment became available and further expanded the musical development of reggae. The best work of the time emanated from three producers: Clement "Sir Coxsone" Dodd, Lee "Scratch" Perry, and Leslie Kong.

One of the most significant events in reggae occured when Coxsone Dodd came back from England equipped with a two-track recorder, tape delay and assorted other gadgets. The two-track enabled him to record complete rhythm tracks separately and possibilities multiplied. Suddenly it was possible to add a solo vocal, harmony vocal, instrumental solo or deejay rap over the same rhythm track, which was now perpetually available for every imaginable permutation and combination. That same rhythm track could be used for any number of different

success as a singer or even toaster. So his vast musical imagination had to be channeled into producing and arranging. When the Wailers came to him in 1969, he was ready to unleash his accumulated rhythmic sense and make some of the greatest records of the era—arguably the best Wailers records also.

By 1969, the Wailers had left Dodd and temporarily disbanded. When Bob Marley returned from America, they re-formed with their Impressions-derived harmonies, sounding better than ever, with their songwriting at an absolute peak. The thirty-or-so tunes they cut with Perry appeared on *Soul Rebels Volume I and II* on Perry's Maroon and Upsetter labels in Jamaica. (In England they were released as *African Herbsman* and *Soul Rebels,* the latter later re-titled *Rasta Revolution).*

The Perry-produced version of "Lively Up Yourself" takes all the usual elements of proto-reggae and delivers them in a superior package, anchored by stunningly effective bass-led rhythms. On "Small Axe," Perry's trademark chopping guitar figures and ticking percussion

ker and the Aces, the Wailers (who recorded with him briefly after leaving Perry) and Bruce Ruffin dominated the Jamaican charts from 1968 through 1971. The Pioneers and the Maytals, whose greatest recordings were made with Kong, epitomise Kong's style during this period.

The Pioneers' "Long Shot Kick De Bucket" (the tale of a popular racehorse's demise) and "Samfie Man," both included on *King Kong,* an excellent sampler of Kong's greatest productions, pit chopping guitar and bubbling organ in tandem against doubled bass and single-note guitar figures as the drums hit the one-drop bass and swirl accents around it. The actual rhythms themselves do not stand out, but all the elements are so well balanced and cleanly recorded the earthy performance is irresistible. It's a typical Kong session we see in *The Harder They Come* with the Maytals doing a relentless, joyful version of "Sweet and Dandy." The groove is so strong and the sound so warm that one wishes it would continue forever.

By the early '70s, the foundations had been laid for most major innovations in reggae. The

Left: Producer Leslie Kong was one of the early pioneers of recording Jamaican music, launching the careers of Bob Marley, Jimmy Cliff and many others. Kong was also a key figure in the international dissemination of Jamaican music, producing the world-wide hit "Israelites" and supervising the Paul Simon sessions in 1971 that put Jamaican studios and session musicians on the map. Kong died of a sudden heart ailment in 1971. Some say obeah did him in.

Center left: Bob Marley and the Wailers, San Francisco 1973.

Prince Buster and Jimmy Cliff at Buster's shop, 1976.

ines, versions of the same tune or bare dub ylings. Thus was born the huge library of udio One rhythm tracks—still being used on t records today.

Lee Perry started out working in Dodd's udio as a kind of freelance arranger and prod-ction assistant. His first records as a solo artist evealed his vocal range to be too limited for

(he often added African percussion devices), played by Perry's house band, the Upsetters (the nucleus of which became the Wailers' band), took the music to a new level of sophistication. The rhythm section of Aston "Family Man" Barrett on bass and his brother Carlton on drums was the most innovative combination in reggae at the time.

At the other end of the proto-reggae spectrum, we find the productions of Leslie Kong, a small businessman turned producer. While Kong, like most Jamaican producers, had little or no musical expertise, he did have an ear for quality and a willingness to take time to get the music right. Moreover, the sessions which he oversaw have an identifiable signature in the clean production, bright, choppy rhythms, and melodic, soulful vocals. Although Perry's depth and Dodd's innovations were not matched by Kong, he stripped the music down to gimmick-free, formulaic essentials.

Leslie Kong's recordings with the Pioneers, Maytals, Melodians, Ken Boothe, Desmond Dek-

Kong sound bathed Kingston, blaring out of homemade speakers and transistor radios everywhere. Pop reggae was born. Lee Perry had opened the way for African rhythms to become an important constituent of the reggae pulse, making overt what had always been beneath the surface. Coxsone Dodd had established a storehouse of rhythms with new recording technology, which he used as the basis for dub music —a new emphasis on bass-and-drum rhythm which sparked an addiction among sound-system dancegoers that continues to this day.

Reggae had opened up for infinite degrees of improvisation. The freedom sought in the lyrics had been achieved in the music. By 1972, it was time for reggae to attack.

—*Randall Grass*

Bruce Ruffin

Producer Lee "Scratch" Perry at the Black Ark studio, Washington Gardens 1976.

Sir Coxsone

Sir Coxsone at Studio One, 1976.

The young Dennis Brown

John Holt, lead singer of the Paragons. His song "Tide Is High" was a big hit for nuevo-wavo group Blondie in 1981.

Anyone who even casually explores the last 25 years of Jamaican music will constantly stumble across the name of Clement "Sir Coxsone" Dodd, proprietor of the famed Studio One label, pioneering record producer, and a leading sound system operator from the early ska days on.

Nearly every reggae artist of note has either begun a career with him or recorded for him at some point, including the Wailers, Toots and the Maytals, Burning Spear, the Wailing Souls, Dennis Brown, Joseph Hill of Culture, Marcia Griffiths, Rita Marley and the Soulettes, Johnny Osbourne, the Heptones, the Gladiators, the Skatalites, Dillinger, Dennis Alcapone and dozens of others.

The Studio One catalog of recordings, encompassing every era of Jamaican music since the late '50s, continues to be popular in Jamaican communities everywhere. Dodd was one of the first to market dub in the form of LPs and the first to introduce two-track recording to the Jamaican scene. His trove of rhythm tracks contains so many classic rhythms that Studio One continues to have hits using newly over-dubbed vocals on tenor 15-year-old rhythm tracks.

Yet Dodd has remained a somewhat elusive figure, releasing virtually no all-new recordings. Like most Jamaican producers, he is cast as a villain in many musicians' tales of mistreatment and exploitation. Yet many artists acknowledge that he has been one of the few producers to work with them to develop their artistry. Above all, he is a survivor, one who has withstood the often violent challenges of rivals (Duke Reid was a notorious nemesis in the ska days), the determined demands of musicians and the uncertain swings of the Jamaican economy.

Perhaps his survivor's instinct has led him to maintain a low profile. The conversation that follows took over a year to arrange—and even then almost did not take place. Finally, we

agreed to meet at his wholesale shop in Brooklyn on New Year's Eve. The shop—as hard to locate as the man himself—was, until recently, situated on a run-down block in Bedford-Stuyvesant, dominated by boarded-up buildings, many of which harbor so-called "social clubs"—dens of drug trafficking and illicit entertainment. Rumbles of reggae bass vibrate from the basements of some of these buildings.

Q: *What inspired you to get involved with recording?*

Coxsone Dodd: We realized that we were not getting enough stuff [from America] so we had to make our local sound. I had a couple of sessions, basically tango and calypso and some rhythm and blues-inclined sounds.

Where were these recorded?

It was Federal Records. Well, after a couple of times in the studio, I found a sound that was popular with the dance crowd in Jamaica, and we worked from there. And, as a matter of fact, I didn't realize that this could be a business. I just did it for enjoy-

ment! So we had the demos being played on the sound systems—this is what we called "dub"—and it got so popular that we realized that it could be business and I released a couple of my first songs. This is when Duke Reid came into the production scene. Before then, the only local music that was being made was strictly calypso or a slow tango type of thing.

So, were you among the first sound system operators then?

No, there were others. Popular sounds like Tom "The Great" Sebastian and Nick. They were the top sounds that one could remember. But one of the earliest sounds was a sound named Waldron. At that time I was a fairly young kid.

Why were instrumentals bigger in the ska days than vocals?

Well, it was much more artistry in it because you had a nice melody going and when it came time for the solos, each person could solo and so forth. And that was important because it was really based upon dancing.

Back then, there were all those talented soloists. But now there doesn't seem to be much room for

soloists.

I'd say that production has fallen in Jamaica in the last ten or twelve years. You see, the earlier music, there was more arrangement. Now, it's just strictly drum and bass and . . . the unexpected, you know?

Production effects?

Yes, anything comes up and it just goes. Earlier, we had to have strict rhythm going and the whole song has been built up. You've got a nice introduction, then the singer comes in, then you have place for soloing and then get back to the singer again.

What are some of the things you did in the studio, involved with creating arrangements and things?

Well, . . . in the studio, it was more like leftover ideas from the night before, because I'm always planning for the next day in the studio. Even tape recorders weren't that easy to get in those days—they were very costly. Being handicapped by not being a writer, a musical writer . . . I've got to find ways of recording my ideas so that I can look back and think of what I was thinking of at that time.

Your own contribution has to come through . . . the arrangement?

The arrangement. The main thing was the use of a lot of rehearsal before recording so all the arrangements were done in rehearsal . . . We were well rehearsed . . . we have an idea of what the sound would be like . . . the whole structure.

I've heard that at one point Bob Marley worked for you as a kind of A&R man, had an office in your place and found new talent.

No, no, never. You see, when Bob Marley started with me, they were very young artists. I gave them a lot of direction. But they never really reached that far, to be a A&R man, and select.

How about the Heptones?

Yes, they did, they did. A very good group. Some of them played [on sessions]. Leroy played bass on some of them, Barry plays percussion.

How did you get the singers you wanted?

Every Sunday was my audition day. During the run of the day, there may be a person who was from the country or whatever. I always made myself available to check it out and see whether the person made sense or not. Maybe a man might have a good voice but didn't have a good song but you night figure you can get a good song written for him.

I've heard it said that of all the producers in Jamaica, only you and Lee Perry tried to work with the artist and develop the artists.

I think that is true . . . I would really say a word for Lee Perry because he is a hard worker and has been in the business for years. But Perry started by me and was by me for years, before he had any idea about production.

In the middle to late '60s, when the music seemed to be changing, the beat was changing from what is called rock steady to what is called reggae. What was behind the changes?

Yes, well, idea come along. But I remember what changed the whole sound from rock steady to reggae. We did a recording by the name of "Nanny Goat" By Larry [Marshall] and Alvin. A very popular record. At that time, I had been in England and came back with quite a few gadgets . . . like a delay. After "Nanny Goat," we had a series of recordings with that sound but it was like the guitar being on the delay meshed with the organ shuffle. This was coming on as something new, and this is where the change came from rock steady to reggae. And you can listen to the guitar change in "Nanny Goat" and quite a few of the Cables' tunes. But rock steady is a beautiful music. You can dance it, you can rock it.

Why did the Wailers leave Studio One?

Well, they started to move into this Rasta thing and, you know, I wasn't ready to go with that. Then they broke the contract 'cause they figured that they were underage [when they had signed] and I'd taken them to my lawyer to straigh-

ten out certain things. Bob Marley was more or less like an adoption, 'cause he used to stay by me, you know, and I used to provide whatever . . . Let's face it, the artist, it's hard for them to really have a steady work. Most of them, I encourage them to find a part-time work and not just depend on the recording because it's pretty tough in Jamaica.

The Wailing Souls were around pretty early and they grew up in the same neighborhood as the Wailers. Did they start recording with you way back then?

They started recording for me as a group first, but the lead now, Pipe, he had done some recording for Prince Buster. He was in a group called the Schoolboys. But that wasn't really happening for them. They were discouraged early by Bob Marley 'cause we could really relate to him. He [Bob] was really scared of him [Pipe]. But comparing them to [the Wailers] when Tosh and Livingstone were together, they [the Wailers] had a really unique sound. But I think these guys [the Wailing Souls] need more guidance.

In the early days of the sound systems, it must have been an exciting time in Jamaica, with the competition and so on.

Well, the sound system days are always referred to as the good old days, because the behaviour and discipline was on top. You just go to the beach and have fun!

You didn't have the trouble then that we have now (at dances)? Cause a lot people think of them as rough and tumble days.

No! No! (chuckles) Those were the nice days!

—*Randall Grass*

Perry Henzell, The Harder They Come

Perry Henzell

The headlines screamed off the front page of the *Daily Gleaner* on Thursday morning, September 2, 1948: 2 KILLED, 4 SHOT BY ESCAPED CONVICT; GUNMAN TRAPPED IN HOTEL; SHOOTS WAY OUT OF POLICE CORDON, SLAYS WOMAN; POLICE HUNT DESPERADO AFTER RUNNING GUN BATTLE IN CITY'S WEST END. Rhygin' the bandit, Jamaica's most feared criminal, was on the loose.

Rhygin'

Later, after he had been brought to rough Jamaican justice, the *Gleaner* would rhetorically ask on its front page: "Who was this Rhygin'? This man with a price on his head, whose twisted mind made him an enemy of society. Who was this five-feet-three of ruthless killer who at the turn of last September blasted a blood-spattered path to newspaper headlines with seven falling before his guns, and three of the seven dead?"

His real name was Vincent Martin, and he was born in the parish of St. Catherine in 1924. When he was 14, he arrived in

Kingston like so many ambitious country boys, on the back of a produce truck. He turned to a life of crime, and was sentenced to whippings and brief terms in jail for wounding the victims of his robberies. In the ghetto he had many names—Ivan Martin, Ivanhoe Martin, Ivan Brown, "Alan Ladd," and "Captain Midnight." But mostly he was known as Rhygin,' denoting a *bwai* who's always number one.

According to the *Gleaner:* "He picked up a smattering of blacksmith's work. Long hours of swinging a heavy sledge built tough muscles into his small frame. And, like most small men, Rhygin' was very active on his feet . . . Underworld women heard of his prowess and obliged with their dubious affections. He took to flashy clothes and somewhere on his forays on St. Andrew houses, he acquired guns . . ."

Not only did Rhygin' acquire guns, he flaunted them. Convicted in January 1948 of possession of a revolver and burglary, he escaped from the General Penitentiary in

Bottom left: The Heptones in Kingston, circa 1975. From left: Barry Llewellyn, Earl Morgan, Leroy Sibbles.

Jimmy Cliff as Rhygin'. Vincent Martin, the real-life gunman of the late 1940s, stuck up a photo studio at gunpoint and sent the pictures to the **Gleaner** so his fame as a master criminal would spread; and it did.

April of that year, jumping out of second-story slit window. In May, he stuck up a photo studio and demanded a set of glossies showing him posed with a pair of revolvers and sporting baggy zoot pants and a rakishly slanted fedora.

On September 1, he foiled a nighttime raid on his hideout, the Carib Hotel in Hannah Town. Dur-

The real Rhygin', 1948.

ing the raid Rhygin' blew away two detectives, Edgar Lewis and H. E. Earle. (Lewis died at the hospital.) Rhygin' jumped out of a window and vanished into a block of tenements.

Police reinforcements were called in, but during a running gunfight Rhygin,' wearing only his underpants, shot another police-man and escaped. Three hours later, Rhygin' showed up at a house on Spanish Town Road, where he thought he would find a man named Eric Goldson, who Rhygin' thought had stooled on him. Goldson wasn't home, so Rhygin' shot his girlfriend, Tibby Young, and for good measure shot two witnesses, Estella Brown and Iris Bailey.

Rhygin' laid low for six weeks. He may have been slightly woun-ded when he shot his way out of the raid in Hannah Town. Needless to say, he was the object of one of the biggest manhunts in Jamaican history. He was almost caught on October 7 when he emerged from a swamp and crossed Spanish Town Road at Red Water Bridge and fled into the hills. With two other gunmen, Rhygin' sat in the hills and watched the police search for them far below. They had to keep on moving.

At Cockburn Pen, Rhygin' split

from his friends and headed into the city for a new hideout. Finally, his gang members found him a canoe, and Rhygin' was rowed out to Lime Cay, a desert isle seven miles off Port Royal. The plan seems to have been that he would be picked up by a boat bound for Cuba. Rhygin' never made it.

The *Gleaner,* October 9, 1948: RHYGIN' KILLED BY POLICE; GUN BATTLE ON LIME CAY THIS MORNING; KILLER TRAPPED AFTER FLIGHT FROM CITY. When the police caught up with Rhygin,' they ventilated him. Dozens of Mark 7 bullets were taken from his "ghastly" corpse. But to some, Rhygin' was a hero. He was the first rude boy. Thousands gathered at the Kingston morgue when word of the killing spread. When the van bearing the body approached at noon, pandemonium spread among the people, and police had to fire in the air to keep order.

That day, the *Gleaner* editorial-ized: "It must have occurred to Rhygin' several times as he watched the police close in on him that 'Crime Does Not Pay.' " And perhaps it did. But one can't help but wonder if Rhygin' had any inkling that his spirit would even-tually apotheosize into the stuff of Jamaican legend. More than twenty years after his execution, Rhygin's story would put Jamaica, and even-tually reggae music, on the world cultural map.

In Perry Henzell's Garden

In 1973, a strange little film about Jamaica made its American premiere in Milwaukee. Cut in a thick Carib patois (subtitles are used early in the film), using King-stonian musicians and actors (two of whom were murdered during

production), *The Harder They Come* recreated a fearsome world of reggae music, outlaw icono-graphy and Third World revolt. Predictably, *THTC* became *the* reggae cult film. It ran for seven years in Boston before the theatre semi-retired it in 1980. In the film, Jimmy Cliff played Rhygin.'

The Harder They Come has proven to be one of the most important films in the cultural history of our time. It created an

interest and a market for reggae. Jamaican stars like the late Bob Marley, Burning Spear and Jimmy Cliff easily filled the demand for Jamaican roots music created by the film. And, most importantly, the reggae movement focused its unsparing lens on a troubled, verdant, endlessly fascinating island corner of the Caribbean called Jamaica, where 700 inno-cents and gunmen can be killed during a national election that turns into urban civil war.

The man who shot *The Harder They Come* in 1971 is Perry Henzell, a true man of the Caribbean (born in Aruba of Dutch descent) now in his early forties. Many people have told me over the years that Perry Henzell knows Jamaica's secrets; so, desirous to know them myself, I went to visit him one morning not long ago at his tropical studios in one of Kingston's tonier neigh-borhoods.

The compound on West King's House Road has a gatehouse that serves as a kitchen and the head-quarters of Island Records. Down a green path redolent of oleander and ginger lily, I found Perry working in a house whose walls were open to the slight breeze. He was screening rushes from his new film on a Betamax. Further in the garden is another building with a film lab and editing room. Henzell was harried; he was shooting that afternoon on the beach with his young French crew, and so couldn't really talk. "Come back for supper," he yelled over his shoulder. "Around 8:30."

When I returned that night, crew and staff had departed and Henzell's garden was dark, cool and quiet. We talked over cold Red Stripe beer, sitting on an open upper veranda, as palm fronds clacked against each other in the breeze and the tiny hummingbirds Jamaicans call "doctor birds" drank from the crimson bells of trumpet vines growing along the railings. If anyone has his finger on the island's national pulse, it is Perry Henzell, speaking in a soft Caribbean burr:

"Right now, Jamaica is a country rejuvenating itself" he says with the trace of a smile. "It's an incredibly exciting time to be living here. In spite of all the bad things you or anyone may have heard about Jamaica over the last years, I don't think I would have missed it for anything."

Why, I wondered, had Henzell taken almost eight years to complete his new film, *No Place Like Home,* considering the success of *The Harder They Come?* I guessed the delay might have had to do with the rigors of the unsuccessful socialist revolution Jamaica has just passed through.

Perry explained that his problems weren't as simple as that. During the early phase of production, his local financing collapsed while *THTC* foundered on the international market. Then he discovered problems with his story, in which a bourgeois American woman is introduced to the mysteries of the island by her amorous local driver. And then the hard times involved with Jamaica's socialist experiment began to hit in 1976.

"This became an incredibly confused country over the last five years," says Henzell, somewhat ruefully. "Toward the end of Manley's government, people here were literally walking around in a daze. So much had to happen before people like myself could find our way again. That's why I'm so proud to be a Jamaican, because I believe that any other country

would have gone to all-out civil war over the kind of politics we have been through. And that's why I'm so grateful to the American cult audience."

At this, one of Henzell's retainers poked his head through the door and announced dinner, which he had on a large tray. "Put it over there," Henzell said, and we sat down to a meal of spicy roast pork, white rice, salad.

As the food quickly disappeared

and we licked the grease from our fingers, I asked Perry about the future, now that *No Place Like Home* was finally finished. He answered that he has in mind a Jamaican trilogy of films. "The three films assume two Jamaicas, the Jamaica of the city and the Jamaica of the country. So *The Harder They Come* was an examination of the city through the eyes of a country boy. The new film, *No Place Like Home,* is an examination

of the countryside by an American woman. And the third, which I'll call *The Power Game,* will be a clash between these two spirits for control of the island, seen through the eyes of six characters, each of whom thinks he or she has the power, in the crunch, to take over Jamaica."

Did he think, I asked, that this last film would be a realistic scenario or a paranoid scenario?

"Absolutely realistic," he said vehemently. "In Jamaica, it has *already* happened. The center here has gone soft, and basically we are still up for grabs by whoever can amass enough firepower on his side."

Later, after supper, we sat in front of the video and watched parts of *No Place Like Home.* The plot is simple. An intelligent and attractive American woman is sucked in by the relentless lure of this exotic jungle isle. More subtle than Henzell's first movie, *NPLH* relies on nuance and strong acting rather than on the cartoon imagery and blistering reggae soundtrack of *The Harder They Come.*

When he flicked off the monitor, I asked Henzell why Jamaican culture was so interesting to outsiders like myself and the thousands of young people who kept his movie playing in Boston for eight years. His reply was exactly what I was looking for, a true secret of Jamaica.

"If you take as your cultural polarities Africa on the one side, and North America on the other side, you have two *extremely* heavy cultures balancing each other. And there's this one little, tiny connection between the two, in which you can see both. And that connection, I think, is Jamaica. So think: you have a huge quantum of cultural energy on each side, and one very small connection that's glowing red-hot. That's Jamaica, glowing like a red-hot wire.

"So somebody like me—or you, for that matter—you touch that energy and you get a shock! It's a live wire. It's almost as though all you have to do is do your work, *transmit* what is already there, and it's automatically interesting because this culture is so full of energy and human life. So I feel incredibly lucky to be here in the middle of it, just to have the *privilege* of tapping it."

—*Stephen Davis*

The Reggae Arrangement

Reggae is rhythmically spaced like the natural sounds you would hear any evening in Jamaica, outside of town: a lacelike pattern of beeping tree frogs and crickets over the night hush. The pace of it is natural, unhurried and altogether *human*, indicative of a people who have to walk instead of drive and whose disregard for the strict, workaday time-sense is epitomized by the now-legendary attitude "soon come."

The critical factor in arranging music with many parts and instruments is rhythmic syncopation and order: If there really is a rhythmic place for everything in the group pattern, and everything's in its place, you have a tight and tidy sound. And this is the overwhelming virtue of the reggae music approach. In reggae, if each musician strays from his pattern enough, it just ceases to sound like reggae music and changes form.

Reggae's approach is to have fewer instruments play fewer parts. The arrangement can nevertheless accommodate many instruments, because the muscians will double up on a handful of parts. The result is that the rhythm pattern retains its character and spaciousness, but tonal qualities become richer and more complex as the various timbres mesh to form compound timbres. Each instrumental role in the ensemble, except for melodic signatures, is in fact a syncopated drum part. This is a very African aspect of reggae, and accounts for the intrinsic tightness (without stiffness) of most Jamaican arrangements.

Reggae, like most of the world's popular music, is in 4/4 time, four main beats to a bar of 4/4. However, in almost all of Jamaican music since the '50s, the strongly felt beats, or "downbeats", are *not* 1 & 3, but 2 & 4. This is one of the main reasons, besides lack of exposure, that reggae has had a difficult time gaining acceptance in America and Europe, where the public is used to feeling the downbeat emphasis on 1 & 3. Hence the fairly common com-

Sly Dunbar and Robbie Shakespeare, currently the master rhythm section in reggae.

Leroy "Horsemouth" Wallace, a key drummer in the history of reggae. A graduate of the famed Alpha Boys School, Horsemouth became involved in Jamaica's spirit religions—pocomania and kumina—and went on to play with Studio One, the Soul Syndicate, Jack Ruby's Black Disciples, Marcia Griffiths, Inner Circle, Now Generation and many others. He was the principle musician/actor in the film **Rockers**.

plaint, "I just don't know how to dance to reggae."

Reggae took over from the prevailing rhythms of rock steady around 1969, with a rounder, fuller rhythm. It was not all that much faster than rock steady by the metronome (still 72–90 beats per minute), but the change in feel, especially the shuffle parts (see pages 54 and 55) made it sound peppier in pace.

By 1971, the pace of reggae had slowed down again and Jamaican music began to introspect slightly; there were not perhaps as many major musical developments as before, but reggae was consolidating all of the previous forms. The early '70s was the time of great diversity and experimentation.

The Ensemble

It was between 1974 and 1976 that

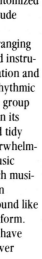

two new styles of drumming became extremely influential. First, under the producership of Bunny "Striker" Lee, who had already given Jamaica batches of rock steady and reggae hits, Lee's studio band (the Aggrovators) drummer, Carlton Davis a.k.a. Santa, was one of the originators of the "flying cymbal" or "flyers" pattern in reggae: his right hand would play on the half-open hi-hat in a sizzling pattern of sustained afterbeats (upbeats). Actually, the pattern had appeared a few times in rock steady. Coincidentally, Trinidadian calypso drummers also used a similar maneuver, but at a much quicker tempo.

It was typical of the Jamaican music scene that just as the Aggrovators saturated their own "flyers" market after two years, another studio, Channel One, and its house drummer Sly Dunbar (mostly with Aggrovators' Robbie Shakespeare on bass) kicked off a style they called rockers. Channel One continued the oldies revival, even printing "Revival Sounds" on their labels, and remaking mostly rock steady but also ska material from the 1960s catalogue of Coxsone Dodd's Studio One label.

The Channel One house band was called the Revolutionaires or the Revolutionaries; this was at a time when political wars in Angola and Mozambique were drawing a lot of concern in Jamaica. They put out a very successful horn instrumental album called *Revolutionary Sounds* which included the hit

"M.P.L.A." What really made Channel One's music distinctive, though, was Dunbar's drumming, which they appropriately called "militant style:" More strictly patterned than before, it featured a fat, muffled and very military-sounding snare sound on top, and a straight ahead marching figure from the bass drum on the bottom, on all the main and afterbeats (eight eighth-notes to the bar).

Credit for the style should be equally shared by the inimitable Leroy "Horsemouth" Wallace, Dunbar's mentor, who had been the house drummer at Studio One in the late '60s. Once again, like the flying cymbal, this bass drum

figure had been precursed at Studio One six years earlier by another drummer named Ducky, but in the mid '70s it appeared that the inspiration for this eight-to-a-bar figure was disco.

Technically, this stepping bass drum pattern is eight eighth-notes to a bar, but it is played at the same tempo as the four-quarter-notes-to-a-bar bass drum in disco. It sounds best at around 130 beats per minute, sounding rushed, even busy, at faster speeds. This means that the four main beats of the bar occur at half the frequency, or 65 beats per minute. A lot of the rock steady songs that were remade as rockers had been played originally at 72–90 beats per minute, but in order to comfortably accommodate the new rockers bass drum at the right tempo, the songs had to be slowed down considerably. This

took the life out of a few of the tunes, but most of them actually benefitted from being stretched out like this, now unfolding with a new lyricism and liquid elegance. The real revelation was to hear how absolutely ingenious so many of the old bass parts really are.

Looking back over trends in Jamaican drumming, the drummer, like so many other kinds of drummers, has held the role of time-keeper, but at different times has enjoyed varying degrees of freedom from pattern. Once the players get the groove, the rest of Jamaican band is rhythmically self-sufficient enough to allow the drummer a stylistic shift towards almost jazz-like freedom of movement and colour. Ska and rock steady were very reserved styles: strict patterns, a few accents and punctuations, but not many long breaks. When rockers came along, the drummers went to patterns that were almost as strictly disciplined as the bass lines to which they were closely tied.

Nowadays, the patterns have changed and are still quite strict, but there are more breaks than ever before from all instruments, not just the drums. Since 1979, there has been a trend in drumming towards playing the four main beats on the bass drum. The bass drum has also started to play slow American funk syncopations and is mixed like funk bass drum with more treble than ever before, so that it has a rather loud punching or flapping attack.

Now the snare plays mostly just the 2 & 4 beats, a somewhat deadened sound bathed in reverb. It's almost as if the snare and bass drum are reversing the roles they played in early reggae. There is also a tendency now to pile on several tracks of solo clutter on the records. This will no doubt alienate purists inside the reggae market, while winning new converts outside it.

It was during rock steady that the bass, the most important instrument in reggae, assumed its full importance and its unique place in Jamaican music. Reggae bass is merely the latest and strongest expression of a cultural predisposition for bass sounds that *predates* the arrival of American records and electric instruments in Jamaica.

The Jamaican fondness for bass is clearly present in mento groups, where the hollow branch of the trumpet tree used as a crude trumpet to produce tuba-like bass patterns of mainly rhythmic value with a loose melody, mostly out-of-key, but *in rhythm* with the rest of the song. Tourist-oriented mento bands on Jamaica's north coast, often include a "rhumba box," a large thumb piano ("kalimba") called a *sansa* throughout Africa. Its long metal blades, sometimes hacksaw blades, provide a bass accompaniment when plucked, though they are not always tuned to the rest of the music.

I have heard two hill farmers in Portland parish, Jamaica sing a duet accapella (without instrumental accompaniment). One sang the words and tune in a definite key,

while the other man hummed, grunting out a bass part completely out of key with the song, but which was extremely supportive and enhancing rhythmically. These examples of folk bass culture point to a bass aesthetic in which rhythmic statement and strength take priority over melodic/harmonic considerations. It means that, in this case, the bass is a

drum that plays a definite rhythm, but may or may not play a distinct melody line; in fact, reggae bass lines are called *riddims* in Jamaica.

A Jamaican riddim is an underlying statement of its own. It is equally supportive of itself and, at the same time, of all the other elements in the music. Like other types of bass playing, riddims give arrangements "bottom," and complement the chords, melody and lyrics of the song. Yet each riddim has its own distinctive and strict melodic and rhythmic pattern which has a recognizable identity and can be listened to as a *separate composition unto itself.*

Riddims are highly intuitive, delicate and strategic exercises in

balancing "space" (or silence), and "matter" (or sound) with reference to pitch, so as to make a communication with an intimate, conversational quality. The bass "says" a phrase, then pauses for "breath" like a person speaking. The pause "frames" the phrase and gives the mind of the listener time to absorb it. After a string of notes, the listener becomes accustomed to the

presence of the bass in his ears and body. At this point, a cleverly placed pause creates a minute "gap," a momentary emptiness in the bottom of the music, which regains the full attention of the listener.

Wherever bass pauses occur, other instruments are unveiled and "pop out" of the arrangement. Where a pause coincides with the stronger divisions of the rhythm (any of the main beats) it will emphasize them.

So there is an ingenious element here of pausing for emphasis, as well as playing for emphasis; some say the glass is half-empty, some say it is half-full; riddims acknowledge both views.

After a pause, the bass hits the

listener again, this time with renewed strength. Physiologically, depending on its pitch and loudness, bass resonates the the facial mask, the abdominal cavity and even the pelvic area. Riddims, being low in pitch and under the arrangement, tend to bypass the intellectual mind and *communicate directly with the heart by actually massaging it in rhythm.* It's no accident that all over the world reggae is proclaimed "music of the heart." In fact, the tempo of Jamaican records compares remarkably with the human pulse rate.

There are many groups of basic rhythm patterns in reggae which, with much variation, are used repeatedly over the years as models for nearly all the bass lines; these form a sort of culturally sanctioned bass orthodoxy, which very few of the bass players choose to depart from. But it *is* a matter of choice, not inability: orthodoxy is highly respected in the Jamaican music community.

A good, solid riddim goes down through the years, as the musical backing for new songs, deejay scat-singing, instrumentals and dubs. In this sense, Jamaican music continually treasures its own past. It bears mention that a great number of the most seminal bass lines in Jamaican music are the work of one man, Leroy Sibbles. Sibbles, though better known as lead singer for the Heptones, is an expert bass player and with Horsemouth Wallace on drums, they made up the house rhythm section at Studio One, nicknamed "Coxsone University," during the late '60s.

For a number of years, Sibbles composed the riddims that backed the most influential hits and artists in Jamaica. This makes Sibbles a true giant in Jamaican music, equal in stature to Bob Marley. Whatever advances the Wailers have made for the vocal consciousness of reggae, Sibbles has done at least as much for the musical development of the music's most important instrument. He brought much of his African heritage as a "West Indian" to the Jamaican bass style. As one man, he is really a bridge between Afro-Jamaican and Afro-American musical values.

As a riddim goes from bass player to bass player, either over the years, or at a specific time during one of reggae's frequent crazes over one particular riddim, the riddim's melody and phrasing may mutate slightly. Or, as is the case nowadays, two traditional

Leroy Sibbles

riddims may be intentionally hybrid. The factor that changes the least is that of key: the same riddim recorded ten years apart in different studios by different bass players is likely to be played in the same key. This fact strongly suggests that for reggae players and listeners, key has as much to do with the identity and exact mood of a riddim as rhythmic phrasing and

Frequency ranges and relative volumes

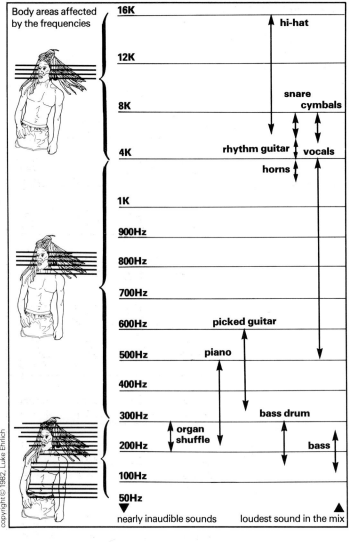

melodic form.

In reviewing a cross section of riddims spanning the rock steady era through rockers, the variety of rhythmic forms is staggering.

Riddims tend to fall into four categories: the first two are those that emphasize beats 1 & 3, and those that emphasize 2 & 4 along with the drummer. With these groups, the placing of the emphasis on alternating main beats is symmetrical within the bar. Riddims of the 1 & 3 group balance out and interact with the heaviness of the drummer on "downbeats" 2 & 4. The 2 & 4 group makes the bottom of the arrangement coagulate around these beats.

The third category is comprised of bass parts that emphasize the beats of the bar in an asymmetrical fashion. These are: 1, 2 & 3; 1, 2 & 4; 1, 3 & 4; 1 & 4; 2 & 3; or 2, 3 & 4. Reggae bass is often described as "loping." This can be attributed to the fact that the bass players sustain and bend certain notes in a subtle way, often playing dotted eighth-notes. But bass lines of this asymmetrical category are "loping" or "lopsided" *in their very form,* because the emphasis on the main beats is unevenly distributed in the bar. The great majority of Jamaican bass lines emphasize the one beat, often preceded and set off by a rest on the fourth afterbeat. The last category is for very sparse or very unorthodox riddims that may accent only one main beat out of the bar, or are very syncopated and emphasize one or more afterbeats or other obscure offbeats.

The simpler, and generally earlier, bass lines tend to be one-bar statements. Some of these contain identical or nearly identical rhythmic figures in each half of the bar and these are most symmetrical parts around—the AA patterns. Other one-bar statements are AB patterns, where B sounds like the lyrical result of A and is somehow a summation. These statements project a "call-and-response" or "theorem"-like quality: "If A, then B."

Later in the development of Jamaican music, the bass gradually extended the range of its statements to two-bar AB patterns and two- and four-bar ABAC patterns. Some bassists play one pattern just for the song's introduction and switch off to another for the main body of the tune.

The Mix

In the recording studio, players create new backing rhythms or use old ones that fit a particular singer's song, or they do an instrumental version of an old song at the request of a record producer. For reggae, as for any studio music, this is only half the story. What happens to the raw music and what the final product will actually sound like depends on the *mix* which is in the hands of the recording engineer.

Today in Jamaica four-track studios are thought to be rather limiting, at least for basic tracks, and everyone wants to work with at least eight tracks. Sixteen- and 24-track facilities also exist. The separation of the instruments onto their respective tracks is achieved either electronically, by running the signal of, say, the electric bass directly into a mixing board and onto its own track of the tape machine; or when using microphones, acoustically, by placing sound absorbent baffles around the mike to prevent it from picking up the other instruments (acoustic leakage). Each mike is then assigned to a separate track.

Another method of acoustic separation is the isolation booth, an acoustically separate and soundproof room, mostly used for the drums or vocals. The ultimate in separation is to cut a set of basic tracks leaving a few tracks open (unrecorded), then go back over the whole thing later, adding extra parts on the open tracks. This is called *over-dubbing.*

During the recording of the basic tracks, the engineer's job is to record the instruments in such a way that they will sound closest to the timbre and pitch of the desired finished product at *flat response.* When we say that a sound is recorded at flat response, we mean that as many as possible of the naturally existing and recordable frequency characteristics of the sound have been included on the basic track without *equalization* (Eq). Eq means filtering out some frequencies or accentuating others with tone controls on the mixing board.

Later the separate tracks are played back into another tape machine and mixed at different volumes with separate Eq for each track. This is called a *mix-down*; the finished product is called the *final mix.*

In addition to the basic volume and Eq controls on the mixing board, the engineer has many other means of altering sounds, which include reverb, echo, phase shifters and flangers. These are produced by delaying a sound, then mixing the delayed version with the original sound.

While the engineers' technique and recording technology advanced and changed the music during the '70s, the earlier traditional mixes are still the roots of today's production values and they reveal a lot about how Jamaicans have generally always liked their music to sound on records. Today, each instrument sounds richer and less tinny than before. This is partially due to technical advances, but also to a shift in production values towards American mixing concepts, those of black American music especially.

The graph on this page is a picture of an "average" Jamaican arrangement. The vertical axis represents the frequency band from bass to treble; entered up and down the band are the different instruments and the frequency band they mainly occupy, after Eq. Frequencies are measured in Hertz (Hz, or cycles per second) or in Kilohertz (one K = one thousand Hz).

The horizontal axis of the graph is a subjective appraisal of the relative volumes of the instruments in the mix. The frequencies that affect parts of the human body are also indicated. People hearing a reggae record on a fairly rich-sounding stereo, but at modest volumes, might only feel the bass part gently vibrating their ears, forehead and throat. But on a large and powerful sound system, such as they have in Jamaica, deeper overtones of the same bass part may be reproduced on the larger speakers and at much higher decibel levels. The listeners would then feel the bass also resonating their chest, stomach and pelvis.

The lowest frequencies on a reggae mix are, of course, the bass guitar and, slightly above it, the bass drum. The bass guitar is mixed to sound "round" with very little treble stringiness, and is among the loudest sounds on a Jamaican record. The traditional bass drum is mixed thinner than the bass, but again not with too much treble content. Its volume is adjusted relative to the bass guitar, so that its punch "becomes" the attack of the bass guitar notes it reinforces. Bass drums tend to "kick to the chest" or knock on the forehead.

Next, around 250 Hz, is the organ. Playing a shuffle part, it's one of the lowest volume sounds besides the piano, in the mix. The louder and/or more trebley the shuffle, the choppier the feel of the arrangement. Many organ shuffles have a muted or mushy timbre that performs a vital function in the sound of reggae. The organ occupies, virtually alone, a specific band of "warm-sounding" lower mid-range frequencies which is like the narrow neck of an hourglass, connecting the rounded, loud bass and bass drum below to everything else, mixed rather thinly and sharply above.

The organ sound becomes an often invisible musical glue of subtle, but formidable cohesive power both rhythmically and texturally. I pulls the mix together by acting as

54

n elusive mediator between the bassy rhythm section and the trebly ska section (piano-and-rhythm-guitar combination playing afterbeats). Because, rhythmically, the notes of organ shuffles are tucked away between other beats of other instruments, and because they are also tucked away in the group texture by their low volume and muffled Eq, organ shuffles are probably the toughest sounds for the untrained ear to pick out on a record, making them the most subliminally perceived of the sounds. Organ melodies, played on a louder, separate keyboard of the organ, are mixed sharper and about as loud as the vocals.

The sound of the piano rides in a slot just above the organ, but overlapping a bit, from 250–500 Hz. It is mixed rather thinly and softly, usually a little louder than the organ. On most of the older recordings, the upper mid-ranges of the piano are brought out, but its bass richness and percussive attack have both been cut. Unless the piano afterbeat is purposely featured in place of rhythm guitar, the engineer normally positions the volume and Eq of the piano to make it a "cushion" which buoys up and melds with the sharp sound of the rhythm guitar.

The resulting afterbeat sound is one entity, neither piano nor guitar. Instead, it is a fresh sound, starting with the clicking attack of the guitar which instantly "becomes" the more etherial, lingering decay of the piano. Afterbeat mixes are delicate balances, and slight adjustments yield surprisingly different results. If the engineer chooses to use reverb or echo on the afterbeats, he can stretch them out, completely changing the rhythmic feel of the entire song.

In the 300–500 Hz range above the piano is the picked or "lead guitar." The guitarist plays a muted, ornamented version of the bass part which is mixed with the same sharpness as the rhythm guitar, but perhaps a little thinner on the bottom, so it does not have that much melodic substance. Its trebly attack melds with the bass notes that it duplicates an octave above, and gives them a percussive attack which, in a subtle way, brings out the riddim but also ends up in the same area of the mix as *kete* (Rasta hand drums) and other percussion.

Vocals and horn intros are next, Eq-ed for medium thinness from 500 Hz to 2K, 2K being a pivotal point for vocals in mixes; at 2K,

the sharp edge or definition of the vocals increases abruptly. Voices are among the louder sounds on a record and are mixed so that they just stick up out of the arrangement enough to be featured, but not overly up front. If you think of the backing track as a post card, then vocals are a postage stamp in an upper corner: it doesn't take up all that much space, but you can't send a letter without one.

The ideal volume of the rhythm guitar is just loud enough to compete with, but not obscure, the vocals. Snare drum, tom-toms, and percussion are mixed slightly crisper than the rhythm guitar and

almost as loud. Cymbals are Eq-ed even crisper, and range in volume from very dim to as loud as the vocals. In the latter case, if the drummer doesn't exercise great care in how he positions his cymbal crashes, he can easily cover up parts of the vocals.

The most treble sound on most Jamaican records is the hi-hat. It is positioned right behind the rhythm guitar and snare in volume. On older Studio One recordings, the hi-hat is nearly inaudible, the snare and bass drum are dim and smokey-sounding, yet the rhythm pattern is still solid—the afterbeats, bass and shuffles carry the

rhythm completely.

Finally, to enhance certain parts of the music, Jamaican engineers have traditionally used a rapid tape-echo, like the vocal echo on so many '50s r&b records. ("Be Bop a Lula" by Gene Vincent is a good example.) Most of the time, it is used to increase vocal definition, but it can also slicken up the hi-hat, snare, rhythm guitar, even sometimes the bass drum.

By radically restructuring reggae music on his mixing board, the engineer fathered a whole new sound called dub.

—Luke Ehrlich

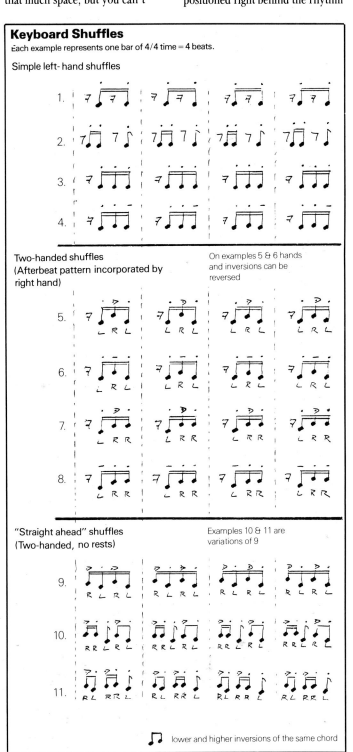

Keyboard Shuffles

Each example represents one bar of 4/4 time = 4 beats.

Simple left-hand shuffles
1. 2. 3. 4.

Two-handed shuffles
(Afterbeat pattern incorporated by right hand)

On examples 5 & 6 hands and inversions can be reversed

5. 6. 7. 8.

"Straight ahead" shuffles
(Two-handed, no rests)

Examples 10 & 11 are variations of 9

9. 10. 11.

♫ lower and higher inversions of the same chord

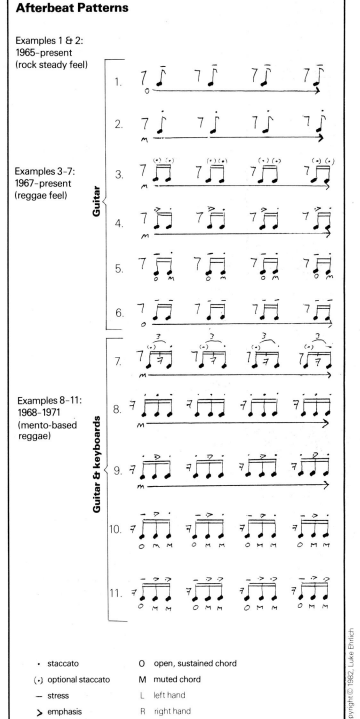

Afterbeat Patterns

Examples 1 & 2:
1965–present
(rock steady feel)

1. 2.

Examples 3–7:
1967–present
(reggae feel)

3. 4. 5. 6. 7.

Guitar

Examples 8–11:
1968–1971
(mento-based reggae)

8. 9. 10. 11.

Guitar & keyboards

• staccato   O open, sustained chord
(•) optional staccato   M muted chord
— stress   L left hand
> emphasis   R right hand

The Rastafarians

5

From the Root of King David

During the 1970s, Rasta became the ideology of Jamaican music. The Rastafarians emerged from the Kingston slums, dreadlocked and millenarian, in the early 1930s as a religious response to Jamaica's racial history. A legacy of slavery and colonial oppression combined with Marcus Garvey's prophesies and the biblical flow of world events to eventually produce a new religion and a new way of life for thousands of young Jamaicans trapped between Jamaica's history and its destiny. In this chapter, **Rory Sanders,** an observer of Rastafari (and a graduate of Harvard Divinity School), outlines the place of Ras Tafari in history, and demonstrates that the ever-changing modern Rasta faith is an avant-garde theology of liberation. Doubters have only to consult their Bibles.

A Rastafarian Primer

Man has a deep need for religious conviction, and Rasta resolves the contradiction of a white man's God in a colonial society . . . I think that the only Jamaican who truly knows who he is has to be the Rasta man.

Michael Manley, *New York Times,* August 25, 1976

"The menacing devils with snake nests for hair." "Cult that worships old newspaper clippings of Haile Selassie." "The Rastafarians—the ones who use manure in their hair." "No good Jamaican bums." "Rastafarian Link Seen in Shootout."

Believe it or not, those descriptions actually reflect popular opinion about the Rastafarian movement in Jamaica. Even with reggae music's recent popularity, it is amazing how little the public knows about the movement's message.

Reggae is the artistic and cultural expression of the Rastafarians, signifying oppression, exile, a longing for home, optimism and Jah love. Since the inception of the movement fifty years ago, its ideologies and belief systems have been in constant flux. However, in spite of the many doctrinal differences within the group, certain beliefs and symbols are uniquely Rastafarian. These are often the messages delivered in reggae lyrics, the soul of the music itself.

The emergence of the Rastafarian movement is most easily understood when viewed as an extension of Ethiopianism:

In the 19th century, when the defenders of slavery tried to divest blacks of every dignity of humanity and civilization, blacks appealed to the fabled glory of Ethiopia. When confronted by stalwarts of religion, philosophy and science who sought to falsify history in the service of Western slavery, black preachers—though for the most part unlearned—discovered in the

only book to which they had access (the Bible) that Egypt and Ethiopia were in Africa, and that these countries figured very importantly in the history of civilization.

Leonard Barrett, *The Rastafarians*

Ethiopianism includes the appreciation of Ethiopia's ancient civilization as well as its role in the Bible. To blacks, Africa (interchangeable with Ethiopia) became a glorious, Biblical home-land equated with Zion. The recognition of African roots and the desire for repatriation has been a central theme in New World black religion before and since emancipation. Ethiopianism became a "black religious reaction to pro-slavery propaganda."[1]

Marcus Garvey's "Back to Africa" movement developed the spirit of Ethiopianism to its fullest extent.

. . . since the white people have seen their God through white spectacles, we have only now started out (late though it be) to see our God through our own spectacles. The God of Isaac and the God of Jacob let him exist for the race that believe in the God of Isaac and the God of Jacob. We Negroes believe in the God of Ethiopia, the everlasting God—God the Son, God the Holy Ghost, the one God of all ages. That is the God in whom we believe, but we shall worship him through the spectacles of Ethiopia.

A. J. Garvey, *The Philosophy and Opinions of Marcus Garvey*

Garvey's words planted the seeds for most "Black God" movements in the US and Caribbean. Stressing the superiority of the ancient Africans and the dignity of the black race, he inspired many successful nationalist movements and numerous African leaders from Kenyatta to Nyerere.

Marcus Mosiah Garvey was born in St. Ann, Jamaica, in 1887, descended from the fiercely proud Maroons. He founded the newspaper *The Negro World,* which took as its motto his nationalist cry, "One God, One Aim, One Destiny." In 1917, he founded UNIA (Universal Negro Improvement Association) in Harlem. Its aims were described in a speech delivered by Garvey in 1924, at Madison Square Garden, New York:

The Universal Improvement Association represents the hopes and aspirations of the awakened Negro. Our desire is for a place in the world, not to disturb the tranquility of other men, but to lay down our burden and rest our weary backs and feet by the banks of the Niger and sing our songs and chant our hymns to the God of Ethiopia.

Garvey's goal of repatriation was expressed in his famous slogan "Africa for the Africans." His well-known Black Star Line steamship company was established to trade and eventually carry New World blacks to Africa. This prophet of African redemption was not always successful in his countless business ventures, but by the 1920s Garvey was the most powerful leader among the black masses in the United States.

In 1916, before he left for his US campaign, Garvey's farewell address to Jamaicans included

Marcus Mosiah Garvey

Haile Selassie's coronation portrait, 1930.

the words "Look to Africa for the crowning of a Black king; he shall be the Redeemer."

On November 2, 1930, Ras Tafari Makonnen, great-grandson of King Saheka Selassie of Shoa, was crowned Negus of Ethiopia. He took the new name Haile Selassie (Power of the Trinity), to which he added the titles "King of Kings," "Lord of Lords" and "Conquering Lion of the Tribe of Judah." Selassie claimed to be the 225th in a line of Ethiopian kings which could be traced all the way to Menelik, the son of Solomon and Sheba.

To a handful of Jamaicans (mostly Garveyites), this was prophesy fulfilled. Thus, the visionary Garvey had prophesied the coming of the Messiah just as John the Baptist had prophesied the coming of Christ.

Many preachers in Kingston began to express their belief in Selassie's divinity. They searched their scriptures for passages which would support their belief that Selassie could be the Redeemer. They found the Revelation 5: 2–5: "Weep not; behold, the Lion of the Tribe of Judah, the root of David, hath prevailed to open

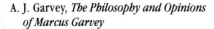

the book, and to loose the seven seals thereof."

Psalm 68:31, a central theme of the Garvey movement, became a chief source of textual proof for these early Rastafarians: "Princes shall come out of Egypt, and Ethiopia shall stretch forth her hands unto God." They also interpreted Revelation 19:16 to prophesy the coming of the King in the person of Haile Selassie: "And he hath on his vesture and on his thigh a name written, KING OF KINGS AND LORD OF LORDS." Other frequently quoted passages are Ezekiel 37:19 and Revelation 1:14,17,18.

These early preachers believe the King's longevity and skin color are prophesied in Daniel 7:9:

And I beheld till the thrones were cast down and the Ancient of days did sit, the garment was white as snow, and the hair of his head like pure wool: his throne was like the fiery flame, and his wheels as burning fire.

Fundamental Rasta

Looking at the early Rastafarian movement, we see the crucial significance of Jamaica's (and Garvey's) Christian roots for its ideology. Ninety percent of the Rastas are ex-Christians, and the Bible provides the foundation on which they form their beliefs. The Rasta "knows that Bible like he knows the back alleys of his shanty town."[2]

But the Rastas reject orthodox Christianity in its existing Revivalist Jamaican form. They see it as a colonial weapon to oppress the powerless and disenfranchised, and view the church as death-worshipping (the crucifix, graveyards, funerals). They also reject the syncretistic, Christian-African cults (Kumina, Pocomania) and Jamaican folk beliefs (Obeah, duppies). These are considered superstitious, unscientific and backward. They are seen as "unreal in the presence of formidable sociopolitical forces."[2]

Thus, the Rastafarian belief system is a rich and complex theology of liberation. The Rastas redefine and reinterpret the Bible. This is necessary because they feel it has been corrupted throughout its many translations from the original Amharic language of Ethiopia. But, when read carefully and selectively, the Old and New Testaments provide meaningful answers to life's fundamental questions. The Scriptures provide the Rasta with an account of his/her cultural identity. It explains past and present suffering. It prophesies the inevitable doom of the oppressor. Furthermore, the New Testament foretells of a hopeful future for the righteous. And both the Old and New Testaments delineate the proper way to live and worship God.

Rastas feel free to interpret the Scriptures insightfully. They add those parts which they believe might have been left out with political motivations. They subtract those portions which might have been corrupted. The result is a viable theology and way of life based on ancient Biblical ways, African culture, and a preference for a "natural" lifestyle.

"Jah" is the Rastas' word for God. It is probably derived as a shortened form of "Jehovah" or "Jahweh." In certain Bibles the form "Jah" can be located in Psalms 68:4. Jah is seen as black. The Rastas use the same Biblical passages as did Garvey and other "Black God" advocates to prove this. In Jeremiah 8:21 we read "For the hurt of the daughter of my people I am hurt; I am black . . ." In Solomon's first chapter of the Song of Songs: "I am black, and comely, O ye daughters of Jerusulem, as the tents of Kedar, as the curtains of Solomon. Look not upon me, because I am black, because the sun hath looked upon me . . . His head is as the most fine gold, his locks are bushy, and black as a raven" (1:5–5; 5:11). If Solomon was of color, then certainly so were David, Jesse and the patriarchs before them.

Based on the premise that Haile Selassie is God and that God fashioned his chosen people in his image (Genesis 1:26) then they, too, are

[1] Joseph Owens, **Dread** (Kingston, 1976).
[2] Leonard Barrett, **The Rastafarians** (Boston, 1977).

The I-Words

In the pure Jamaican creole, the first person singular in all its cases is expressed by the pronoun "me": "Me have me book." The plural of the first person is in all cases "we": "Them see we with we book." The Rastas, however, would seem to perceive this creole pronoun "me" as expressive of subservice, as representative of the self-degradation that was expected of the slaves by their masters. It makes persons into objects, not subjects.

As a consequence, the pronoun "I" has a special importance to Rastas and is expressly opposed to the servile "me." Whether in the singular ("I") or the plural ("I and I" or briefly: "I&I") or the reflexive ("I-self," "I&I-self"), the use of this pronoun identifies the Rasta as an individual, as one beloved of Haile-I Selassie-I. Even the possessive "my" and the objective "me" are replaced by "I" in the speech of the Rastas.

"I&I" is basically a substitute for "we," and indeed a very significant one. It expresses at once the individualism that characterizes the Rastas and the unity which they see among themselves by virtue of their unity with Jah . . .

In a further use of this favourite and significant sound, the Rastas take many key words and replace their first syllable by the vowel "I." The use of such I-words is common in all Rasta speech:

I-cient = ancient
I-ssembly = assembly
I-ses = praises
I-tection = protection
I-tinually = continually
I-ration = creation

—Joseph Owens, **Dread.**

black. Black supremacy seems to be a major belief of the Rastas in several early studies of the movement. The message is definitely more tolerant and universal now. The injustice of African enslavement must be corrected. But the Niyabinghi chant "Death to all Black and White Oppressors" clearly cuts across racial lines. A person of any color can be redeemed if he chooses to live and worship Jah in an "upfull" way.

"And upon her forehead was a name written, *Mystery, Babylon The Great, The Mother of Harlots and Abominations of the Earth*" (Rev. 17:5). The Rastas say "Babylon must fall." Babylon's doom is predicted in Chapter 17 of Revelations.

To the Rastas, Babylon is the corrupt establishment, decadent Western civilization, the "system," Church and State, the police. Rome is considered to be the capital of Babylon. Romans were responsible for the execution of Christ. Rome fought against black Hannibal. Rome fought against Haile Selassie when Mussolini's troops invaded Ethiopia. The Pope is the head of

Rome and therefore, of Babylon. "Kill Pope Paul and Babylon fall," the Rastas metaphorically chant.

Likewise, the Rastas blame the British for the enslavement of the African. Queen Elizabeth I and her reincarnation Queen Elizabeth II are considered personifications of the ancient Whore of Babylon.

When the Battle of Armageddon is fought and the Apocalypse takes place, good will triumph over evil. Liberation from the suffering caused by oppression and deprivation will finally come. "Jah shall wipe all tears from their eyes; and there shall be no more death, neither sorrow nor crying, neither shall there be any more pain; for the former things have passed away" (Rev. 21:2).

These millenial ideas are expressed in many reggae songs.

Must Rasta bear this cross alone
And all the heathens go free
JAH seh no, JAH seh no
Must Rasta live in misery and
*   Heathens in luxury*
JAH seh no, JAH seh no
He's coming to tear down the walls of
*   down-pression*
Drive away corruption
Tear down Babylon
Set the captives free . . .

—Peter Tosh, "Jah Seh No."

When the world destroys itself, only a comparative few (144,000) will be saved. "Many be called, but few chosen" (Matthew 20:16). Those redeemed will have rejected Babylonian life and chosen a path of righteousness and love. This choice is an individual, soul-searching process. It is the "dread" path of knowing and accepting oneself. It involves respecting and not judging other peoples and cultures.

Following God's commandments and maintaining the laws of nature is believed to be part of the ancient "African-Israelite" lifestyle. This chosen path is evident in certain visible aspects of the Rastafarian way of life. Although no two Rastas live exactly the same way, there are certain distinctly Rastafarian features. These serve as symbols allowing us to penetrate the deeper meanings of the movement. Knowing the rationale behind the wearing of dreadlocks, the sacramental use of ganja and the I-tal diet enhances one's understanding of the Rastafarians.

Talking Rasta

Jamaicans speak many variations of patois, from the British-schooled upper-class version to the more recondite "roots" style of speaking. Geographical dialect is also a factor adding to the diversity of speech in Jamaica. But the Rastas speak their native patois with several distinct

characteristics. Added to the dialectical creole is a vocabulary of "I-words" (see margin), created words, transposed words and Biblical phraseology.

In Genesis, Jah created the world through his words. Likewise, the Rastas shape their reality through the use of language. In Revelation 10:13,15 the significance of the Word is stressed: "And he was clothed with a vesture dipped in blood; and his name is called The Word of God . . . And out of his mouth goeth a sharp sword, that with it he should smite the nations . . ." Wordsound is power.

The Rastas have found certain words either unsatisfactory in describing their ideas or else inconsistent with their philosophies. The most evident of these is their disdain for the word "back" or "backward." This concept is considered negative and is therefore always replaced with "forward." Another of these words is "understand." This word does not fit the positive nature of the word and is thus transposed to "overstand." In the same way, "oppressor" is exchanged for "downpressor."

The frequent use of Biblical terms in the everyday life of the Rastas is also quite evident. These words include: fullness, brethren, dispensation, brimstone, Babylon, Armageddon, locks, etc. Other words commonly used by the Rastas are listed in the glossary [see page 69]. Many of these words are used by Jamaican society at large. Quite a few are Rastafarian contributions. To a large extent, these have been absorbed by the general population through constant exposure to the Rasta language in everyday life and reggae music.

Dreadlocks

The most visible characteristic of the Rasta is his/her dreadlocks. The uncombed and uncut hair (it *is* washed) is an outward sign of many of the Rastas' inner commitments and beliefs. However, not every Rasta wears dreadlocks. And not every "Dreadlock" is a Rasta. Some individuals wear them as a sign of their commitment to the Rasta path of knowing themselves and leading a righteous life. Others might be hustlers or faddists sporting their locks for ulterior motives or style.

The Rastas consider themselves to be "Nazarites" and as holy men they follow the ancient commandments of the Bible:

Numbers 6:5: *All the days of the vow of his separation there shall no razor come upon his head: until the days be fulfilled, in the which he separateth himself unto the Lord, he shall be holy, and shall let the locks of the hair of his head grow.*

The Nazarites of old (including the famous "Samson") were numerous during the Maccabean times. They were known as the crowned ones, distinguishable by their mass of uncut hair. The word "Nazarite" means to "separate" in ancient Hebrew. The Nazarites were set apart by

their individual exemplification of pure and holy living. The Nazarite vow stated that one was not to cut his locks, drink alcohol, or deal with any form of death.

Thus, the locksman is continuing an ancient

Biblical tradition in his commitment to the "dread" path. Some Rastas refer to their locks as antennae through which they receive inspiration from Jah. The Rastas believe that the early Israelites and prophets, as well as Christ and the early

Christians, must have worn dreadlocks.

The first Rastas to wear dreadlocks are reported to have been at Leonard Howell's Rasta camp "Pinnacle" in 1935. Those Rastas were inspired by photographs of Masai and Somali warriors from East Africa. Since then, the Rastas have documented the African-ness of the hairstyle in other publications. The December 1970 issue of *National Geographic* is the most frequently cited example, with its photos of Ethiopian monks wearing locks. The Rastafarian publication *Our Own* pictures a Mau Mau leader with a long and impressive set of dreadlocks. Dreadlocks have also been seen on Carib Indians, East Indians and South American tribesmen. Perhaps this hairstyle is a worldwide phenomenon among ascetic peoples.

Besides the African and biblical rationale for wearing dreadlocks, the hairstyle is also connected with the Conquering Lion, Haile Selassie, who is said to have been "natty" as a youth. Dreadlocks suggest the mane of the standing lion, which is the symbol of the Davidic line of kings as well as the national symbol of Ethiopia.

Sociologists have theorized on the defiant, anti-societal nature of dreadlocks, which has made for intense police harrassment. Psychologists have hypothesized on their representing repressed, unconscious feelings. But Rastas don't usually agree with these analyses. To them, dreadlocks are a natural hairstyle with deep cultural meaning, representing their biblical commitment. Only immature or new converts seem to exhibit overpowering urges to flash their dreadlocks in youthful defiance.

Herb

Marijuana is used in some form (smoked, drunk, eaten), by approximately two-thirds of Jamaica's population. This is possibly the highest percentage of national marijuana use in the world.

But, marijuana smoking is not merely a way to pass time or a form of entertainment for the Rastas. They believe that it was given to man by Jah in order to aid his meditations and open his consciousness to a higher reality. To them, it is a sacred herb and smoking it can be a form of religious worship, supported by many biblical quotations. Some Rastas believe that marijuana first grew on the grave of King Solomon.

Marijuana is said to have first appeared in Jamaica with the arrival of East Indian indentured servants in 1845. Other studies claim it arrived in 1545, carried by the Spanish from Asia to the New World. Some say it has always existed in Jamaica and was used by the original Arawak inhabitants of the island.

Its East Indian roots would explain why it is most commonly known by the Hindi word "ganja." Kali (the most potent form of marijuana) is also a Hindi word referring to the Black Goddess of Strength.

Next to ganja, "herb" is the most commonly used term for marijuana. This points to its medicinal and healing qualities. Likewise, it is dubbed the "healing of the nations" and the "wisdom weed" (although the term "weed" denoting marijuana is dimly viewed).

Ganja is also designated other titles depending

on its strain: Sinsemilla, Indica, Lambsbread, Short Day, Goatshit, Jerusalem bread, etc.

"I-shence," an I-word for marijuana, could come from "I-cient" or "I-ciency," Rastafarian modifications of the words "ancient" and "anci-ency." It could be a transformation of the word "incense" to which ganja is often compared.

Ganja is utilized by men, women and children. It is smoked in large "spliffs" rolled with paper, corn husks or tobacco leaves. People drink it for its medicinal and healing properties in a boiled tea. Sometimes it is used as a spice in food. And it is often made into a healing liniment and rubbed into wounds or infections.

When smoked in a chalice or chillum pipe, by a group of Rastas, its use as a form of religious worship can be most appreciated. The water-cooled pipe is passed solemnly from one person to the next as a holy sacrament. Traditionally, before one smokes, he or she respectfully gives thanks and praises to Jah. Smoking from or "licking the chalice" is often called "sipping from the cup." In this respect, it is comparable to the Christian communion cup.

Although not all Rastas smoke ganja, most do. For many Rastas, "drawing herbs" is a common daily practice and growing it is a career. The Rastas consider the smoking of herb a spiritually enlightening and healing practice. It is a criminal offense in Jamaica.

Although illegal since 1913, ganja is a valuable Jamaican export. Even so, ever since the inception of the movement in the 1930's, Rastas have been consistently arrested and harrassed in connection with it.

I-tal Food

Most Rastas prefer to eat "I-tal" cooking. The word "I-tal" refers to the natural or organic, undefiled state of the food. I-tal food is unprocessed, unspoiled and unrefined. As with dread-locks, the rationale for eating this way is in keeping with the Rastas' desire to live naturally and in conformance with the ancient protocol in the Bible. Thus the "vital" I-tal diet is a symbol of the Rastafarian ideology.

Know ye not that ye are the temple of God, and that the Spirit of God dwelleth in you? If any man defile the temple of God, him shall God destroy; for the temple of God is holy, which temple ye are.
—Corinthians 16–17

Some of the Rastafarian dietary preferences are derived from Old Testament "kosher" laws. The Rasta disdain for pork, shellfish and scavengers are of this category. Many also refrain from the products of vine-growing plants because of biblical commandments against them.

Certain foods are considered objectionable for other reasons. Rastas are usually strict vegetarians. Their abhorrence for all meat, called "deaders" by them, stems from the Corinthians message as well as the "You are what you eat" philosophy. Most Rastas regard meat-eating to be a violent, aggressive act which promotes those traits in individuals. They also feel that the slaughter and consumption of animals is barbaric and indicative of the Babylonian mentality.

Fish is regarded as the least contemptible of meats and is often part of the I-tal diet. One

Rasta explained it like this: "It go pork, den beef, den goat, den fowl, den fish—best is pure vegie." He also rendered the same type of list for forms of transportation: "It go like this: first airplane, den train, den bus, den car, den motorcycle, den bicycle, best is pure foot."

Abstinence from alcohol is a crucial part of the I-tal diet. The Scriptures say "It is not for kings to drink wine; nor for princes strong drink; lest they drink, and forget the law, and pervert the judgement of any of the afflicted. Give strong drink unto him that is ready to perish, and wine unto those that be of heavy hearts" (Proverbs 31:4–6). Rastas say they don't care for the sensation of drunkeness and prefer the enlightening qualities of marijuana.

After meat and alcohol, the absence of salt from the diet is part of being an "I-talist." Salt is considered to be an inorganic additive and therefore not necessary.

The extent of how natural or organic an I-talist is depends on a few factors. First of all, if a Rasta is broke, he will eat what he can get and

know that Jah understands this. Second, although he might prefer to eat fresh foods, in certain areas it is more difficult to obtain desired food than in others. Rastas in touring reggae bands are most aware of this.

The Rasta Society

The Rastafarian movement has remained relatively leaderless since its inception in 1930. However, there have been individuals who contributed significantly to it, historically and/or ideologically.

After the coronation of HIM (His Imperial Majesty, Haile Selassie), several preachers became noted for expressing their beliefs in his divinity on the streets of Kingston. They included Joseph Hibbert, Archibald Dunkley, Robert Hinds and Altamont Reed. Meanwhile,

other individuals were developing more repatriation-oriented movements. They also eventually accepted Haile Selassie's divinity. The most successful at attracting a following was Leonard P. Howell during the 1930s.

In essence, many of the Rastafarians' aims and concerns are political. But the Rastas prefer to have little to nothing to do with Jamaican "politricks." Their loyalties lie with the Divine Theocratic Government of Haile Selassie I. Their laws are biblical.

The Rastafarian movement has never united together as one homogeneous political or religious organization. Anyone interested in the Rastafarians who has visited Jamaica recently has probably noticed the many doctrinal differences within the movement. The only clear-cut similarity between those who call themselves Rastas seems to be their vision calling for a world "that will guarantee redress for the oppressed of the earth." As to lifestyle, church or organizational involvement, and outward appearance, each Rasta differs from the next.

However, there are certain visible groups existing today that can be distinguished even though Rasta is a growing, changing movement, not a stagnant, dogmatized religion.

The first group are the *Niyabinghi* Rastas, a traditional, orthodox Rastafarian group (not warriors). The majority of Rastas in Jamaica and elsewhere fall under this category. They tend to believe that the divine Haile Selassie represents the First Coming of the Messiah and that the Babylonian "Je-sus" is a false god. They are extremely suspicious of organization, leaders, churches and governments. They are selective in their biblical belief and concur that most versions have been corrupted.

A number of Rastas are members of the *Ethiopian Orthodox Church*. Established in Jamaica in 1969, this church has branches in New York, Jerusalem and the Sudan. It is one of

"How beautiful upon the mountains are the feet of him that bringest tidings, that publisheth peace; that bringeth good tidings of good, that publisheth salvation; that saith unto Zion, thy creator reigneth.

"Thy watchman shall lift up the voice; with the voice together shall they sing; for they shall see eye to eye when the Lord shall bright again Zion."

Isaiah 52: 7-8

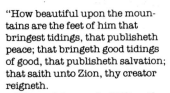

the most ancient and historic of the Christian churches. Representing the glory and history of ancient Ethiopia, it appeals to many Rastafarians. They believe that no other nation has as solid a foundation in Holy Scriptures as Ethiopia. Its Bible contains the entire Old and New Testaments as well as other non-canonical books found in their entirety only in that text. The EOC cherishes other literature including the *Kebre Negast* (Glory of the Kings), the book which traces Haile Selassie's lineage to Solomon and Sheba. The Ark of the Covenant containing the original Ten Commandments is also said to be housed at the Ethiopian Orthodox Church in Addis Ababa.

The Ethiopian Orthodox Church does not stress the divinity of Haile Selassie, especially since his demise in 1975. To them, he was a God-serving Christian. Thus, whether it can really be called a Rastafarian church is certainly dubious. The Ethiopian Orthodox Church is an orthodox Christian establishment partaking in all the pomp and ritual associated with its tradition. Although many Rastas flocked to the Church when it first became established in Jamaica, many have since left. They found it to be too Christian for them and at odds with many of their Rastafarian beliefs.

Another group is Prince Edward Emmanual's *Ethiopian National Congress.* Located in the hills of St. Thomas, this camp tends to be a self-contained commune. The group has been around since early in the Rastafarian movement and began living at this location in the late 1960s. The Prince is the head of the hierarchy claiming to be a priest of Melchizedek's order. He is worshipped along with Haile Selassie and Marcus Garvey. Below these three (and the Prince's wife), are a number of priests, apostles and prophets. The members wear turbans and robes for work and worship. Many do not wear dreadlocks. They adhere to a strict moral code and abide by many rules and regulations. Besides ritual prayer and worship, according to Leonard Barrett, "very strange practices may be seen in this group . . . sacrifice is a ritual practice, the washing of the saint's feet, and prayer by prostration." The scarcity of women within this camp is obvious. This group is very race-conscious. They are black supremacists and don't believe whites can enter the gates of Zion. Outsiders have told me that Prince Edward Emmanual seems to be worshipped above and beyond Selassie and Marcus Garvey.

The members of the *Twelve Tribes of Israel* organization are basically Christians who believe that the Second Coming of Christ has already occurred in the person of Haile Selassie. Whereas Jesus Christ was the "Sufferer," Selassie is the "Conquering Lion." Their proof is HIM's lineage and biblical scripture.

Despite small discrepancies between Bibles, they believe that adherence to any Bible is crucial. Haile Selassie stressed this point in his speech on the importance of the Bible. It should be read "a chapter a day" in order to be fully understood from beginning to end. Answers to all questions about life can be found within its pages if read this way. Thus, the Bible is "life's handbook."

Because Haile Selassie I is the "perfect man," his words are revered and his speeches referred to constantly. The actions he is said by the press to have committed in his later years are considered ill propaganda. Or, they are attributed to the corrupt feudal lords and princes who were supposed to carry out his orders. Instead, members point to his many accomplishments.

Most Twelve Tribes members don't believe "The King" died. "Where is his body? Where is his coffin?" they want to know. Some believe he is in hiding somewhere in Ethiopia. But, even if he did die physically, it would present "no problem" or contradiction to their philosophy. This is because he has a son and grandson both born in July, which would also fulfill the prophecy.

The members of the Twelve Tribes often assume the name of the biblical tribe which refers to the month in which their birthdays fall (e.g. Howard Gad or Karen Levi). References to the scattered twelve tribes of Israel are found throughout the Bible. David is said to have had twelve advisors each representing different

months of the year. And Revelation 22:2 also connects "the Twelve" with certain characteristics: ". . . And on either side of the river was the tree of life, bearing twelve kinds of fruit, yielding its fruit every month. . ."

The organization began in 1968 in Trench Town and has since moved its headquarters uptown. I was not given an estimate of its membership, but it is obvious that the movement has vastly increased since 1974. Bob Marley was a member, known as "Joseph." There are organized branches of the Twelve Tribes in New York, London, Ethiopia, Toronto and Trinidad, as well as members on other islands and cities around the globe. Twelve Tribes members come from all walks of life. Membership cuts across all race and color lines. Many are well educated. They stress the importance of racial tolerance, citing Selassie's famous speech (put to music by Bob Marley) on this topic.

This organization also stresses freedom of lifestyle and appearance. Although many members are I-talist (or used to be), this group as a whole believes that what leaves your mouth can defile you more than what goes in. Many members wear dreadlocks but that is not a prerequisite by any means. "Be all things to all people" is the biblical message they emphasize. Being "Born Again" and maintaining inner faith, along with works, are more important than outer appearance. Although they don't fight against ganja use they ask members to refrain from smoking it during meetings.

The Bible prophesies that when Armageddon takes place, God will assume his rule as King where the Arc of the Covenant is stored. That is, in Ethiopia.

For thou thy people Israel be as the sand of the sea, yet a remnant of them shall return.

—Isaiah 11:22

The remnant constantly referred to in the Bible are these 144,000 men and women who gather in Zion. Although there are many more righteous people, the Bible states that some of them will not make it. Selassie believed that the West would perish first. And Isaiah 11:110–13 mentions that the gathering would begin in the "isles of the sea," which is understood to mean Jamaica.

Although these are the "last days," the Twelve Tribes don't focus too much attention on the date and manner in which the world will end. They know it "can't finish" until the tribes are gathered. Thus, they must spread the word and gather the tribes from the four corners of the Earth.

The Twelve Tribes take repatriation very literally, based on their strong biblical belief. They see themselves as the only group in Jamaica today to be actively working on the repatriation effort.

Fly away to Zion
Fly away home
One bright morning
when my work is over
Going to fly away home

67

Repatriation Is A Must

I say fly away home to Zion
Fly away home
One bright morning when my work is over
Man will fly away home . . .

—Rasta Man Chant

Reggae band the Rastafarians

Some Rastas believe this repatriation is a spiritual event which will inevitably and eventually occur, and they will patiently wait for it in Jamaica. When Haile Selassie visited the island in 1966, he told some leading Rastafarian brethren that they should try to achieve "liberation before repatriation." This might have resulted in what Barrett calls the "adjustment of Rastafarians to the realities of Jamaican life."

There have been both successful and unsuccessful repatriation efforts. A few of the latter were hoaxes. The most famous of these was the responsibility of the preacher Claudius Henry. Orlando Patterson's *Children of Sisyphus* is a

Africa

M
T
A
L
Spanish Sahara
Egypt
River Nile
M
Mali
N
Chad
S
Guinea
U D
N
Gambia
S L I G T
Cameroon
CAR
Ethiopia
E
G C
Z
S
U K
R B B
A
Zambia
T
Mozambique
N
B
Z
Malagasy Republic
S
Lesotho

1. Identify the countries of the African Continent:
2. The source of the River Nile is:
_____
3. Identify the major African lakes.
4. Rivers Niger and Congo flow through which nation? _____
5. These cultures, the Benin, Ibo, Yoruba and Ijagham, are from which nation? _____
6. Ras Tafari is the name of the last monarch of which nation? _____
7. Identify Somalia and the French Territory of the Asars and Issas.
8. Which nation was recently known as Rhodesia? _____
9. Color in (blue) those countries that were part of the British Colonial Empire.
10. Which country does South Africa still rule in defiance of world opinion? _____ .

Their movement is well organized and its members are articulate.

The group stresses: that Haile Selassie is the Second Coming of Christ; the importance of reading any Bible, a chapter a day; actively working on the repatriation program; freedom of appearance and lifestyle; and racial tolerance.

Besides these groups, there are a number of individuals in Jamaica and elsewhere who might be called "secular" or "functional" Rastas. These include those people who sympathize with the humanitarian concerns of the Rastafarians (peace, love, freedom, equal rights, justice), but do not believe in Selassie's divinity. They might engage in some of the Rastas' biblical, African or natural practices and lifestyle (I-tal, dreadlocks, etc.).

And there are a large number of Rasta impostors. These "wolves in sheep's clothing" are those self-serving hypocrites who might wear dreadlocks or use the Rasta lingo as a form of deception. Although many profess belief in Haile Selassie (usually very vocally and defiantly), their actions and motivations contradict every Rastafarian belief in righteous behavior.

The 50-year-old Rastafarian movement is contemporary and holistic. Although it emerged from the Caribbean, its concerns are shared by the entire Third World. Thus, it is relevant to anyone interested in the plight of humanity itself.

—*Rory Sanders*

fictional account of an aborted repatriation attempt.

In 1937, under the auspices of Haile Selassie, the Ethiopian World Federation was established. A Jamaican chapter was set up in 1938. Its goals were to unite black peoples and defend Ethiopia. In 1955, the Emperor granted the EWF a number a acres of land for those who wished to repatriate. Today's Twelve Tribes of Israel is a modern outgrowth of the Local 15 chapter of the EWF in Jamaica. They have succeeded in slowly but surely repatriating its members. They report that

those members who have actually settled there have been very well received by the Ethiopian people. They live a kind of "frontier life," using their individual talents to help the Ethiopians. They teach them agricultural methods, hygiene, housebuilding techniques, etc. In contrast to the young, anti-royalist Ethiopians, they find that many of the country peoples share their belief in Selassie's divinity.

The Twelve Tribes of Israel organization is the least documented and most often misrepresented of the Rastafarian groups active in Jamaica today.

A Rasta Glossary

Armageddon: the biblical final battle between the forces of good and evil

Babylon: 1. the corrupt establishment, the "system," Church and State 2. the police, a policeman
badness: hooligan behavior, violence for its own sake
bag-o-wire: a betrayer
bambu: rolling paper
bandulu: bandit, criminal, one living by guile
beast: a policeman
bredren: one's fellow male Rastas
bull bucka: a bully
bumba clot, rass clot, blood clot: curse words

cha! or cho!: a disdainful expletive
chalice or chillum: a pipe for smoking herb, usually made from coconut shell and tubing, used ritually by Rastas
clap: hit, break, strike
control: to be in charge of, responsible for, to own; to take
cool runnings: a greeting; things are going smoothly
corn: 1. marijuana 2. money 3. a bullet
crucial: serious, great, "hard," "dread"
Culture: reflecting or pertaining to the roots values and traditions highly respected by the Rastas

darkers: sunglasses
dawta: a girl, woman, "sister," girlfriend
deaders: meat, meat by-products
Downpressor: preferred term for oppressor
Dread: 1. a person with dreadlocks 2. a serious idea or thing 3. a dangerous situation or person 4. the "dreadful power of the holy" 5. experientially, "awesome, fearful confrontation of a people with a primordial but historically denied racial selfhood"
dreadlocks: 1. hair that is neither combed nor cut 2. a person with dreadlocks
dready: a friendly term for a fellow dread
duns, dunsa: money

duppy: a ghost

feel no way: don't take offense, don't be sorry, don't worry
first light: tomorrow
forward: 1. to go, move on, set out 2. in the future
fronta: tobacco leaf used to roll herb
fullness: to the fullness; completely, absolutely, totally

ganja: herb, marijuana
gates: home, yard
general: cool operator
gorgon: outstanding dreadlocks
grounation: large, island-wide meeting and celebration of Rastas

hail: a greeting
hard: excellent, proficient, skillful, uncompromising
herb: marijuana

hot-stepper: fugitive from jail or gun court

I: replaces "me," "you," "my"; replaces the first syllable of selected words
I and I, I&I: I, me, you and me, we
I-man: I, me, mine
Irey: 1. a greeting 2. excellent, cool, highest

I-shence: herb
isms and skisms: negative term denoting Babylon's classificatory systems
I-tal: vital, organic, natural, wholesome; refers to way of cooking and way of life
ites: 1. the heights 2. a greeting 3. the color red

JA, Jam-down: Jamaica
Jah: God; possibly derived as a shortened form of Jahweh or Jehovah
Jah know: Lord knows

kali; cooly: marijuana
kouchie: bowl of a chalice or chillum pipe

lambsbread: a form of high-quality marijuana
lion: a righteous Dread

mafia: big-time criminals
mash it up: a huge success
mash up, mash down: destroy
more time: see you later
my baby mother: the mother of my child

natty, natty dread, natty congo: 1. dreadlocks 2. a person with dreadlocks
Nazarite: Ancient Hebrew mean-ing to "separate," consecrated, set apart by choice and devotion
Niyabinghi: 1. "death to all black and white oppressors" 2. East African warriors who resisted colonial domination 3. large Rastafarian meeting and spiritual gathering 4. referring to orthodox, traditional Rastas 5. a variety of drumming
Niyamen: name for Rastas referring to Niyabinghi warriors of East Africa
no true?: isn't it so?

One Love: a parting phrase, expression of unity

ranking: highly respected
ratchet: a switchblade knife popular in Jamaica
red: 1. very high on herb 2. mulatto color
rockers: reggae music
roots: 1. derived from the experience of the common people, natural indigenous 2. a greeting 3. name for a fellow Rasta

satta: sit, rest, meditate
science: obeah, witchcraft
screw: to scowl, to be angry
seen: I understand, I agree
sight?: do you understand?
sinsemilla, sensie: popular, potent, seedless, unpollinated female strain of marijuana
sister, sistren: a woman, a friend, woman Rastafarians
skank: to dance to reggae music
skin: rolling paper
skin your teeth: smile
soft: not well done, amateurish; unable to cope
spliff: large, cone-shaped marijuana cigarette
star: common term of affection, camaraderie
step: to leave, to depart
structure: body, health

tall: long
tam: wool hat
transport: vehicle

uphill: positive, righteous
uptown: the upper classes

vex: to get angry

whole heap: a lot

yard: home, one's gates
ya no see it?: you know?
youth: a child, a young man, an immature man

Zion: Ethiopia, Africa, the Rastafarian holy land

Big Youth in concert, 1981.

Countryman, a young fisherman from Hellshire who became a film star.

69

**His Imperial Majesty
Emperor
Haile Selassie
I&I
Negus of Ethiopia
Elect of Jah
Five by Five
King of Kings
Lord of Lords
Light of the World
Power of the Holy Trinity
Conquering Lion of The
Tribe of Judah**

**I&I
King
Selassie**

Ras Tafari and his father Ras Makonnen, 1903.

Selassie and Ethiopian Empress, late 1920s.

Opposite: Haile Selassie arrives in Jamaica, 1966. Rasta leader Mortimer Planno attempts to calm the frenzied crowd so Selassie can leave the imperial jet.

Haile Selassie

Haile Selassie, Negus of Ethiopia, was the world's oldest and longest ruling monarch when he was deposed in 1974. Often called a "medieval autocrat," he was renowned as an international statesman, and his reign is particularly noted for the modernization of a feudal Ethiopia. Many Rastas still insist that reports of his death in 1975 were mere propaganda.

Haile Selassie was born Ras

Makonnen Tafari on July 23, 1892 in the Harar province of Ethiopia. He died at the age of 83—the last emperor in the 3,000-year-old monarchy. Selassie began his rule as a reformer and nationalist before his coronation in 1930. In 1923, he succeeded in having Ethiopia accepted into the League of Nations. In 1924, he abolished

slavery. He established schools throughout the country and set up a program for Ethiopian students to study abroad.

Selassie's reign was responsible for "leading a largely illiterate, rural and feudal country with 2,000 languages and dialects into the 19th, if not the 20th century," according to an obituary in the *New York Times*. He deliberately moved slowly in this attempt, saying "We must make progress slowly so as to preserve the progress we have already made."

Selassie convoked the first meeting of the Organization of African Unity and supervised its charter. He was also responsible for the establishment of the UN Economic Commission for Africa and was renowned as an international statesman and for his almost magical skill at acquiring foreign economic aid.

It is difficult to find any description of Selassie's reign that doesn't criticize him on a number of points. He was said to have "lost touch with his subjects in later years, showing more affection for his pet cheetahs and dogs than for his human entourage." Critics also say his economic reforms were too slow.

In 1974, Selassie was deposed in a military coup. He was accused of neglecting the peasants during a long drought. He was alleged to have secretly sent vast sums into private Swiss bank accounts.

Any objective analysis of the life of Haile Selassie would probably reach certain conclusions: that Selassie was a great man in years and influence; that he contributed positively and significantly to Ethiopia's history during his reign; that he was not immune to the dreadful problems, both from internal and external sources, which any ruler must face; that he made mistakes.

But, the orthodox Rastafarians

do not see HIM as *any* ruler or *any* human being. Rather, they claim Haile Selassie is God Almighty. He is not a *messenger* of the Lord or an immaculate son.

Jah Rastafari created the universe. He is omnipresent, omnipotent and omniscient. He is the "beginning and end." All of these characteristics are traditionally associated with the Christian God. But the Rastas have attributed them to

a new revelation of the divinity, a belief based on Selassie's lineage, biblical prophecy and faith.

Ras Tafari is the name of the Lord as well as the name of the people who believe in him. By calling themselves Rastafarians, his followers are expressing the belief in their own Godliness. Jah exists in every person but the identifiable part of him is found in "the only King for this time," Haile Selassie. The fleshliness of God is evident in John 1:4: "In him was life; and the life was the light of men."

Rastas consider Jamaican religion to be based on death-oriented Christianity and folk beliefs in spirits and "duppies." The refutation of these concepts is integral to the Rastafarian belief system. Rastas call themselves "duppy conquerors."

In rejecting the notion of God as pure spirit, the Rastaman is rejecting as well a whole system of thought which places God in "another world" or in "another life." The Rastas are certain that God is alive and working in this world and this life and do not have to project another, "spiritual" dimension to see the divine within the human and the natural. Those preachers who draw the eyes of the people away from this world's beauty and potentiality are guilty of leading them towards a false god, not a God who works in and through history. —Joseph Owens

Just as there is no "ghost god," there is also no spiritual heaven. The Rastas discard the notion of a "pie up in the sky." Zion is Africa and it really does exist as a physical entity as well as within the Rasta. In the Wailers' song "Get Up/Stand Up" Rastafarian reality is directly expressed: "If you know what life is worth, you would look for yours on earth."

When asked about HIM's acts leading to the dethronement, the Rastas have much to say. One explanation is that:

. . . . changes and general upheavals were inspired by the Emperor himself. The fact that in the early stages of the crisis the Armed Forces claimed loyalty to the Emperor was interpreted to mean that Selassie was putting his own house in order, the implication being that he could not seek to put the rest of the world in order if his own house were corrupt.

Some Rastas compare Selassie's problems as a man to those of Christ, citing Hebrews 2:9-10 as their text:

But we see Jesus, who was made a little lower than the angels for the suffering of death, crowned with glory and honour; that he by the grace of God should taste for every man. For it became him, for whom

are all things, in bringing many sons unto glory, to make the captain of their salvation perfect through sufferings.

Most Rastas feel that all the bad press about HIM was propaganda, and that his death was propaganda too. They don't believe in the Christian view of death.

The issue of the Roman system is to show people that Christ is dead, but the principle of the orthodox is to show to you that Christ is alive, incarnate with man—within man— so that your soul, your mind, your body, your structure becomes one.

Death is considered the wages of sin. It is a destructive force which will destroy those who fight against the forces of life. Man must choose

between creation and "everliving" life or else destruction—and death. This is clear in the contrast between the slave song "And before I'll be a slave I'll be buried in my grave, and go home to my Lord . . ." and the Rasta version: "And before I'll be a slave I'll skip over my grave."

And so, Jah lives. "Ethiopia has existed for 3,000 years," said Haile Selassie; *"in fact, it exists ever since man first appeared on the Earth. My dynasty has ruled ever since the Queen of Sheba met King Solomon and a son was born of their union. It is a dynasty that has gone on through the centuries and will go on for centuries more. A king is not indispensable, and besides, my succession is already ensured. There is a Crown Prince and he will rule the country when We are no longer here. That is what We have decided, and so it must be."*

—Rory Sanders

Important Dates in Reggae History

Continued from page 23

1930.—Haile Selassie I crowned Emperor of Ethiopia.

1934.—Leonard Howell arrested for selling photographs of Selassie as passports to Ethiopia.

1935.—Italy invades Ethiopia. Jamaican press reports on Niyabinghi warriors of E. Africa.

1938.—Bloody labor strikes on Jamaican sugar plantations lead to unions and political parties.

1940.—Marcus Garvey dies in London. Leonard Howell establishes Rastafarian commune at Pinnacle Estate.

1948.—Rhygin' the bandit (Ivanhoe Martin) gunned down on Lime Key, October 9.

1954.—Pinnacle closed by police. Rastas scatter throughout Kingston.

1958.—First Niyabinghi convention held by Prince Edward Emmanuel for 21 days at W. Kingston Rasta stronghold Back o' Wall.

1959.—Clement C. Dodd (Sir Coxsone) sets up his recording business in Kingston. Beginning of ska era.

1962.—Jimmy Cliff, Skatalites, Wailers and Maytals begin careers. Jamaican independence from England.

1963.—"Holy Thursday Massacre," clash between police and Rastafarians near Montego Bay.

1965.—Height of rude boy era.

1966.—Haile Selassie I visits Jamaica, April 21. On July 12, police bulldoze Back o' Wall, causing Rastas to again disperse throughout Kingston. An especially hot and humid summer slows Jamaican dancers, and the rock steady era begins.

1968.—Twelve Tribes of Israel organization formed.

1969.—Ethiopian Orthodox Church formed in Jamaica.

1971.—*The Harder They Come* in production.

1972.—Island Records releases the Wailers' *Catch a Fire*. The modern reggae era begins. Michael Manley's socialist People's National Party wins control of Jamaica.

1975.—Reported death of Haile Selassie in Addis Ababa.

Continued on page 179

"Today, we look to the future calmly, confidently and courageously. We look to a vision of an Africa not merely free but united. In facing this new challenge, we can take comfort and encouragement from the lessons of the past. We know that there are differences among us.

"Africans enjoy different cultures, distinctive values, special attributes. But we also know that unity can be and has been attained among men of the disparate origins, that differences of race, of religion, of culture, of tradition, are no insuperable obstacle to the coming together of peoples.

"History teaches us that unity is strength and cautions us to submerge and overcome our differences in the quest for common goals, to strive, with all our combined strength, for the path to true African brotherhood and unity."

—HIM Haile Selassie I, *Addis Ababa African Summit Conference,* 1963

Rebel Music

6

Rebel Music

Most people who love Jamaican music cut their reggae teeth on Bob Marley and the Wailers. During a 20-year career, Bob Marley became for much of the world something more than mere musician. By the time of his passing in 1981, he had achieved a powerful moral and prophetic authority. In this chapter, writer **Timothy White** digs into the history of the band, drawing on research he did as an editor at **Rolling Stone** and **Crawdaddy** magazines. The long interview with Bob Marley by **Stephen Davis** that follows was one of the last such conversations he was to have with a journalist.

A History of Bob Marley & the Wailers

We're gonna help our people
Help them right
Oh lord, help us tonight!
Cast away that evil spell
Throw some water in the well . . .

"Smile Jamaica," 1976

It was the birth of a new day.

The smoldering red sun crept over the Gulf of Aden and the Somalian freeport of Djibouti, traveling west across the torrid Danakil desert, past the winding Awash River and onto the mountain-collared plateau beyond the rift valley where stands Addis Ababa, ancient capital city of Ethiopia.

The pale rays of morning light fanned out over the gray miasma, illuminating the putrid ochre tannery basins, the silent marketplaces, the leprosarium, the cigarette factory, the dessicated government plazas, and eventually seeped into the Jubilee Palace nestled in the central district of the city. Inside, a clock struck 7 a.m. on Wednesday, August 27, 1975. But the man who lived there was not at home.

On the streets, word was spreading of a great change. His Imperial Majesty, Haile Selassie I, Power of the Holy Trinity, sole surviving legitimate son of Governor Ras Makonnen of Harar, 225th Emperor of the 3000-year-old Ethiopian Empire, Elect of God, Lord of Lords, Kings of Kings, Negusa Nagast, Heir to the Throne of Solomon, Conquering Lion of the Tribe of Judah, was dead at 83.

He was born Lij Ras Tafari Makonnen on July 23, 1892, under a humble roof of mud and wattle in Ejarsa, Gora. Outside his father waited tensely while servants supplicated themselves or loo-looed in the hot wind. The tawny baby's lips were daubed with ritual butter, and soldiers and loyal tribesmen emptied their rifles skyward as

Peter Tosh, 1981.

Trench Town Rock
You don't look back
Trench Town Rock
If you are big fish or sprat
Trench Town Rock
You reap what you sow
Trench Town Rock
And only Jah Jah know
That I'm just grooving
This is Kingston Twelve . . .

the hills shook with the first whimpers of his sacred might.

Although a thin, frail man, he rose in 38 years to become the medieval autocrat of a sprawling kingdom the size of Texas, Arkansas, Louisiana and Oklahoma combined. On the morning of November 2, 1930, Archbishop Kyril anointed the new emperor and lifted the temple crown of a timeless monarchy into place as thousands bent down low. Selassie ruled his realm with an iron hand from that year until 1974, excepting a three-year exile during World War II when the country was occupied by Italian Fascists and then the British Army. In 1974, Selassie was deposed.

Now Selassie was dead and gone, the street rumors proclaiming that another propitious symbol of deliverance had been reduced to dust. Suffice it to say that several million wretched and much-maligned souls shrugged heavily and turned their hungry gazes to the new Marxist regime of Mengistu Haile Mariam.

Years from now, it will serve as a quirky footnote to history that thousands of miles from his defunct empire, on the West Indian island of Jamaica, a number of syncretic religious sects grew up around this hallowed monarch. Known as Rastafarians, these oppressed and downtrodden black disciples believed Selassie to be "Jah"—The Living God; or maybe the Son of God, or, at the very least, a God-sent black liberator and Redeemer . . .

Bob Marley's reedy form is scarcely visible in the dim, bare-bulbed light of Harry J's Recording Studio on Roosevelt Avenue in Kingston, Jamaica. Dressed in a brown cotton shirt, dungarees and expensive calfskin boots, he is standing with his arms akimbo in the middle of the cluttered studio. A wispy ribbon of smoke drifts up from a bulbous ganja spliff in his hand, encircling his dreadful head as he concentrates. A clock overhead reads 10:30 p.m. on this September night in 1975.

The sessions for Bob Marley and the Wailers' *Rastaman Vibration* album have slowed to a temporary crawl as the group's leader psyches himself for the task at hand. Engineer Sylvan Morris, burly and solemn, sits hunched over the

16-track board on the other side of the soiled glass window that separates the grimy control booth from the studio proper, sipping from a bottle of Dragon Stout and waiting for some signal to start the tape. There is no sound, except Sylvan's labored swallowing, followed by a stifled burp.

Marley draws a pair of headphones onto his tiny Medusa's mane and signals Morris with the barest nod. An instrumental track begins to ooze from the studio monitors and the rhythm is an arcane one to non-Caribbean ears: the bass drum hits the backbeat, rather than the downbeat as in American funk. The hypnotic time signature is propelled, trance-like, by noodled organ phrases, cuffed electric guitar and a numbing electric bass.

Marley steps quickly to the boom mike and paralyzes observers as he sings with a passion that disesteems all mortal concepts of space and time:

Selassie lives! Jah-Jah lives, children!
Jah lives! Jah-Jah lives!
Fools saying in their heart
Rasta, you God is dead
But I&I know evaaa more,
Dread shall be dread and dread!

Slouched behind me is Aston "Family Man" Barrett, attired in Army surplus and a woolen ski cap of the sort worn in the streets by dreads wishing to avoid harrassment by a constable. Family Man is the master bassist of the Wailers and one-half of perhaps the finest rhythm section in all reggaedom. His partner in syncopation is his gangly brother Carlton "Carly" Barrett, presently leaning stiffly against the opposite wall under a red day-glo NO SMOKING sign, an ambitious spliff tight between his thumb and forefinger.

The faces of both brothers are frozen in a wide grin they share with all present: the Wailers' American guitarist, Al Anderson; co-producer Lee Perry and his wife; keyboardist Tyrone Downey; guitarist Earl "Chinna" Smith; conga man " Seeco" Patterson; and the I-Threes, the group's vocal back-up trio, which consists of Bob's wife Rita, plus Judy Mowatt and Marcia Griffiths, all of whom are top local recording artists in their own right.

Without warning, Marley suddenly whirls about and explodes with a raspy, primal exultation that roars in upon us like a roundhouse tidal wave. The umber statues around me leap to life; they buck-and-wing with furious abandon and then begin to mambo back and forth from an anteroom as Marley shifts his sandpaper tenor into highest gear:

The truth is an offense, but not a sin!
Is he laugh last, is he who win!
Is a foolish dog, barks at a flying bird!
One sheep must learn to respect the shepherd!
Jah lives! Selassie lives, chill-drannn!
Jah lives! Jah-Jah lives!

That's how it's done, Wailers-style. Led by Bob Marley, they became the most potent purveyors of an almost 40-year West Indian evolution of shuffle 'n' soul now known as reggae. Almost from the start, the Wailers played a vital role in

the development of this unique sound. They didn't know it at the time, but their *Rastaman Vibration* album (on which "Jah Live" failed to appear), proved to be one of the best-selling reggae records in history.

Jamaicans have a marvelously vivid word—*blue-swee*— to describe those who are wiley and hard to pin down: the Bob Marleys of the world. In Jamaican folklore, these qualities of cunning are personified by Anancy, a legendary figure whose name comes from the Twi *ananse,* meaning spider. The Anancy stories, derived from the Ashanti and brought to Jamaica in the 1600s on slave ships from the Gold Coast, are fables wherein the small, weak spider man befuddles and outwits a host of his adversaries, among them Brer Monkey, Brer Tiger and even Brer Death. Relying on his guile (and a mystical faculty to alter his appearance at will), brave Brer Anancy illustrates the ability of the downtrodden to overcome the mighty—an inspirational bit of symbolism for the thralldom in slavery days.

Like the blue-swee spider man, reggae, as played by Bob Marley and the Wailers, is both a wellspring of homespun adages and a canny cultural tool with great facility for adaptation and innovation. Tracing the Wailers' growth from the falsetto vocals and languid r&b/jazz-tinged shuffle of their seminal ska era in the early '60s, on through the percolating soul of rock steady, the raw, late-'60s stutter beat of reggae, to the rise of the dub-wise march cadences popularly described as *rockers* and *militant,* the band's evolution is so dramatic that one realizes the music has never lingered in any stylistic camp for more than two years. In fact, the Wailers are the only group to have thrived during these many phases, producing reggae as desperate as the souls who fill Jamaica's hills, savannas and ghetto streets.

For the multitude of Jamaicans, Bob Marley was Anancy incarnate, a sagacious shantytown hero whose concerts evinced the fearsome ballet of a black widow spider and boasted a musical artifice seemingly shrewd enough to sidestep Brer Death himself. Indeed, Marley narrowly escaped assassination in December 1976, while rehearsing for an outdoor concert in Kingston . . .

The torpor of the quiet tropical night was interrupted by an eerie noise not quite resembling a firecracker. Bob Marley was swallowing a sweet/sour segment of grapefruit when a dull *crack!* caused him to drop the fruit. And that's when Don Taylor, Marley's manager at the time, felt the first bullets enter the backs of his legs.

"I couldn't believe it was gun shots," remembers Taylor. " I sorta rushed toward Bob to figure out what was happening and then the rest of the gunfire flew in from the doorway behind me! I was standing in front of Bob at that point, so I got most of the shots. I went down but I stayed conscious and I heard a lot of fire around me, some of it from what seemed like a machine gun! Then I blacked out. . ."

As the rifle-wielding assailant exited, a con-

"Father Spider once created things, but now he hangs above the fire and the smoke has blackened the spider, the smoke has smoked the spider."

– Akan proverb

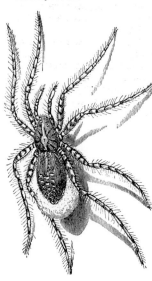

Yes, me fren
Dem set me free again
Yes me fren, me fren
Me deh pan street again

(The picture of Bob Marley is circa 1972.)

federate outside yelled, "Did you get him?"

"Yeah!" he was told. "I shot him!"

It was a dozen minutes after 9 p.m. on December 3, 1976, as Don Taylor lay in a heap on the dirty kitchen floor, bleeding internally from four slugs lodged in his upper thighs and another at the base of his spine. He was unaware that because of his casual proximity to his employer, he had shielded and thus saved the life of the Caribbean's first international music

business cynosure since Harry Belafonte, and Marcus Garvey's successor as Jamaica's international firebrand: Robert Nesta Marley, the sovereign of Reggae.

Only moments before, the six-odd musicians that made up the Wailers' band had been assembled, along with the Zap Pow Horns, on the side porch of Marley's palatially shabby headquarters at 56 Hope Road, Kingston. They were rehearsing in earnest for a free outdoor "Smile Jamaica" concert festival, co-sponsored by the group and the Jamaican Cultural Ministry, which was scheduled for that Sunday at the city's National Heroes Circle Arena. A short break had just been called when Don Taylor, who had been detained in business discussions at the nearby Sheraton Kingston Hotel, entered the house and began searching for its owner.

Unbeknownst to Taylor, two white Datsuns loaded with at least seven men had been following minutes behind his car. While he strode into the house they slipped through the rusty gates at the bottom of the driveway, one vehicle blocking the exit while the other swiftly approached the building. In an instant, the cars had emptied out and the gunmen were peppering the place with a barrage of automatic-weapons fire, shattering windows and splintering plaster and wood on the first floor.

According to Jeff Walker, then press officer for the Wailers' Island Records label: "They were shooting blindly, wildly."

Combining his own on-the-scene evaluation of the assault's aftermath with the eye-witness descriptions of percussionist Seeco Patterson, Family Man, and Tyrone Downey, Walker recounts that "four gunmen rushed the house on all sides and two others stayed in the front yard, guarding. It was one of these guys that, after the shooting started, shot at Rita [Marley], Bob's wife, as she was trying to escape in a car with five of Bob's children and a reporter from the *Jamaica Daily News.*"

Neither the children nor the reporter were hit but Rita took a bullet in the head; it burrowed into a space between scalp and bone but did not

penetrate her skull.

"At the same time," Walker says, "the second gunman standing guard, who was a young kid with a revolver, pushed into a side door nearest Hope Road. Tyrone Downey's girlfriend was standing right behind him—the boy didn't even see her—and she described him as a '16-year-old kid, scared to death.'

"The kid's eyes were closed; he pressed up with his face against the wall and blindly stuck a gun around the corner into the area where some of the musicians still were. Bullets struck the organ and the ceiling—you could see the holes all over the place. Then the kid stopped firing and ran out."

Meanwhile, a man armed with an automatic rifle had burst through the back door off the kitchen pantry, pushing past a fleeing Seeco Patterson to aim at Bob Marley—who made no move to dodge the assailant.

"See, Bob was still not aware of all the shooting going on, Walker explains. "He saw the weapon coming through the door behind Don

Taylor and even relaxed for a second because it was an automatic, one of the typical police weapons. It was not unusual for the police to be around at that time because they were assisting with the preparations for the cultural program that weekend. But when Bob saw that the gun was *raised,* he realized it wasn't the police."

The gunman got off eight shots. One bullet went wild and hit a counter, another ricocheted and passed into the sagging ceiling, and five tore into Don Taylor. The last creased Marley's breast near his armpit and then went clean through his arm.

Miraculously, no one was killed in the night-time raid. A passing police car happened on the scene at the height of the pandemonium, frightening the would-be assassins into a high-speed exit. If the night riders had sought to murder Marley and his clan, they had failed. But Don Taylor was seriously wounded; friend Lewis Griffith and Marley's wife Rita were injured and the post-melee mood was one of defeat and static terror. It was the same brand of violence-bred

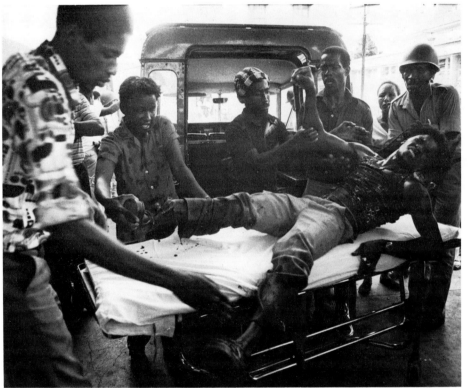

Don Taylor and Al Anderson. Taylor was Bob Marley's manager from 1975 to 1980. Al Anderson played lead guitar for the Wailers beginning in 1974 and continuing through the group's last tour in 1980, with a stint in Peter Tosh's Word Sound and Power band in the middle. When Marley met Anderson in London in 1974, the reggae king told the young guitar from New Jersey to just play the blues.

See them fighting for power
But they know not the hour
So they bribing
With their guns, spare parts and
  money
Trying to belittle our integrity . . .
Ambush in the night
All guns aiming at me
Ambush in the night
Protected by His Majesty

paralysis that had been spreading across the 146-mile-long island throughout the last year in anticipation of general elections, now just weeks away.

Albeit conceived as a non-political, non-partisan celebration, the "Smile Jamaica" concert the Wailers were slated to headline was to cap months of efforts by beleaguered Prime Minister Michael Manley to defy a wave of fierce partisan disorder and death-dealing which had gripped his country.

Tragically, all the incendiary elements of Jamaica in 1976 converged with the brazen attempted murder of Bob Marley. Although his local appeal cut across political lines, Bob was known to be sympathetic to Manley's People's National Party (PNP, see page 173), just as the Prime Minister was openly solicitous in his encounters with Bob's ganja-smoking religious brethren.

And so, while his manager hovered on the critical list in Kingston's University Hospital, a scarred, bewildered Bob Marley had to make a decision on a matter which could have an irretractably profound effect on the current gloom in his homeland, on his thoroughly harried career—and on his very life: Should he still appear at the "Smile Jamaica" festival?

"At that point there was no real intention of going through with the concert," says Jeff Walker. "When I saw Bob as he was getting his wound dressed at the hospital, he was very, very shook up and convinced that the gunmen—whoever they were—were trying to kill him, and not simply scare him."

After being released by the attending physician, Marley was hustled away under police escort to a secluded encampment high in the Blue Mountains above Kingston. Heavy protection by plain-clothes officers stationed around the retreat was supplemented by machete-toting Rastas who kept a constant vigil, some hiding in surrounding trees after nightfall. Jeff Walker was

Michael Manley, Bob Marley and Edward Seaga onstage, 1978.

Bob Marley and the Wailers (sans I-Threes), in an elevator in London after returning from performing at Zimbabwe's independence celebration, April 1980. Standing from left: Tyrone Downey, Junior Marvin, Earl "Wia" Lindo, Alvin "Seeco" Patterson. Crouching from left: Carlton Barrett, Bob Marley, Al Anderson, Aston "Family Man" Barrett.

one of a very few who knew the head Wailers' location. The evening after the shooting, Walker joined Marley in the mountains for a conference.

"We all talked from eight p.m. until two in the morning about all the various aspects of what had happened and what it meant," says Walker. "We discussed whether or not he should play, considering that if the gunmen had been trying to stop the music, then whether Bob had died or not, they were still accomplishing what they'd set out to do if he didn't play.

"Bob was extremely upset and a lot of things had to be pointed out to him. Even so, it was his decision, and at the end of our talk it was left up in the air whether the band would appear the next night. Besides, they were scattered all over the island and Bob wasn't really in contact with them."

Spirits at the hideout lifted a bit on Sunday morning with the news that Don Taylor's con-

dition had improved, although he would eventually have to be flown to Miami's Cedars of Lebanon hospital for removal of the bullet lodged against his spinal cord. If complications arose during the delicate surgery, Taylor might never walk again.

There was also considerable concern over the fact that the gunmen had not yet been apprehended. One of the getaway cars would be found abandoned in Trench Town, but the identities of its occupants remained a mystery.

As the day wore on, conversation concerning the festival was minimal but the camp stayed in touch over walkie-talkies with developments at the site.

Manning the unit at Hero's Circle were Ibo and Cat of the Third World Band, which was expected to open the show in the absence of Bunny Wailer, Peter Tosh and Burning Spear—none of whom ever showed for their scheduled sets. Nonetheless, the early turnout at the track was estimated at a staggering 50,000 people and their mood was a buoyant one.

"Originally, Third World wanted to wait until Bob committed himself before they decided to play," Walker confides. "Ibo and Cat spoke with Marley on the walkie-talkies about the feel of the crowd, the vibes, and it was so astoundingly beautiful that they convinced themselves—if not Bob—to go on. He was able to hear the audience's reaction to Third World over the walkie-talkies and then listened to the woman MC's warm, tribute-like message to Bob Marley from the people. It was odd that so many horrible vibes could be transmuted by so many good, positive ones—but they were.

"We started trying to get the band together and sent someone over to the Hope Road house

to see if we could turn up some of the musicians. We found [guitarist] Don Kinsey, Tyrone Downey and Carly Barrett and each spoke to Bob. He basically told them, 'Get over to the arena. I think we're gonna come down.' Every member but Family Man was eventually found. Cat called us from offstage and volunteered to play his bass."

Marley still had misgivings, however. Sources said that a final pep talk from none other than Tony Spaulding, a powerful government minister, tipped the balance, sending Marley and his escort into a red Volvo waiting behind an idling police car. As the impromptu seven-car motorcade made its way down the narrow mountain roads, Jeff Walker, who rode in a car behind Marley's, informed the concert site that the Wailers were on their way down.

"We could hear the people were exultant over the walkie-talkie, and as we were tear-assing down into the city, we sped past—of all things—a rival JLP (Jamaican Labor Party) rally that was dispersing. The people lined along the roadsides were actually cheering, 'Bob Marley! Bob Mar-ley!' It was incredible."

Attendance at the thoroughly-garrisoned festival site had swelled to 80,000, yet the approach to the stage was remarkably clear. Bounding out of the Volvo, Marley was met at the microphone by Michael Manley, who hugged him with emotion and then stepped to the sidelines, where he stood for the duration of the show on the roof of a Volkswagen van, fully exposed to any would-be sniper.

Shaking his dreadlocked mane in exhilaration, Bob Marley offered a timorous homily to

the throng: "When I decided ta do dis concert two anna 'af months ago, dere was no politics. I just wanted ta play far da love of da people . . ."

Prevented from strumming his familiar brown solid-body Gibson electric guitar because of his arm injury, Marley murmured that he would sing "one song." He thereupon launched into what became a 90-minute *tour de force* opening with "War," from *Rastaman Vibration*. Its lyrics are a virtual transcription of a speech His Imperial Majesty Haile Selassie delivered in California in February 1968:

What life has taught me
I would like to share with
Those who want to learn . . .
That until the basic human rights
Are equally guaranteed to all . . .
Everywhere is war.

The proceedings were further electrified by the presence of Rita Marley, who sang dressed in a nightgown and duster with a scarf covering her bandaged head—the decision to perform had been made so swiftly she had no time to change clothes. At the close of his performance, Bob opened his shirt and rolled up the sleeve to show his wounds to the vast crowd. The last thing they saw before the reigning king of reggae disappeared back into the hills, was the image of the man parroting the two-pistoled draw of a frontier gunslinger, his head thrown back in triumphant laughter.

Legend has it that Jamaican producer Ken Khouri got the ball rolling for the island's recording industry in the late '50s when he re-turned from a trip to New York with one of those *Record-Your-Voice!* booths that filled the pinball parlors in Times Square. From that humble beginning he started Federal Records and recorded almost anybody who wandered in. All you need-ed was a reasonably good song, a creditable voice and a producer who agreed with you on both counts—since he was the one who payed for the session time, hired the musicians and owned the record after the artist got his payment —maybe twenty pounds and his own master.

It was during this period that 16-year-old Bob Marley was introduced by Jimmy Cliff to producer Leslie Kong. Bob went into Federal and cut a raw version of a song he'd written for Kong called "Judge Not (Unless You Judge Yourself)." It saw some scattered play, but it wasn't until the record was picked up by Island Records and released in England in 1964 (under the misnomer Bob Morley) that he began making a name for himself. By that time, he had assem-bled a vocal group called the Wailers—the only band besides the Maytals that would flourish during the twenty-year ska, rock steady, reggae and rockers eras.

"Some child says he wants to be a doctor, but we couldn't even tell ourselves lies like dat," says Bunny Wailer. "Gettin' into music with Wailers was a natural progression for all of us. When I was a yout' I used to play a homemade guitar. I took the strings for it from some electri-cal wire—electrical wires 'ave fine wires inside; I took the rubber off them and used the fine wires. I took a sardine can, nailed it to a piece of wood and the bamboo pole was the neck of the guitar. At the time Bob and I were living together on Second Street in Trench Town. We finally got a real guitar from Peter Tosh and by singing together over years, we made a childhood t'ing grow up and happen.

"In the start, it was jus' Peter Tosh, me and Bob Marley—nobody else. We jus' sat around in quiet places in Trench Town and harmonized. Dis was the period when we nicknamed de Wail-ing Rudeboys or the Teenagers but we never recorded wit these names. The Wailing Wailers was a name Coxsone Dodd give us further on, in 1966."

[There is a widespread misconception that the Wailers also recorded under the name Wailing Souls during this period. Actually, Wailing Souls was a group of younger youths that Bob Marley took under his wing in the late '60s. While the Wailers never sang or played as a group on Wailing Souls records, they did supply a good deal of guidance that reportedly resulted in a certain amount of artistic give-and-take—Bob is known to have written such Wailing Souls songs as "Back Out." The group itself issued singles on the Coxsone label, among them "Back Out" (1969) and "Without You" (1970). In the early '70s, Bob Marley started an unrelated record label called Wail 'N' Soul and released singles by Fam-ily Man Barrett and the I-Threes, among others.]

It was during the scuffling days of '62 and '63 that the boys first became friendly with Joe Higgs, a veteran on the music scene who recog-nized the trio's potential.

"We looked up to Joe Higgs," Bunny admits. "He was something like a musical guardian for us. He was a more professional singer, because he was workin' for years wit' a fella named Roy

Peter Tosh, Rita Anderson (Marley) and Bob Marley pose in 1966, the days of "Bob Marley and the Wailing Rudeboy Wailers."

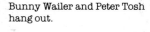

Bunny Wailer and Peter Tosh hang out.

Joe Higgs, the Wailers' early music professor and harmony master.

Bunny playing football, 1980.

Wilson as Higgs & Wilson. They had a lotta hits ["Manny-O," "There's A Reward"] and they had the knowledge of the harmony techniques, so he taught us them. And he 'elped in the studio, to work out our different parts."

Higgs must have been an able instructor because they learned fast.

"The Wailers was first recorded successfully as a group," says Bunny, "when we met Coxsone, and it was Bob, me, Peter—and we had a brother, name-a Junior Braithwaite, singing tenor, and two girls."

A hit single in Jamaica traditionally sold in the neighborhood of 6,000 to 8,000 copies, and the Wailers always managed that much. But having a hit in Jamaica didn't mean you were making any money. Unaware that royalties even existed, most of the artists recording during the ska era were street urchins and poor "yardboys," and they never really complained about the setup. Marley was the first to admit that "me just wanted to hear myself over the jukebox," and he felt privileged to pocket a few pounds and play his own acetate of the record until it wore the needle to a nub.

The Wailers' first single, the 1964 hit, "Simmer Down," was a natural. The rude-boy plague of gang violence was the talk and the terror of the island in the mid-'60s, and while the Wailers' song was an admonishment to "Simmer down/Control your temper," it nonetheless romanticized the rudie scene.

The Wailers filled the instant demand for their rude boy music with a succession of similar 45s, all cut for Studio One during the period ('64–'66) that Peter, Bunny, Bob worked with Dodd. Two of the best to appear on the Coxsone label were "Rude Boy" (also released later as "Rebel's Hop") and "Jail House" (which has likewise been issued as "Ruddie Boy" and "Ruddie").

"Rude Boy" was a percolating performance that sprang from a harmonized bedrock of "Why, why, why, why" and "Dibbie, dibbie, doo, ba, day." The lyric, or what passed for one, concerned a rude boy wanted by the police who's

"got to keep on moving." The sense of desperate flight is offset by a moralistic chorus that chides the young criminal with an old Jamaican folk-saying: "Wanty, wanty, can't getty. Getty, getty, no wanty." In other words, you only want what you can't have, and vice versa. The Wailers would later use the same hills adage in an early-'70s single they cut for producer Lee Perry on the Upsetter label, "Craven Choke Puppy."

"Jail House" had a slower tempo, the narrative lyrics painting a bleak picture of the future for rude boys, and their victims, should their misdeeds go unchecked:

Jail house keeps empty
Rudie gets healthy
Baton sticks get shorter
Rudie gets taller

Can't fight against the youth, now
(Cause it's wrong)
Can't fight against the youth, now
(Cause it's strong)

Prediction: The people a-going wild
Dem a rude, rude people . . .

The Wailers also cut a number of blues-tinged ballads in their ska days. The first was "It Hurts To Be Alone," written and sung by Junior Braithwaite and released in 1964 on Dodd's Coxsone/World Disc label. Similar singles included "I am Going Home," an arrangement of "Swing Low, Sweet Chariot" that featured an extremely nasal lead vocal by Bob Marley, and "I'm Still Waiting," a corny Bob Marley composition in which Braithwaite considers the pangs of teen angst:

I'm still waiting for you
Why-o-why? Why-o-why?

I said my feet won't keep me up anymore
And with every little second my heart beats girl,
 it's at your door . . .

Pretty dismal fare. When the Wailers cooked, it was usually on the up-tempo numbers like

"Dancing Shoes." Even a ripoff of Junior Walker and the All Stars' "Shotgun," retitled "Ska Jerk," worked well; if not for the vocals, then for the first-rate instrumental accompaniment.

In the beginning, the Wailers and their contemporaries were primarily vocal groups. Instrumental backup for the Wailers was usually provided by members of the Skatalites, Beverley's All Stars (during their rock steady explorations) and, from 1969 to 1971, by producer Lee Perry's Upsetters (the band included future Wailers Aston Barrett on bass and brother Carlton on drums). With the possible exception of Peter Tosh, none of the original Wailers was an instrumentalist of any special merit. Rather, their strengths lay in singing, songwriting and arranging. Ironically, one of the most acclaimed performances by a Wailer is the lead guitar on "Concrete Jungle," the opening track on the group's 1973 Island LP *Catch a Fire.* Though there's no mention of him on the two versions of the album's cover, the brilliant lead was overdubbed by American session guitarist Wayne Perkins.

The notable rock steady material by the Wailers was cut for Leslie Kong. The beat was usually there but the lyrics were lame, lacking the nasty, calypso-rooted cleverness of Alton Ellis' best performances. "Can't You See" is indicative of their miscomprehending approach with its insincere rhythm and tepid refrain: "Can't you see/what you doing to me?/I am bound/Won't you set me free?"

A perky arrangement of "Caution" fared a bit better, propelled by an agitated lead-guitar line and Marley's wisecracks: "Hit me from the top! You crazy motherfocker!"

These and other songs were gathered together by Kong in the late '60s and released under the dubious banner, *The Best of the Wailers.*

"I told him, 'Don't do it, mon,'" Bunny Wailer remembers fiercely. "'It cannot be the *best* of the Wailers,'cause our best is yet to come.' And I promised if he did that, he would *die.*"

Such threats are not taken lightly in Jamaica, where ancient "balmyard" voodoo superstitions go hand in hand with the righteous fire-and-brimstone ethic espoused in rural Pentecostal churches.

"He went ahead anyways and that album came out," says Bunny. "A month afterward, Kong fell ill in the studio and went home—and he died. He was tryin' to kill us and it bounced back on him!"

"Bunny really does have an obeah capability," Chris Blackwell asserts. "He knows how to completely control any situation, and then alter it at will, often somewhat mischievously.

"When I first attempted to sign Bunny to a record contract in 1976 for *Blackheart Man* [i.e., the "bogeyman"] he was being very difficult. What it finally came down to, was that he did the deal with me personally, rather than with the company. He told me he wanted a clause in his contract whereby if I should die, he'd be out of the contract. I said, 'Well, I don't know, really, about that.' But at last I said, 'Okay, I suppose we could do it.' There were a few moments of hesi-

tation and then Bunny said, 'Good. That means I can get out of my contract at any time.'"

By the time [1969] the Wailers first threw their lot in with Lee Perry, Lee had built up a well-deserved reputation through his stewardship with Clement Dodd and his own solo material. While working as an "idea man" with Coxsone, Perry helped run his original mobile sound system and then assisted at Dodd's primitive console when Dodd began to make his own records. As Studio One prospered, Perry and Skatalite organist Jackie Mittoo became two of Dodd's right-hand men—auditioning artists, producing and engineering the instrumental tracks for the vocalists and mapping out record distribution.

In those days, "Little" (as he was known early-on) demonstrated the bold temerity to notch his *own* hits with discs such as "Roast Duck," "Open Up," and "Old for New." He cut a track that indulged the latest dance rage, "The Chicken Scratch," and his admirers christened him "Scratch." By 1968, Perry was rude and cocky enough to thumb his nose at a titan like Clement Dodd and strike out on his own. Two of his trial balloons were vengeful singles directed at Coxsone, "Run for Cover" and "The Upsetter," which became a smash hit.

It was at this Olympian juncture that Perry and his crack session men began celebrating their success by tripping down to the Odeon or the Bijou to catch the latest Clint Eastwood spaghetti western. Galvanized by the gory orgies of death, they cut violent instrumental 45s like "Clint Eastwood" and the tumultuous "Return of Django."

Perry ended the Wailers' ragged, random studio tactics and honed them into a Rock-influenced unit that typified the *best* in early reggae and rock steady meanderings. It was Lee Perry who redirected the group musically and vocally and while his primitive recording facilities held them back technically, he pushed Bob to eschew his lazy singing style. Marley's approach suddenly became urgent, plaintive, unencumbered by the silly vocal gymnastics that sometimes marred the Wailers' ska and rock steady singles.

Perry advised the group to minimize its hackneyed falsetto harmonies and work on unobtrusive backing vocals that would serve as a cushion for sharp, assertive leads. Peter Tosh had an errant baritone he'd long tried to contain, and both Marley's and Bunny Wailer's tenors were fluid, but untempered and sloppy. It didn't matter, Perry told them, be genuine and go for the gut. And Perry wasn't obsessed with horns, as were so many other Jamaican producers; he pre-

ferred a hard rhythm guitar that was "cuffed" in sharp counterpoint to the bass, which he allowed to belly to the foreground. The tempo was thud-heavy, volatile and as insistent as a nagging child.

Together, Perry and Marley crafted the songs that would forge the Wailers' gutbucket reggae attack when they rerecorded most of them—"Small Axe," "Trench Town Rock," "Duppy Conqueror"—for the prospering Island label.

Even the most avid ska and reggae fans outside of Jamaica are unaware of the fascinating shades of meaning in most of the songs. For instance, when Bob Marley intones in "Small Axe" that "If you are the big tree/We are the small axe . . ./These are words of my master," he is not just admonishing the Third World's oppressors that their days are numbered. The song refers to the rival "big three" Jamaican studios—Federal, Dynamic and Studio One—that Lee Perry's Upsetter Records sought to surpass, and the symbolism is derived from the days of British colonialism, when Jamaican slaves would splash rum on the roots of the stately silk-cotton trees before felling them. This was done to placate the "duppies" (ghosts) within the huge trunks—the slave simultaneously singing to assure the spirits that such destruction was not of his own doing but the orders of his master.

In 1978, I ran into Bob and Perry in a Los Angeles hotel room. Perry was lounging around contentedly and seconding Marley's emotions with graceful contriteness as Bob fretted about the way Perry had ripped off the Wailers by taking their tapes to England and selling them to Trojan Records for what would become *Soul Rebels, Rasta Revolution, African Herbsman* and *Soul Revolution Part I* and *Part II.*

The talk turned to the artwork of the latter two records, and Bob and Lee reminisced about the ridiculous cover photo session supervised by noted singer Glen Adams. Perry and the group were depicted lurking around back yards wearing heavy coats and brandishing toy sten guns.

Bob giggled and then pressed his finger to his temple. He had a habit of doing that, both in concert and in conversation, when he wanted to

Chris Blackwell of Island Records relaxing by the pool of the New Kingston Hotel. With him is associate Denise Mills. Blackwell parlayed good taste in pop music and a gambler's instinct into what even his critics concede is the best record company in the world.

Bob and Peter, Los Angeles 1978.

shift gears or introduce a new idea, and the movement would immediately be picked up by those around him. He could alter the mood of a room at will. People fell silent, as if on command.

"I don't like guns, and I don't want to fight," he said evenly, echoing something I'd heard him say years before. "But when we move to go to Africa, if they say no, then I personally will *have* to fight. I don't love fightin' but I don't love wickedness either. My father was a captain in the army; I guess I have a kinda war thing in me, but is better to die fightin' for our freedom than to be a prisoner all the days of your life."

His face was stony. Then he lifted his finger from his temple and placed it on mine.

"Peace," he said, his voice scarcely above a whisper. "There is no fear or anger here, mon."
Open your eyes and look within
Are you satisfied with the life you're living?
We know where we're going
We know where we're from
We're leaving Babylon
We're going to our father's land
"Exodus," 1977

Marley was equally distraught over what he saw as the racism and ignorance of critics who damned his music along thematic lines while making no attempt to investigate its underpinnings, to learn that it was steeped in folklore, in the country maxims he had been raised on, in Rastafarian tenets. But what cut deepest was when some black deejays and station programmers in the United States called his records and those of his colleagues "jungle music" and "slave music."

Still, Bob Marley was one of the most revered figures in the Third World. Wherever he traveled in the Caribbean or Africa (and Europe, for that matter), he sparked enormous outpourings of affection and admiration. A hero of mythic proportions in his own country, where he was honored with a state funeral, Marley had been given a special citation by the United Nations in 1978 on behalf of Third-World nations. And it was no accident that when Rhodesia became the independent state of Zimbabwe two years later, the first words spoken following the order to lower the British flag and raise the new standard were,

"Ladies and gentlemen, Bob Marley and the Wailers!" The government had invited Marley and his band to perform at the ceremony marking the birth of a nation. An inspiration for black freedom-fighters the world over, he was mobbed in Nigeria, Gabon and every other African country he played in or visited.

The pervasive image of Bob Marley is that of a gleeful Rasta with a croissant-sized ganja spliff clenched in his teeth, stoned silly and without a care in the world. But, in fact, he was a man with deep religious and political sentiments who rose from destitution to become one of the most influential music figures in the last twenty years. His records have sold in the multi-millions and have been covered and/or publicly adored by Eric Clapton, Paul McCartney, Mick Jagger, Linda Ronstadt and Paul Simon, among others. Marley was also incredibly prolific, writing and releasing hundreds of songs that were bootlegged under nearly half as many labels in an equal number of far-flung locales. There was hardly one kid in the Caribbean who did not want to meet, if not *be,* Bob Marley.

"My Cup/Runneth Over . . ." 1973

With Haile Selassie, 1976, and, 18 years old, with mother Cedella Booker and baby sister Pearl at Nine Mile, St. Ann, 1963.

When Bob Marley was happy, he smiled like he had a rainbow in his pocket. When he was sad, he was as woeful as an orphan. And when he was angry, he was especially fierce.

During a 1977 US concert tour, Marley was sitting in a Manhattan hotel room, reading a newspaper article that ridiculed his patois. He slammed the paper on the table. "Fucking hell!" he raged. "Tell me, why do they make fun of me? Why do they make fun of Rasta!" He began to spew out his frustration with those who mocked his dreadlocks, his dialect, his religion, his heritage. He said that he once gave an autograph to a journalist who then told him he was surprised Marley could write, and that he pointed out errors in a story to another reporter who could not conceal his amazement that this rope-haired Rastafarian knew how to read.

Bob and Peter with Mick Jagger, 1978.

On the day before his triumphant Madison Square Garden concert in 1978—a sold-out event that would prove to be a turning point for commercial recognition of reggae in this country—Marley talked about his first record, the solo single "Judge Not." He recalled how excited he was when he sang it at a talent show in Montego Bay. He was sixteen then, just another poor country boy in Trench Town who dreamed of hearing his voice blare out of a jukebox. That same year, it happened. And less than two years later, Marley would be a founding member of the trio known as the Wailers, harmonizing with boyhood friends Neville O'Riley Livingston, now known as Bunny Wailer, and Winston Hubert McIntosh, a.k.a. Peter Tosh.

"I was a skinny child with a squee-ky voice," he said, erupting in the creaking sandpaper cough that was his laugh. "*So* skinny, mon! Skinny like a stringy bean!"

Bob Marley was born in the rural parish of St. Ann, Jamaica, on February 6th, 1945, to Norval Marley, a white Englishman, and his 19-year-old Jamaican wife, Cedella.

"I was about seventeen and livin' in St. Ann," says Cedella Booker (she remarried in 1962), "when I met Bob's father. He was a handsome white man, in his fifties, a captain in the army who worked as a foreman over the Army property contingent, a place for people who are back from war. You see, Jamaica wasn't independent then, and the British army was still there. St. Ann was farm country, a beautiful place, but Norval was not a farmer; he was a soldier."

St. Ann *is* a beautiful place: miles of lush jungle, spectacular waterfalls and rolling, verdant hills in whose misty creases duppies are said to lurk. Called the Garden Parish, its rich soil is perfect for the cultivation of ganja, citrus, bananas, pimento, sugar, coconuts, coffee and sisal, and its vast chalky-beige beaches are magnificent. Even for a poor boy, it was a great place to grow up.

Marley was efficacious in his ability to straddle his bloodlines. "He was just like any other little boy, always playful, lovin' and cooperative with his friends," Mrs. Booker recalls. "But sometimes he was a little selfish. And he always looked at me like he was hiding his true feelin's."

Bob was six years old when his parents parted for good. His mother decided to give up her tiny grocery store in Alva, a village near Rhoden Hall, and move to Trench Town. His father died two years later. "I believe it was malaria or cancer," says Mrs. Booker.

In their early days in Kingston, Bob's mother made ends meet by working as a cook or servant. Although the two lived modestly, Mrs. Booker, disliking the area's inferior public school system, struggled to earn enough to send Bob to private schools.

But she wasn't breaking her back doing other people's wash so her son could boot a soccer ball off the tumbledown walls of Babylon, and as soon as Bob completed grammar school, she insisted he settle on a trade.

"I really didn't choose anything special as a job for him," she says. "I knew men who were doing welding for a livin', and I suggested that he go down to the shop and make himself an apprentice. He hated it. One day he was welding some steel and a piece of metal flew off and got stuck right in the white of his eye, and he had to go to the hospital twice to have it taken out. It caused him terrible pain; it even hurt for him to cry."

At the time, the Marleys were sharing a roof with best friend Bunny Wailer and his father, Thaddius Livingston, a welder and carpenter. Once his eye healed, Bob convinced his mother that he could make a more comfortable living pursuing a musical career with Bunny. "Bob wrote little songs, and then he and Bunny would sing them," his mother says. "Sometimes I'd teach him a tune like 'I'm Going to Lay My Sins Down at the Riverside.'"

Bunny says that he and Bob made do with the crude (bamboo-cum-sardine can) instrument until Peter Tosh, who lived on nearby West Road, joined in with his battered acoustic guitar. Tosh had come to Kingston from Westmorland, a tall and haughty youth who sang deep bass. They formed a group and called themselves the Teenagers, the Wailing Rudeboys and then the Wailing Wailers, playing in local "yards" for tips

and eventually in small clubs and talent shows in Kingston theaters.

In 1963, Mrs. Booker emigrated to Delaware and moved in with relatives. Because of the expense, Bob stayed behind in the care of Mr. Livingston and other friends. Moreover, he was committed to his musical career in Jamaica, since the Wailers had grown, with the guidance of Joe Higgs into a group worthy of a recording contract. Mrs. Booker sent for her son in 1964, just as the Wailers were establishing a relationship with Studio One, one of the top three recording outfits on the island, so he asked to remain in Jamaica.

Finally, in 1966, he paid his mother a visit, but he had little use for the United States and Delaware in particular. By his own admission, "Everything was too fast, too noisy, too rush-rush." Nonetheless, he prolonged his stay to earn money to start his own record label back home, and thus put some distance between himself and the predatory producers he and the Wailers were forced to deal with.

Among the jobs he held, under the alias Donald Marley, were a stint as a DuPont lab assistant, a short stretch on the night shift at a warehouse, and on the assembly line of a nearby Chrysler plant. The introverted singer made few friends, preferring to merely tolerate the present and fantasize about the future. In his mother's words, he was "lost without his musician friends."

On weekends, he lolled around the house, picking out simple melodies on a cheap acoustic guitar and writing lyrics in a little book, a combination diary and songwriting ledger that he guarded judiciously. One of the songs that emerged from that private journal was "It's Alright," a caustic, exhortatory dance tune he cut in the late '60s for Lee Perry's Jamaican record company, Upsetter.

When Marley first recorded the song, it featured a bouncy, whoa-whoa chorus and antagonistic taunts of "Do you like it hot or cold?" His temper had cooled by the time he recorded the song as "Night Shift" in the mid-'70s, but the words changed only slightly, the power of one young man's determination shining through as he described his lonely, ass-backward work schedule:

The sun shall not smite I by day
Nor the moon by night
And everything that I do shall be upfull
*   and right . . .*
Working on the night shift,
With the forklift . . .

Marley's stay in Delaware reportedly came to an end when the draft board discovered the lean immigrant worker after he applied for Social Security. But when asked about his departure, Bob would shrug and maintain that the ultimate impetus for his flight came from a far less mundane quarter.

While asleep at home one afternoon, he had a dream wherein a man attired in khaki and weathered hat appeared, described himself as an emissary for the deceased Norval Marley and presented Bob with a ring set with a curious black jewel. He awoke from his mystical reverie and described the vision to his mother. She then produced the very ring in the dream, and Marley slipped it on his finger.

But it made him extremely uncomfortable to wear it, and he reasoned that he was being tested by God to ascertain whether he was more interested in personal gain than in spiritual fulfillment. He removed the ring and handed it back to his mother. After he returned to Trench Town, the message of the dream was interpreted further by Mortimer Planno, a Rasta elder and longtime adviser to Bob.

Bob Marley subsequently embraced the beliefs of the Rastafarians. Slowly but surely, Marley let his Sam Cooke haircut go to seed, allowing the lengthening tresses to wind themselves into dreadlocks. He shunned alcohol, tobacco, meat, shellfish and food prepared with salt. Anything, in short, that was not I-tal.

Bob's mother, Cedella Malcolm, was born in St. Ann in 1926. She married Bob's father, Norval Marley, in 1944. In 1962 she was remarried to Edward Booker and moved to Wilmington, Delaware. Today she lives in Miami, a queen mother of reggae.

Initially distressed, Cedella Booker eventually adjusted to her boy's dramatic transformation. "I was surprised at first by the locks," she said. "I have some photos of Bob without them, and he hates to look at them. I've gotten used to it, and it doesn't bother me anymore. He started to grow them in 1966, cut them off and had an Afro in 1968 that grew into locks again. When he told me he was a Rastafarian and believed Selassie was God, I thought he was wrong. I'm a Christian, a member of the United Church of the Lord Jesus Christ of the Apostolic Faith.

"One night in the kitchen here, Nesta sat me down with the Bible, striking the table and talking about Selassie from nine o'clock until three in the morning as he quoted from the Scriptures. He pointed to where it says, 'What is hidden from the wise and prudent is not hidden from children.'"

Several years after returning to Jamaica, Marley sent his mother a touching note, along with some money, intended as "a token of love." He told her about his burgeoning career and tried to convey the excitement he felt when he

Rita and Bob and their children in 1971. The children are Sharon, Ziggy, baby Stephen and Cedella Jr.

Bob in a hallway at 56 Hope Road as it was being rebuilt, 1975.

performed. It was a short note but full of emotion from a son who had so often behaved with a perplexing aloofness. Mrs. Booker wept over every word.

Marley was always open in his gratitude to Chris Blackwell, the white Anglo-Jamaican producer and founder of Island who rescued him from the shark-infested Caribbean record industry and staked him through thick and, often, thin. Island leased and reissued "Judge Not" in England in 1964, as well as a succession of Wailers singles, but the initial Island LP, *Catch a Fire,* didn't appear until 1973.

The first Wailers album to see widespread international distribution, it was not an immediate commercial smash. But critical reaction was overwhelmingly positive, with much praise for the record's hypnotic, sulfurous songs. Intriguingly, the loping, hiccuping beat that propelled

them was the inside-out counterpart of funky American r&b tempos. Blackwell and Marley were thrilled with the response, and a long-term alliance was forged.

Jealousy and internal power struggles ultimately plagued the Wailers, and Peter and Bunny departed in 1973 after the follow-up LP *Burnin'* to pursue solo careers. "Jamaica is a place where you easily build up competition in your mind," Marley said of the break-up. "People here feel like they must fight against me and I must fight against you. Sometimes a guy feels he should do that because he might never have no schoolin' and I went to school, so he feel he must sing some song to wipe me off the marker or I should do the same. Jealousy. Suspicion. Anger. Poverty. Competition. We should just get together and create music, but there's too much poverty fuckin' it up. People don't get time to expand their intelligence. Sometimes I think the most intelligent people are the poorest—they just want to *eat.*

"God created the earth for us, but people wonder, 'Who owns the tree? Who owns the

ladder? Who owns the ganja pipe?'" He shook his dreadlocks in disgust.

"When the thieves took up with reggae music, mon, they have it *made*! It *easy* in Jamaica for any guy who have a few dollars to rent a studio, go in, get a recording, ask the engineer to mix it. The hustlers move in as soon as he's gone into the street; the record goes into stores and Jojo knows nothing about what happened! Jamaicans go slow, everything is 'soon come,' but if there's one thing Jamaicans rush about, it's making a recordin'!"

When he finished, Bob sat quietly for a moment, and then burst out laughing. "Ahh, nothin' is important that much, eh?" he said with a bobbing nod and a shrug.

Marley's stepfather Booker passed away in February 1976, and on his deathbed made Bob promise to look after the children. Marley kept

that vow, spending increasing amounts of time in the States and using his mother's home (she later moved to Miami) as a headquarters whenever he toured America or visited on business.

Marley had fled Jamaica following the 1976 shooting, and while he retained his property at Hope Road and built his Tuff Gong record concern into a thriving business that developed local talent, there was a new restlessness in his lifestyle that kept him away from Jamaica much of the time.

However, he spent the better part of 1980 in Kingston, working feverishly to realize a long-time ambition: the transformation of Tuff Gong into a completely self-sufficient recording company, complete with its own pressing plant. Shortly before cancer sapped the better part of his strength, he succeeded in his dream, but he occupied the small private office on the top floor of the Tuff Gong complex only briefly. The administrative work soon fell to Rita Marley as her husband fought for his life.

I first met Bob Marley in the fall of 1975, at his home on Hope Road in Kingston. At the time he was working on *Rastaman Vibration,* the twelfth album with the Wailers and the fourth of the ten he would issue on Island Records during his lifetime.

"You find that most people, when they get money, they get withdrawn and foolish," he offered. "Money is not my richness. My richness is to live and walk on the earth barefoot. Richness is when your mind can tell you to get up and do something you *want* to do—and you can do it!

"Some say I talk too much about this, that Rasta speaks too much about it. The intelligent but innocent are poor, hungry and get brutalized Daily. The thieves, they are rich, but only moneywise. Hear me! Before I knew Island and Chris Blackwell, I had some albums out in England, three albums of my music on Trojan Records that I *didn't even know about*! It's so weird

That's why some guys get knots in their heads."

Bob's wife Rita appeared on the lawn with Robbie, one of his children. Bob Marley hiked up his torn jeans, nudged me playfully and began to rhapsodize about his heroes: Elvis Presley, Jimi Hendrix, Stevie Wonder and the Beatles.

"I covered one of the Beatle songs, 'And I Love Her'!" he announced, falling briefly into a goofy warble: " 'I give you all my love, that's all I *doo . . .*'

"The guys are brethren, those guys are *roots.* Money hasn't spoiled them to where they cannot be friendly. Billie Holiday sings, 'when your money done, you ain't got no friends.' If the money's done, you may not have a woman either!"

Robbie ran over to give his dad a hug, and Marley kissed the little boy on the nose, then tickled him into hysterics.

Marley lifted his hand in a sign of solemnity.

"Children are wonderful," he said. "It don't take plenty, you know? Just a nice girl who don't take birth control. Sexual intercourse is a lovely thing." He burst out laughing.

I have rarely seen any man so happy.

The saddest I ever saw Bob Marley was on the day before his magnificent Madison Square Garden concert in 1978.

I had stopped by his hotel to say hello, and we began to discuss his career, focusing on his early days.

There was a knock at the door, and the manager of the hotel was admitted with a lovely young black woman walking sheepishly behind him. The manager apologized for the interruption and explained that the young woman had always wanted to meet Bob Marley and had begged him to introduce her.

It's no secret that Marley was something of a lady's man, having squired such stunners as the former Miss World, Cindy Breakspeare. I'd heard more than a few women describe Bob as "the sexiest man on two legs." Besides his four children by Rita, he never concealed the fact that he'd fathered seven others.

But he was not at all amorous toward this young woman at the hotel. He sat her down, kidded her sweetly about her infatuation with him, and then asked about her family, where she came from, what she wanted to do with her life.

After she left, Bob curled up on the couch, staring off into space; his mind had a tendency to wander, and there was nothing offensive about his periodic lapses into mute contemplation. This one, however, lasted longer than usual.

"I have a sister, ya know," he finally said softly. "My father was her father, but she has a different mother. I knew about her since I was a youth, and alla time I search for her. One time, when I was in my twenties, Rita find her. She was workin' in a dry-cleaner's in Kingston. Rita talked with her for just a few minutes and then they said goodbye, Rita thinking she was gonna see again. But when I go back a few days later, she is gone. I never found her again. It was a painful thing, not to know her."

"When the time comes, people will seek the truth in all things," he added wistfully. "They get it when they are ready to hear it."

Bob at the board, Tuff Gong studios, Kingston 1979.

to Rita Anderson. Looking over Blackwell's shoulder, gazing at her slight son as he lay in a Miami hospital bed, his dreadlocks gone due to the illness, Bob's mother remarked that he looked the same now as he did back then.

"Once a man and twice a child," Chris Blackwell said later, quoting a Marley lyric. "That's the way it was."

My final encounter with Bob Marley was in the fall of 1980, the day after his second concert stand (opening for the Commodores) at Madison Square Garden. I was unaware of it at the time, but he was about to undergo diagnostic treatment for cancer at New York City's Memorial Sloan-Kettering Institute. Stretched out on the bed at the Essex House, he looked drained, frail, and annoyed by the flock of hangers-on that filled the numerous rooms of his suite, guffawing loudly and helping themselves to room service.

The aura of joy that had always surrounded him had begun to dissipate. His payment for the previous night's show arrived, and he looked pensively at the crisp stack of bills as if studying

Bob Marley loved women and the feeling was mutual. He fathered eleven children with seven different mothers. Top: Dancing with a model after a concert in Paris, 1977. Bottom: A back-rub at the Essex House, New York 1980.

Every man thinketh his burden is the heaviest
But he who feels it knows it Lord. . . .
I've got to protect my life,
And I don't want to live with no strife
It is better to live on the house top
Than to live in a house full of confusion
So I made my decision, and I left you
Now you coming to tell me that I'm
      running away
But it's not true, I am not running away
"Running Away" 1978

Death took Bob Marley in his sleep on May 11th, 1981 at the age of thirty-six. It was around noon, just forty hours since he had flown to Florida after checking out of a Bavarian clinic, where he had been treated for lung and liver cancer and a brain melanoma. A few days earlier, Chris Blackwell had shown Marley a photo taken of him when he was sixteen, on the day he was married

Center: **Bob & Family Man rehearse at a sound check.**

Bob at a sound check, Providence Rhode Island, 1980.

Bob and singer I Jah Man Levi, and Rita and children at Tuff Gong.

Center: The view from Tuff Gong Studios

an old gimcrack to see if it still held meaning or should be discarded. He absently passed the money to a band member.

Several months later, I was told how sick Bob was. I began to think back on the pleasurable years I spent immersed in Bob Marley and the Wailers.

I remembered hunting through the basement of Daddy Kool Records in London in the winter of 1976. A contact at Island had told me it was a particularly good place to locate vintage ska,

challenge, "Don't try to show off/For I will cut you off/I will take your rass off." I've never found a band as compelling as the Wailers and a singer who could fire my imagination like Marley.

What I will remember most about Bob Marley is how his music was so much a part of his life. Near the end of the our first meeting, in Kingston in 1975, he began to speak about children, how close he felt to them, how their presence always strengthened him and how blessed he was by his own brood.

"Peace, peace! he is not dead, he
    doth not sleep—
He hath awakened from the
    dream of life—
'Tis we, who lost in stormy
    visions, keep
With phantoms an unprofitable
    strife"

Shelley, **Adonais** (part of
stanza 39)

rock steady and reggae. Sure enough, there were tiers of singles and LPs stacked halfway to the ceiling and spilling out of broken bins. I waded into the confusion and located two of the many treasures I was after: a copy of "Simmer Down," and the original version of "Duppy Conqueror," which the Wailers recorded in 1968 while under contract to the Upsetter label. As Peter Tosh once explained to me, "The Wailers were more interested in 'reality music' than 'I love you darlin','' and all that," and the raw, rancorous call to arms that was "Duppy Conqueror" closed with the

I told him how I had shuddered when I'd read a story in the Jamaican *Daily News* about the plight of local youngsters who forage through huge trash heaps on Causeway Road outside Kingston for food and clothing.

He nodded slowly and then told me he had recently written a song called "Children of the Ghetto." "When my children are old enough to sing it," he said, "I'm gonna record it with them. ("Children of the Ghetto," since retitled "Children Playing in the Streets," was released on Tuff Gong in 1979 by the Melody Makers, a group consisting of children of Rita's and Bob's.)

Slumped against the great, gnarled tree beside his house on that sun-splashed day, their father began to talk-sing the lyrics:

*Children playing in the streets
In broken bottles and rubbish heap
Ain't got nothin' to eat*

*Only sweets dat rot dere teeth
Sitting in the darkness
Searching for the light . . .
Moma scream, "Watch that car!"
But hit-and-run man has gone too far . . .*

When he was finished, Bob turned away to watch Rita and son Robbie cavorting on the lawn, and he slipped into a trance. He picked up a stick, rolled it in his palms: his arms tensed and he broke the stick in half with a loud *crack!* Then he relaxed, and his lips wrinkled in a weary grin. "Ahh, Jamaica," he sighed. "Where can your people go? I wonder if it's anyplace on this earth."

I saw his eyes; he knew the answer to that question.

Bob Marley—
A Final
Interview

I saw Selassie
I stretch forth his hand
To take I cross
Jordan River
I'm on my way to Zion

from "Jordan River" (author unknown)

The following conversation was taped in September 1980, in a hotel suite at the Boston airport on the eve of what would become the last, aborted Wailers tour. Bob was in an expansive and philosophical mood, surrounded by friends and entourage monitoring the conversation, one of the last major interviews

From left: the late singer Jacob Miller, who perished in a Kingston auto accident in 1980; Bob Marley, guitarist Junior Marvin, and unidentified musician.

Bob would give. The talk could serve to commemorate the positive, testifying spirit that took Bob Marley from the ghetto of western Kingston to a position of worldwide moral and prophetic authority.

We began by talking about the forthcoming Jamaican election . . .

Q: This is an election year in Jamaica, and there've been more than 700 political killings so far. You narrowly escaped assassination yourself. What's going on?

Bob Marley: Why you ask me these things, bwai? Is not good to talk about it. Certain kinda dem really have plenty . . . equipment. You no ask me these kinda things, really. Me no like it, y'know? I don't like it.

Is it too personal to ask who you might support in the 1980 Jamaican election?

No mon, axe me anything you want axe me, I'll answer you the best I can. Well, I would not support anyone. I'll support myself. A Rasta, you know wha I mean? Only Rasta. No one else is what the people want. Everything's our territory.

Have you been approached for support by various politicians?

Me? Well, tell you the truth, any

political party in Jamaica would *love* our support. And, it might not just come like that, but it come some time. See, all we see happening in politics in Jamaica is that a lot of youths—youths that can't even vote—*die!* Y'unnerstand? Politicians don't care. I mean, maybe you're sick, maybe you want see a doctor, but him don't care about that, him want you to vote. So me no defend politics deh.

In Africa recently I counted several different versions of your song "Zimbabwe" by African musicians. What do you think of what Africans are doing with reggae?

No, me no hear a lot of it. Some things from Nigeria and Senegal, that's all. Some youth trying something. The group we really hear from Africa is Fela, from Nigeria, y'know.

The introduction to "Could You Be Loved" from your Survival *album sounds a lot like Fela.*

Well, me listen to him, but I couldn't tell you which song might sound like him.

You took the band to Zimbabwe for the independence ceremony, right?

Yeah. We were invited by one of the ministers in the new govern-

ment. Yeh mon. We go to the ceremony to play, and we watch the whole thing. Watch the British flag go down and the Zimbabwe flag go up. *Tell ya, bwai* . . . We hear all dem 21 cannon go off, about 60 yards from where we're standing, y'know. You can just imagine that, and how we felt. And then alla musicians from all different African countries.

Was that your first trip to Africa?

No, that was my second.

Do you feel comfortable there?

Africa? Yah mon. Africa nice, mon.

Did you think when you wrote "Zimbabwe" that it would become a folk anthem and that you would perform it at the actual independence celebration?

No, and that's the truth. Hee hee. Now I want to write a song about Ethiopia. Maybe one that could make something happen over there. Yeah.

Who paid for the Wailers to fly to Zimbabwe?

We pay all ourselves, 'cause it mean a lot for us to be deh.

In Jamaica you have your own label, Tuff Gong Records, that records a lot of the island's up-and-coming reggae talent. People who

know you describe you as a shrewd entrepreneur . . .

Wha mean so?

A smart businessman.

Yeah?

Yes, and this is what people used to say about Marcus Garvey as well. So is this accurate? Are you a good businessman?

Well, I don't know business, y'know? That's a thing I don't know too much of. Business. But there's a reality of justice, y'know. If you get justice, I&I get justice.

Do you make the decisions for Tuff Gong, or do you delegate authority?

No, Tuff Gong is *young*. It run by people who don't even know the business that much. But it has a lot of potential because it's one of the few places in Jamaica where the youths can get free development for their talent within music.

It can help them. Yah mon. Pure *children* recordin' there these days.

I know that you and your wife Rita have four children who record as a quartet called the Melody Makers. Who else are you recording?

Yeh, well we have a girl called Nadine Sutherland. She's about nine or eleven year old. I don't know her age there. Very young. But she has an amazing voice. Then you have Junior Tucker, and plenty young youths, y'know, because youth dem know for some reason everything what going on.

So you're like a professional sports team that builds for the future by teaching younger players the game . . .

Yah mon. It can work that way.

Is there a lot of young talent coming up in Jamaica?

Yeh mon. I see it as a place with

so *much* talent that I don't know how I can even *begin* to develop it. So many people go to waste for lack of opportunity. In Jamaica you have a *lot* of good musicians, folk type of musicians, spiritual folk. Yeh mon. People with *incredible* natural talent, but it's hard for them to get heard. We trying to change that. Yeah. And then we also work with great artists, like Burning Spear. We do little of everything.

People who love reggae pay close attention to the texts of your songs, what the lyrics say. What about that lyric in "Redemption Songs" about atomic energy?

"Have no fear for atomic energy / Cause none a dem can stop the time."

That's hard to interpret.

Time is where we are, what we have. Y'know? And no one can

and sometime Delroy Washington. Y'hear 'bout him?

What about Linton Kwesi Johnson? He's very hot these days.

Ahh, I like Linton too, y'know. In Jamaica the interest in his music is that him really no seh "Rasta." But me love him still. Yah mon! Him say great things, otherwise still. And then there's a guy in Jamaica named Oku Onuora, wrote something called "Reflection in Red." It's a new kind of music.

As a religious Rastafarian, I thought you might be interested in Bob Dylan's most recent album. "Saved?"

Yes, and on the album he quotes Jeremiah 31: "Behold the days to come, saith the Lord, when I will make a new covenant with the house of Israel and with the house of Judah."

Of course. Good, sir. And him

Rise ye mighty people
There is work to be done
So let's do it little by little
Rise from your sleepless slumber
We're more than the sand on the
Seashore we're more than
    numbers
Wake Up and Live

Leghorn Coghill, the long-time Wailers crony credited with writing "Them Belly Full."

From left: guitarist Al Anderson, Tyrone Downey & Son, Donald Kinsey, the Indiana musician who played guitar for the Wailers in the **Rastaman Vibration** era, 1976.

stop the Time. So I say, "have no fear for atomic energy" to those who would put the fear into mankind that everything must be destroyed. Now dem seh, this atomic thing can do it. But me seh, "have no fear," because man have hopes. No one can stop the time. Y'know you have to live within Time. So time is important.

Who are you listening to these days? Who are your favorite artists?

Well . . . me listen to . . . listen to Dennis Brown, y'know wha I mean? Me listen to a lot of new artists, lots of new youth. Like Black Uhuru. Like Meditations dem. In England I listen to Steel Pulse,

mention Judah . . . Now in reality, I'm knowin' who Judah is—Haile Selassie! Because him the only man who can say him is Conquering Lion of Judah. So when Bob Dylan says "Judah" immediately I hear him say "Rasta." Ha ha ha. It just *link-up,* y'know. What a revelation. In reality, it's Haile Selassie that is Judah, 'cause Judah is Leo. Right, mon! Him right. Bob Dylan *right*. And y'know which song I like? "Everybody Gotta Serve Somebody." Ya know dat one?

Yes. Many of Dylan's old fans really hate his religious gospel music.

Mmmm. I glad him do it, though. Yeah. Because there comes

a time when an artist kyaan follow the crowd. You have be *you,* and make the crowd follow *you.* If you start follow the crowd, bwai . . . bad thing. So even though dem might not like it, him still do it. Like when we was doin' *Kaya* [an easy flowing dance album dealing with ganja and sex] we knew that plenty people was gonna say, '*Kaya* blah blah blah.' But we *still* do it, y'know. Everyone must take the pressure some time.

The only people who don't like Kaya are people who don't like to dance.

True.

You're just starting a long tour of America.

Yeh. What do you call it? About three months.

How many people travel with you?

'Bout 21.

Do you still travel with body-guards?

Yeh mon.

Do you still travel with an I-tal [natural food] chef?

Yeh mon.

How does that work. Do you carry around a kitchen for him?

Well . . . most of the time we find some hotel what have kitchen and dem things. But now we're thinking about getting one of those kitchens on wheels. But food is no problem, mon. Man shall not live by bread alone y'know. So if we can get no food we stay without food. I can live without food for a period of time, not for a long time, but for an amount of time. Y'know?

Does a touring reggae band have difficulties maintaining its supply of herbs?

Yeah. Cyaan get enough. Sure. And that's bad when you can't get it. And when you get it, you must

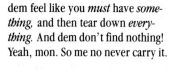

get the good stuff, 'cause if you only get the middle stuff, bettah you go smoke a cigarette. Ha Ha.

Does a dreadlocks like yourself get hassled in customs?

Well it depends through which customs, y'know. Suppose I come through America customs straight from Jamaica. Dem seh, "Weh ya comin' from, mon?" I say "Jamaica." Dem seh, "Ahhh, that's where the good stuff is from." Dem search me as if customs want it for themselves. Ah ha ha ha. If I comin' from England, you just go through easy. Coming from England, seh "Alright." Just go right through. Germany? Dem search,

dem feel like you *must* have *something,* and then tear down *everything.* And dem don't find nothing! Yeah, mon. So me no never carry it.

You just finished a tour of Europe . . .

Yeah. We played Milan. Fifty thousands of people.

Why has reggae caught on more with Europeans than Americans?

Dem like it. I feel Europe nearer to a certain kind of consciousness what we have. For instance, we going down to Germany me can see the people farming and working on the land. I mean, you can see it in America too and every other place, but in Europe me can see little farm on every hillside. Dem nearer to the earth and ting. Y'know? I figure maybe that's why dem have a more easier feeling to us . . . Whole big green piece of land spread out and fertile and with wheat. We going down the road in Germany and all we see is pure wheat everywhere . . .

Why do you think black Americans are the last to catch on to reggae music?

Well y'know I have a way of saying something about it and I

don't know if I am right, but y'know, reggae music is just like anything else. It's a business. Record companies sell the music, right? Our record company is an English company who is set up in America to sell English rock music. To sell that English rock music dem never have to go down to black people town, so dem don't know how fe really reach those people deh. Dem never really have the equipment fe go to the people and let the people know that something new is here and blah blah. But it's great music, right? If black people in the States can hear it more, they like it more, like Stevie Wonder who is now making hisself into a reggae artist . . . Right?

Now that you have a lot of money, what are you going to do with it?

Heh heh heh heh.

Well?

I don't know if I'm going sound funny to you, but I really have no expectation in life, y'know. Y'know wha I mean? Me always grow, and the things that I grow with, I never give them up. Like the trees, the sweet smelling trees where you take em, boil tea and drink. Bush tea? I kyaan give up that which gives happiness, . . . There's a lot of things me really love, and money kyaan buy dem things. Y'know wha I mean?

What about using your money to help people?

Well, yeah. We deal with community development y'know. But we 'ave fe be careful in Jamaica cause Wailers so powerful. If you do that kind of thing in a political country like Jamaica, you become too . . . *big.* Y'unnerstand wha I seh? People expect you take over the country. And people might come and shoot at you . . . If you do good you have to be careful

Gillie, Bob Marley's I-tal cook, on tour, 1977.

Seeco at Tuff Gong. Known in the old days as Francisco Pep, Seeco was the Wailers' rhythm mentor. After 1975 he served as the band's anchor-like hand-drummer and elder.

Right: Family Man, master reggae bassist and musical director of Bob Marley and the Wailers.

An old friend of Bob's from Trench Town.

Bob, Pam Nestor and I Jah Man

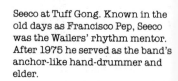

One Love, One Heart, One Destiny, One God. Me plan no answer. This is free talk. Now how 'bout a nice big spliff? . . . heh heh heh heh. Yeh-hoo!

where you do good, 'cause everywhere you go, somebody control that vicinity. If you want to leave Trench Town and go down to Tivoli, some minister control Trench Town and a different minister control Tivoli. So any community you go into, it's a problem. It's like in prison, because there's a politician near telling the people which way to vote, and here comes a man like me saying, "Don't vote!" Rasta no vote.

It must drive them crazy.

Ha hah hah. Yes! Don't vote! No voting here!

Do you still drive your big BMW?

No, it gooone.

So what do you get around in?

Me? A jeep. An *old* jeep, so nobody will say I'm driving a BMW any more.

That car got you into a lot of trouble.

Yah bwai, I couldn't *stand* that BMW. Ha ha ha. Bee-Em-Dubya make pure troubya!

What are you reading these days?

I'll tell ya one kind book that I love, the first book is the Bible. Next book I ever read that I love is *The Late Great Planet Earth.* That's the second book I ever read where I really *interested* in reading. Y'know? *The Late Great Planet Earth.* 'Cause all dem prophesy is true. Y'know wha I mean? Ya can't want anything nearer to the truth.

You use a lot of Biblical references in your songwriting, recycling Biblical wisdom back into folk culture. What part of the Bible have you borrowed the most from?

Solomon. Proverbs. Dem talk some things weh . . . whew! Y'know wha I mean? Revelations. Yeah. The whole thing link up. It line up y'know. The New Testament tell ya about Old Testament. Read the Bible, mon. Most populous book in the world.

I understand there's an organization of Rastas in Jamaica called the Twelve Tribes of Israel . . .

True. Me is a member of that organization. Me name Joseph. The revelation of the Bible. We are the 12,000 people who know we are of the tribe of Judah. Just like today—y'know why Rome control the world so much? If you go there and say you want 12,000 people from

Aquarius, you get dem! Because Rome know who is Aquarius. But if you ask them what is Aquarius, dem tell you bwai that dem don't know. And a wise man like me now, who was a fool so long, can tell you that . . . Aquarius . . . was a *Roman god!* So pick sense out of nonsense—if I am Aquarius, then I am a children of the Roman god. So it don't link me up properly. I don't feel the linkage. Y'know? I feel more *Jerusalemish.* Y'unnerstand?

So instead of being the twelve signs of the Zodiac, we're becoming the twelve tribes of Israel. Y'know? When we finally know this is true, there will be no more color prejudice, and then human being become *one family again.*

Many prophesies revealed in reggae music over the last ten years have come true. What do you think will be happening in the next ten years?

Well, I know dat, way I figure seh, maybe tings get worse for the better! Y'unnerstand? they just get . . . *worse for the better.* That is the solution. Worse for the better. What we do is check the conscience of mankind, and we find that there's a great amount of selfishness, because right now you might have millions of people a-starving someplace, and all it takes is transportation to get the food to them. But, that *care* is not there. It's a lapse in the conscience of mankind.

Do you own land? Plant any crops?

Yes, me is a planter by art! Me grow up in it, y'know? That's the first thing me ever do—farming. Me grow up inna it, and is it me really love. And me love it more still now.

But the farming I used to do, it was slave farming with the machete and a hoe. Or we'd dig it by hand. We didn't have dem ting that you drive and plow it up.

You mean a tractor?

Yeh. An' a plow.

Most people look at you as the king of reggae. Do you ever get tired of all that? Do you ever want to take a vacation for a couple of years?

From the music? No, me love music too much fe really. Y'see, music is not hard work to me. I

siddown, and a song come *nice as that.* It's very nice, very relaxin,' especially when a new song comes, y'knowwhahmean? And if ya know how fe do it then ya record it. So ya know.

What do you think of white reggae?

Well, I hear "Police and Thieves," you know dem Clash?

And me hear some more, y'know? I hear one, it musta been the Police. Some I like, some . . . ah . . . (*aside to aide:* Skill, roll me a spliff!)

Does white reggae sound right to you?

Depends on the feeling. Reggae music is a feeling, but reggae music is not the first time that feeling come to the earth. That feeling is always there with the people, black and white. Even with ordinary people who nuh deal with making no music. If dem hum something, it reggae dem hum, I mean, without even knowing. Ya can just tek it, and hear dem hum something while they wash or while they work. It's the same feeling like all the blues and the folk music come from. Lot of the same feeling deh.

So I say dat the feeling was *always* there, y'know.

Many people at first identified with the raw anger in the Wailers' music; some now claim that you've become rather mellow. Any response?

No mon! It might mellow to the outside people, but where I come from it is more *militant* than it ever used to be. Our music is there to *deal* with the conditions where we come from. The music is like the news. The music influence the people, the music do everything fe the people. The music tell the people *what* to do, in Jamaica. So . . . it's stronger than it used to be, mon! Y'know? But to the outside . . . no, dem might not know what is going on. Let dem come to

Jamaica and see. In Jamaica we deal with struggle and presshah every day.

Did you try any of the African herb?

Herb vary, y'know. Some good, some very good.

When at home, what do you like to smoke?

Well, I prefer Lambsbread, y'know. Or Jerusalemsbread. Dat is something like cotton. We used to call it Goatshit. Strong herb. Real good stuff, mon.

Any shortages of herb in Jamaica?

Das the only one dat place have plenty of, bwai. Plenty herb! Plenty herb sah!

What about the herb in Zimbabwe?

Yeh? One night we go to a soldier place, and a guerilla call out to me, and give me a touch of something . . . and that was it. No wonder they won the war! *Tell ya bwai*—Dem mon smoke some good herb mon! Good herb demma smoke mon! Dem tell me they smoke that herb and feel brave. I axe dem why they smoke, and dem tell me it make them . . . *invisible.*

Good herb from African soil, not ruined with fertilizer. Authentic herb, like we used to get in Jamaica in the '50s and '60s.

What's the difference in the herb of then and now?

Because dem bring in a ting, dem fertilize, and so it come up, and look big and pretty, but . . . no good.

But now we have a ting, sinsemilla, but that take a lot of work, constant work. But it takes so much work it's as expensive in Jamaica as Miami. Cause a mon must stay in the field, must really *live* with the plant to make it become sinsemilla. Cause one bad plant can spoil the whole thing.

—*Stephen Davis*

7

Iron Sharpen Iron

he year was 1968 and the first rush of dreamy visions from San Francisco was losing its freshness as rock began to concretize into monolithic slabs of sound and rhythm. **Randall Grass** suddenly found himself in the South, where time seemed to stand still and the easy lope and warm harmonies of early-'60s soul—Maurice Williams and the Zodiacs, the Tams, the Showmen, Willie Tee and more—still cast a familiar spell.

Flipping on his car radio one day, he heard a nearly acappella, droning doo-wop harmony with a hair-raising edge. Suddenly, a rim-shot kicked a rhythm section into an odd, loping rhythm, the likes of which he'd never heard. The lead singer's charged tenor sailed up into falsetto and broke into staccato Buddy-Hollyish phrases as the harmony singers droned an inevitable, relentless refrain: "Israelites!" America was introduced to reggae.

Randall tells the story of the harmony trios of Jamaica, the roots of reggae, and the chapter includes conversations with the Meditations, the Wailing Souls and Toots Hibbert of the Maytals.

The Great Jamaican Harmony Trios

I was mystified, enchanted, delighted with "Israelites," but who in hell *were* Desmond Dekker and the Aces? Their name sounded like some '50s streetcorner group, but I'd never heard of them and no '50s group had that insidious rhythm. Their chant-like call-and-response seemed primal and timeless, instantly reducing everything else on the radio to so much fluff.

Desmond Dekker's freak one-off American hit introduced a lot of American ears to reggae; quite a few reggae fanatics date their obsession from "Israelites." Die-hard r&b fans heard again the emotive solos and vibrant harmonies missing from American music since the early '60s. "Israelites" completed a circle of sorts, by giving back to America the harmonies once beamed down to Jamaica from the States. From the late '50s on, American radio touched off an explosion of harmony singing in Jamaica that became an indispensable element of reggae in

Opposite: **Black Uhuru**

Below: **The Meditations**

Roots

Anyone who tells the story of reggae harmony is creating a myth. No one can say with any assurance why, for instance, harmony singing has hung on in Jamaica long after it passed out of fashion in the US. No one really knows why the preferred vocal configuration has been the trio for Jamaican vocal groups, but quartets or quintets in American r&b. It's a safe bet, though, that American radio instigated a sudden flurry of harmony singing in Jamaica during the late '50s. Most of the outlets for aspiring young singers were talent contests and local shows featuring myriad acts doing "blues" (Jamaican-ized r&b) versions of American hits. No Jamaican recording industry existed at the time. Oddly enough, duos (such as Jackie & Roy, Higgs & Wilson, Derrick & Patsy, etc.) were more common than any other sort of singing group.

As one-half of Higgs & Wilson, one of the most popular duos of the late '50s, Joe Higgs began an extraordinarily influential but chronically under-recognized singing career. He has helped coach such groups as the Wailers and the Wailing Souls with their harmonies, replaced Bunny Wailer on a critical Wailers tour in the '70s, and toured with his former pupil, Jimmy Cliff. Higgs' songs have won numerous competitions but he has enjoyed few financial rewards and languished in relative obscurity while his former students became famous. He remains fiercely proud of his worth.

"We, Higgs & Wilson, our songs were more to the root of what we were thinking," Higgs told *Black Music* in 1975. "We swapped over in harmony, do things that shift from lead to the other band back each other up. We practised a lot of things. For the next nine months, we were about the top pair of harmonizers on the island as well as the West Indies. We met the Blues Busters about eight times in all kinds of contests and we beat them eight times."

Higgs & Wilson made "Oh, Manny Oh," perhaps the first record pressed in Jamaica, for West Indian Records (owned by Edward Seaga, now prime minister of Jamaica) in 1960, helping to launch the Jamaican recording industry. A series of popular records followed, but a total lack of career management or financial gain led to the dissolution of Higgs & Wilson by 1964. The legacy of their vocal inventiveness should not be surprising. Higgs once listed Thelonious Monk, John Coltrane, Ray Charles, and Marvin Gaye as influences and acknowledged listening to country-and-western and classical music.

That Jamaica-America connection was a two-way street from the beginning. "Sweet As An Angel," an r&b tune by the Jamaican group the Jivin' Juniors, so perfectly reproduced American stylings that it became a highly prized item for American record collectors. Formed in 1958 by Derrick Harriot, the Jivin' Juniors were a four-man harmony group who sang American

the '60s. The exhilarating sense of freedom and emotional outpouring of American streetcorner groups came from unpolished, unpredictable bursts of creativity unfettered by any set of harmonic "rules." The harmonic outbursts from the concrete jungles of America flew directly into the hearts of Kingston youths.

Walk into a good Jamaican record store (in the US or Jamaica) and you'll see the American soul influence on the walls. Besides Jamaican Studio One pressings of Huey "Piano" Smith, Professor Longhair and Shirley & Lee, you'll likely find classic '60s r&b LPs by Solomon Burke, Percy Sledge and the Impressions. Look at the cover photo of the *Wailing Wailers* LP (their first, circa 1965). It's a ringer for early-'60s Impressions LP covers: cool Peter Tosh with shades as Sam Gooden, Bunny Wailer as Fred Cash, and Bob Marley as Curtis Mayfield. Then listen to the Wailers' version of Mayfield's "Keep On Moving." Close your eyes and it could be the Impressions.

The Wailers first became wildly popular because they were the best *harmony* group being recorded in Jamaica during the mid-'60s. All this explains why Gregory Isaacs, Barrington Levy,

94

hits until Duke Reid and Clement Dodd recorded the group's original material for their respective labels. One of the group's massive hits, "Lollipop Girl" ("you could go to a dance and hear 'Lollipop Girl' 15 times straight" says Harriot) became a hit for Harriot (now a respected producer) in a new version in 1980.

By the early '60s, three-man vocal groups had superseded duos as the standard vocal configuration; in all of reggae music, there haven't been more than a handful of quartets. Trios seem to produce a mystical effect—the power of the Trinity as it were. Harmony singers speak in just those terms.

"Three is a divine spirit, a harmony," Winston Watson of the Meditations once told me. "When you say three, you say power, righteousness. The Bible says so."

In musical terms, the special qualities of trio harmonizing stem from the trio's penultimate flexibility. Harmonies can be relatively full—a triad fulfills the minimum requirements for a chord—but never opulent. Yet the harmonies

Roberts formed the original Gaylads and made a few sweetsounding mento records. By 1960, they'd recorded "Rub It Down" and "Lady In a Red Dress," both hits, which kicked off a 12-year recording career spanning ska, rock steady and reggae. Most of their hits were tortured romantic sagas put across by creamy harmonies (directly inspiring the Paragons, Heptones, Melodians, Techniques and others) and irresistible Studio One dance rhythms brewed up by the Skatalites and the Soul Brothers.

By the time of the ska era, trios were the dominant vocal form, but most ska was preeminently instrumental dance music. The rise of great vocal trios as the Wailers and Toots and the Maytals is now a familiar story, but such lesser known groups as Desmond Dekker and the Aces, Justin Hines and the Dominoes and the Clarendonians responded to the energy of ska with buoyant, post-Independence vocalizing. Though a duo, the Clarendonians won the hearts of Jamaicans with a harmony sound patterned after the close, lazy New Orleans style popularized by

Gene & Eunice and Shirley & Lee. The Rude Boy era had arrived, so Ernest Wilson and Peter Austin's first hit was "Rudie Gone a Jail" in 1963. No amount of hisses, pops, or missing frequencies on a primitive recording can diminish their fresh, exuberant harmonies riding so easily above the cymbal-and-horn-driven ska beat. It's no surprise that Ernest Wilson still records today; his "Truths and Rights" single showed up at shops in Brooklyn and London recently.

Rock Steady Romance

When the ska beat began to metamorphose into rock steady in the mid-'60s, groups really came into their own. Less-predominant horn lines gave the singers more space, and less-rigid beat offered more possibilities for rhythmic subtlety in vocals. The Stateside soul explosion offered less-mannered, gospel-driven vocal styles for inspiration (Toots Hibbert had been ahead of the times in this regard) and the Temptations, Marvin Gaye, and the Impressions were now heroes in Jamaica.

create a very open sound with wide intervals or, alternatively, two harmony singers can drive the lead with dynamic two-part harmonies.

Then again, reggae trios often seem to present three distinct personas, a psychic trinity: comic extrovert, solemn judge, and prophetic teacher. The lead singer preaches while the others act out comic/tragic flip sides of everyday existence.

The archetypal reggae harmony trio may be the Gaylads, a group named by many reggae groups as their model. Most probably they popularized the trio format. They began, like so many groups, with informal harmonizing sessions in streets, yards, alleys and vacant lots in both Jamaica and America. Harmonizing is a social activity—most groups have family-like relationships—and for poor, urban youth it's a cheap method of musical instruction.

In 1958, Seaton, Delano Stewart and Maurice

Like so many other harmony groups inspired by Stateside soul, the Heptones were neighborhood buddies who harmonized for fun. When Leroy Sibbles, Barry Llewellyn and Earl Morgan decided to pursue singing on a serious basis, they experienced almost instantaneous success. Their earthy, sexy "Fatty Fatty" ("I'm feeling rude, I'm in the mood for a Fat Girl tonight") became an immediate hit, kicking off a string of winners that has never really stopped, although 1966–1969 was their peak.

The Heptones took the smoothness of the Gaylads to new heights on both romantic material ("Pretty Looks," "Why Must I") and message songs ("Equal Rights," "Heptones Gonna Fight") penned mainly by Sibbles but sometimes by the others. Sibbles' singing had a mellow edge that contrasted sharply with many other singers of that era, thus adding another dimension to the vocal group tradition Morgan and Llewellyn sailed above, often in falsetto harmony, as Sibbles relentlessly poured out anguish, passion or determination, as the song demanded, between the punctuating response of the harmonized lines. With the Heptones, a rough call-and-response merges with a smoother romantic

The new Heptones. Naggo Morris replaced Leroy Sibbles in 1978.

Justin Hines and the Dominoes

Leroy Sibbles

95

style. Their classic 1974 hit "Book of Rules" is probably the most tuneful piece of philosophy ever recorded.

Many thought the Heptones would fall apart when Sibbles left for Canadian exile in the late '70s (he was the most prolific writer, lead vocalist and frequent bassist on recording sessions). But Naggo Morris, who had begun singing during the Heptones' formative era, stepped ably into his shoes and the Heptones continued to record, creating another masterpiece in 1980 with "Streets Of Gold." Their professionalism stems from their early jobs as salaried session singers at Studio One, an experience which reflects the informal transmission of skills among harmony groups.

While the Heptones combined raw feeling with precise harmonies, the Paragons, led by John Holt, left no rough edges. The Paragons, along with the Techniques and the Melodians, challenged the Heptones and Wailers for rock steady supremacy and probably gained the widest audience. Ironically, their greatest global

recognition probably came in 1981 when the rock group Blondie made an international hit of "The Tide Is High," a 1966 Paragons hit. This astonished Jamaicans who saw the old Paragons

tune (not even their best) trumpeted week after week as Number One on the "Solid Gold" television show broadcast in Jamaica.

In 1964, the Paragons were a quartet, but when star singer Bob Andy left to pursue a solo career, Holt, Tyrone Evans and Howard Barrett began a series of Treasure Isle recordings that epitomised the rock steady era. Such was the potency of those Treasure Isle rhythms that U. Roy used them for his ground-breaking deejay hits in 1970.

With memorable melodies written by Holt and Evans, the Paragons created close, lockstep harmonies that bathed a tune with warmth rather than charging it with energy. When meagre monetary gain forced them to disband, Holt went on to become the king of MOR reggae, his soulful delivery swathed in strings rather than harmony.

While the romantic rock steady groups began streamlining their harmonies, some of the roots groups continued to produce rough, unpredictable vocal blends, often in a hypnotic call-and-response format. The Ethiopians' "Train to Skaville" (1966) and "Whip Them" pitted falsetto bleats against interjections by the lead singer, a style which flowered into the open harmonies of "Selah" and "Everything Crash." By the '70s, their country-ish vocals were set in the context of reggae riffing, a change which capsulized the metamorphosis of rock steady into reggae.

Reggae Riffs

Where most rock steady seemed to thrust slicker, romantic harmony groups forward, the advent of reggae seemed to bring out more chant-like, message-orientated singing. When the Abyssinians recorded "Satta Amassagana" in the late '60s, the almost modal, wailing harmonies found little favor. Yet, by the early '70s, the booming bass line and *akete*-style drum patterns of the rhythm became one of the most widely used rhythms in reggae. Its hymn-like lyrics about Africa ("There is a land, far, far, away . . .") became an anthem. All this reflected the growing influence of Rastafarianism and Africa-consciousness in general.

Winston Rodney's Burning Spear, the archetypal roots vocal trio, transformed this approach

into a personal style, working solo against the rhythm track in the late '60s but using Rupert Willington and Delroy Hines as chorus by the early '70s to make some of the greatest trio music ever with such songs as "Slavery Days," "Marcus Garvey," "Man In the Hills" and others.

Hines and Willington would step majestically in place, arms swinging easily as they stared unwaveringly ahead as if fixed on some otherworldly reality. Winston Rodney would bend toward the earth, gesticulating insistently as he

sang a tortured phrase into the microphone: "We used to work so hard. . ." Hines and Willington would intone the inevitable chorus line as if uttering an inescapable, prophetic historical reminiscence: "Do you remember the days of slavery?" Their spellcasting found its perfect foil in those unvarying, insistent harmonies—a Greek chorus out of African griot tradition.

By the 1970s, with rock steady grown into the militant drive of reggae, the trios were as strong as ever. The array of magnificent singing groups is staggering, but most of them were unknown outside of Jamaica at the time and some barely were recognized there. Even today, many of these groups are known to only a handful of connoisseurs and roots people. The Gladiators, Slim and the Uniques, the Twinkle Brothers, the Tamlins, the Royals, and the Wailing Souls (who usually had a fourth member) joined the Wailers as prime creators of exquisite harmony.

Most of these newly emerging groups (as smooth, established groups as the Paragons, Techniques, Melodians and Pioneers broke up or

Burning Spear as a trio, 1976.

John Holt, original lead singer of the Paragons.

Far right: The Mighty Diamonds

Bottom right: Winston Rodney, who took the group's name from Jomo Kenyatta's *nom de guerre* during the Mau Mau rebellion.

The Sons of Negus

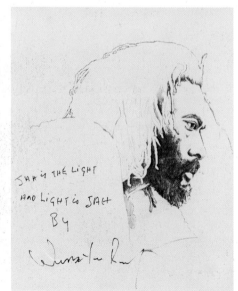

JAH IS THE LIGHT
AND LIGHT IS JAH
BY

began to fade) reflected the growing influence of Rasta and African cultural awareness. For these groups, the traditional hymns of grounation ceremonies, the African retentions in folk music, and the call-and-response fervor of church groups were as influential as the classic r&b harmonies of American groups. The new, young dreadlocked groups decided they could sing about *both* love and prophecy.

This strange mixture of love and revolution, African roots and smooth crooning, came to dramatic fruition with the emergence of the Mighty Diamonds. If 1975 was the year of Channel One rockers rhythms, then the Mighty Diamonds were the rockers extraordinaire with such tunes as "I Need a Roof," "Them Never Love Poor Marcus," and especially "Right Time." Leaping onstage in army fatigues (and sometimes brandishing machetes), the Diamonds sang some of the most militant lyrics with some of the sweetest harmonies this side of heaven. Imagine the Spinners with machine guns. Their vocal style came from sweet soul groups, The Philadelphia Sound as much as Motown. They'd wheel and spin with almost Temptations-like choreography, but suddenly lead singer Tabby Shaw would dance to the edge of the stage in an exhuberant jig.

These days, the Diamonds are just as likely to perform in three-piece suits—outrageous lime, apricot and eggshell blue, for instance—but their unfailing melodic gift continues to produce a couple of masterpieces a year. A massive hit in Jamaica and England, "Pass the Kouchie" shows the continuing vitality of this odd mix of earthiness and dreaminess. Harmony is as relevant as ever.

The Latest Wave

As self-contained bands become more prominent —Third World, Steel Pulse, Black Slate blazing the way—the old harmonies are being transplanted into a new environment. Meanwhile, many of the hottest young artists seem to be solo singers (Barrington Levy, Tristan Palma, Barry Brown) or deejays (Lone Ranger, Ranking Dread, Michigan & Smiley). So why do the classic harmony groups—especially trios—persist? For Roy Smith, formerly of the Westmorelites and the

Itals (perhaps the best new harmony group —they were show stoppers at 1981 Sunsplash), it's back to that indefinable magic.

"Harmony has to still keep going, especially in reggae," he mused from his Philadelphia home. "The combination [of voices] has to be there. It's like a family thing. The trios became a tradition. The producers used to say [to four-man groups] 'it's too full, too relaxed.'"

Too full, too relaxed. Reggae may rock easily with the rhythm but it needs to be charged with emotion, with spirit. And harmony singing is still the most straightforward way to unleash the spirit. So despite the trends, several magnificent harmony groups have emerged since 1975. Many of them have been around for a long time (the Royal Rasses, the Tamlins, the Itals, Wailing Souls, the Prophets) but others date from a younger generation (Culture, the Morwells, the Meditations, Black Uhuru, Israel Vibration, Te-track, the Congoes and, on the female side, Light of Love, Brown Sugar and 15–16–17).

For sheer unpolished inspiration born of free spirits, no harmony group can outdo the Morwells. Formed in 1973 by Roots Radics guitarist Bingy Bunny and eccentric producer Morris "Blacka Morwell" Wellington, the Morwells proceeded to reconstruct the world of harmony according to their own inspiration on such records as "Crab Race," "Crazy Baldhead," "Don Morwell" and "Mafia," many of them issued on the Morwell, Esq. label. Their voices leap intervals unexpectedly, veering near or far according to their mood. Many of their recordings have an offhand inspiration that can only come from spontaneous harmonizing sessions.

For sheer versatility, you can hardly do better

The Mighty Diamonds, Cambridge Mass. 1980, and Tabby of the Diamonds examines an herb stalk.

Skelly from Israel Vibration.

Producer Vivien "Yabbo Yu" Jackson, once part of the harmony trio the Prophets.

Toots and the Maytals, in business since 1960, when they first recorded as the Vikings. Their band is Hux Brown & the Dynamites.

The Congos

Culture

The I-tones

than the Meditations. Winston Watson, Danny Clark and Ansel Creigland have taken a few faltering steps into the global arena but have netted little attention after three fine LPs and a handful of excellent singles (especially the exuberant "Rasta Shall Conquer"). They write all their material, moving easily from rather sophisticated political insights ("Tricked," "Running From Jamaica") to comic parables ("Woman Piabba," "Marriage"). Look at the sad mish-mash of lettering and barely intelligible liner notes on their self-produced *Guidance* LP and then listen to the music. You see raw talent groping for its proper channel.

Against all odds, contrary to every trend, harmony singing survives. The "overnight" success of the Wailing Souls proves the point. They'd been present at the creation in the early '60s with Marley, Tosh, Livingstone, Higgs and Dodd, yet, until 1979, only one Wailing Souls LP had been released (the magnificent Studio One LP *Wailing Souls*) and, until 1981, they had never performed outside Jamaica.

The Wailing Souls' harmony, produced by one of the few four-man groups in reggae history, is full without being saccharine. They sing dynamic, almost modal, intervals, picking notes that drive the melody harder rather than merely flesh it out. The harmonies are the crucible for a lyric and sonic imagination that enables them to compose song after inventive song. That special group chemistry of communal creativity could not be duplicated by a single composer notating "interesting" harmonies. Like all great harmony groups, spontaneous combustion causes them to break the "rules" as they pursue their vision.

As reggae grows in sophistication amid the electronic wizardry of Babylonian technology, the continuing survival of harmony singing is problematic. Very likely, it will become unfashionable sometime in the near future. But as long as poverty and oppression exists, people will need to sing from their hearts, having no other means of expression than their own voices.

—*Randall Grass*

Message from the Meditations

Along with Culture and Israel Vibration, the Meditations constituted the second great wave of reggae harmony trios that broke in 1977, the year the two sevens clashed. Patterned in many ways after the ethereal and authoritative sound of the early Wailers, the Meditations thundered into reggae immortality in late 1976 with an album of now classic songs (*Message from the Meditations*) that included biting social polemics ("Tricked"), anti-Papist Rasta arcana ("Rome") and unapologetic analyses of the war between the sexes ("Woman Is Like a Shadow")

In the years following their initial success, the Meditations continued to record as a group. (*Wake Up, Guidance*) and as Bob Marley's occasional backing trio. More popular abroad than at home, the Meditations' travels had taken them by 1982 on somewhat different paths. While Winston Watson and Danny Clarke based themselves in New York, working as the Meditations, lead singer Ansel Creigland was living in Kingston, recording excellent 12-inch singles under the nom de reggae Ansel Meditations.

We interfaced with the three Meditations during the summer of 1980, during one of the group's infrequent tours. The gigs we saw were at a nightclub called the Hot Tin Roof on the resort island of Martha's Vineyard, off the coast of New England. The Meditations were backed by an at-first anonymous band of Gotham-based Jamaicans.

Warming up the crowd on a hot Friday night in July, the band performed a right-and-tight medley of Wailers hits, revealing the roots of the Meditations as the junior adjunct of the older group. The ratchet-sharp guitar was played by Robert "Billy" Hall, who played on all the classic Meditations hot stuff. The rhythm section was an 18-year-old graduate of Alpha Boys School in Kingston, Drummy, and bassist Alan "Jerry" Walsh.

All three Meditations are excellent singers, and the trio traded

leads all evening, with the group chaotically executing typically goofy Jamaican harmony trio choreography with great aplomb. They had gone on with the show that night without a rehearsal or a sound check, but both trio and band were as tight as sunburned skin after the first two numbers. The Meditations' groove kicked in almost at once, and within ten minutes everyone in the club was in a trance.

The following interview was done in an old farmhouse in West Tisbury that the club uses to house visiting musicians. The Meditations sprawled on an old four-poster bed, rolling spliffs, laughing and interjecting on each other . . .

Q: *Where are the Meditations from?*

Winston ("Mighty Dread"): Kingston 11.

Danny ("Fire One"): I am from Kingston 12. Yunno. "Trench Town Rock"? Fifth Street. And Ansel is from Westmorland.

How were the Meditations formed?

Danny: Well, y'see, the three of us were on our own, in Kingston. I

used to sing with a group called the Righteous Flames. Then I quit and come down to Kingston 11, where I met Winston and Ansel. Winston used to move among groups like the Termites and Lloyd Parkes and We The People. Ansel used to lead a group called the Linkers. He was the lead singer.

When was that?

Ansel ("Scandal"): About 1974, ah, no, '75, I think. In Majestic Gardens. After I left the Linkers I went by myself as a solo singer. I had a little box guitar, and after living there for a couple of months I saw Danny come around, yunno? Well, there's music all over, so we get to meet each other and start to rap and Danny start to show me one or two chords more that I didn't know about.

And from there we would follow his band around and try to do one or two songs with them, trying to create something in Majestic Gardens, with another friend of ours named Winston Harewood, who was the leader of a group called the Hombres. So we get hooked up with him and started to do a lot of little gigs for him. Then we split up, and Danny

and I went around and did harmonies for each other's songs. Then after that I met Winston, and Winston and I started to go around, yunno? Going around, trying to look a break.

So one day, before we did "Woman Is Like a Shadow," Danny said to me, "Let's go up to Channel One, they're doing an audition up there for recording." So I went along with him also and it happened that I sing "Woman Is Like a Shadow;" it was a song I wrote in 1974 and which was played as a dub at dances. People came up to me and dem seh: "Dat song *baard.*" Then we did "Tricked" and were on television one Saturday night when whole Jamaica saw us, and that was how we begin our career. Eventually we released "Woman Is Like a Shadow" as a single and it sell its first pressing of 2,000 copies in the first three hours. After a month it had sold 26,000. That was the beginning of the Meditations.

There was some reaction to that song by women who didn't like it. For instance, Marcia Aitkens did an answer song called "Narrow Minded Man."

Ansel: I want to tell you that the women buy that record *more* than anybody else. They bought it instead of *food*. All over that record do well. Because of it, Meditations got their first tour when the record hit big in Bermuda. So we go to Bermuda.

What was the inspiration for that song?

Ansel: It's a long story, but I will try and cut it short. I was involved with this girl for five years. One day I had the opportunity to see my father, who I hadn't seen since I was a likkle kid 'cos he went to the States. In 1973, I was in the country with him, up and down, and when I get back in town and I call her—she was in a place called Edgewater staying with her uncle—she tell me that she going back up there for the night. I said, "But I was away, and now I am here." She said no, she had to keep her uncle and her relatives company. I said, "Well, I'm a lonely man, what about *me*? Lonely, and your uncle have so many kids there." Then she tells me that she has been talkin' to another guy. So before she leave, I said to her, "If you go tonight, over there, you not gonna see me again." So she laugh and seh to me, "Ansel, you dunno, whenever time a man love a woman, that man will do *anything*

The Meditations, 1980 ". . . And a man is like an arrow."

99

to make up with a woman mistake." I said, "Ahh, *that* is why you keep hurtin' me!"

So after she leave I'm walkin' down Marcus Garvey Drive and something in me said, you *can't* get her outa your mind, you're lovin' her too much to lose her. Another part of me seh, you've *got* to let her go, or you'll never be happy. Yunno? So I'm walkin' and lookin' at me shadow and stepping on it like this; and I seh, you know, it's a funny thing, but a woman is just like this shadow.

So I went to my work, which was spot-welding, and the machine is a ting that go like this—BONG BONG BONG BONG—moving in rhythm, so I'm sittin' there singin' to the beat of the machine, yunno, and the song come together.

Your first album was very political . . .

Danny: Yah, mon! And that's what we wanna keep, cause I&I kyaan sing no likkle folly. We got to sing songs to uplift people because our name is Meditations.

Winston: Yes! The Meditations, with *elevation!*

How do Meditations songs get written?

Ansel: Each one get their inspiration differently, OK? Danny and Winston and I have different inspirations, but when we combine them, then we get Meditation.

Winston: We bring ideas to each other and discuss it.

Ansel: Sometime we go to the studio and record improvised harmony, without rehearsal. It always fits.

Do the Meditations argue with each other?

Ansel: No, we discuss, yunno?

Winston: Everyone got to have a little discussion yunno. It's not always nice, yunno, no group can go on just like that. Some people think that their burden is the heaviest (*seems to indicate Ansel*).

Ansel: The main thing is that as Africans, we don't have to go to school to learn to play the music or anything. It's a thing that we *born* with, a thing that is *in* us.

Danny: As Africans, we feel a lot of tribulation, and for you to know yourself, you got to feel tribulation. Tribulation come down from our first generation unto this time. We get a message, and it falls onto our head to go out and teach the people.

Winston: It's like, every time I feel the spirit moving in my heart, *I praise God* yunno.

Who wrote "Rome Is a Wicked Place?"

Ansel: Danny wrote it. Well, y'see Rome? Rome was the first place that all evil things start from. Jah know that, that's why you see him destroy that place.

Danny: You see the Crucifixion in the Bible? Dem was *Roman* soldier! Dem was gamblin' for his garments!

In many ways, we still live in the world the Romans left us.

Ansel: Yes!

Danny: Right! Look at Sunday. Pope Nicholas changed the Sabbath day to Sunday.

*On your most recent album (*Guidance*) you are backed by the* Wailers.

Ansel: That is because we know Tyrone Downey from when we are very young. But we had also done sessions with Bob Marley for "Rastaman Live Up" and "Blackman Redemption" as backing singers. Also "Punky Reggae Party." But mostly we are friends with the Wailers, and also wherever we go in Jamaica people tell us we sound just like the Wailers. The first thing that we do is, we don't imitate. We come with our own original, for without a builder you don't have a home.

Winston: Meditations don't do Imitations. Always do Originations.

Danny: Once Ansel tried to change his style and started soundin' like Bob Marley. So I said, "Watcha doin'? Keep the same way. We got this far already!"

Ansel: It's true. So many people said I sounded like Bob Marley that I got upset and wanted to change my style. Winston and Danny said no.

To us, the singer that really sounds most like Bob Marley is Pipe (Winston Matthews) from Wailing Souls. Who have the Meditations been influenced by?

Ansel: For love feelings and dealing with a woman, John Holt. For inspiration about suffering and those things, I listen to Bob Marley. For learning about harmony, I listen to Impressions, Curtis Mayfield.

What about rub-a-dub?

Winston: The only deejay we regard are U. Roy, Big Youth and Dillinger.

Ansel: These new deejays, dem not teaching people nothing. When they tell you, "Come here girl, and I'll dub you in the corner," you're not teaching the children nothing. The more the children grow, the more the children learn. So you got to teach them something. That why we like Big Youth, 'cos he always deliver message.

Winston: Big Youth takes the Bible into the studio to record.

Ansel: The name reggae is a sound which everyone has to try to get involved in.

Danny: Reggae means revolution, peace, and unity amongst all man. That's the word reggae meanin'.

Winston: Reggae music shall be the last trumpet sound. And there shall be no other music around.

—*Peter Simon & Stephen Davis*

The Wailing Souls; "Y'see, deejay music now . . . I dunno."

The Wailing Souls

A performance at the Reggae Sunblast in Berkeley during October of 1981 capped a startling year of hits that finally brought the Wailing Souls to the world's attention. They teamed with rhythm meisters Sly & Robbie for two magnificent singles, the sticky-sweet "Sugar Plum Plum" and the wryly delivered "Old Broom," and scored in England with a string of hits.

A flurry of releases is nothing new for suddenly hot reggae artists, but for the long-suffering classic harmony group Wailing Souls, fate seemed capricious indeed. Why should they suddenly find an audience after 18 years of struggling to produce a precious few under-appreciated gems? Right time come, as they say.

Q: *What were those sessions like when you just got together and sang and played with Joe Higgs and Bob Marley (in the early Trench Town days)?*

Winston Pipe Matthews: Those sessions was like all of us come from the same community and we had a house on First Street in Trench Town. We'd get together mostly from around eight in the morning, and we had a little jamming, we call it "jamming," 'unno, for everyone just get together to sing.

That early in the morning?

Lloyd "Bread" Macdonald: Yah, mon. Harmony practice and different t'ing like that.

Pipe: And that would go on till around midnight.

How were your voices at eight o'clock in the morning?

Bread: No, mon, we used to that. Naturally. Let me tell you something. You see what happen really. You see inna Trench Town now, when we was little boy, you always have bigger singers like Bob, or Wailers-dem, right? Joe Higgs, Alton Ellis, why him can go on for hours. So, mostly when I&I come from school and dem thing, in the evening time is just cricket. So you see from cricket done now, from sun gone down, is just run to the house-corner weh de big man dem dere smoke and-a sing, me just around gone and sing. You just naturally join in and start hold harmony, so we get used to that from we small, we sing for *hours*. I just used to it, it's a habit.

Would Joe stop you in the middle of a song and say, "Wait a minute, you were flat?"

George "Buddy" Hayes: Yah, mon! He's the most serious person I've ever met with music.

Some people have written that your harmonies are so similar to the Wailers because you had the same teacher?

Bread: And not even that alone, as I say we grow up in the same environments, 'cause sometimes you would find us and the Wailers-dem singing, rehearsing. You have a kitchen and everybody just jam in the kitchen, when you go in the kitchen you have Bob and you have all 15 man in de kitchen, and is just pure singing that. Everybody a-sing and hold harmony. Sometimes it was Joe and Bob alone dere 'bout, and every man hold harmony. Or we alone may be about, me, Pipe, Buddy and Vision mostly. This is the foursome there mostly. Even if we a-sing, sometime Bob-dem come and join we sing.

And then there was the confusion in those days over who was who, because there were the Wailing Wailers at one point, and the Wailing Souls. I've seen books that actually say that Bob Marley was the Wailing Souls and be did "Mr. Fire Coal Man."

Pipe: Yeah, I saw it in a book too.

Now which name came first, the Wailing Wailers or the Wailing Souls?

Bread: I guess it's the Wailing Wailers. Cuz here we always had the Wailers. What really happen, it was the Wailers, just Wailers, you know. Me nuh know who grow up the name Wailing Wailers, maybe Coxsone. Because, you know them early days dere, right, after we go Coxsone, Joe Higgs passed through Coxsone and tell we about Coxsone; Bob go Coxsone and tell we about Coxsone; we go Coxsone and find out about Coxsone. And then we left Coxsone, and we form an organization with Wailers and the Soulettes, and we form one name, Wailing Souls. We actually do some record on Tuff Gong label, "Harbour Shark." And that is when we change the name to Pipe and the Pipers then, due to the confusion with the Wailers and the Wailing Souls.

Where does the name Classics fit in here?

Bread: It start first with Coxsone, because Coxsone realized the similarity with the sound and with the name, so him say "Bwai, is best if you come up with a new name," remember, Pipe? And we just start look around, and we say alright, "The Classics." But we no in tune with the Classics, really, is just Wailing Souls me a-love, because that was our original name. But him suggest we change.

Pipe: You see, the word "Wailers" really mean a messenger.

Bread: Like a soul crying in the wilderness, wailing soul like John the Baptist. First Wailing Soul, that; John the Baptist.

Buddy: Every man is a living soul. But we are just *wailing* souls. Wailing out against oppression and depression.

Pipe: When you are wailers, you know the people always going to be listening to you because, at all time, you always there above the others. Because there are certain vibes that you might get that others don't get.

You're more attuned?

Bread: You have to bring it out, express it good, so the next man can see.

We just a sing for a joke, in the early days. It just come natural. Just a sing really, we never take it serious. We no really start take the business serious until about four years ago [1977]; then we give up work and start a-deal with it

seriously. Because me and Pipe start sing from about nine, him first recording; I did mine about 15, 16.

You had a kid record out, Pipe? What was it?

Pipe: "Little Dilly" by the Schoolboys, on Prince Buster.

How do you explain in a time when some of the greatest groups in Jamaica (like the Dominoes, the Heptones and the Wailers) have all broken up, you've basically been singing together for over 15 years. How come you're still together?

Pipe: Is the oneness that we all have. As I said before, we are above certain levels.

Buddy: I&I have fe think upon higher plane.

Pipe: Cuz, a clean hand and pure heart—well, we figure more than less, we already have that livity.

Rudolph "Garth" Dennis: You have seen when people come together in unity, they can build a lot of things. Look at the Chinese and other people over the world, how them work, and a million people come together and dig a dam out of the earth.

Pipe: All it takes is, I don't have, Garth have; he gave what he have to me. If I have, and Garth don't have, I give Garth what I have.

It's really living out a Rastafarian livity, isn't it?

Bread: It come natural, it come natural to I&I, cuz me a show you, we always been together, from boy, even before we start singing, we have always been seeing each other, and we have always gotten on, on good terms.

Pipe: We know how to get around things, you know.

Bread: Just Jah really.

Pipe: Because everything I&I do, is just the works of the Father. We couldn't do anything without Him right now.

—Roger Steffens

Toots Hibbert— Talkin' de Psalms

Frederick "Toots" Hibbert: Five four four six was his number.

Q: *Toots, you have a lot of new work coming out after more than a twenty-year career as the leader of the Maytals.*

Toots: Even longer than that, but that's de time dey know of.

So you're in the Guinness Book Of World Records *now, and there's this new video coming out and the Maytals are revered as a still very strong creative force. Can you tell me why you and Raleigh and Jerry have been able to do it for so long?*

Yeah, we just deal wit love, one love . . .

It's been going on for more than twenty years: do you ever dispute among yourselves?

No, everyone understand themselves.

Are the three of you all still in the same church?

Still in de Coptic Church, yes, de Coptic Church is the one main whosoever do de right thing. We pray every day, night, mornin', yu know? Everytime and do de right thing. Dats where my performance coming from, spiritual vibrations so I vibrate de heart of de people and bring dem to be one. In de spiritual words, de way I sing, and de way I perform my own way, you know, I get de message to de people dat way.

The Maytals have probably travelled more miles than any other reggae band. Has that affected your music at all?

No, it don't affect . . . Sometime when we travel we just have to travel and most of the time I don't travel much, but when I travel I travel to a lot of places and spread glad tidings of great joy that I bring to everyone, yuknow?

The Coptic Church uses herb as a sacrament, is that not true?

Like what I'm usin' right now . . .

Do you find that you get a lot of inspiration from using herb?

It is not an inspiration—it is from crea*shan* dat we mus use herb for the use of the prayer, for the use of your body, for the use of everything which is good unto you. You use herb: boil it, tek it mek tonic. It's good for asthma, is good for bad cold, is good for cleanin', it clean you physically and spiritually, it mek you seek out where God is, seek out where the King of Kings is, it let you know dat de Kings Of Kings is in you, and which is the breath of Life, is de Father . . seh, de breat' of Life is Father from creashan. He's a spiritual man dat dwell in every man.

When you use de herb you see all dese things knowin' dat it is not de right to mek people suffa, it is not de right to use birt' control, it is not de right to kill white people, it is not de right to kill black people,

it is not de right kill chiney people, it is not de right to kill no one.

Toots, the herb you're using now, does it have tobacco in it or do you just use straight herb?

It's of a right and yu have a right to use it wid tobacco, for is a man and woman creation. De tobacco called female and herb called de male, so they always go together.

As creation . . . . if you use it widout cigarette, it a-go mek yu drink water much, it dries yu out, dries out your veins, your blood because it don't have nothing to really flavor, it need to be cook properly, so mix it up and mek they blend together as wife and husband, yuknow? Then when yu cook it up dat way wid de tobacco and de herbs—yuknow, so you have to know how much cigarette to use for it is not good to use a lot of cigarettes. When yu smoke herb and you talk your psalms, like I'm gonna draw my herb now and mus say a psalm. And de one dat come to me right now, it is Psalms One, seh:

Blessed is the man that walketh not in the counsel of the ungodly, nor standeth in the way of sinners, nor sitteth in the seat of the scornful.

For our delight is in the law of our Lord; and in his law do we meditate day and night.

And we are the tree that's planted by the rivers of waters dat bringeth forth our fruit in due season. Our leaves also will not withered and whatsoever we doeth will prosper.

The ungodly are not so: they are like the chaff which the world driveth away.

Therefore the ungodly will not stand in this judgement, nor sinners in the congregation of the righteous.

For our Lord know de ways of the righteous: and the ways of the ungodly will perish. Selah.

Whatever open our lips to Allah Jah and our mouth which offer thy praise, for in the congregation of the saints we are blessed O Lord. Allah into thine hands do we commit our spirit, thou art redeem us, O Lord God of Truth and Man, de Coptic Church exalteth the nation. Love.

Toots, there are millions of people who love your music but who know very little about you. Could you tell us a few things, like where you're living right now?

Well, where I'm livin now, I'm livin', in my Father and my Father is living in me. Physically I living in Kingston.

Are you married?

I'm married all the while, man, I'm married all the while. Married

is not only one day, yu know? *(pauses to light his pipe)* Pwffft . . .

Do you have children?

No, I don't really "have," but I create de children! I created, yuknow?

What do you think when you hear white groups like the Specials in England who record your songs like "Monkey Man"? Have you heard that?

Yeh, I heard it and I saw them doin' it too and I love it very much! *(laughs delightedly)* yeah, man!

Do you feel that you were properly paid for their using that song?

Yes, really well de way dey do dat song, de way dey did it really I cannot don't get pay: I mus get pay all de while, y'knowhamean? De way how we set it I always gettin' pay from anyone do my records. I would love fe have more people who know bout reggae, who know how reggae originate, who feels such about reggae, yu know? Can do more reggae! For de reggae cyarry de message, yuknow?

So you like seeing European or American groups playing and taking up your music, spreading it more and more?

Yes, I do dat too, and also I will do some of *dem* song too, if it touch me, yeah, but the song mus touch you before you want to do it. Like if a Ray Charles song touch me I say well I'm gwine do it. Even if is not him write it, but so long as he sing it and it reach me I will just do dat song. And so like I'm doin' this one "I Can See Clearly" by Ray Charles, though Johnny Nash is the writer, I did like [Ray Charles'] version and Johnny Nash is one of my favorite, too.

Some people say Bob Marley actually might have written it while under contract to Johnny Nash . . .

Mmmm . . . hard to say . . . and I really want to know something about Bob, I want to know if he feelin alright cos I wanna give my message to Bob dat he could feel alright—my bredrin, yuknow? So I always say special psalms dat he could uplift.

You keep him in your prayers?

Yeah! Cos is really not the death of a sinner, but the sinner to repent, so therefore when one of the bredrin ill we all feel it, yuknow? So therefore, we say psalms of redemption for him dat he could be uplift. Like *(recites 121st Psalm, and goes on to Psalm 19:14).* Amen. That was for Bob.

—*Stephen Davis*

Toots in Kingston, 1981. "Let the words of my mouth, and the meditation of my heart, be acceptable in the sight, O Lord, my strength, and my redeemer. Amen. That was for Bob."

Make It JAMAICA. Again.

8

X-Ray Music

Look at the B-sides of Jamaican 45s beginning with rock steady, and you'll notice that many of them say "Version." This is "dub," a simple instrumental remix of the A-side that may also include a few scraps of the vocals. The singers are "dubbed out," but in most other respects the version is identical to the A-side. Begun as a test for sound levels during the record-mastering process, version later became vogue. The Jamaican public developed an avid taste for version, and the scat-singing sound-system deejays took to recording their master-of-ceremonies raps over hit-backing rhythms.

Dub is a peculiarly Jamaican musical texture, and **Luke Ehrlich** tells the story of this art form of the sound engineers—insights into a song's innards. Musical X-ray. Then we talk to Scientist, one of Jamaica's top dub engineers, who explains his views on the "good mix."

The Volatile History of Dub

"This station rules the nation with version."
—U. Roy, "Ace from Outer Space."

Early dub was recorded using a two-track recording, with the vocals on one channel and the rest of the band on the other. From the producers' point of view, version probably became as much a money-saving consideration as an aesthetic, a way to get more mileage out of each tune. Musicians and singers were getting paid by the song, as a rule, not by how many mixes of that tune were released.

The question of extra royalties to musicians and singers for versions or dubs is still unresolved, but usually the producer gives the musicians "a moni" (pocket money), and once he has paid the session men their fee for the song, he owns the music outright. If a producer decides to scrap the singer and his song for local release, he can always salvage the tracks by mixing a version of it, perhaps adding a solo horn or a rapping deejay. As a result, tapes of basic tracks change hands quite a lot. Some tracks cut in Jamaica never get released there for years; meanwhile, they surface in some other form on British "prerelease" albums or 45s.

The musical turning point for version came when a record cutter named Osbourne Ruddock (alias King Tubby) began to dub out the band track right after the intro of the tune and during the first few bars of vocals, leaving the singers acappella. Then he would abruptly shut off the vocals, sometimes chopping off words, and let the band roll. The chief pioneer of dub music, King Tubby, explains what he discovered:

"I had a little dub machine and I used to borrow tapes from the producers and mix them down in a different fashion. You see I used to work on the cutter for Duke Reid and once a

Opposite: **King Tubby** at the controls, 1976.

Scientist, dubmaster extraordinaire.

105

tape was running on the machine and I just drop off the voice y'know; it was a test cut. Well we take some of these test cut and carry them home and the Saturday we was playing out and I said alright I going test them 'cause it sounds so exciting the way the records start with the voice, the voice drop out and the rhythm still going. [We] carry them go ah [to] the dance man and I tell you 'bout four or five o' the tune them keep the dance 'cause is just over and over we 'ave fe [to] keep playing them you know."

Lee Perry, a.k.a. "Scratch," "Little," "Upsetter," "Pipecock Jakxon."

That special moment in a version when the band drops back in from the acappella vocal passage, was, and still is, a thrill. Why? Because the vocals by themselves are thin, high and brittle, rhythmically suspended without the band beneath. This creates a mounting suspense for the listener and a thirst for fullness and motion, which is immediately quenched when the band drops back in with its rich bass-and-drum-propelled forward drive.

Think of the reintroduction of the music track as a "plunge": During the acappella vocals the abdomen is not being resonated by the bass, and the head is occupied by the singing. When the band track drops back in, the awareness of the listener is quickly diverted down towards the abdomen for a moment and the cerebral stimulus of the singing ceases. Plunges, created by withdrawing and then reintroducing the bass part, can plainly be heard for fleeting moments in other, mostly black, musics.

One '60s r&b disc, "Cool Jerk" by the Capitols, is a good example. "Now let me hear the drums all by himself," shouts the singer around the middle of the song. After a four-bar drum solo the singer demands a "a little bass on those eighty-eights" and the piano and bass drop back in over the drums. It's exciting.

Dub

This is the church, this is the steeple,
Open the doors and see all the people!

—Children's hand game

Dub is really a display of musical shadow-boxing by the recording engineer which allows us to hear isolated passages of parts that normally interlock with others, but with the other parts dubbed out of the recording. The advent of four-track studios in Jamaica made possible more separation of the instruments onto different tracks, and with the work of King Tubby and Lee Perry, dub was the logical step from version. Using the same plunging technique as version, the ska-section (see p. 55) track was now dubbing out, plunging into the bass-and-drums rhythm section which was seemingly playing all by itself. It had the effect of sounding like a very cool rhythm-section jam. In very short doses of a few bars, the same idea had appeared on late '60s American r&b records.

Dub, however, was a contrivance of studio technique, not a musical arrangement. Jamaican engineers were extending the bass-and-drum texture to make it the main body of their B-side mixes, replacing the vocals as the center of attention. They called this texture "dub," from the recording lingo for copying off "dubs" (doubles)

of tapes.

With dub, Jamaican music spaced out completely. If reggae is Africa in the New World, then dub must be Africa on the moon; it's the psychedelic music I expected to hear in the '60s and didn't. The bass and drums conjure up a dark, vast space, a musical portrait of outer space, with sounds suspended like glowing planets or with fragments of instruments careening by, leaving trails like comets and meteors. Dub is a kaleidoscopic musical montage which takes sounds originally intended as interlocking parts of another arrangement and using them as raw material, converts them into new and different sounds; then, in its own rhythm and format, it continually reshuffles these new sounds into unusual juxtapositions.

The focus and center of the reshuffling process is one particular juxtaposition that is of more cultural importance than the others—that is, the bass riddim and drums, regarded as the foundation and bones of the songs. In Jamaica there is an acute awareness of the riddim as the inner message of the music and a distinct value placed on it. Dub is therefore the natural result of a Jamaican cultural tendency in music—a fondness for bass—evolving over the years into an entire musical art form and dominion of its own. It is also a clearing of space, a removal of familiar barriers and divisions.

Over time, many other studios besides Tubby's began mixing dubs in various styles and dub soon became stylistically and structurally as formulaic as the rest of reggae. There are countless formats for dubs, too many to go into fully but here are some standard moves.

The intro of a tune has traditionally been the focus in several types of Jamaican folk music, and in reggae is crucial to the proper send-off of a dub mix. In Jamaica's countryside, farmers exchange labor, working on one another's hillside cultivations. To make work more enjoyable and to set a group pace for blows of the pickaxe, they sometimes sing "digging songs," which are preceded by a rhythmless introduction called the

bobbin. During the bobbin, the farmers fix the musical key and the distribution of harmony parts, usually by humming long notes until things sound right to the song leader. Then he gives the word and they start the song.

The bobbin provides both a psychological and a musical unity preparation for the work and the song. Most reggae songs start with a drum roll of some kind, and a lot of the intros are like modern bobbins, sometimes without a distinct rhythm, or else with a different rhythm from the rest of the song.

In dub, the engineers also use intros like bobbins, as launching pads for their dubs, and then find tricky ways of getting from the intro into the first dub passage. Echo is a favorite ingredient for this transition. King Tubby introduced a slower pace of tape echo than the common 1950s type of echo already in use. He used it as a way of making the more trebly textures climax and wash over into the dub texture. The intro might start out identical to the A-side mix, becoming increasingly echoed or reverbed until it's jangling and feverishly metallic, then peaks and slowly subsides, unveiling bass and drums.

Another intro format, this one a tactic from version, has the intro mixed "dry," then dropping out as the first line of vocals is dropped in acappella. The voice then echoes out and the dub passage drops in.

Still another approach is to let the drum roll start the tune, then cut it off, and leave the band to play the intro without bass and drums. This almost always sets up a burning, tense mood which breaks off, with or without echo, into the first dub passage.

Echo techniques include doubling up the density of the drum pattern by finding just the right echo-rate, and cutting off cymbal crashes or drum rolls halfway through them, then echoing the cut-off point. Because the echo intensity and echo volume are set quite high as a rule, the first few echoes sound just like the original sound. When this is applied to cut-off drums, it can give off some curious steam-hammer racket. The same technique applied to vocals can have some really humourous results—it makes the singers sound as if they're stammering. The last word of a line is a favorite point for echoing out.

The most popular style of echo, Tubby's, has an echo rate of about 168 echoes per minute. This is a very outer-space or wilderness sound. In nature, the same echo would result from a sound bouncing back and forth between hard, sound-deflecting surfaces at least 200 feet apart. Dub echoes of this "slow" type are typically mixed with sufficient echo intensity to leave long, fading trails over the music. The effect of one of these climaxing and long-fading echoes is very like a blinding rush of blood to the head from standing up too fast.

Reverb, which Tubby introduced before slow echo, is a primary ingredient in most dubs. Even on the most conservative dubs, where the equalization (tone control) of the tracks is identical to the A-side mix, there is almost always a telltale dash of extra reverb, at the very least, on the snare and bass drum downbeats. On more daring efforts, hi-hat, afterbeats and singer get drenched in reverb as well. Reverbed downbeats contribute a lot to the "heavy" quality of the bass and the whole dub, sounding like distant gun- or cannon-fire, and at the same time suggesting a rather dark and ominous cavelike space. Another dubbing technique has the engineer dubbing out every other afterbeat, leaving in the first and third or second and fourth afterbeats, glowing with reverb. The fourth afterbeat is always a good pickup for the bass-and-drum texture, especially when echoed out. The metal spring of a spring-type reverb unit emits crackling peals of "thunder" when the unit is physically jostled; it's used sometimes on "fire-and-brimstone" Judgment Day types of tunes, both at sound-system dances and on record.

In the early '70s, the other great dub pioneer, Lee "Scratch the Upsetter" Perry, injected sound effects into his versions and dubs. The idea didn't exactly take over, but later resurfaced on rockers dubs, notably "Crown Dub" (Channel One label), a 12-inch 45-rpm EP of four dubs that features factory buzzers, barking seals, babies crying, pistol shots, police whistles and breaking glass. Also, electronic cue tones, usually reserved only for testing and marking tapes in the studio, began to make their atonal appearance on the dubs, heavily echoed. Deejay producer Mikey "Dread" Campbell is very keen on the use of sound effects; check out his LP *World War III*. My favorite dub using sound effects is the B-side of the 45 by Culture, "I'm Not Ashamed" (Joe Gibbs label), mixed by one of Jamaica's best engineers, Errol Thomson. Near the end of the record, the long trail of an echoed vocal fragment transforms into a baby's cry with spine-tingling surrealism.

How does a dub engineer accomplish all these fancy moves by himself? He either has very fast hands, like Lee Perry, or he has an assistant. Another method is to mix down a dub in stages, back and forth between different tape machines. The drawback to this method is that each time a tape is mixed down onto another tape machine, it represents one more "generation" of tape. With each generation, not only are a lot of high frequencies lost (as with tape echo), but electronic hiss and tape hiss is added, detracting from the "cleanness" of the production. Also, any small irregularities in the speeds of the tape machines are compounded with each generation and result in audible waverings of pitch known as "wow" and "flutter." In dub, this can enhance or ruin a piece of work, depending on the feel of the riddim.

The most successful dubs are ones that have a solid internal organization and atmosphere all their own. They might be expansions of the original songs or nearly unrecognizable, unpredictable transformations of them. But they must have a naturally unfolding continuity and they must captivate, not bore. The engineer must assert and efface himself at the same time, and let the song appear to perform what amounts to a striptease. Many dubs closely follow the verse structure of the original tunes, while others totally abandon it. No matter. If they have their own recurring sequence of textures, they attain a higher degree of character and consistency than disorganized or haphazard dubs. The idea is

Sly & Robbie outside Channel One studio.

to mesmerize the listener, but also, with a change in texture, to periodically rivet his attention before it wanders.

Another approach that helps develop consistency is for the engineer to pick out one or two of the instruments to be featured over the bass and drums. This is very often percussion, and these dubs offer a unique opportunity for us to hear the brilliant work of percussionists like Sticky and Scully. Until you hear them stand out on a dub, you have no idea how much these percussion parts contribute to the feel and texture of the A-side mix, where they are embedded in the arrangement and mixed so ingeniously that you can barely pick them out.

Imperfections in the mixing process (like mechanical or electronic problems with the mixing apparatus, or sloppy timing by engineers) can at times deflate the worthiest of dubs. Like seeing how a magician does his tricks, it spoils the illusion. At other times, the same kinds of "mistakes" take on great curiosity value, with a unique kind of homeliness. The studios seem to delight in including recording and mixing session in-jokes and bloopers on dubs. We hear false starts to tunes and the drummer counts off again. Or you can hear the engineer shouting, "The tape is rolling!" or "Go deh!" A common practice at sound-system dances is for the disc jockey to lift the needle off the record in the middle of the intro or first verse, exclaiming, "Lick it back from the top to the very last drop!" or "Sounds so nice ah have to play it twice!" Musical coitus interruptus. The same thing happens in dub when the engineer suddenly rewinds the tape during the intro, sucking up the music backwards like Donald Duck caught in a vacuum cleaner.

Poor basic tracks are to blame for a lot of dub's shortcomings, especially if the bass plays an uninteresting riddim or is very out of key, either with itself or with the rest of the band. Still, I've heard some out-of-tune basses sound sweetly strident and poignant: Listen to "Show Us the Way" by Hell & Fire (Channel One).

Live in Ocho Rios

Dub has two definite drawbacks that hinder it as far as getting airplay on the radio. Many disc jockeys shy away from it as "too boring" and say they don't want to lose their audience. The other problem is that the bass line doesn't reproduce especially well over small portable- and car-radio speakers; during the bass-and-drum passages, it can sound as if only drums are playing. To be sure, dub finds its ideal medium in the gargantuan sound systems run by Jamaican, and now American, entrepreneurs, wherever there is a demand for reggae music. It's with these massive columns of colourfully decorated "bass boxes" and "steel horns" that Jamaican music comes closest to First World heavy-metal music for sheer cathartic power.

Over the years, people have often said that they have had direct encounters with something deep in themselves through reggae music in general, and through dub especially. Reggae, and even more so its skeletal alter-ego, dub, are musics that are on all levels spacious enough to include and stimulate the listener's mind and body, while still allowing him enough reaction time and space to continuously absorb and realize the music and his own relationship to it.

It has also been reported that dub seems to distort the sense of time; a three-minute dub might seem to last twice as long. Because the ska section is missing for most of the dub, a familiar division of time, the afterbeat (upbeat), has been removed. The time-frame provided by the lyrics (the number of verses and choruses that have elapsed) is also missing, replaced by the time-frame of the riddim, which is often twice as long as a bar-long line of lyrics.

By the mid-'70s, dub had firmly planted itself in the hearts of Jamaicans. Sound-system disc jockeys from Kingston to Montego Bay couldn't flip their 45s over fast enough to satisfy the dub-hungry crowds. Dub fanaticism became so pronounced that stories began to circulate about gunmen threatening to "mash op de dance" if

Lee Perry and session men, including Errol "Tarzan" Nelson, Boris Gardner, Deadly Headly Bennett, Winston Wright, Robert "Billy" Johnson (holding guitar case), Dirty Harry Hall and Herman Marquis. Cedric Myton of the Congos stands at right.

even a single A-side vocal were played. Even in the remote hills, men would seriously debate the relative merits of full-mix vocals versus dub: "Well, me is a man who like him dub fi to play first and then de vocal . . ."

Studios began to prerelease (sneak-preview) new material in dub form by giving sound systems exclusive limited pressings or acetates called "dub-plates." A sizeable market now existed for dub albums, often poorly pressed affairs with blank labels or covers, and sometimes, inexplicably, at twice the price of a normal album. Some dub albums have unifying thematic titles like *Herb Dub;* the title of each cut has something to do with herb—"Quarter Pound of Ishence," "Lambsbread," "Kali Dub,"

"Chalice," etc. Other themes include astrology, world politics, Rasta doctrines, video games, guns, famous gangsters, Jamaican or African place names, revolution, and western or spy movies. There's even *Rassclaat Dub* (literally "ass-cloth," old-fashioned toilet paper). Some albums are dub versions of entire vocal albums or combinations of two such albums; some make no mention of this fact, others use it as a strong selling point.

Dub Ikonography

Channel One introduced 12-inch 45-rpm records to the reggae market in 1976. They called them "disco 45s," since 12-inch singles were already in full swing on the American disco scene. The 12-inch format allowed record cutters more room on the vinyl to master the grooves of the record wider and louder. Ordinarily on a regular 7-inch 45, the cutter must limit the width and side-to-side motion of the groove, because if one groove overlaps another, the phonograph needle will skip. The 12-inch 45s have greater, more live-sounding dynamic range; that is, the soft

sounds are softer and the loud sounds are louder (the opposite of compression).

Channel One's first 12-inch 45 was "Truly," an old Marcia Griffiths hit for Coxsone, this time remade by a vocal group called the J-Ayes. The flip was another Coxsone tune, originally by the Viceroys, called "Yaho." Besides the unusually impeccable sound quality, the real musical contribution of this 12-inch was to present a seven- or eight-minute rendition of each song that transformed itself halfway through into a dub. "Truly" featured deejay Ranking Trevor chanting over the dub.

At first they achieved the transformation from full mix to dub by echoing out the vocals near the halfway mark and then splicing the dub mix

onto the end of the full mix smoothly and in rhythm, without skipping a beat. This made the dub seem like much less of a separate flip-side entity and more like an extended jam. The plunge into the dub, at a point in the music where listeners were conditioned to hearing the song fade out, was electrifying and there was no waiting around for the dub to be announced or for the record to be turned over—dub gratification was immediate! The momentum of three minutes of full mix spilled over into the dub.

During the 1977 period of fiscal crisis in Jamaica, Channel One issued singles labeled "Economic Package." This was a 7-inch 33-rpm disc with the same full-mix/dub combination that the 12-inch 45s have on each side. Some were spliced, others simply featured the song, followed separately by its dub, with or without a chanting deejay. Unlike the disco 45s, the sound quality on the "Economic Package" was abysmal, and they were a short-lived phenomenon. The most recent packaging of dub is the "show-case" 33-rpm album, with two to four songs per side. Full mixes are followed separately by their dubs, or each cut is a full-mix/dub combination with or without deejay.

In 1976, Channel One put out 45s on which the mix behind the vocals on the A-side is a dub, instead of being full. "Woman Is Like a Shadow" by the Meditations was one of the earliest and best of these vocal/dubs. When the material appeared later on albums, it had the straight full mix: "Woman Is Like a Shadow" is well known to many Americans by now because of the widely distributed album *Message From the Meditations*, but they are not hearing the same 45 mix that was such a hit in Jamaica. After Channel One, Joe Gibbs was the next major studio to follow suit with vocal/dub. But there had been hints of dub mix spilling over onto the A-side as early as 1973–4, with records like "Do Right" by Jackie Brown, "Irie Feelings" by Rupie Edwards and some material produced by Lee Perry and Niney Holness the Observer.

What is remarkable about vocal/dubs is the way the arrangement constantly changes texture under the lyrics, plunging and climaxing with echo trails, creating different moods that underscore the singer. One great mixing maneuver in this area belongs to Lee Perry and involves tricking the listener. Coming from a full-mix passage, Perry dubs out everything but bass and drums for just the first beat of a bar, usually in the first bar of a verse. This is a plunge and leads the listener to believe that the tune is going "dubwise," as they say. But no sooner has the listener become comfortable with this feeling for a split second than Perry drops a full mix back in for the rest of the bar, "faking out" the listener completely. On *Message From the Meditations* you can hear this on the tunes "Running From Jamaica" and "There Must Be a First Time"; also on Lee Perry's own 45, "Dreadlocks In Moonlight."

Singers gradually began to follow in the footsteps of the deejays, recording new songs over dubs of other tunes. If the backing track is already in dub form when the new singer voices the song—that is, if the dub mix of the tracks is what the singer actually hears through his headphones when he records his vocals—it can bring musical problems. It is very difficult to gauge singing pitch from just bass and drums; singers normally gauge their pitch from hearing the keyboards and guitars. So there are vocal/dub records where the singer starts out in key, but begins to go sharp or flat whenever the ska-section track drops out. This problem shows up most frequently with deejay artists because their particular form of music incorporates elements of both singing and talking.

Dub International

Dub has heavily influenced other musics besides reggae. In the mid-'70s, disco created its own version of dub, leaning on bass, drums and the use of echo. Some say this was merely coincidental with Jamaican dub, but direct influence is probably more likely. For one, the undeniable Jamaican presence in the New York and Miami areas since the mid-'60s has exerted a direct, though subtle, influence on American black communities and their music.

Key figures in disco production were also quite aware of Jamaican music. Disco engineer Tom Moulton has even remixed early Coxsone tracks of the Wailers for American release. Steve Alaimo, former soul singer and president of Miami-based TK Records, loves Jamaican music and even recorded a thoroughly authentic ska album back in 1963, featuring Jamaica's Blues Busters on back-up vocals. Rap records, a newer trend in American black music, are without a doubt America's answer to the Jamaican deejay.

Up until the end of the '70s, Jamaican music had been largely a recorded studio art. Live music shows were an afterthought, not the primary focus that they are on the American music scene. But with the growing market for reggae, especially outside of Jamaica, stage-show tours assumed more importance. At the same time, dub was an increasingly popular and musically familiar aspect of reggae. What happened is an

interesting reversal of "art imitates life": This time, live bands began approximating a form that originated as a purely studio technique.

Live reggae bands everywhere now perform live dub, though many still have yet to attempt it. When a live band can smoothly execute dub, it becomes a supremely enjoyable kind of musical volleyball, the players tossing around the different patterns with body-language and eye-contact cues. Vocalists sing their own echo trails; guitarists and keyboardists have developed strums and fingerings to approximate echo, or they actually use echo- and reverb-units right there on stage. Drummers have learned to stop and start abruptly and also to cut short cymbal crashes and double up patterns to sound like echoed drum tracks.

Dub is useful most of all as a learning aid for aspiring reggae musicians, in particular bassists and drummers, because it clearly illuminates aspects of the parts and the players' technique which are normally covered over, or not included at all, in the full mix. The separation of the tracks disentangles rhythmically interlocking parts for individual scrutiny and understanding. For example, it's apparent from dubs that a great many Jamaican bassists purposely lag a split second behind the drummer. This is not the same as slowing down; rather, the attack on each note is consistently late ("soon come"?). Nevertheless the pace of the bass pattern is right with the drummer. This subtlety is very powerful. The overall effect is that the rhythm section sounds rounder, more rolling and natural, and this is baffling—it makes time seem to last longer by heightening the vividness of the riddim.

Without dub music, or at least version, the art of reggae music might have stayed confined to a select group of studio musicians in Kingston, perhaps forever. But by now several generations of dub-tutored amateur reggae musicians have emerged from their basements in New York, Boston, London, Kingston, Toronto and Dakar to form and record their own reggae groups.

Version focused the attention and admiration of the common people on the musical forms behind the singers. Once this orientation was established, dub enabled an increasingly large segment of the Jamaican population to become aware of, and later completely fluent in, the language of the many riddims behind their national music. Through dub, hundreds of the prototype bass riddims have truly become folk music. It's now very common to find Jamaican non-musicians, even schoolchildren, who know their reggae riddims just as some preachers know their Bible, chapter and verse.

Masters of Dub

One person in particular deserves a prominent place in the dub Hall of Fame, as the most prolific and influential true dub artist. He is Augustus Pablo (Horace Swaby), famous for his distinctive melodica playing over dubs and his keyboard work on recording sessions. A melodica is a hand-held reed instrument similar to a harmonica, but about a foot long and with a single mouth-piece at one end and a small keyboard like a piano. Pablo is also a tasteful producer of other artists, such as Hugh Mundell and Tetrack, and has done more than any other single musician to promote and develop dub in Jamaica and abroad. His personality really comes out in his hauntingly minor-key melodica compositions in what he calls the "Far East" sound. Pablo's many hits include "Java," "East of the River Nile" and "King Tubby Meets The Rockers Uptown."

The top dub engineers of 1979–81 have to be Prince Jammy and Tubby's young protégé, Scientist. A whole series of albums produced by Henry "Junjo" Lawes has Jammy and Scientist in various showdowns for the title of Heavyweight Dub Champion. Both engineers work mostly out of Tubby's studio, with its characteristic sound, yet Jammy's dubs are a bit busier, less hollow and fatter-sounding than Tubby's. The basic tracks are mostly by the Roots Radics Band.

Scientist goes for a dryer, punchier sound than either of his influences, and indulges in trickier patterns, too. His specialty is a wicked sledgehammer emphasis on the 2 & 4 downbeat snare drum: first, he mixes the snare into a potty-sounding gunshot, thickly daubed with a pasty reverb. Then he sends this through a flanger which turns the elongated snare slams into twanging screen-door springs!

My own favorite dub album of all time is probably still *Garvey's Ghost* (Mango), a dub treatment of Burning Spear's album *Marcus Garvey*. Without using much reverb or long echo at all, this record is the essence of tasteful simplicity in dub. Interestingly, it was mixed in England under the supervision of Spear's then-producer, Jack Ruby, but by engineers, possibly Englishmen, who are not well known to the Jamaican dub scene.

Keyboardist and session wizard, Augustus Pablo.

Errol T, veteran engineer, at the board at Joe Gibbs studio.

—*Luke Ehrlich*

109

Scientist

Scientist: I really got involved with music by electronics. I came up with an idea about building a mixing board, a studio console, and I wanted to really see how my idea would work towards it, meaning that the same idea that I am thinking about, it is the same principle which they use at a studio. So I went up to King Tubby's studio and was asking him some question about a board.

That's approximately three years ago. And he used to tell me that how I'm thinking about it, it cannot work becaa de ting that I am thinking about towards music is a bit impossible at dat time. So it happen dat he went on his face when he didn't have a next engineer when Prince Jammy left there. And it start dat I just did go into the studio now start recordin and so forth. I got involved . . .

Q: *How many tracks did Tubby have then?*

Four.

And he's still recording basically on four-track?

Yeah.

But you're at Channel One now, right?

Yeah.

So how did Scientist begin to build his reputation?

Scientist's name is Overton Brown. Born Kingston, 1960.

Well, by givin de people-dem a good mix . . . I would say you have to know certain tings about music. When I say dat, I mean dat to give somebody a good mix, you have to try to get de ting sounding as clean as possible, and try to get de music to sound deep and use de bass to form de foundation of de riddim, a strong bass without distorting it. It's a hard ting to do fe get a mix like how I would mix.

How did you come by the name Scientist?

From Tubby's. He was de one who made it popular but from school days. I used to mek certain lickle tings and cyarry to school and they used to call me Scientist.

In Jamaica, the word "scientist" also has another meaning, like someone who's involved with magic.

It depends on what you call magic becaa almost anything can work out as magic.

I've seen quite a few albums in the States with your name on them. Who did you make those records for, Tubby's?

No, the producers who come there and rent the studio. It's just that dem come to the studio and seh that dem want I mix a dub album for them. And I mix it, and change up de music.

What producers have you worked for?

Well, a lot of producers. I started with Henry Junjo Lawes, he was the first person who put out [one of my] dub albums. Bunny Lee, Al

Campbell, all o' de producers dat you have in music.

What other dub artists do you check for, who else do you like?

You mean, as engineers? Barnabas. Well, you see, all of them yunno, becaa next ting about it is a different style, but to really get it as how you people like it, dat it have a certain feelin to it, is a very technical ting—is a ting more kinda have to born into you, is not something that you can show somebody. Is not a ting like say you can tell a man "do this" or "do this" or else if you gwine tell a man do this and that, you gwine find say de music is nah gwine have any taste.

Someone once described dub as like a musical X-ray.

And it come in like you just examinin that particular body of the music . . . Yeah well dat mek sense—the ting about it is not tek it out: It's *why* you tek it out, *how* you tek it out, das de important ting. When like say yu tek out de bass line, yu tek it out to create a certain feel and how yu put it in and why yu put it in, dat is de ting. Dat is a ting dat yu ave to study.

When did you start building things? When did you start working as a scientist?

From when I was about 12, 13 comin up. I build something as a form a security, when you put it on de gate and if anybody come there it shock dem (laughs)!

Did you ever try it on anybody?

Huh? Yeah man! Dat was one of the process, dat. And yunno I used to experiment on lizards, cut them and so forth, freeze dem and see if dem would after dem thaw out, come back to life, a whole heap o' lickle tings; I used to mek crystal radio.

So have you ever worked at a studio that has more than four tracks?'

Yeah, Coxsone.

How many tracks does he have?

Sixteen.

Did you find that you were making better music with more tracks or did you find that the four tracks were enough?

Well, at the moment, for the ideas that I have about music, sixteen and twenty-four tracks come in like that is a lickle bit o' tracks. To my idea, I need about two hundred tracks!! (laughs)

—*Stephen Davis*

9

Long Time I No Deejay Inna Dance

Deejaying is reggae's oral folk journalism, part nursery doggerel, part shrewd social analysis. During their relatively brief careers, Jamaica's deejays serve as the nation's street poets, oracles and phrase-makers. Deejaying is a kind of human buffer between reggae music and the great mass of the people. Deejays are conveyers and interpreters of the music, reggae's greatest fans as well as relatively high-ranking members of its priesthood. In this chapter, veteran writer **Carl Gayle,** editor of **Jahugliman** magazine in Kingston, celebrates some of his favorites. He starts by taking us to a sound-system dance somewhere in Kingston, one night back in 1979 . . .

Nice Up the Dance

". . .Your life depends on how yu corporate . . . Dam right . . .You always ever make things great yu pop on thru the gate . . .True true . . . Pay the musical rate an take a pop on thru de gate with a smile upon your face . . . Heh heh . . . Das what I appreciate yeah . . . Go deh . . . Say long time I no deejay inna dance . . . Long time I no chant inna dance . . . Me come to nice up de areaaaah . . . Me come fe nice up Jamaica . . ."

A record called "Nice Up The Dance" by the best in de bizniz, Michigan an Smiley. The biggest selling record for the year 1979, sounds from de ghetto making celebration in time of war. "**But watch ya man, dance ha fe cork dance ha fe cork . . . Plate gwy sell out, plate gwy sell out . . . People who really keep it have to laugh . . . Oh Lord . . . Promoter an his Idrin have to laugh . . . How dem laugh? Sha la la la la la la la laaa . . . Tra la la la la la la la laugh . . .**"

Fairclough and Bennett, otherwise known as Papa Michigan and General Smiley. A deejay duo dat establish demselves with talkin music. Inna de *rub-a-dub* style. A thing dat existed from Adam an Eve went up my sleeve an never come down till Chrismus eve. Lissen . . . ". . . **Born an me grow in Jamaicaah . . . Man a say Ah naah leave me ghetteoh . . . Me say me naah leave Jamaicaah . . . But watch ya man, Pawn yu crocus bag go on a dance scene . . . I an Papa Mich go on a bizniz . . . Say I a sell rolls . . . I sell Wrigleys . . . Man, how yu keep yu pickney, Smiley, tell me how yu keep yu pickney? But Papa Mich, love is all I got tell yu love is all I bring, tell yu bout de thing keep rockin an swing, cos every man throw a thing . . . An ting an ting . . . Keep yu rockin an swing . . . An swing an swing, Long time I no deejay rub-a-dub . . . Long time I no deejay rub-a-dub . . .**"

Papa Michigan & General Smiley

Ranking Joe at Skateland

111

De music a bubble. Like all music from Studio One. A bubbling dance rydim. Bass player name Bagga. Anything him play on sound good at Studio One, de original dance hall sound. Established by Clement Dodd known as Sir Coxsone in the roots dance world of sound systems, the mobile discos of Jamaica. Once again, the best in the bizniz, Michigan and Smiley, one tall one short.

"**. . . Started to talk an de dance really cork. Gate man a laugh and de cashier a laugh . . . Cyaahn find a bottle with a cork . . . Me say me cyaahn get no place to walk . . . Ah want a food before de pudding selll offf . . . De cane man an him Idrin a laugh . . . Promoter an his Idrin have to laugh . . . How dem laugh? Tra la la la la la la la la laa . . . Oh Lord, tra la la la la la la la laa . . ."**

Dey dress for stage like veterans of showbizniz. With white gloves an de ole-time fish-tail suit an top hat favour Louis Armstrong. Dem move with experience cos is just natrality. An dem enjoy demself cos de whole Jamaica love dem talkin inna rub-a-dub style. Cos every tune dem mek reach number one. Lissen . . .

"**. . . People outside cyaahn get into de dance . . . Dem really ha fe dance on de street tonite. People inside say dem want me photograph. Some a dem say dem really want me autograph . . . yaahn really work tonite . . . So Smiley rockin inna resident area . . . Papa Michy in a resident area . . ."**

The roots of deejay music are found in the excitement of the ska, a fast foot-shufflin music for dancers with stamina. Ska music saw the birth of the recording deejay. Those days yu call the live deejay a toaster. He toast for his sound system on de live wire pulling the crowd with his loose lip, so his reputation spread like wildfire. Eventually, he go to studio. One early deejay disc was Lord Comic's "Ska-ing West" (1966). Tho even Baba Brooks precede that one with "One Eyed Giant." And "Lawless Street" by the Soul Bros., noted for its vocal scatting riff all the way thru. In "Ska-ing West," Lord Comic begins "*. . . Adam and Eve went up my sleeve and they never came down till christmas eve/come on you cats, we're going west . . .*" The rhymes spur on the dancers cos the comments suit dem. "*Okay daddy we're going west . . .*"

Any artist can make a talking tune, but the real toaster emerges from the world of Sound Systems, the school for deejays. Sound systems have consistently promoted and popularized Jamaican music ever since Jamaica had a music of its own, and even before with American r&b. A contribution to the Jamaican recording industry of crucial importance. King Edward, Sir Coxsone, Duke Reid, V Rocket, Prince Buster, King Tubby, Jah Love. The names of the most renowned and rated sound systems.

The Jamaican sound system is custom-made, with amplifiers built for power, and heavy wooden speakers built to wage the bass and drum war of roots reggae. The Sounds, as we say in JA, used to thrive on more competition in the earlier days of r&b; but politics discouraged such clashes in the election-filled '70s, until today the best-known and best-loved sound, Jah Love, restricts playing and never competes. By tradition, sound system operators titled their sound after the ranks of the British aristocracy as a show of power and prestige. Nowadays, this attitude is changing; the Sirs and Dukes have vanished. Only one king remain in memory, the unforgettable King Tubby's.

But the colonial influence still exists. For whereas Jah Love sound discard all British ascendancy as a part of the organization of The Twelve Tribes Of Israel, Movement of Rastafari, yet still its beloved deejay is known as the Brigadier. A non-stop toaster with a British army ranking and the ability to entertain dread an baalhead, police an thief, members an nonmembers, up an down town with the latest in slang and street talk, while promoting The Twelve Tribes Of Israel organization itself upon the live jive wire.

Sound systems become popular and successful by simply playing good music, rare music not heard on radio or anywhere else. To stay in the ratings yu have to make your own sounds to satisfy the crowd who demand new music continually. After graduating from the dance halls to the studio, the sound system man starts to make dance hall music. None has been more successful than Clement "Sir Coxsone" Dodd, whose records are the foundation of all sound system music, and will continue thus. To stay on top each sound needs a good deejay, someone with something witty an nitty-gritty to say. Someone to talk aloud to pull the crowd . . . His reputation fly by word of mouth soon as he start to shout . . . Becos of his wit they call him King Stitt becos a quick word dat rhyme is golden as a stitch in time . . .

King Stitt: The Ugly One

Sunday afternoon, October 1976, Kingston, Jamaica. Sun is shining. Tribal war still hot but not so loud. We upstairs on de corner of King Street an Beeston Street, I an Udson, Keith Hudson. Him point down to de corna goin' toward Love Lane showin' where Coxsone ujually ave him record shop first time. Him see King Stitt reasoning with another one so him sen' and call de deejay. Stitt come thru de door an siddung. I ask Stitt if him not doin no deejayin. Him say no him naw do no deejayin. So Udson ask him wha mek?

"Right now, breeda Keet, me no like how some a de promoter dem a go on, yu know, a de trute!"

"Is juss a money ting dem after, an dem naw think bout de welfare o' de artist dem," say Udson.

"Yeah, a de trute, das why me juss kinda back out, yunno," reply Stitt.

"Yeah," say Udson, "but yu no back out! Cos a man who learn a ting never feget it, yunno. An right now dem time ya a your time. Is time dem ya now when yu should a really try mek some money out a de bizniz becaw de bizniz reach a stage . . ."

"Well de bizniz reach a stage now whey a man can mek money," say Stitt. "Ah don't even know which one a de promota dem fe check, cos wher yu check it out de whole a dem gwy tell yu a thing."

"Yu no ha' fe check no one, me deh ya, yunno," say Udson. "Me deh ya yunno! I an I deh ya. Who dont know you Stitch? Your name deh everywhey. De people dem who know yu, dem *talk* bout yu. Dem tell other people bout yu who never know, yu yunno."

The Ugly One him start play sound system inna de '50s, about 1957. Sir Coxsone Sound. Dose times Coxsone set up at de corna of Love Lane an Beeston Street. Stitt started as a second to King Sporty, de star deejay. Stitt took over when Sporty go to America. Stitt was inspired by Count Machuki, the talk of de town deejay with Coxsone some time before Stitt mek him debut a a toaster. "Him show me a lotta things yunno," say Stitt. "Him show me de techniques. Like yu know yu play a selection, yu must watch de crowd dancin to it. Well de toastin now, I never generally use another man thing. I try my own ting yunno, an it ketch on. Well dat time it was mostly rydim an blues, an yusee yu had to present some picture to de people cos yu have certain places whey yu play where de crowd can't just stay outside an know dat inside full. S yu juss use someting . . . live jive an all dat an yu get de people dem. . . . like how de box move when de bass note drop an yu see it yu sa LOOKIN GOOD! So people outside get excited now, dem want to see what lookin good inside. Yu undastan! Sometime nobody no really inna d

dance hall but to how de weight a de music drop an de box start vibrate an move, yu just create something off a de box . . . so dem juss pay an come in, come see wha lookin good."

"De powa o' yu amp a shake yu dance yu box dem!" say Udson. "Then man de thing deh, de battle o' de giants wid him an U. Roy man, yu never hear bout it? Yes man Stitch mash it up."

"Dem did ave a show at Arena," say Stitt. "Ah think is '74, yeah '74 July. De three bess disc jockey, which was Big Yout, U. Roy, an meself . . . When I started recordin de scene was juss becomin live . . . alive. Well de first tune dat I make, it was a hit."

Dat was "Fire Corner," recorded for producer Clancy Eccles in 1969. All his top-ten tunes were for Eccles: "Lee Van Cleef," "Vigorton Two," "Herbsman Shuffle." "Vigorton Two" was a tonic, a stitch in time. Stitt do some music with Coxsone studio but dem never reach anywhere, never take the market. "When sayin dem never tek de markit," say Udson, "dat did ave a involvement wid de radio station wherein yu coodn't get no play."

"Coodn't get no play," agree Stitt.

"So de song dem coodn't get no promotion," say Udson. "So is not dat de ability a de song wasn good . . . but it was de concept between him an de radio people dem. An yu know de radio is de medium for promotion!" Stitt do live deejayin for Coxsone, the number one sound system from '57 till '69, then he record "Fire Corner," his best seller to date. **No matter what the people say. . . these sounds lead the way. . . it's the order of the day from your boss deejay. . . I King Stitt . . . up it from the top to the very last drop . . ."**

"An Ah want tell yu yu *hard* yunno!" shout Udson. "Yu *haad* man. Right now me a plan fe chuck him inna de studio early." Udson want to put Stitt on the recording track again with some of his own dub music as the backround for The Ugly One's toasting. But the plan never did work out. "An mek we mash it up!" Udson declare. "Cos people love Stitch out deh, is juss thru dem no hear him. Dem naw hear de man. A juss dat. But him no have fe do music fe people tell yu bout him or talk bout him. . . ."

"Up to de other day a man come check me fe control stage show," say de deejay. "Me say, right now me no really. . ."

"Noh yu can't," say Udson. "De benefit, de benefit too poor. An yu see what appm? When dem used to de freeness it hard fe dem pay money."

"Haaad fe dem pay munny," repeat Stitt.

"And dats it now, yu can't do it so again," say Udson. "Dis time ya now is munny. Money, cos everyone haffe live. Everyone waahn live. Is a man who ave responsibility juss like any other man out deh."

"Serious ting," say Stitt.

"Right now Stitch," say Udson, ". . . I a go mek yu do a music. Cos me know yu entikle fe earn some good munny. An entikle to be out dere 'mongst de ress a dem, cos him was dere from before dem come."

"Yeah!" say Stitt.

"Cos when him record tune, U. Roy no record no music yet," say Udson. "I. Roy no record no music yet. Big Yout no record no music yet."

"When me record 'Fire Corner' is long after dat before U. Roy do 'Old Fashan Way,' " confirm Stitt. "Dynamic Fashion Way" was one of Roy's first recordings, using the original song titled "Old Fashioned Way" as the backdrop for his toasting. This was before he recorded for Duke Reid. "And dat a U. Roy," say Udson. "Cos 'Ole Fashan Way' a him fuss tune."

"Yes" say Stitt, " 'Ole Fashan Way' a him first tune."

"First tune," say Udson, " 'Dynamic Fashan Way.' But is de competition wha build up inna de last part of it deh, Stitch, cos is me . . . Me a de first man put U. Roy inna studio, de fuss man put Dennis AlCapone inna studio, de fuss one fe give Big Yout a hit. So is de competition wha build up thruout it, yu no seet?"

"Dat is true yeah," say Stitt.

"An de pace wha me did a set," say Udson, "no man wouldn't try fe come in between me and de deejay dem. When me bring U. Roy, him go out deh wid Duke Reid. An Duke Reid a mash it up with him an me say, A wha de blood claat me a gwaan wid? So me go inn de Lane (Chancery Lane), go find Dennis AlCapone an bring out Dennis AlCapone come giv U. Roy a blood claaht competition."

"True, true!" say Stitt. "An him switch an go to Duke too."

"An him switch an go to Duke," Udson repeats. "So me say A wha de blood claaht do hoonoo? Come Big Yout number one 'S-90'. . . Right now Stitch me hav fe carry yu inna de studio nex week, yu hear sah!"

"Dat cool," say Stitt.

"Yes man," say Udson, "me ha fe do dat. Put yu pan a ridim name 'Treasure Of De Worl' dubwise. Ah ha ha ha! Me a go mek yu hold some money, munny inna de bizniz man."

"A whole heap a money inna it yes," say Stitt. "Right now de way me see some a de promoter dem go on me juss say watch ya, hoonoo hold hoonoo tape an me will hold my voice. Cos me can't afford fe run go a studio from half past eight go wait till six a clack. NOH!! No, in my time of doin recordin' Clancy Eccles come tell me say we a go a studio today. So me can siddung 'mongst me bredrin an build two spliff an juss cool."

"Right now Stitch me a go lick yu out deh man, cos a my time dem ya time ya," declare Udson.

"Yeah," say Stitt. "Me wi go a studio but . . . when me do a ting an it sell out deh a man juss ride an me can't even walk when yu check it out. Dat no mek sense."

"Right now dem no ave argument like you a blood claaht," say Udson, "yu mussy ave de whole a dem inna yu head. Stitch ave argument to mek certain people who no buy record fe do past three years come out come buy record . . . wi mek man who no buy record fe de past ten year come out an say him want Stitch record. I a go gi dem suppm name 'De Collector's Item.' Wha de blood claaht do yu Stitch? 'De Collector's Item' from King Stitch de original. Ridim to dem head."

"An Stitch, when me a come wid yu is hit record me a deal wid yunno," say Udson. "Hit me a deal wid dat mean me naw go even sell it meself, me juss gi it to de Chineyman and GWAAN, lick dat fe me sah!"

King Tubby's Legacy

As with Coxsone, Prince Buster, King Tubby and Jack Ruby, the sound system man can make a success in record production once he step up. Out of the old-time rivalry between Reid and Coxsone emerged the strongholds of home-grown reggae, the roots sounds. Reid and Coxsone have been responsible for the discovery of the best artists in reggae music, for the earliest, and many of the best records in reggae.

But they belonged to the '60s in the sound system world. Today's sound is technically better equipped to please followers of roots entertain-

Prince Buster

ment. Dance fans still support their sounds, but their zeal might be waning due to lack of rivalry and competition between various sound systems. The last recognized or confirmed ruler of the sound world, King Tubby, no longer studies dance hall sound war, but now enjoys the freedom of his own small and compact recording studio that he himself set up to experiment with electronic sound production on record, mixing instrumental sounds with vocals in a way that established, in the minds of all who hear, the real meaning of dub.

Tubby, the electrician. Studio engineer formidable. Those who know his works call him Scientist. He claimed the title in the roaring '70s as the world's number one sound, which no one can dispute on Earth. A master of sound recording and playback. The man who first dubbed the vocals of U. Roy onto an already tried and proven rydim, the major move in the rise of dub music and deejay recording.

Using reverb and delayed echo to cut in and

113

U. Roy

out of the music at key points, he distorted the sound of all the instruments and vocal in turn, producing a new instrumental sound dominated by the rydim of bass and drum. Nowadays dub music is sold as the instrumental version of the song after going thru the engineering process pioneered by Tubby. But dub is unlimited, for anything added on to something already existing is called dub. It takes two to dub it. So rub-a-dub style is a way of talking about coming together to the sound and moving to the rydim right on time. Is like mixing up; when yu dub it with your dawta, you mix it up like a good engineer.

King Tubby is the man who gave the great deejay U. Roy an audience, and so delivered him to Jamaica as the most exciting musical experience since ska days. "You have more man nowadays a listen to sound system than first time," said Tubby in December 1975. "Them times, man used to have sound system as hooligan bizniz but now it can even nationalise. Yeah man, becos is dat dem use fe help win election yuknow. Sound system come in such a demand that every weekend if a man naw go to no session is like some part o' him life gone. Man not going a club again, no even waahn hear jukebox again.

"We never really get famous until around May 1968. But I used to fool round sound system from 1964 as a hobby. Coxsone and Duke Reid was still there but dem was losing dem name. Top sound those times was Sir Mike, Sir George, Kelly, and Stereo from Spanish Town. Then we come on as Tubby's Home Town Hi Fi. We say we wasn't going in it that big, just play in we home town area which was Waterhouse. But eventually we get big.

"We introduce a different thing to the sound system world. This amplifier here have chrome front and reverb. That's the first time a reverb was introduced in Jamaica is when my sound come out. And it get de people so excited that everywhere we go we have a following. And then U. Roy come on with a style . . . he wasn't a professional at the time, I hafe teach him bout the sound bizniz too.

Early in 1970, U. Roy had three records ("Wear You To The Ball," "Wake The Town," and "Rule The Nation") in the top three positions on both radio stations for several weeks. A marked achievement where deejay music had not been even recognised as worthwhile music by Jamaican critics. The preceding year, King Stitt had appeared with three good records, the best known being "Fire Corner," followed by "The Ugly One" and "Vigorton Two." But the peak performances were not sustained, the promise of this new wave of music not fully realised until U. Roy burst on the scene. U. Roy was not the originator as he toasted on record, but he was the bright spark, chief innovator, a true original. Immediately infectious, devastating with speed, deejay music was never like this before. A self-induced excitement, shouting, screaming, singing, reaching a pitch of intensity between '70 and '72 that has not been matched since.

U. Roy

December 1975. U. Roy is on the verge of a new breakthrough. Over the last two years or so, he's been in Limbo, making only one or two records worthy of his name and staying away from the recording studio in general. Then Bunny Lee the producer brought him farwud as a force with some moderate sellers. Now his new producer is the youthful Prince Tony, a lover of deejay records since Winston Scotland gave him his first hit production with a thing called "Buttercup" a few years ago. Tony sees the full potential of the new-styled U. Roy backed by the reigning heavy dub style rydims of today, with the voices of Delroy Wilson, Barrington Spence and even The Gladiators to respond to. Since the emergence of Big Yout with this heavy dub style of message deejaying, the daddy of deejays had not shone so bright. But still the great U. Roy only needs one good LP to once again set him free.

But it is ironical that the man whose music once went straight to the nation's head soul and feet should face a struggle due to competition from less original or enterprising toasters. But what separates U. Roy from the rest is the fact that he gave reggae this live jivin dimension which is so electrifying, and not his successors or predecessors. With his will-of-the-wisp Kingston jive talkin he turn the tables on a Jamaica recording scene full of singing talent. And brought excitement, paving the way for a dance hall full of imitators.". . . U. Roy is a lickle name give to me by my cousin yuknow," he says, "when I was a youth in Jones Town. Like I used to tease him an him say, 'Behave yuself URoy!' From dat time de name just stick on . . ."

U. Roy is otherwise known as Ewart Beckford. He live in the ghetto. Earn his livin with music . . . recordings, live deejayin, putting on his own dances. Used to be a timekeeper in a cement company before his sound system life started.

"Half of my direct works is sound system strictly yuknow, since I left school. The first sound me play is Dicky's Dynamic, then Sir George Atomic, then Coxsone Downbeat, then Tubby's.

"Yu have a certain amount o people who really love me yuknow," say Roy. "Anywhey me sing dem go swing."

A modest, reluctant talker. "My religion is like I dont really run joke with it much, yuknow. To me most man just use Rasta as a money-makin thing. I used to do Psalms long time, the same tune name 'Earth Rightful Ruler.' "

With the vital emergency of Big Yout, U. Roy's sound and style aged rapidly. Yout's sound, fresh and vibrant, was a slower heavier rydimic pattern featuring drum and bass as never before. A bigger gun of a sound.

Most of Roy's records for Duke Reid, if not all, used an already recorded rock steady style song as his backing music. So by clever deejaying Roy's shouted phrases fitted in like jig-saw with the words of the song, call-and-response style, as if everything was recorded in one go. It was a melodic, most danceable sound, de beat bouncy, melody sweet, toasting fast and fleeting.

"I never used to love de dubwise ting," admits Roy. But yu juss haffe rock yu thing steady according to de movement o' de rydim . . . Well right now Big Yout is de ratings. Jah Yout hav fe juss get dat. Him ave some good timin'. Not sayin I. Roy and Jazzbo don't have still, yu know, but . . . Jazzbo hav fe come third too cos I. Roy is a man who ave a style. But as soon as him personally herar me with a style him gone with it. But a deejay don't bother me much yunno. De most important thing to me right now is dat I imitate no one."

AlCapone

In the wake of U. Roy came many imitators until the sudden burst of Big Yout. Even Dennis AlCapone was swept forward by U. Roy's current. So was Scotty, another good deejay who ran out of things to say all too soon. Yet these two were the only real competition to U. Roy in his prime time, Capone being the most successful.

"People didn't really recognise the deejay stuff untill U. Roy took over," said Dennis in December '74 when his popularity was waning. "King Stitt did a good thing wit things like 'Fire Corner' but it didn't really get off until U. Roy came along.

"I came on de scene about three months after U. Roy, then Lizzie came. Then you had Scotty. But I was in the shadows at that time. I was selling but . . . I rate U. Roy up to now as de greatest, yeah! I used to go and listen to him and I admired the sounds he put out. He used to play King Tubby's sound. Dat was an is de best, it ave everything a system should have.

"But when you siddown and lissen to dat man U. Roy playin dat sound, it really blow your mind . . . The only reason why a good Jamaican artist don't keep up to expectation is because of exploitation. The producers they're not givin you any money an you keep on doin stuff for dem makin dem richer an richer everyday an you not gettin anywhere. If a man ask you to do a tune an you ask for 500 dollars which is very small, he start to screw (face). And if you don't want to do it there will be someone else ready to do it for 100 dollars or less. But you can't go on doing things without any reward. And as soon as you stop they spend money on dat one an bring him up till he become popular."

Dennis AlCapone Smith did welding and played El Paso sound system in his spare time until he made his first recordings: "El Paso," "Spanish Omega" and another for producer Keith Hudson. "The children really turned on to dat sound ["El Paso"] in Jamaica," he recalled. "Everywhere you went they were singin 'A wha so el paso . . .' The sound system was such a success dat I didn't even have to start playin. As soon as I touch de needle de place full! People come from all over yuknow."

He switched to producer Coxsone for a tune called "Nanny Version" with the name Al Capone as he was long well-known. "Home Version" and "Power Version" followed. Then Capone do a thing with producer Bunny Lee called "It Must Come," and one called "Mosquito One" for Duke Reid, as well as the big one "Teach The Children." "Power Version" was number two on both radio stations in JA for several weeks, then "Teach The Children" took over Jamaica.

"You couldn't stop dat one," said Dennis. "The reason why it went to de top is becos I got payed for it as soon as I finished recording it. And in the space of three weeks it was number one on both stations for about four weeks. Then I got a tour to Guyana with Boris Gardener Happening."

Capone was good but still considered in the shadows of U. Roy, at his very best. Tho U. Roy found it hard to switch from rock steady to dub, Capone did not. His nursery-rhyming style was sometimes self-effacing, but his popularity continued chartwise after Roy's had waned. "Teach The Children" was a reggae version of "Mister Big Stuff," the soul tune, called "Sister Big Stuff." **Teacher teacher I beg yu ring the bell . . . teach the children teach dem how to spell . . . r-a-t rat, m-a-t mat, c-a-t cat . . ."**

"It was educational for the children, yuknow, cos you have a lotta children like to listen to music," said Dennis. "They learn the words of a song quicker than learning in school lessons."

Unlike the other deejays, Capone's phrases were clearly audible but lyrically mediocre. Rhymes for children delivered without speed, repetitive and catchy. "Master Key," "Out Of This World," and "Cassius Clay" were notable exceptions dat sounded more like Big Yout brand of music with Dennis AlCapone loosening up his tongue, diggin deep to come out heavy dubwise.

Early Big Youth

January 1975. Jamaica is a record shack, dancin floor, music man. "House of Dreadlocks" by Big Youth and "Marcus Garvey" by Burning Spear are the tunes Jamaicans a dance to in the new year sunshine. De music man is ahvin a ball. When you listen to reggae in Jamdung yu feel the sun hot an de cool breeze simultaneously. Yu see de pickney dem a dance an prance pan de street. Tourists lap it up an drink it down with Red Stripe beer, or jelly coconut water. Reggae *created* Jamaica, made it what it now is. Now dey come from the ends of de earth to see hear

More recent photographs of the great Jah Youth, Manley Buchanan.

and feel it for themselves. Dey hear it on de radio . . . Every time dem hear de soun' uptown, downtown, all roun town . . . an country too. An how dem *love* it. Dey heard about Big Yout. **"Said it was I Jim Screechy . . . an me bredda Dilly Dally . . . say we gone down de alley down whey we smoke up de colly. . ."** dey heard Big Yout . . . de deejay with de rebel sound . . . **"John Coltrane died in vain of a love supreme"** says Jah Youth, aping the Last Poets, but now he give it new meaning . . . **"so John Coltrane blow so white people blow black people mind every time, Church an State . . . hypocritical system . . . Said it was I Jim Screechy an me broda Dilly Dally. . ."**

"House Of Dreadlocks" is still selling but in Jamaica you have to strike while the iron hot, yu cyaahn dilly dally! So on this particular morning Big Yout an producer Prince Tony are upstairs in

Randy's Studio, North Parade. Yout is about to voice his next hit, a ting called "Mummy Hot Daddy Cold." Skin Flesh and Bones (featuring Lloyd Parks on bass and Sly Dunbar on drums) have already laid down the rydim for the producer, and now Big Yout, the star of the show, is ready to go. The most popular hipster in town is calmly tinkling a few notes on the studio piano. His bredrin are well attended. A Big Yout session isn't under the control of a producer, especially one so eager to record de dread and exploit him to their mutual benefit.

Yout begins slowly, lacking inspiration. He says he don't like the concept of the song but Tony (whose idea it is) is positive it's a big hit . . . when it comes. But Tony have to contend with about three other "producers," Big Yout's bredrins, in de studio. "Tony, it too commercial man, me waahn do some *creative* lyrics!" says de deejay, acting unwilling. Tony perseveres, keeping cool, aided by Randy's toast engineer Errol Thompson. A white American harmonica player begins blowing to de rydim at the producer's suggestion. Suddenly the studio catch-a-fire. "De guy hard man!" one man shout. Everyone agree. Him catch de riff in de right tone blowin' his blues straight to the soul an feet of all present. Big Yout light up with inspiration. The rest is butter.

"Big Yout blow my mind bad bad man," say Prince Tony. "You say something to him, he say suppm better to you. I'd like to see him have his own lickle house in a nice clean area. He really want to go ahead but because of de people round him and de environment he's in, it kinda hard fe him. But sometimes I think it's good becos I don't know if it's becos he's from de ghetto and he's a dreadlocks dat de public like him so much.

"The kind of thing Big Yout doin is someting different from everybody. I would say he's a great entertainer, and actor, yuknow! When yu see dat man work man yu see someting. We plan to do an album [*Dread Locks Dread*] and I hope he'll be successful. I'm not planning to rob him. I pay him ten cent royalties. He know he gon see at least 1,000 dollars. You have a lotta people who will take an advance but Big Yout want royalties, and he's better off. He's a smart bloke."

Jamaica is a record shack, music man, Big Yout fan. His popularity is due as much to his immense capacity for self-promotion as to the quality of much of his music and lifestyle. They call him Jah Yout now. And like Caesar, de messenger speak of himself in the third person, revering the ego as a ruler of thousands upon thousands.

"Is de world me a cater for me bredrin, me say me hard man. If me get de opportunity fe express meself me shake de world. Bredrin, hear me, me not talking no bias. You see dis brother Ken Boothe, him hit de chart an him up dere. You put de two o we on a show, I tell yu dat Big Yout is de dynamite! De man out of de charts is de rass claat show! Right now Bob Marley hard man. See him on a Jackson Five show comin out here now. But dem can't put me pan it cos if me go sing "Natty Universal Dread," "House Of Dread," and "Every Nigger Is A Star," just dem three songs . . . Big Yout, right now Jamaica is *mine* . . .'"

An almost legendary living enigma of reggae Jamaica. With his tongue running he is spokesman of the rebellious ghetto youth who he inspire with word sounds. Knowing he speak for many who crave better living conditions, work, pay. How could he ever run out of real things to say? Big Yout have found de work he love to do, he gladly eat the cake called reggae music. He don't need no tools he just talk what he know from the things life show in de language of the ghetto. De dread dem love it. "House of Dreadlocks" is a soccer team.

Manley Augustus Buchanan is the name he's not known by. Used to be a mechanic by day, while playing Tippatone sound system by night. "I start doin dem music and see de people *move* man. I enter Jamaica charts with seven record when me burst man! Five in de top ten an de other two 29 and 30. I had one, two, four, five, six in the two charts RJR and JBC. All of dat was juss a name, fame where I concern cos with all my famous songs, "Cool Breeze," "S90," "Chi Chi Run," that go number one in the chart down here an me dohn get not money."

When you start you record for . . .?

"Gregory Isaacs. I do 'Movie Man' from de movie *Movie Star*. It sell a few copies. At least de people's faith was in me. I follow up with another Errol Dunkley rydim name 'Cinderella.' Dat again I don't get nuttn but me just glad to hear me name. Till I get involved with the Upsetter, Phil Pratt, and Gussie Clark who make de first album.

"Like all dem album sell in England an America an me never get a cent. A guy give yu a hundred an fifty dollars, two hundred dollars. Dat is when yu wait six months. Maybe yu wait on a man for a year. De best yout me really encounter is Prince Tony becos in de space of no time, him do it de right way. Is a long time him want me to sing for him an I wouldn't do it becos like I juss don't trust people no more. Nobody trying to help me. Over de past year, with lack of promotion, people trying to fight my music style. When I get some money it will go back into de bizniz and das just to keep me alive."

I. Roy

I. Roy and Prince Tony are playing skittles in a bar on Slipe Road. It's after two in the afternoon, October 1975, not too hot but hot. October in Jamaica means sudden rain, heavy downpours dat not even taxi drivers can afford to be caught in. De bar is de bast place in town for those who got time an money to spend. Record sales are slow, producers taking stock, loading their guns for December when things begin to fly. The local favourites on the two airwaves are "Jah Live" by Bob an de Wailers, "Jailhouse" by Mighty Diamonds, "Black Star Liners" by Fred Locks, and many of I. Roy's current stock. The deejay is one of the few artists who can afford to laugh, buy yu a drink, if yu want it, and play skittles in a bar. He is the year's most successful deejay, I. Roy. He live in Spain Town, but you can hear him everywhere.

"Go get a pen and write down Carl Gayle," says I. Roy the boaster host. 'Natty Down Deh,' 'Dread In The West,' 'Welding,' 'Teapot,' 'I Man Time,' dat make five. 'Roots Man' mek six. 'Time Bomb,' 'Straight To Prince Jazzbo Head,' 'Jazzbo Ha Fe Run,' 'Mad Mad Hatter,' 'Fire Stick,' 'Padlock,' and 'Forward On' mek 13. A 13 tune me have out deh a sell man!"

Roy been living in England between November '73 and June '74 when he returned. He remained silent until February 1975 when the first of his current sellers was released. While in England Trojan released the LP *Presenting I. Roy,* containing his best shot so far—"Black Man Time"—and others just as good and better. Fresh music, exuberant rhythmic patterns giving de deejay plenty room to toast.

I. Roy de most skillful jive improviser until this day. Rhymes dat say suppm, with a easy pace, ready with vocal tricks to match de drummer. The next LP, *Hell And Sorrow,* was heavier in bass an drum and in the lyrics of black awareness. More echo, less horns. I. Roy still shinin thru in his own inimitable smile, phrasing in clear diction so yu hear every word he say even at fourt' gear. Cos only U. Roy have dat extra accelerator. Things like "Sugar Candy," "Monkey Fashion," "Forward I Man" were comic strips of Jamaican humour whereas "Deep And Heavy," "Jah Lion Jungle," and "African Descendant" were black history an culture clear-cut and accurate, from a serious tongue. Not a dance hall alone.

Not another run-of-the-mill deejay. Not an imitator in spite of the name. A original, wit a good-enuff education and superior air of a distinguished guest. Begun dejayin wit a sound system name Sounds Junior. In 1970, he made "Musical Pleasure" for producer Harry Moodie, plus "The Drifter" and "Let Me Tell You Baby." But his status rose thru "Magnificient Seven" and "Rose

I. Roy (Roy Reid), 1978.

Of Sharon," then "Black Man Time." And by dee-jaying for King Tubby's sound.

With a pleasant array of shots on the skittle table, Prince Tony sink de balls into the 100 and 200 holes regularly. But, as he does in the first game, he fails to put the red into the 200 hole and knocks down the skittle instead. Roy, with the gates closed, sinks the remaining balls laughing, teasing the producer, urging a 200 dollar wager on the next game. Tony half agrees on a smaller layout. "Me say from February till now me no give no artist no break," says I. Roy. "Tony can tell you, from de gate open me just gone clear. Everybody go pan de rail an me go a de winning post. An me naw ease up neither, yuknow. Next time me come from Prince Tony stable . . . "Me just a watch de crowd becos me ave some ideas that if me give a man, him have to go write me a big cheque. Charts, no miss. Me ave a A-to-Z tune, alphabetical tune, an anybody get dat, him certain of even £50,000 when him done, yuknow."

His run of hits has boosted his confidence to the tip of his tongue. Words flow like rain outside. Out of that 13, the one named "Welding" (released by Phonogram in England) sold well at a nationwide level, almost penetrating the big charts.

"When me come back out ya, things wasn't all dat right," says Roy. "Have to start a new life, yuknow, set up meself in all different phases. Me leave me car out here and dem swap it. My baby mother she spoil up part of my life by givin the whole a my clothes to har friend dem.

"Right now Carl Gayle a my time now. Me know why a my time too. Yusee, me give every man a concep' of me morality and culture. Most people have wondrous talent yuknow, some no ave none. Some get dem talent an hide it under de grung.

"A in a de ghetto me graduate . . . Princess Street, Rose Lane, Beeston Street where yu haffe meet every man . . . who come from Mongoose Town, who come from Salt Lane, him still haffe come deh so. Dats whey me graduate, fight, vandalism . . . some use dem wits, some use dem strength. Dats how record bizniz go. Producer who use him wits will always be de better producer. De one who use him strent can't reach far.

"Me come back from England an me sit down an use my wits. Me watch record bizniz and me hear dem say talkin' dead. Me ask who kill it. Dem say Sonny Bradshaw. Well me just make a tune straight to him head name 'Natty Down Deh,' and call him Lockjaw Lockjaw. And show him say it is easier fera camel go thru de eye of a needle than for a version [deejay record] to die."

Bradshaw, an eminent Jamaica jazz musician, is the chairman of the Jamaica Federation of Music, a musician's union, and agent for stage work, but otherwise not so enterprising. Bradshaw is deemed the man responsible for preventing many deejay records from being played on the air.

"Most people mek dem money out o singin but I mek it out o talkin. And as long as yu ave talkin tune what go inna de charts like 'Monkey Spanner' and 'Deck O Cards,' a million seller dat yuknow. Nobody can't stop talkin man, talkin was from creation. Jamaica people *love* version,

a it mek record bizniz interesting. De biggest promotion on Jamaica record bizniz been done by sound system, and sound systems play versions.

"Record bizniz owe every artist a living. Me no play no direct sound system right now, me only play Tubby's sound sometimes becos U. Roy leave it go play Soul Attorny. But yu get inspiration from sound system. When yu go dance hall sometimes yu hear certain little lyrics, ghetto lyrics yuknow. It catch on. And ghetto people like ghetto bizniz. Me come inna record bizniz fe mek it interesting. And whether de man waahn sing, whether him waahn talk, whether him waahn bark, whether him waahn name Johnny Clark, or if him even don't skylark, me no waahn find myself asleep inna Victoria Park. Me need a roof over my head and money pan my table man, so if a man a go stop 'talkin' him a go stop I. Roy from live."

Prince Tony love I. Roy's impromptu rhyming. "Jeezas Chrice bwoy, yu have lyrics fe kill no rass," he exclaims. "Whey yu get dem ting from? But Roy yu suppose to can sing if yu can write all dem ting deh."

Tony sink de red in de 200 hole and laugh. Whats yu biggest seller dis year? " 'Welding' and 'Teapot' and 'I Man Time' a de three biggess tune," reply Roy. "Dem a de giant seller."

"Yeeaaaaaah!! earthquake!! Jeezas Chrice!!" screams Tony as he knocks down the 200 points skittle and loses 1,200 points, leaving only five balls on the table, the gates closed, and I. Roy to play. The producer has been sinking the balls in every hole and from every angle but again he fails at the final fences.

"Can't give yu a chance again Tony," says Roy sinking in a white ball, "you shape too pretty a while ago. If yu never shape so pretty I would a give yu a chance. But a while ago yu get me nervous to rass claat . . . yeeooow!!!"

He sinks two more balls, laughing boasting toasting and teasing Prince Tony all thru his performance. "Jeezas Chrice!" says the producer again in disbelief.

"Too pretty men, too pretty," taunts the deejay. Suddenly he goes wild as he sinks the last two balls in one shot to win for the third game straight. "Yeeeow!" goes I. Roy. "Hey, me is a Cassius Clay in skittle, yuknow."

"Naw, naw but yu can't play me fe money man," say Prince Tony, who has been urging only a small bet since they started. "No but if me ride my pony yu hav fe stay back as Boney Maroney becos me dangerous," toasts the deejay, teasing de producer. "De shocks dem me have a pure boney man; no Prince Tony, me dangerous. Money? Well dat funny. If me tek your money yu really have fe go take bus . . . an me no want yu check yu pocket and find dust, becos de conductress will start fuss and cuss, no Prince Tony me dangerous. Me nah tek yu money Tony man. Beat yu three nice game heh?"

Me nolike when people beat me, yuknow," says Tony, lost for words. "Well inna my game yu havfe win an lose, yuknow," replies the deejay. "But even if yu blow de fuse yu still hav fe move to de blues. Cos right now me a put sand inna yu shoes Tony, three games straight. I wouldn't play yu a next game, no it ave to remain de same."

Dillinger

Before Dillinger hit de Jackpot wit' "CB200" I&I used to see him all around town always flashin' him tongue. Him walk an talk an mouth. Is a street poet of de ghetto where he spring from. Everyting de yout dem pan de corner talk about yu hear inna Dillinger record. Yu hear it same way dem talk de slang, any new slang? Check Dillinger. Is a man who do de town. When it come to rhyming, check Dillinger. When it come to de good joke check Dillinger. When it come to lip, check Lester Bullocks. Him start life wit music like "Ensom City Skank," "Crashie First

Dillinger: "MURDER!!"

Socialist," "Jah Jah Dub," then "CB200." Never mek a boring record yet, so yu can check Dillinger. Him music last for generations. Don't hear no latest Dillinger for de past three year or so but when it come to Deejay, check Crankface. Him ave a nice phrase, not easy to mistake for anyone else. Who sound like Dillinger? Har to imitate de sound dat flow like water, whose words drop like honey. Muss be de cocaine runnin aroun him brain.

Made many 45s and several LPs, among them one for Coxsone and one ("CB200") for de Chineyman. Listen to "CB": **Mercy Lord, Lord ha mercy, hold me tight yaah . . . say one dread two dread, satta pan a CB200 . . . I say to one dread yu better show me yu natty dread . . . a so de dread flash him locks an a lightin clap an a weak heart drop . . . we come ya fe dread we no come ya fe dead, we come ya fe knot we no come ya fe platt . . . say set up yuself dreadlocks for natty dwell on de mountain top . . . a**

natty dwell on de mountain side, where peace an love abide yaah. . . ."

Singer sing deejay talk. His music is de rydim girded about him in his saddle. His stirrup is his whip, his tongue. A talking ace from space setting de hot pace reggae music race. Dillinger is a commentator who can mek dem laugh it off an cuss dem same time. ". . . **Star yu waahn see first day I man give de gal I ganzee fe wash yuknow star, an yu waahn see de gal starch I man ganzee an iron it pan top a it skip, me vex!"**

A loose tongue dat chat nuff, the best rhymer in town? Come into Channel One studio straight from cold ground bed first night, come tear dung Rome with a thing called "Death In The Arena." **"For out of Garvey pistol Bag O Wire get shot, Mother Mushet betray it an she pick up two tack, say death in de Arena . . . fire bun in de Arena . . . blood run in de Arena . . . blood run in de Arena . . . no one cyaahn come in de Arena I would say . . . so lef out a Mafia, then yu come in a de house of dread . . . Hotter de battle de sweeter de victory, an dey say dat de Prophecy reveal an Swallowfield shall be de battlefield . . ."**

Babylon enemy number one. This Dillinger, the word-slinger with powaful sounds like hand grenade from a fist. Punch it out quick with a flick of the wrist. Inspiration come fast and the tongue can't resist. **"Saturday a race day a Caymannas Park, tek a lickle walk dung a Caymannas Park fe go check Arthur Sharpe, an him give us two horse. Him give us two double say it a mek trouble, fe mash it up a town, Lord . . . An when we dally up a Apex, say de bookie dem vex up a Apex, me kotch ten dolla! an dem started to holler up a Apex . . . Say me look thru de window say me sight sista Linda . . . Gal hop up pan me Fender yu saaf an tender, hop up on me Fender yu saaf an tender, yu bound to surrender cos you're a feminine gender, an I'm a masculine gender, yu too hard fe surrender . . ."**

Dillinger in action, 1978.

Prince Far I (seated, right) at Channel One.

Jah Woosh

Him burst on the scene in 1974 brimful with the toaster disease infecting his soul. He blew out his caged-in energy like a youth ready to step into badness because he can't get de food de clothes de shelter an de money in him pocket dat each an every yout desire. With a fresh new LP produced by the then-hit-maker Rupie "Wandering" Edwards. Sounds from the guts of frustration and hunger. Sounding like the Big Yout they look up to when they raise their voice, until one day they become their own giant. With tunes like "Teh Wanderer," "Crooked Skank," "Famine On Teh Land," "Chucky Jean," "Liberation," Woosh was on top of the peak. Free-roaming toasting dat was so real. Not jive talking, more live wire walking. Not a rehearsed sound, a sound of de ghetto Saturday night dance for all sufferers.

Woosh was a deejay for a small sound system name Prince Lloyd. In 1973, he cut "Angela Davis" for a small producer, then the LP for Rupie Edwards. The LP *Chalice Blaze* established Woosh as yet another toaster of ability with some steady rockin dub reggae dealing with the toaster and him dawta dem above all else. But "Weak Heart Feel It," "Peace And Love," and "Ital Forces" still carried the message of right and wrong among the poor. "Psalms Of Wisdom" was the rehearsed toaster in full bloom, able to call on the knowledge of the Prophecy for wisdom and understanding. A LP using popular rydims of the day as background music. Of his 45s, two stand out, "I'm Alright" and "Love Jah And Live," that are easy to recall.

Prince Far I

Full of surprises. The elder statesman of toasting, not becos of a long history but becos of the experience and wisdom evident in the sound of his voice, which belongs to man of maturity. The Louis Armstrong of reggae, but it's not gravel in his throat, it's a throat parched by the heat of flames of smoke of herb. The sound is the heat of Kingston, dry and husky and lazy. But is not real lazy, just the right pace, cos Far I is the slowest toaster in town. The oldest lookin. *Friendly* lookin when he show teeth, otherwise he frighten pirates away. Everyone love Prince Far I cos there ain't no choice cos the voice don't need music cos de voice is Cry Cry. They call him so cos das what they heard when he spoke. "**. . .You better love your brother as you love yourself, do unto others as they would do unto you . . . Man stand firm on the ground shall never be eaten by worm, yeah . . . hold dem Jah me say hold dem, hold dem Jah me say hold dem, I art weak but thou art strong . . ."**

With records as "Who Have Eyes To See" and "Heavy Discipline" ("**Discipline is what the world needs today, an etiquette yuknow. . . for one of the noblest things a man can do is to do the best he can . . .**"), Prince Far I begun to make himself fully heard around 1976 with Joe Gibbs as producer. Now Far I is loved and admired everywhere his records go. He represents the city of Kingston in the everyday heat of survival.

When he open his mouth to sing, the breeze do blow and the sun shine bright and whoso

hear the music start to smile. He sound like he is doing the thing he love best, to sing about a lovely girl he have a invitation from cos his desire is to be loved by everyone. Like he's dictating a letter, he sound like the old time ballad singers, so mature, so mature. Prince Far I with the feeling of love which is down on him. He chant the Psalms so he rise to fame abroad, still at home they don't regard his name. These hoarse sounds of wisdom with rydims that kick up dust, Prince Far I riding thru the valley of the shadow, the name of the songs matter not: just make sure yu hear Prince Far I before you talk bout deejay an deejay music.

Ranking Joe

The deejay carrying the swing in 1977, starred with Culture on a disco release called *Baldhead Bridge*. A quick steppin tune based on dat old song school kids in England love to sing. The one about London Bridge falling down.

Last year the deejay was known as Little Joe, and he was so good at imitating other toasters that it was easy to mistake him for another. Today he's easily detectable as the deejay who tells Mr. Finnegan not to send him no telegram. As a school yout, Little Joe started to take more than average interest in music, the music of the

Tappa Zukie

"Special livicated to all de lickle sista dem whey a wind up dem battam inna shorts . . . Oh Lawd!"

Me say de man a crash it inna Eart Iya. Tek him voice fram him toe come up thru him conscious, come up right out a him mouth an spill it out like a batterin ram fe ram de souns inna yu. Word soun powa. Fast sounds. Workin souns. Drivin souns. Him keep up de pace. Bwile it up. Ridin de ridim . . . Hot gettin hotta. Nuff ting fe say Rasta. Inspired. Chune name "Different Fashion."

Ranking Joe and friend

Tappa Zukie

ghetto, promoted and played by sound systems with regular followers. His father was a deejay and now he is one also, having been inspired by his audio-visual experiences of U. Roy, the man with his jiving talking tongue which put a nation under its spell.

He studied the records of his favourite talkers and emerged in 1974 with the debut record, "Gun Court" for the Studio One label, a sound using the song "Love Me Girl" by the Heptones as background music. His friend, a singer named Carl Dryden, encouraged the little yout, helping to tutor him in the art of jive talking in time with rydim, until the yout was ready.

"Him carry me go a Bohemia Club one time," says Joe, "a talent show ting. And me just go deh and win dat show deh. And from me see how de people react to me, an ting, me just check out Studio One."

Joe practised his art as a sound system deejay, starting out with a system called Smith the Weapon and then the famous El Paso. Nowadays, he plays Ray Symbolic.

Him is not a man falla other deejay. No, him mussy ave too much pan him brain fe do dat. ". . . Buck Buck Fish Yunno . . ." Is a man can hold yu attenshan. Caa him comin from a deep well within. *Full* to de brim wid ridim. Heat boilin over like as if time runnin out. An is too much ting fe sing right ya now fe go follow a nex man style. Afta dem nuh ave de inspiration like de I right now.

De I King Zukie. Typically Tappical Tappa. Tropical Clappa Jooky. Boilin ova. Keep it up me bredda. Keep it up. Then yu nuh hear de school pickney dem how dem love Tappa Zooky. Lickle beeny pickney cyaant even walk good an him loves Tappa Zooky. Becos I sight him a walk with him madda, holdin har hand. Have on him lilly short pants suit dis Friday nite. An him hear de chune start. Comin fram inside de bar. An Tappa say "People are you ready" an him say "Blohy" wit him lickle voice. An him madda hear him. But she never surprise. Becca she know him loves dat deh chune. Knows it by heart Rasta. Yu waan see de lickle Yout. Ka Ka!

Dillinger

But is a long time de I a mek dem way out deep down souns deh. Dem souns deh comin fram a livin reality. Caa yu feel it? Know wha Ah mean? Yeah, caa yu feel it. Come een like a batterin ram. Like a new breed a music fe come mash dung Rome. Caa Roman nuh love dat. But I betcha dem nuh teach dem dat a school. Naah man, dem teach dem bout Christopher Columbus instead. Instead of tings dem know fe demself becos dem see it pan de street. Battam inna shorts. Caa Tappa is Tappical. An Tropical.

Is a man who wear pin-stripe three-piece pan stage inna London. Place dem call Lyceum Ballroom as I would tell yu. An stirrup de crowd wid dem type soun deh. Fa dem feel it boilin over fram de deep well within. Is a man who sing say "Simpleton Simpleton Simpleton leave out badness badness badness . . ." Me say yu waan hear it man! Is a man who try fe help him bredrin an de yout in de ghetto naybahood whey him live. Doin it fram de heart. Pleadin his cause. Judge I, O Lord. Accordin to de works. Is a man who sing say "Don't eat pork it's not good for you . . ." Becos if yu nyam pork yu naw go able fe cross de Jordan River out of Babylan.

Say me respect a man who sing like how him really chat, Iya! Who chat like how him really chat, Iya . . . Is dat I a defend, Iya. A culcha dat, Iya. Love dat man. Derefore I do appreciate de I King Zooky. Ave to call him dat becaa him tek him mout an rule dem: ". . . Ya so Missa Marty A ya so Sah. A nuh whey never sweet like ya so Sah . . . Run run come fore de nite run dung, let's ave some fun and sekkle dung . . . Ya so Missa Marty ya so Sah. A nuh whey never sweet like ya so Sah. A tan ya Missa Marty yu tan ya Sah . . ."

Him juss open him mout an everyting come out fine. Keep yu on yu toe. Kip yu up . . . Kip yu movin. Mek yu waan hear more. Keep yu rockin an swing and mek yu do yu own ting. Suppose yu stick a B . . . Yu do de reggae! When yu find dat someting yu been searchin for. Or dat someone!

So go deh natty go deh with a Princess. A natty go deh natty go deh natty go deh natty go deh natty go deh natty go deh wit a Princess . . . Come with har. No one is dere to take har away . . . De dawta dem love it. Fat gyal a moggle inna shorts!

Tappa onstage, Paris.

Doctor Alimantado

U. Brown

A good deejay but many prefer the original who inspire Brown, who without shame or pride still continue in the manner he begun as a follower of U. Roy. He is fast and accurate with a sound of his own but a style that is not. Made a hit or two in the JA charts and cannot be ignored as a skillful fast-talkin toaster who appears on shows and toasts at many dances all over the island. A regular and persistent deejay in the flick of the wrist jist style.

Doctor Alimantado and his Bredrin

1976. Somewhere in the heart of Kingston, Jamaica is a dread who go by the name of Doctor Alimantado. Alimantado, he says, is pertaining to some kind of vegetable, and was the name of an ancient African prince. A name never written on a birth certificate but has been handed down thru generations. The medical part of his title was accrued while at school.

"Every school I went only my name went, I never go. I always be findin time to do suppm else. So at one stage I was kinda involve in de medical work. I did kyna sit in at de university one time. I just worm my way in, like. But becos of de feelings for music, I man couldn't learn neither. I man leave it an go play sound system a night time. But de doctor thing was forced on me by me parents becos dem did want to get me off de streets out of bad company."

Tado make records. To keep him an family going, and to tell people what he want to say about the life he see. His time an money he invest into the sound of his voice accompanied by reggae dub music. People all over buy his records. He is a serious artist. Those who have seen him on stage enjoy themselves, becos of him. He chose to be unusual, to ketch de eye. The act is good.

"How I man future look pan de scene up so?" ask Tado.

"Well, is only one tune yu ever release in England, right, is 'Best Dressed Chicken.' So unless yu get yu records released out deh your market just remain a small section of people who mostly buy import record . . ."

"Well is not dat I man wouldn't put out a record every week if I man did ave some contacts fe sell it fe I. I would even have me album on de road a'ready. But because de people who dealing with bizniz not really throwin no weight."

"Best Dressed Chicken" is a deejay tune dat use sound effects like dirt and still succeed. Music from the machine. A sound of confusion based on a gutsy rendition of the song "Ain't No Sunshine." Tado's echoing shout rises above the other voices and sounds of the machine and make itself understood. The other chickens juss flee away . . . "I call the bessed- . . . the bessed- . . . the bessed dressed chickin in de town, town, town . . ." Echo like dirt. Quality of sound whose roots dig deep into the Doc's experience. The best dressed chicken is Doctor Alimantado, who else!

Tado says he was the first to deejay for Tippatone sound system. Later toasted for Syntone, Unitone, and Intone. He cut some music around 1969 for Lee Perry. Becos of those chicken voices, Tado usually prevail upon his music with sound effects. "They add a different touch to the music," he says. In a praise unto Jah, a record called "Jah Jah Great," the voice is like a battering ram, the sound effects as lightning and thunderbolts. In 1976 came the inimitable, the effervescent "I Kill The Barber." A menacing sound delivered with the air of violence evident in the title. Balanced by humour justifying such action. Gunshots burst thru the air as Tado shouts, **"Everyone goin around saying they know who shot the barber . . . I know who shot the barber, it was Tom . . . Tom the Piper's son . . ."**

"All the records I did for producers is talking records," say Tado. "Since I start produce myself I start singin. I never get no bread off a none a dem. But becos I usually ave something doing to achieve some bread, I never have to run dung producer."

A solo operator. His discs have appeared on seven different labels owned by him. His records are sought by those who know de good reggae music in cities across the Atlantic. Despite their unsophisticated, inexpensive production they are regarded as the pick of any crop. They run out of stock. His music is dynamic, his stagework exceptional. "I man is de first local artist who go on stage inna dirty water boots and crush up pants and crush up shirt, dat was signifying one time when I used to work for the KSAC [Kingston And St. Andrew Corporation]. Clean street, yuknow, cos dats one of de many things I do to raise money to enter the recordin bizniz . . ."

"If people could just sit down and listen to my records they would have a good idea of de scene in Jamaica becos I always try and build a scene. The reason why my music have so much effect is becos I man reason wid Jah. In every walks of life, every minit of de day. So Jah really guide me, tho I guide myself. So whenever time I go to do music I ask him for some inspiration. Something dat can really help a situation.

"Like how yu have so many suffering people in the world today, I don't really think is right for me to make some whole heap a song dat really don't make any sense. So I try to do music with a certain amount of sincerity towards meself, my people and God, wherein yu have de three in one. They are the forces of the Earth . . .

"I is de son of the Father who come to teach. And to doctor the wounds of me bredda and sister out deh. Heal dem soul wid music. For I man music is a meditation dat can heal your soul and make you know yourself."

Trinity

Trinity and neighbour Dillinger shared de mutual interest in music. Dillinger was a recording artist; Trinity was not. In March 1976, Dillinger took Trinity to Channel One studio and he made his first disc, a thing called "Set Up Yourself."

So de yout become a deejay. But fame don't come so easy. He remain in the shadow of his neighbour who was riding high on the sounds of freedom.

Meanwhile, Trinity was still waiting his turn listening keenly to de sounds of Big Yout which he enjoyed more than any other. Then one day

Trinity heard the sound of music . . . "**I'm still in love with you boy. . .**" It was sweet and mellow, rocking steady. "**. . .You don't know how to love me, not even how to kiss me . . .**" It sounded like a challenge. A few days later, the deejay made a tune called "Three Piece Suit." With it he discovered something in himself, which sound those who heard wanted to hear again and again.

A short stocky youth with a dark tan inna Babylon, and a pair of dark shades. He does not struggle to attain his lyrics. His studio sessions are well attended right now, his performances well favoured. He dresses according to current style to catch the eye. Imported three-piece suit from London courtesy of former producer Prince Tony, again!

"From me a lickle yout around 12, 13, or so, me is a man usually go around sound system and hear whole heap of deejay like U. Roy and dem man deh. So me just come and me find dat it inna me too. So me just try a thing an me

succeed!"

Trinity is a good deejay. His audience which was a handful of friends now become a nation of radio listeners with the success of "Three Piece Suit." ". . . Deejay thing is a pattern thing but I don't like when a man hear yu wid lyrics and him go and do it pan a different tune. De slurring is different. De more original you come, the better yu do. Dillinger is a talented youth, him 'ave him own style. Sometimes me is a rhymer too. Still, me is a plain man. But de way Dillinger rhyme yu must laugh, dat mean him records must sell.

"You see Leroy Smart?" asks the deejay. "Is a man who live in him three-piece suit. All de while we mouth one another and thing yuknow. Sometimes we see a fat girl and me say to him 'Leroy, see a fat ting deh!' And him say to me, 'Boy, I waahn tour wid har in me three-piece suit an ting.' So me rhyme it off and say 'Up A Constant Spring.' So me kinda build it up. And me have a Earth Man shoes and diamond socks. So when yu have on dat yu kinda look way-out. So

me and Leroy mouth one another so till we make a tune."

The background music for the "Three-Piece" hit was supplied by Marcia Aitken's version of "I'm Still In Love," a song that never fails.

"Me just hear it and just love it," say Trinity. "De first day me go to Errol T and tell him dat me have a nice lyrics fe dat rydim him say me must come back another day because no time no deh today. But when I start to chant de lyrics while de rydim a play in Joe Gibbs record shop, it hold him so dat him hug me up and say 'Come now, yu can do it now.' So from de time we do it everyone inna de studio start jump so me know is a seller. It come a road now and hit, play five time a day pan radio."

Unlike other toaster Trinity doesn't want to be a singer too. "If you try to concentrate pan two things," he say, "it throw you off." In certain rural areas of JA where electricity has recently arrived, the yout show appreciation for the record-playing machine by feeding it continually

Jah Stitch

Him rip thru the crowd like a bullet with a thing called "The Killer," then de deejay himself pick up a shot in his head that turned his face, to meet the increased demand of photographers. With speed of tongue to match the pace of the flying rydims of producer Bunny "Striker" Lee, Stitch rush to the front of the deejay spirit with words like "**A natty how yu come over, a natty how yu come over, a natty jump right over an das how yu come over . . . Sayin yu were down in de valley for a very long time an a how yu come over?**" Toastin for a sound called Black Harmony, he rise up with the passion of the ghetto whey all deejay come from, and players of instruments too. And those also that live by the sword which is revealed in the music. The sound system life is the heart of the poor. Anything that spring from there spread like wildfire. Jah Stitch, the dread, don't mince words, he talk fast without rest cos it urgent. Made some good 45s but not a hit record deejay. His sounds deal strictly with the dance hall.

Trinity

with ten-cent coins. The music stop only to start again. For the sake of a lickle enjoyment the yout flee their gates to a modest little grocery shop on the hill, the one that houses the jukebox. To meet each other to make ends meet. Masculine and feminine gender seeking some kyna surrender. Whether you know or have been to Constant Spring or not, it make no difference; Trinity's disc hide no secrets."

"**Man, yu should a see me an de big fat ting, tell yu when me dub har inna Constant Spring . . .**" The tune that made Constant Spring famous. Not for its waters but for its dawtas. They don't have to be big an fat, some are not, but it's uptown. Downtown sons and uptown dawtas. "**Tell yu when me dub har pan de big bed spring, inna me three piece suit an thing, tell yu wid me diamond socks an thing, tell yu wid me Earth man shoes an thing . . .**"

121

Mikey Dread to Yellow Man

Mikey Dread

When Mikey Dread was on de radio Friday night, de whole town stay awake in dem bed. Yu hear de best an de music don't stop an de deejay know sound effects an he surely use dem, an every singer an deejay hear his tune play. Is not a dreadlocks but him name Michael "Dread" Campbell simply becos of de music he play an de way him drop dem. He wake de town wit sound.

A radio disc jock who became known throughout JA due to his roots approach. Before

Mikey Dread

Papa Kojak & Mama Liza

him mek a big hit with a ting called "Barber Saloon." When there was a gap to be filled, "Barber Saloon" fill it. The whole Jamaica laugh, an de yout dem sing it all round town.

"... **Now here come de musical disc called the barber saloon, an I'm a gemini an I was born in June**," said Mikey Dread. In a sly mocking tone he went on, "**Come ya natty dreadlocks come ya man, mek me tell yu a story ... I was walkin down de road one afternoon. I sight a natty dread in a barber saloon ... him a cut off him head an him a turn baalhead ... tell yu what a rude lickle dread like dat, dis ya dread him a ediat, him no love Selassie I, cos him no know Rastafari ...**" A funny little thing for a baal head to sing an say.

But it was a big hit for de radio deejay. His next shot, "Natty Red In A Bull Bay," was even better, the year 1978. "**Ah say I know a lickle lady out a Harbour View ... she gave dem some broth she no give dem no bread, an**

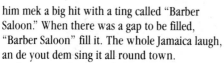

Jah Thomas

dey all become de natty dread locks dread, an so dem satta inna Bull Bay ... A so me say de natty red inna Bull Bay ..."

It speak of de plight of de poor, showing yu where and how Rasta originate. Cos de reason why natty red (plentiful) inna Bull Bay is becos de ocean charge no tax for de fish man catch, neither light bill have to be paid, neither gas nor rent. Mikey Dread say, "**Jamaica is an island in the sun, so mek we all get togeda me we sekkle dung ... out of many people we all are one, whether dreadlocks, baalhead or babylon, come mek we satta inna Bull Bay ...**"

Jah Thomas

Remembered for a tune called "The Ugly One," goes something like dis: "**Me say you may so pretty and I may so ugly but de girl say she love me ...**" A deejay with a heavy voice and a witty chant you grow to like, coming in de wake of Trinity, also from Joe Gibbs' stables.

Nigger Kojak

With a broader voice, boastful and tongue in cheek, Floyd Perch otherwise known as Pretty Boy Floyd and now Nigger Kojak, de number one baalhead deejay in JA, shave his head clean like de movie star and proudly deliver de neighbor-disturbing sounds called "Hole In The Bucket," a well-known song all over de globe. In de same line, also a big corker for eager sparring partners of rub-a-dub was "Fist To Fist Rub-A-Dub."

Papa Kojak & Mama Liza

Papa Kojak say a hundred gyal have to brush him teet', so he expect admiration. Along with sidekick Mama Liza, both from de ghetto, and she build plump and favour a shinin star for de future. Kojak can't tek de mash mout gyal dem cos after him "**fix har mout an carry har out him see her at rum bar with man a drink stout.**" And Liza she can't tek de cast-eye boy dem. But Mama Liza a dub it sweet so a thousand

bwoy haffe rock to de beat. An a million boy haffe clean out dem teet'. "Sky Juice" the cheapest drink in de city. It captivate de imagination and side with the youth by talkin bout de thing dey demand from de juice man at de school gate. Kojak and Liza are lively and dangerous, watch it!

Michigan & Smiley

Iron sharpening iron in tune with the people of dem community. When natrality flow, you find dem community. It's de sound of freedom. Like when yu free fe talk and yu know how to tek advantage, so dat your lecture become de chant of a nation, like a anthem. Things dey say dat touch de people heart an soul. Like "One Love Jam Down," which as dey say "cause a controversy in dem community ..."

It says, "**De social barriers bruk down, togeda inna one love Jamdown ... de foreign an de local a dub to de Rastaman vocal ... de reggae an de jazzband tune een pan de same one band stand ... de Risto (aristocrat) an de dreadlocks come togeda in a ital wedlock ... if yu rich, poor, wise or dumb, we all rock togeda in reggae Jamdown ... if yu black, white, yellow or brown, we all rock togeda in reggae Jamdown ...**"

So dem tongue chant in time and every line in rhyme. They began in 1978 with a ting called "Rub-A-Dub Style." Backed by Alton Ellis bubbling Studio One rydim of "I'm Just A Guy," they climb till dey reach de top cos de sound flow nonstop and everyone love rub-a-dub.

At Reggae Sunsplash 2 MoBay JA, the duo star de show with full crowd approval while recording a live version of "One Love Jam Down" called "We Need A One Love" with new lyrics speaking for everyone: "... **About de sound dat cause de controversy in de community becos of I an I ability ... Brothers and sisters here come the musical counter reaction for your musical satisfaction yaah ... We need a one love inna Jamaica, we need a**

lone love inna Jamaica . . . cos things an time really gettin slow, a strictly reggae music mek de money flow . . . so reggae music in Jamaica, it control de nation out ya and aaah . . ."

Errol Scorcher

A big success with "Roach In The Corner," a tune using de same rydim and melody as "Nice Up De Dance," but Scorcher's tune was still an original. **"A roach inna de corner . . . bim kill him!"**

But de roach is known among yout in town as a germ carrier among certain female. Talking about those who go from man to man. An when yu go dance if yu open de toilet door an look inside, yu will see all de roach dem flyin about. But Scorcher say him no romp with de roach, him use Baygon spray. A very fast-selling tune, tho banned by radio becos of scornful lyrics. But all schoolchildren know it by heart. Bim kill him! Scorcher say **"If me use Real Kill me a go see dem still, use Baygon dem a run ration, say me naw leave me Baygon . . ."**

General Echo

De deejay was shot and killed by police in Kingston on November 23, 1980. Two of his sound system colleagues, Flux and Big John, were executed with him. Police said they stopped Echo's car and demanded a search but the occupants opened fire on dem. The police returned fire killing all three. A .38 revolver with three live rounds and three spent shells was taken from the body of one man.

Echo was a top-ranking deejay who predicted in his massive number one hit "Arleen" that "dis ya sound ha fe reach number one." Using the same rydim as Big Yout's "All Nations Bow," it sold and sold and would not move from number one for weeks. Echo used to have his own sound, Echo Tone Hi Fi. His first good seller was "People Are You Ready" in 1978, then "A Little Dis A Little Dat." "Titanic" and "International Year Of The Child" get nuff air play as minor hits. But all his tunes have a catch lyricwise, the witty "Miss Falla Fashion," the informative kung fu song "Drunken Master," which was another chart-scorer. A pity he go so soon.

Lone Ranger

A talker with a bounce in his voice, with a roll of de tongue in "Barnabas Collins," the vampire tune which go high on the national charts and so established the clever toaster from the Studio One stable. Listen to "The Answer," yu will hear the influence of Dillinger. But de yout full of vibes, he love his trade. And so "Love Bump" prove it as the best selling rydim right now in Jamaica. Cos he know how to tell de story bout love bump. A reggae hymn to herpes. Yu ever hear it?

"**. . . How de love bump stay sah. How de love bump stay sah? Say dat it come out pan yu face like a dyam disgrace . . . come out inna boil mek yu features look spoil . . . bruk out lickle more an den it tun out inna sore, a love dat a love love bump . . ."**

A deejay with a future, a lucky lip. **"Say dat me walkin down de street an a sexy girl me meet, walkin down de street an a sexy girl me meet, first me say me like then me say me love . . . de gyal say she say she waahn go show . . . So I took her to the show that she wanted to go, took her to the show that she wanted to go . . . a lot of entertainment, nuff excitement, lickle after dat she she say she waahn refreshment . . . A wha yu gi de dawtaah Ranger, a whey yu gi de dawta? Ice mint an ice waatah, Rasta me did bruk! Ice mint an ice waata."**

Not his own original, but de best is de best. Like a actor he toast de reydim with interpretation, as one gifted to do so. With de right rydim from rock steady Studio One, home of Coxsone. De tune get yu singin till yu surprise to find yu know every line.

"**. . . Kiss me neck, say when me reach home she back a cutlass, when me reach home she back a cutlass, she say AH gwy chop yu kill yu cos yu nearly mek me dead wid gyas! Ah love dat a love love bump, a love dat a love love bump. . . ."**

Right now, every lickle yout who can mumble de name of Bob Marley are quick to say "Bob Marley, Bob Marley!" as soon as dey sight a dread. Juss becos de dread is not around for dem to see in person. Becos of all de news an views and photos an music publicisin the Reggae Prophet. And now Errol the Roach Scorcher put out a version called "Tribute To . . ." and every time I hear de sound, every day, music increase, reggae music increase. Love Bro B.

Lui Lepke

Lui "Elecric Chair" Lepke is de talk of deejays after a triumphant Reggae Sunsplash 1981 in MoBay. Lepke is a tall dreadlocks crouching and bending at his knees, trampling the stage floor with a mike to his mouth, word flow easy. Audience love it. Can't buy his records anywhey in dis town, got to go abroad. Lucky Lui, dey love de way he toast himself **"My name is Lui Lepke . . .!"**

He put words togeda, give dem de right tone, a born talker, love to win crowd applause. New on the scene with de right tune at de right time, his tribute to Bob, which the people salute as they take kindly to the dread with the ability to call himself Lui Lepke without apology. And when he go on stage him really put on a good show cos de crowd love every word and call him back for more. Cos he keep sayin, **My name is Lui Lepke!** an he rhyme it with what he have to say line by line.

But right now, who can keep up with these

Lone Ranger

Errol Scorcher

Althea and Donna

123

word-sellers of the loose lip on the jive wire? There's one born every minute. So many have not been named. Who am I to dictate or judge or select to mention? What of Ranking Devon who chant "All Nation Have To Bow" whose title tek yu forward to Big Yout, talkin about "**Go dung pan yu knees an pray to Mahssa God . . .**"

Eek A Mouse

Yu only as good as yur latest music, an de charts nuh partial. Still, in JA exclamation dey frown when de deejay chant up the nation. And when dey play dem charts dey have to play a yout name Eek A Mouse, a name from a comic exclamation. Cos dey say no one in dis world will understand what him a say. Dem fool, eeh? Even in Japan dey will sing like Jamaican without fullness of overstanding. Cos dem feel it, dem know it. Like de lickle yout dem.

Yes, in the hands of de toasters grown men an women become but children. A Wa Do Dem? Dem love reggae music, das all. Some don't like

to admit it. But it put corn inna dem pocket, so dem can't stop it. Now how can you resist a natural yout like Eek A Mouse singin a thing name "Wa Do Dem"? Listen, he talkin bout de way people watchy watchy, de way how some a dem watchy watchy! How people love to judge, in JA. ". . . **Me tek a walk go a Kingston Mall, whole heap a people juss a start to laugh, becos a she too short an a me too tall, she too short an a me too tall . . . hey, a wa do dem a wa do dem dem dem, for me no kno oh . . .**"

Some sit on jury to stop some from gettin thru an dey do . . . at first. But when de people buy de record and demand to hear it on the radio all patron have to bow. And dey want to dress up reggae music for de tourist trade. How do dey feel when de dread Mutabaruka get up in front of de tourists an tell dem "**Black man nuh fe stay inna white man yuntry . . .**" Like yu insult yu guest. Soon dey bring a jury fe stop certain singer go pan stage . . . but the voice of the people say dem waahn hear deejay. Cos when

deejay record play, de whole crowd start to swing an sway.

—*Carl Gayle*

Update:

Yellow Man (Winston Foster) exploded Jamaica in 1982 with his wry confidence, effortless crowd control and albino persona. By the summer of that year he had achieved cultural power unmatched since U. Roy was at his peak, able to work a crowd anywhere in the Caribbean better than any other deejay. Yellow Man is of course being over-recorded at this writing, but his talent is still expanding and should survive the abrasive exploitation of talent to which all deejays are prone when they get real hot. Deejays have taken over reggae now; as this is written, even Gregory Isaacs or Dennis Brown would have to open for Yellow Man, or risk embarrassment. A recent headline in the *Daily Camanian Compass* (Cayman Islands) said it all: "Yellow Man—Just Cool."

Yellow Man (Winston Foster); Eek A Mouse (Ripton Hilton), the greatest improvising scat-singer in deejay history; and Lui Lepke with young deejays Ruffy and Tuffy.

10

Feel It in the One Drop

The Kingston recording studios are the laboratories and research facilities in which reggae music is nurtured and developed. In the studios the musicians, the producers, the singers and the deejays interact to form a cultural cottage industry whose craft has enticed the whole planet. In this section, **Stephen Davis** looks at the world of the Kingston studios to see how many musicians they can support, and how reggae music actually gets made. Producer/shaman Lee Perry is interviewed in a vain attempt to procure information. And **Crispin Cioe** monitors the influential riddim battery of Sly & Robbie. These days, those two are carrying the swing for reggae in general.

Notes from the Kingston Studios

Kingston, Jamaica, West Indies, in early 1981. Somewhere in Germany, Bob Marley is rumored to be either dying or already dead. Nobody really knows for sure, and those that do aren't talking. The silence, the deathwatch, makes people jittery. Everyone who cares is aware that with Bob gone, some things are bound to change for the reggae culture. The denizens of reggae's high stratosphere are whispering that Island Records boss Chris Blackwell hath proclaimed: if Bob dies, reggae *mosh*. Meaning, one can only assume, that the reggae force field could be in trouble without its dancing, leonine figurehead. In Kingston's studios and reggae yards, the attitude is a nervous *wait-and-see*. And during cocktail hour by the pool at the New Kingston Hotel, a band called the Caribs is playing subdued but letter-perfect Wailers songs in tribute to the great legend who is known to be suffering so far across the sea.

Kingston itself is half closed down, still recovering from the violent *rigor mortis* of destabilized socialism. Many of the Jamaican capital's citizens are abroad, in New York or Miami or Toronto or London, widening their horizons. With a new government enthroned, there's a pervasive vibe of businessman's optimism in the smokey air, a feeling of relief and survival, of hope and some semblance of national unity. The big song of the moment is Hugh Griffith's happy roots trance-rocker "Step It in Ballet" (pronounce the final t) on the Greedy Puppy label, glorifying and celebrating the black, wonderfully cheap-chic flat-soled shoe the Chinese mainland exports by the billion and which hit Jamaica like a hurricane last year:

Yu nuh hear?
Man and woman justa step it in ballet
Man and woman justa step it in ballet

Hugh Griffith

Tuff Gong studio

Me wife Paulette she a step it in ballet
Me sweetheart Annette she a step it in ballet
Me sister Yvonne she a step it in ballet
Me brother Devon him a step it in ballet
Yu nuh hear?
Man and woman justa step it in ballet

Jamaicans call these Chinese slippers ballet shoes; they're such great shoes that I'm wearing a pair as I type this up.

Despite being semi-shut-down, the Kingston reggae world still manages to hum along at its own pace. Right now it seems that singer Gregory Isaacs is the undisputed and supreme Cool Ruler of roots reggae. (Gregory has his own spectacular African Museum billboard display downtown.) Up on Hope Road, Marcia Griffiths is recording by night at Bob Marley's Tuff Gong studio. Judy Mowatt, supported by Freddie Mac-Gregor's One Vibe Band, is playing a soulful revue called "Black Woman Experience" in a theater across town. Bunny Wailer is in the city to record (he has a farm in Portland parish), and can be occasionally glimpsed cruising Slipe Road and Orange Street in his Land Rover. At Channel

Gregory Isaacs, 1978.

Opposite: Earl "Chinna" Smith, avatar of reggae guitar.

Him get a bullet in de left lung
At de Washington Hilton
Him get a bullet in de left lung
At de Washington Hilton

Later on, at four thirty in the morning, you can get curry goat and rice and Red Stripe at an all-night joint uptown called Gino's. The spicy and delicious meat, almost completely free of fat, is noisily sucked off the bone and washed down with the cool light-tasting beer. As the hot orange tropic dawn comes splashing over the twi-lighted black mountains to the east of the city, you realize . . . that it's *great* to be down in Kingston town once again.

In the early days of ska and rock steady, the studios were dominated by a small handful of professionals who played on almost every recording session. During the 1960s, the prominent session musicians included such local stars as the late Don Drummond and Rico Rodriguez on trombones; Roland Alphonso, Tommy McCook and Gaynair on tenor sax; Lester Sterling, Karl "Cannonball" Bryan, and Deadly Hedley Bennett

One studio, a young dub master named Scientist is digging new psychic tunnels in dub music. His sound seems like a lantern swinging at the bottom of a mineshaft.

The big dance hall of the day is Skateland, and the action there gets very steamy after midnight on a Friday. The sound system is rocking to a horribly obscene catechism over the rootsiest bass culture dub music imaginable. A young deejay who calls himself Lui Lepke (after the late founder of Murder Inc.; the television series "Gangster Chronicles" having been extremely popular among Jamaican youth in the preceding months) is on stage toasting away for hundreds of adoring, chanting fans who know every word and nuance of Lui's every rap, and frolic and pour beer over each other as their hero churns out good-natured doggerel at the expense of U.S. president Ronald Reagan, who had nearly been assassinated that very morning:

on alto sax; Baba Brooks, Raymond Harper, and Johnny "Dizzy" Moore on trumpet; Theophilius Beckford, Jackie Mittoo, and Gladstone "Gladdy" Anderson on piano; Ernest Ranglin and Jah Jarry on guitar; Lloyd Brevette, Cluett Johnson and the legendary "Blues" on bass; the great Lloyd Nibbs, Drumbago, and Hugh Malcolm on drums. From these musicians came the various all-star bands of the '60s: the Skatalites, the Karl Bryan Orchestra, Rolando Al and the Soul Brothers, the Don Drummond All Stars, and Tommy McCook and the Supersonics.

By the time American pop star Paul Simon travelled to Kingston in 1971 to record under the supervision of producer Leslie Kong, the ska boom had passed and the available session talent had boiled down to a smaller group of players. Among the personnel on the Simon sessions were Hux Brown on guitar, Wallace Wilson on rhythm guitar, Neville Hinds on organ, Jackie

Jackson on bass, Winston Grennon on drums and Denzil Laing on percussion. (Today Hux Brown and Jackie Jackson are in Toots and the Maytals' touring band, while drummer Grennon is a resident of New Jersey and mans the battery for Kid Creole and the Coconuts.)

Since then, a new generation of players has risen to dominance in the reggae world (see *Session Musicians*).

The amount a hard-working studio musician can make playing reggae sessions in Kingston varies from player to player. There are very few standards in terms of session fees, because the musicians' union is only still growing in influence and producers generally pay whatever the traffic will bear. Until and through 1980, the standard musician's fee was simply $50 per tune, with session superstars like Sly and Robbie charging $100 per tune (although both Sly and Robbie will play for union scale or even for free if they happen to like a particular artist).

In 1981, the union decided vaguely that session fees were supposed to go up, and relative chaos ensued in the studios. Some players started charging $80 per tune, some $70, some $60, and some would play for as little as $40 per tune as well as a big draw of herb on the side.

There's a pecking order in reggae, and the musicians (like those all over the world) form themselves into cliques and informal brotherhoods. The absolute session elite consists of Sly & Robbie, Ranchie or Duggie on bass, Ansel Collins on piano, Keith Sterling and Robbie Lyn on keyboards, and Sticky on percussion. These musicians (basically, the old Revolutionaires) are reggae Right Stuff, along with a couple of other veterans like keyboardist Winston Wright.

The rest of the musicians are roughly divided into amorphous Uptown and Downtown cliques. Downtown is Channel One and the area around the North Parade and Chancery Lane, an alley off the Parade that contains Gregory Isaacs' African Museum record shop and the legendary Idlers' Rest, a hangout where musicians roast fish, roll spliffs, and reason with one another. Poorer musicians, and those who haven't as yet made it, tend to be Downtown musicians. Roots Radics, the intense young band that backs Gregory and Bunny Wailer, are a decidedly Downtown band. Uptown is Joe Gibbs studio, Tuff Gong and Harry J. A good example of an Uptown band is Lloyd Parks and We the People.

The interesting thing about the singer, deejay and musicians' cliques is that they have very little interchange. It's the usual petty rivalry one finds among musicians all over the planet. In Kingston, the session players look down on the singers and the deejays; the singers think they're superior to the rhyming and rapping deejays, and the deejays tend to sneer at everyone else because they're not roots enough.

By the end of 1981, sessions fees had theoretically gone up again, to roughly $100 per tune. Residual payments to musicians are still unheard of. One result of the price hike was that fewer recording sessions included horn players while the producers got used to the new fee scale.

Recording Studios*

Channel One

Channel One is considered by most musicians to have the best sound in Jamaica, especially for dance hall-style music. The emphasis here is on classic dry and heavy bass and drums. However, some musicians claim Channel One is the most poorly maintained studio. The piano is never in tune. The tape recorder stops in mid-take. The direct boxes never work. The bass amp and the organ are said to emit strange noises, and one or more of the guitar amps are usually on the blink. They either don't use or don't have an alignment tape for their 16-track recorder, which is roughly analogous to an auto mechanic doing a tune-up without a timing light. Musicians say it is also rather difficult to hear the other instruments while they're playing because they don't get earphones, and the amps are turned down very low and hidden behind baffles. Consequently, working at Channel One is often a slow process due to equipment trouble.

Yet, in spite of all this, most musicians say it's a lot of fun to play there. The sound they get on the playback is the best in Jamaica, and the psychic vibrations in the studio are very comfortable. Despite its location in the heart of the ghetto, Channel One is one of the nicest studios at which to hang out. This is because the owners, the Hookim family, have lived in the area all their lives (and some are said to still live upstairs). All the people in the area, and many of the musicians as well, have also been around for years, so the general atmosphere is akin to that of a giant extended family. Channel One's engineers are especially known as great dub masters, and this somehow spills over onto everything produced at the studio. Gospel music, disco tracks, slow ballads—everything eventually sounds like *Ital Dub Vol. 9*. Bunny Tom Tom, who engineered most of Sly & Robbie's Taxi hits, was the best engineer there, but eventually moved over to Compass Point studios in Nassau. (He started out fixing motorcycles for the Hookims in the other part of Channel One, which is a combination bike shop and jukebox and slot machine servicing area.) As an engineer, Ernest Hookim is supposed to be very good, but rarely works a session now unless specifically requested. Moxie (Lancelot McKenzie) is currently the most versatile and competent engineer, as well as the easiest to work with, according to many musicians. Others say his ears aren't as yet of the quality of Bunny Tom Tom's. Another engineer known as Solgie is also said to be very good, but rather slow. Barnabas (the drummer) is great as a mixer, but not so hot at recording a live session. At this writing, Scientist is one of the principle engineers at Channel One, and is

Producer Harry Johnson and Sheila Hylton

considered by some musicians to be a real pain. He came from King Tubby's (replacing Bunny Tom Tom) on the strength of his international reputation as a dub mixer. But Tubby's is only a four-track studio that doesn't record live sessions, so Scientist came over unfamiliar with a 16-track facility and the art of recording musicians live. To his credit, he is the reigning dub mixer in Jamaica.

Joe Gibbs Studio

According to many seasoned session players, Joe Gibbs has the next best sound in Jamaica after Channel One, and is also one of the best places to work. Whether they like Joe Gibbs or not depends on whether they like engineer Errol T's sound. Most do, but a few say that everything recorded there sounds just like Errol T and nothing else. Musicians actually get earphones at Joe Gibbs, although several guitarists complained about the quality of the lead guitar amp. Errol T is the best engineer at "punching in," and works very fast and efficiently. The sound he gets from

Singer Rudy Thomas in the control booth at Joe Gibbs' studio.

the guitar is very stylized and unique. Some don't care for it, especially guitarists, but it does fit well in Errol T's contracted sonic universe and is a valid creation of its own. Some musicians find recording at Joe Gibbs to be difficult because strange and unsavory types are always running in and out (the place is a big hangout), yelling and banging on doors. Errol T's two assistants, Rudy Thomas (the singer) and Oswald "Trini" Palmer, are both very talented, although currently very much in the shadow of the mighty Errol T. Many players say that in terms of engineers and layout, Joe Gibbs is the most pleasant studio to work at. The troublesome hangers-on are offset by the presence of a terrific foodshop next door run by Mother D, a world-weary ghetto housewife who is a marvelous (if slightly unsanitary) chef.

Harry J Studio

Several players maintained that Harry J has the worst sound in Jamaica and is poorly main-

tained. Bass notes can barely be distinguished upon playback. They don't have two guitar amps, so lead and bass guitars are both taken direct and both played back through an inferior monitor which makes it difficult to tell one from the other. On the other hand is the beautiful location (on Roosevelt Road in uptown Kingston) and the presence of Sylvan Morris, a great engineer when he wants to be. In other words, if he doesn't like a musician or his song, that musician will get a lousy recording. If he respects a player or singer, he'll do state-of-the-art work. Morris is especially known for the high quality of his live sound and mixing abilities. One guitarist who has worked all over the world reported that Morris got the best acoustic guitar sound he had ever heard, comparable to the most advanced Los Angeles studio, and especially astounding considering the general state of affairs at Harry J. The studio vibes are also very relaxing, and the place itself is a nice hangout especially when the boss—Harry Johnson—is around. He's a funny and very human man. And it was in his studio

that Bob Marley and the Wailers recorded what many believe was their best music.

Tuff Gong

This is the studio built for Bob Marley at his former residence on Hope Road. Tuff Gong has fantastic equipment and is very well maintained. However, some musicians say that actually doing sessions there is very claustrophobic, as seven musicians, a lot of instruments and equipment, and three or four keyboards are squeezed into a tiny, even miniscule, space. The engineers are uniformly excellent. Steven Stewart, a former musician himself, is one of the best engineers in Jamaica, always seeming to get everything sounding hot and right and tight. Errol Brown is very good as well, and Chiao Ng is pleasant to work with but is said to still be developing his ears to the level of the other two. Some musicians claim that Tuff Gong is no fun as a hangout because a lot of phony dread-style hustlers congregate there, as well as a lot of Back-to-

Africa types with big chips on their shoulders. Some players have said they don't appreciate Tuff Gong's rhythm sound particularly, but the studio does get superb keyboard, horn and vocal sounds, and the guitar never sounds anything less than great. In general, an extremely professional and well-run recording facility.

Dynamic Sounds

This is the studio-of-choice of foreigners (Stevie Wonder, Rolling Stones, Joe Cocker) who choose to record in Jamaica. Surrounded by barbed wire and under close guard in a bad area of Kingston, it's impossible for musicians to hustle sessions because one can't get in unless one is expected. Inside, the control room is on a lower level than the musicians, and the studio proper is brightly lit with fluorescent light and furnished in what looks like Swedish modern. One musician felt the place was like an operating room. The equipment is modern and well maintained, and the whole layout is very spacious and cozy-seeming.

It's also slightly sterile, and wealthy pop stars can forget they're in Jamaica at all, so detached is the inner studio from the local reality. Geoffrey Chung is widely acclaimed the best engineer in Jamaica. Horn players say he's the only Jamaican to know how to record horns properly. In terms of sound, one hears many of the same comments as those concerning Tuff Gong—very clean, clinical, precise, and without much funk; but Dynamic has a wonderful aura of spaciousness, especially when Geoffrey Chung is at the board, that no other studio seems to get. You can hear this on the Rolling Stones' *Goats Head Soup,* which was recorded there.

Studio One/Downbeat

Clement S. (Coxsone) Dodd's studio, the scene of some of the greatest moments in reggae history. With Dodd semi-emigrated to Brooklyn, the studio is no longer open on a regular basis.

King Tubby's

A four-track studio used mostly for voicing and mixing. Tubby is the father of Jamaican engineering, but the studio is antiquated and live sessions aren't played there.

Aquarius

A studio with a poor reputation. Musicians say the place is ugly, clinical, unpleasant, and has poor sound. Many people say they never heard anything come out of there sounding good. Mostly used to record commercials and other non-reggae material.

The Black Ark

Lee Perry's studio, located in his back yard in the suburbs of Kingston. Great music has been recorded there, but Perry himself, one of the greatest of Jamaican producers/engineers, often displays erratic behavior and the studio is said to be closed.

Joe Gibbs (second from right) with Jacob Miller

A Word on Producers

Anytime you see the words "produced by" on a reggae record, that indicates who put up the money. It rarely has any artistic or technical meaning these days. Most of the producers don't really know much about that side of music. An example is Harry J, of whom one musician said: "He doesn't know how to tell you what he wants, but at least he knows what he wants. He'll just have you sit in the studio and fiddle around until you come up with what he wants. He *knows* it when he hears it."

Another musician describes the role of the prominent producer GG (Alvin Ranglin) in a typical recording session: "Basically, GG lets [bassist] Ranchie run his sessions. And most musicians appreciate GG because he doesn't know anything about music, and he knows he doesn't. He might come into a session, say 'how yuh doin', we're doing this artist and this artist, we're doing ten tunes today, you're playing and you're playing,' and then he leaves to go to the bank. Ranchie makes sure it's a good take and tells the engineer how to balance it, and keeps track of who played on what song. Then GG comes back and listens to it and says OK, or work a little faster, or whatever."

Aquarius studio

Manning the record stamper at Federal.

Rhythmic Formats

Before Sly Dunbar revolutionized reggae drumming by introducing new rhythms, the standard reggae format had the drummer playing in a style called *one drop,* characterized by the bass drum coming on two and four. This was the old rock steady style of drumming, and its masters were Carlie Barrett of the Wailers, Santa Davis, and Horsemouth Wallace, the last having played on many of the primordial Studio One sessions that had literally invented modern Jamaican music. One element of this style was what might be called a West Indian *clave,* a variation of the

Sly Dunbar, the father of modern Jamaican rhythm.

classic Bo Diddley rhythm—*dum de dum de dum, dum-dum.* (Some Latin drummers maintain that they hear *clave* in *every* reggae song.)

Post-1972 reggae drumming is synonymous with Sly Dunbar. He played a good *one drop,* but he also added a sheet-lightning cymbal style he called *flyers.* In 1975–76, Sly started playing eight to the bar on the bass drum compared to 16 or 32 on the high-hat cymbal. That's the beginning of the style called *rockers.* One got a faster feel from the high-hat action, but the tempo of the music was actually slowing down a little. The other term for this style was *militant.*

This mode was changed again by Sly in 1979–80. The new style was known by some as *rub-a-dub,* though some people (like Bob Marley) were calling it *one drop* again. Here the bass drum didn't play eight to the bar anymore, and the tempo is sped up almost to that of rock steady. An example is the big J.C. Lodge hit from 1981, "Someone Loves You Honey." For the first time in reggae, the bass drum comes *off* two and four.

Now, every time Sly goes on tour somewhere, he comes back to Jamaica (or Compass Point,

Dean "Youth Sax" Fraser, one of Kingston's top ranking reedmen.

Nassau, where he usually now records) with a new drum style, and everybody follows him. This is the reason that Sly & Robbie literally *are* reggae music these days. They tour a lot, listen very carefully, and pick a lot of things up. Musicians who have been to Sly's house in Kingston say there isn't a reggae record in the place, but a lot of American funk and disco records: War, Kool and the Gang, Chic, Rick James. A guy asked why, and Sly is supposed to have said that since he *is* rockers, he didn't have to listen to it at home.

The point is that all these rhythms co-exist in the studios. There's even a new style just breaking, a sort of reggae-funk beat where the bass drum comes in on one. Any drummer who wants to work has to play it.

In reggae, there are certain familiar bass/drum formats that have their own names—*Chiang Kai Shek, Charlie Chan, High Fashion, Joe Frazier, Bush Master,* rub-a-dub, *Satta Amassagana;* but these are not standardized, since so many records have been made from variations of these rhythms. For example, *Queen of the Minstrels* is also known as *rub-a-dub* style. *Bush Master* is now called *M-16,* taking into account advances in technology. *Satta* is always called *Satta.* A rhythm might be named by any of the records made from it, or just conveyed by the first part of the bass line. Rhythms generally, but not always, stay in the same key as the original version, unless the singer who happens to be working the session can't sing it.

A Typical Roots Session

Seven musicians, the standard reggae configuration, are on the date. Bass and drums, piano and keyboard, rhythm and lead guitar, percussion. If it's a typical ($50/tune—ten tunes/day) roots session, they'll be recording on four tracks: drums on one channel, bass on another channel, everything else on the third channel, and the singer on the fourth channel.

Take a typical roots singer who comes in with a tune, maybe Barry Brown or somebody else. The singer doesn't play an instrument and usu-

ally has no idea what key he sounds good in (although most Jamaican singers can sound good and on pitch at any interval). He'll have no idea of the bass line for his song, no idea of an arrangement. He'll start singing his song to the piano player, who might be Gladdy (also known as Jah Stone), who will work out chords for the song within three minutes, if the singer has anything worthwhile together at all.

Then the piano player will tell the chords to the other musicians and they'll try to thrash out the song. Often Gladdy will also tell the singer when to sing and will try to keep him in time. Most singers have problems with time because they want to squeeze so many words in. So in reality, Gladdy is the co-composer of many of these songs. He usually composes the bridge and writes the words for it too.

Sometimes the musicians will insist on doing introductions. Then they'll run down the tune twice, and then record a take. Maybe half an hour has elapsed since the singer walked in.

The drums usually foul the first take. The second take is more often than not the version you hear on record. A great deal of that pure roots reggae feel comes from the musicians not really being familiar with the song, especially on rootsy sessions downtown. If you listen to many reggae singles under headphones, you can usually hear someone saying *"bridge."* The reason you might hear so many wrong notes or missed notes on reggae records is because you're hearing so many first and second takes.

Despite all the various myths, ganja use is not all that pervasive among musicians in the studios. It's the ubiquitous hangers-on whose brain-fogged state creates the impression of terminal chaos. Sessions are interrupted by hardcore dreadlocks smashing at the door screaming "LION OF JUDAH! LET I IN!! LION OF JUDAH!!! KALI HERB!!!!" On hearing the playback, the dreads flash their locks, step high in time and more shouting and testifying ensues. " LION OF JUDAH! MURDEROUS STYLE!!!!!"

—S.D.

Reggae Bands †

Session Musicians

The Wailers: Bob Marley's recording and touring band.

Word Sound & Power: backing for Peter Tosh; individual musicians play sessions.

Lloyd Parks & We the People Band: backing for Dennis Brown; backing for most Jamaican stage shows; they release their own records and individuals play sessions.

Zap Pow: dormant; the horns occasionally record as a group; individuals play sessions and stage shows.

Soul Syndicate: backing for Big Youth and U. Roy; the group occasionally releases its own records; some musicians have emigrated, while some still play the Kingston studios.

Fabulous Five: stage shows, musicals, revues, Rita Marley's backing band.

Generation Gap/Twelve Tribes Band: stage shows, some sessions.

Inner Circle: dormant since Jacob Miller's death.

Revolutionaries: a.k.a. Revolutionaires. dormant; used to back Culture; individuals play sessions.

Roots Radics: the only group to play sessions regularly *as a band;* plus backing for Gregory Isaacs and Bunny Wailer.

Chalice: own stage shows, records, dances; along with Roots Radics, Chalice are the hot newcomers.

In Crowd: own records and tours; rarely appear in Jamaica.

One Vibe: stage shows; backing for Judy Mowatt and Freddie MacGregor.

Gladiators: own records and tours; occasional sessions as a band.

What follows is a census of active session musicians and singers/deejays in Kingston as of 1981. As a precise list it is, of course, already outdated because the comings-and-goings of musicians in general are notorious. However, it does represent a general picture of how many active musicians can support themselves on the Kingston music scene. While not being exhaustive, the musicians who helped to compile the list feel nobody has been left out. Some famous names (Family Man, for example) are missing because they have given up doing sessions for other people. The singers and deejays were chosen for the frequency of appearances at stage shows, on dance posters and in the recording studios. Again, many famous names are currently inactive and aren't included *only* for that reason.

The names are listed in *approximate* order of their popularity with established producers and other musicians, but this is an *extremely* sensitive area and it should be noted that these are subjective judgements at best. Names appearing after the dotted line are in no special order, and are people who, for one reason or another, play less frequently. This has nothing to do with ability, as a musician like Cedric Brooks or Steve Golding might be a master musician, but also might not look for session work very often. Bands are listed in no particular order, with special areas of influence in parentheses. Spellings are 95 percent accurate. It should also be mentioned that there is a fairly high turnover rate in session personnel, but not as rapid as the turnover rate of singers and deejays. Three years ago, this census would differ by 30 percent.

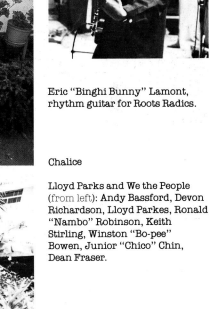

Eric "Binghi Bunny" Lamont, rhythm guitar for Roots Radics.

Chalice

Lloyd Parks and We the People (from left): Andy Bassford, Devon Richardson, Lloyd Parkes, Ronald "Nambo" Robinson, Keith Stirling, Winston "Bo-pee" Bowen, Junior "Chico" Chin, Dean Fraser.

†One reason relatively few young reggae bands are on the scene is because the austerity programs and import restrictions effective in Jamaica from 1976 through 1981 made it difficult or impossible to import electric instruments into the country. And it's hard for young musicians to learn to play without them.

Drums

Lowell (Sly) Dunbar[1]
Carlton (Santa) Davis
Mikey (Boo) Richards
Lincoln (Style) Scott

- - - - - - - - - - - -

Barnabas
Calvin McKenzie
Devon Richardson
Leroy (Horsemouth) Wallace
Eric (Fish) Clarke

Bass

Robbie Shakespeare[1,2]
Val Douglas*
Bertram (Ranchie) McLean
Lloyd Parks[2]
Errol (Flabba) Holt

- - - - - - - - - - - -

Gibby
Bagga Walker
George Fullwood*

Percussion

Uzziah (Sticky) Thompson
Zoot (Skully) Sims
Christopher (Sky Juice) Burtt

Guitar

Eric (Binghi Bunny) Lamont
Willie Lindo[3]
Earl (Chinna) Smith
Mikey (Mao) Chung[3]
Winston (BoPe) Bowen
Dwight Pinkney
Rad (Duggie) Bryan
Andy Bassford
Steve Golding[9]
Geoffrey Chung[4]

- - - - - - - - - - - -

Lennox Gordon
Leonard Smith
Sangie Davis
Dalton Brownie
Junior Marvin
Noel Bailey[3]*
Tony Chin*
Hux Brown

Keyboards

Harold Butler
Franklyn (Bubbler) Waul[3,7]
Ansel Collins
Robert Lyn
Winston Wright[2]
Gladstone Anderson
Keith Sterling

- - - - - - - - - - - -

Errol (Tarzan) Nelson
Pablo (Dreadlocks) Black
Bobby Kalphat
Steely Johnson
Alla from Chalice
Peter Ashbourne
Richard (Jamaka) Johnson
Bernard (Touter) Harvey
Tyrone Downie
Earl (Wia/Wire) Lindo
Theophilius Beckford

Trumpet

David Madden
Junior (Chico) Chin
Arnold Brackenridge
Bobby Ellis
Delvon Campbell
Clive Hunt[5]

Trombone

Ronald (Nambo) Robinson
Joseph (Bubbles) Cameron
Vin (Trommie) Gordon*

Saxophone

Dean (Youth Sax) Frazer
Egbert Evans[5]
Headley Bennett
Herman Marquis
Cedric Brooks[9]
Tommy McCook
Glen DaCosta

Other Instruments

Augustus Pablo (*melodica*)[8]
Jimmy Becker (*harmonica*)
Peter Ashbourne (*violin*)
Harry T (*repeater drum*)
The Gladiators (various)[6]

Singers[10]

Dennis Brown
Gregory Isaacs
J.C. Lodge
Rod Taylor
Jimmy Riley
Barrington Levy
Michael Prophet
Barry Brown
Junior Tucker
Junior Delgado
Tristan Palma
Sheila Hylton
Barbara Jones
Carlene Davis
Beres Hammond
George Faith (Earl George)
Sammy Dread
Pablo Moses
Madoo
Tyrone Taylor
Tinga Stewart
Nadine Sutherland
Ruddy Thomas
Cornell Campbell
Bongo Herman
Freddie Mackay
Keith Poppin
Badoo
General Plough
Bunny Wailer
Peter Tosh
Rita Marley
Judy Mowatt
Marcia Griffiths
Tony Tuff
Ronnie Davis
Leroy Smart*
I Jah Man Levi
Freddie MacGregor
Hugh Griffiths
Sugar Minott

Vocal Groups

Wailing Souls
Tamlins
Israel Vibration
I-Threes
Culture
Mighty Diamonds

Deejays

Eek A Mouse
Yellow Man
Lone Ranger
Lui Lepke
U. Brown
Trinity
Kojack
Welton Irie
Nicodemus
Big Youth (*semi-dormant*)
U. Roy (*dormant*)
I. Roy
U. Black
Sassafras
Ringo
Patrick Irie
Ranking Joe
Prince Mohammed (George Nooks)
Prince Hammer
Prince Far-I
Lee Van Cleef
Papa Michigan & General Smiley
Jah Stitch
Errol Scorcher
Tappa Zukie
Prince Jazzbo
Brigadier Jerry
Jah Scott
Ranking Trevor
Jah Thomas
Dillinger

*These musicians have emigrated.
1. During the period covered by this census, Sly Dunbar and Robbie Shakespeare constituted reggae's primary rhythm section. To the outside world, Sly & Robbie in 1981 **were** reggae music, moving from Peter Tosh to Black Uhuru to Gregory Isaacs to Bunny Wailer to Grace Jones to their own multitudinous productions on their own label, Taxi. Eventually, Sly and Robbie became rare sights in the Kingston studios, preferring to record at Island Records' Compass Point facility in the Bahamas.
2. Robbie Shakespeare, Ranchie MacLean, Lloyd Parks, and Winston Wright (l) have all been known to play guitar on sessions.
3. Franklyn Waul, Willie Lindo, Mikey Chung and Noel Bailey occasionally play bass.
4. Geoffrey Chung plays everything.
5. Egbert Evans and Clive Hunt sometimes play piano.
6. The Gladiators (Clinton Fearon, Albert Griffiths and Gallimore Sutherland) play occasional sessions, switching instruments around.
7. Franklyn Waul plays syndrum and percussion tracks on many of Joe Gibbs' records.
8. Augustus Pablo plays most other keyboards.
9. Cedric Brooks and Steve Golding have excellent reputations as hand drummers.
10. Some singers, such as Madoo and Tristan Palma, also work as deejays, while some deejays (Prince Mohammed, Big Youth) also sing. Some singers (like Barry Brown, Barrington Levy and Sammy Dread) often sing along with dub records at dances, sometimes improvising new lyrics. Here, the line between singer and deejay tends to blur.

Bassist George Fullwood, Ansell Collins and Winston Wright.

Master drummer Barnabas and Jimmy Backford, Bernard "Touter" Harvey, and

singer/bandleader Freddie MacGregor.

An Outerview with Lee Perry

Lee "Scratch" Perry started out in the '60s as an arranger and engineer for Coxsone's Studio One and quickly became the premier avant-reggae producer in the world. His hard bumpity groove and use of African rhythms drew the absolute best from the best musicians of the classic mid-'70s, from the Wailers to the Heptones to Max Romeo. In addition to providing Jamaicans with interplanetary dance music, the Upsetter also invented some of the more arcane dubbing techniques, spewing out a music so retarded and *off* that listening to it exposed one to brain damage and mental turmoil. Perry's dub was the light at the end of the tunnel, always there but never quite within human reach. In time, Perry was widely regarded as the reigning Grand Master of reggae production.

After a series of reversals in the late '70s (including a sanitorium stay and the closing of his legendary Black Ark studio in Kingston's Washington Gardens), Perry went to Amsterdam to live and record. But this potentially fruitful alliance was musically and financially disappointing for Perry, and he returned to Jamaica to take up various projects. A correspondent found him recording an album for Joe Gibbs in late 1981: "At the studio Lee had any number of small children who fiddled with instruments, the board, and headphones with alarming proficiency while the session went on. Occasionally Lee would space out and his wife would take over, doing much of the actual work. While singing, Scratch had laid out before him and around him the following items: Sagittarius horoscope, a small gold-painted statue of a lion, a set of hand exercise grips, a book on Buddhist yoga, a note pad full of lyrics, several Lee Perry records with weird phrases scrawled on the covers, a hammer, a pink plastic airplane, a grater, a book on space oddities and a couple of other objects that were beyond identification. He had a gym bag in

the corner full of other personal talismans which I did not dare investigate. He wore a blue denim suit with the top open, a number of copper chains and ornaments, a blue guitar cord around his neck, and no shoes. During the session he stood on books and occasionally annointed his feet with some cléar, sweet-smelling liquid from a small rum bottle. The session included several Bob Marley tunes, to which Lee improvised new lyrics. The phrase "Coconut Excalibur" was repeated frequently. Despite his eccentricity, Perry was very coherent in giving instructions to the musicians, and very demanding. He knew exactly what he wanted. His singing sounded like a Jamaican Curtis Mayfield on acid reading transcripts from Bellvue Hospital . . ."

In 1981, Scratch toured U.S. cities, fronting a white reggae band from New York called the Terrorists. Several people who caught the shows said they were the worst in reggae history. But no matter. We caught up with Scratch the day after his Boston show in the suburban home of the promoter. At six o'clock that morning the promoter had gotten a call from the local

police, as panicked neighbors had reported a black man jogging through their exclusive neighborhood with a machete. It was Scratch.

With us and his beautiful blond girlfriend as his rapt audience, Scratch began by interviewing us.

Lee Perry: This is an outerview from the Upsetter himself, he that speaketh and he that praiseth and he that doeth all things. Seein' this book in front of me, *Reggae Bloodlines,* which is the blood, means virgin blood, and the sign mean virgin sign and de time mean culture, time dispensation; well, now I feel this the time that the artist start to interview de books writers. For years the books writers been interviewin' the singers, now de singers start interviewin' de writers. What are you doing Mr. Simon? It's a pleasure meeting you in Boston. And good evening, sir. Your name?

Q: I'm Mr. Davis.

Pleasure meeting you. And I wish you success on dis new book, but hope you make it fair this time, a straight line, no despair, fair within love compassion under-

standin' love knowledge overstandin', no more war in your mind. I now destroy the mentality of war, atomic energy from your mind, I give you de blessing of love and order if you obey me in eight nine O zed. That's the power of their computer controlling. Thankyou sah.

Are you a member of the Masonic Temple, Mr. Upsetter?

De Misanic Temple—I art de temple, I art de future, I art de mirror, I art de music and de music art I, and I live in the music and de music live in I de Father—this is de harp, Sam Sharpe.

What did you say last night on the radio, when the deejay asked you if you ever worked with Bob Marley?

I've never worked with anyone. Any time I see myself working with one, then I'll know I like myself to sleep to death, make you see, I'm not fit to live anymore. I wish de day never come when I work with anyone.

And you mentioned you had a teacher-pupil relationship with him, is that true?

Well, if you think I'm not de teacher, test me.

No, I do think you're the teacher, but I was just wondering if you had any comment to make about it?

About what? His vision of slipping out?

About your teaching Bob Marley.

I'm not here to teach Bob Marley, I'm here to teach the universe.

How did you get the name Upsetter?

Because I am *the* Upsetter. That's answer for itself. I am the Upsetter. One take onto himself what he think he is, and I think I know I art the Upsetter, so I *am* the Upsetter.

So would you call this tour you're doing now the Return of the Upsetter?

This don't mean the return of the Upsetter, this mean the tour, the mental power to destroy the mind of the undermind. The overmind is here to destroy the undermind. The overmind control by water, which is here to water de garden and de flowers, to let the trees grow, and let de children sing and let de birds fly and let the air be free from pollutions.

You mentioned something about Dr. Syntax?

That's my idea. My idea is to criticize all tax collectors and my idea is to execute all thief, all liars and vampires, *mentally;* not in a physical form, I can do it physically by my exercise, cramp and para-

lyze, cos I know it is the Master Dance, I art a ballet sounds. Music! Water in here you got to splash if you're drinking rum, lotta people don't love rum, but I love rum very much cos rum is the spirit that was here before the holy—(sings) "Glory be unto the Father and to the Son and to the Holy Ghost, as it was in the beginning now and ever shall be world without end" but you see de rum? Rum is de power of the tom-tom and the tom-tom is the power of the one hundred drums that control the neighborhood at de root. If de baby born and had no navel string then he shall surely die but if he has a navel string then he gonna live. Rum is my navel string, that's where de spirit dwell and I like to have the spirit in me.

How did you first become involved with doing production work in Kingston?

To discuss my original force of life is totally impossible for me to tell you how I got involved. I'm not a man who has kept memory of anything I've done. I'm a miracle man, things happen which I don't plan, I've never planned anything. Like I say, I never try, I never plan. And if there is a day that come that I have to try, I will ax the Almighty to let me die. I hate trying.

You just like doing?

Instant. Whatsoever I do, I want it to be a instant action object, instant reaction subject. Instant input, instant output. If it's not the way it gonna work, well kiss my rass; if it even God, God would have to kiss my rass because we never work to a God that I don't get paid instantly. I believe in getting pay instantly.

What albums are you producing now?

Albums!! Zillion and million and trillion and billion records. I art de camera. I art de future. I art de worlds without end, I don't think to talk, man, do y'understand? So if I want albums, I hatch them because I art Scratch the beginning.

Did you start from scratch?

All de time. If you don't start from scratch, then you in trouble, you don't start nowhere.

Can you explain the unique sound you get on all the records you produce?

Would you give away your secret? If you give away your secret, you may be a very stupid man. I will keep mine. Because I want to live.

Why are most of your record-

ings in mono?

Well mono mean one heart, one thought, one love, one destiny, one aim, one alternative. So I defend only the one; anytime is a split personality I know there can be problem and danger and I don't support it. I support all-in-one, one communication, one Itation, one Iration, one faith, one human destiny. Anytime you come out with that, then I don't think you're parallel. You're confused, you're a mascot! And I don't defend mascot.

Which musicians are you particularly fond of?

At this moment? Well, most of the good thing always pass away, cos sometime I say to meself, "How come de good t'ing die?" Thinkin' of all this, I wish the spirit of Otis Redding could come back alive, a vibration that can never die. I wish the spirit of Fats Domino would come back alive. I wish the spirit of King Cole would come back alive. I wish the spirit of King Solomon Burke, I wish those spirit could come back alive. I not in for the madness, because I can't take it. I don't defend fuckeries. Dig!

Fats is still alive—

I know, and he's in another form, but those are the vibration that I want to come back alive, not to come back but to come forward for the use of mankind because without those spiritual guidance, then Man dead.

So Scratch, you don't feel like shooting the barber and burying the razor anymore?

I think the barber should live, because there's lots of dreadlocks who want to trim. They need a new vibration. Let the barber live.

And dig up the razor?

Of course, the razor gotta come back alive. Heh-heh! Nothing wrong with the barber trimming a man because I think I might takin a trim in a short while to change my vibration. Too much dread things not too good. I love good things. I want to see things happening good for me, no more dread foolishness and fuckeries. Clean hair I think is the honor, because man should respect his hair very much, keep it clean, brush it minutely.

Did you at one point wear dreads?

I was getting involved with it. If I wasn't careful, I'd have got captured by the Devil, but I was careful that I didn't get caught by the Devil. I was the only one that escape the trap. It's war!

—*Stephen Davis and Peter Simon*

Sly & Robbie

working in the studio with Joe Cocker and James Brown.

I first heard Sly & Robbie live in the late '70s, when they were touring and recording with Peter Tosh. Even at that point, their sound combined reggae's African roots with a thoroughly modern, r&b-based attack and attention to form. But it wasn't until I saw the

The beauty of a great rhythm section—like a great director/cinematographer team—is that it colors everything without drawing too much attention to itself. In pop music, and jazz for that matter, a significant bass/drums groove is a very tangible thing, and can have as much to do with setting the pop cultural tone of an era as any box-office blockbuster. For instance, Motown's first-string rhythm section of drummer Benny Benjamin (who was Little Stevie Wonder's early musical mentor) and bassist James Jamerson created a factory-funk, 4-beat, sledgehammer of a groove that virtually dominated most of the prosperous '60s: the sound of high employment.

In these recession-wracked '80s, there's a certain poetic justice to the fact that one of the most influential rhythm sections in the world today is a duo that got its start in the Kingston ghettoes. In the past decade, Sly Dunbar and Robbie Shakespeare have not only become the premier reggae drums/bass duo—producing and playing on a succession of hits by such as Peter Tosh, Gregory Isaacs, and Black Uhuru—they've also stamped their funky groove on non-reggae hit records by Grace Jones, Ian Dury, Joan Armatrading, several international r&b dance smashes, and have recently been

pair several times in 1981 with vocal trio Black Uhuru—whom Sly & Robbie also produce—that I began to realize how deeply their groove has channeled.

At one concert in particular—at New York's Ritz club before a dancing crowd of 1,500 people—the drums and bass were virtually the lead instruments behind Michael Rose's keening lead vocals and Puma Jones' and Ducky Simpson's plaintive, modal backups. The other musicians onstage that night were no slouches either: guitarists Billy Johnson and Daryl Thompson provided metalically precise chording and snaking single-string lines, while Sticky Thompson's percussion —from glockenspiel to cowbells and chattering woodblocks— blended symphonic technique with Ivory Coast syncopation. But on songs like "Sponji Reggae," it was the bass/drums thrust that you felt, always.

Shakespeare uses more rock and roll-style high frequencies in his bass tone settings than, say, a traditional reggae bassist like Family Man, so Robbie's sound probes into the head as much as the chest. Meanwhile, Sly combines mind-boggling rhythmic accuracy—his tom-tom fills sound like distant machine gun reports—with a relentlessly unhurried backbeat.

Sly & Robbie

Lee Perry ascended a tree to be photographed.

Their groove is repetitious, tonally thick, and body-oriented—in the manner of a soulful EKG—with guitar fills acting as funky oscilloscopes. The music is obviously more than conventional reggae, but it's also not reggae-funk (like Steel Pulse) or reggae-rock (á la Third World).

What it all comes down to is a very conscious assimilation of several international influences, often stripped to their barest outlines, so the sources are blurred and run together. In other words, Sly & Robbie are well on their way to defining *the* potential world-groove of the '80s and '90s.

Not surprisingly, both Sly and Robbie emerge in conversation as musicians' musicians. When I visited their hotel suite the day after their Ritz show, Sly had just returned from Manny's Music Store on 48th St., where he'd gone on an extended drumstick-buying spree. They were both as eager to talk about the music I listen to as their own: I mentioned a Jaco Pastorius album I'd just heard, and Robbie immediately jotted down the title, saying "I check it out later."

"When I was young," Robbie began, "I listened to country & western and blues a lot; at first, all you could get was one radio station in Jamaica, and that's what they played in the way of music. Then transistor radios got better and we began to pick up some American stations, soul and rock stations. Jamaicans love sad music, music that makes us want to cry. So, the singers with feeling were the ones we liked when we were growing up: everybody from Marty Robbins to Frankie Laine and Bobby 'Blue' Bland.

"As I started to play bass, my first and longtime hero was Family Man, of the Wailers. He was the first to play really strong, simple, melodic lines with a deep feeling on records—this was after the ska era had passed in the '60s. As I began to work in bands, I really followed in Aston's footsteps: after he left a band called the Hippie Boys, I took his place; when he quit the Aggrovators, I joined that group. I even played on some Wailers cuts, like 'Stir It Up,' and it got so Family Man and I couldn't really tell the difference between our sounds on record. But then I started searching to find my own style, and what I came up with was to make my playing even simpler, to play as simple and direct as I can, so that the people, the real

audience, can all relate to my sound.

"I met Sly after we'd both been playing awhile. One night he was playing at a Kingston club called Tit For Tat, and I was up the street at Evil People. We heard each other on our breaks, and liked what we heard. I'd already been doing a good deal of studio work, more so than Sly, but gradually we began to get on sessions together—I started recommending him whenever I could. Then we played together in a band called Revolutionaries, and then a band called Word, Sound & Power, which became Peter Tosh's back-up group. We did his first album, *Legalize It,* with a very roots, message kind of style; on the later albums, *Bush Doctor* and *Mystic Man,* we meant to record more commercial sounds, especially with the single 'Don't Look Back.'

"All along on those early sessions where me and Sly were playing together, we were already thinking about producing. Me personally never liked the bass sound on older reggae records—the sounds they gave me—and Sly never liked the drums sounds in those days. The musicians would play some nice things, but because the records themselves weren't very well produced, you couldn't hear the true sounds of the players. So, first off, Sly started to really get into tuning his drums, and I worked on my bass sound, my amplifier settings, that sort of thing. Then we started trying to produce little things ourselves—we'd rent some cheap studio time. The way we began working was to just build everything from the bass

and drums, first getting our own sounds just right as the foundation, then adding the other instruments and voices.

"At one point, in the mid-'70s, we just decided we wanted to make a record and start our own label, which we called Taxi, and we used the techniques we'd been working on for a few years. We saved some money from our sessions that we played for other people, bought the tape and booked some four-track studio time. Then we called up our friend Gregory Isaacs, whom we'd backed up many times in the studio, and asked him if he would do a song with us. He said, 'Yeh, mon, *anytime,'* and we said, 'How about now?' That song was called 'Soon Forward,' our first single, and it was the number one hit in Jamaica for eight weeks straight. So that's

how we began to record reggae in our own way. In Jamaica, people like to dance, and they will accept any music if it makes the foot move, whether it's calypso, boogalu, funky, disco, moon-rock, stars-rock, sun-rock, anything.

Basically, we work the same way on everything we produce—constructing the groove. Sometimes we can even recycle a groove! For example, the song 'Pull Up To The Bumper' on the Grace Jones album we did (*Nightclubbing*) was actually another tune we'd done with Junior Tucker called 'Peanut Butter.' The words on that earlier tune weren't right for Grace, so they were rewritten."

Sly Dunbar has what can only be

described as bowl-cut dreadlocks that fall in bangs over his eyes, an infectious smile, and metronomic time. He listened silently, often smiling, while Robbie talked, but when I asked the drummer who his early musical influences were, he didn't miss a beat with his answer: "Al Jackson, Jr.—of Booker T. & the MG's—was my first real hero on drums, along with Roger Hawkins of Muscle Shoals, who played on those Atlantic Aretha Franklin records, and Benny Benjamin on early Motown sides. I especially like Al Jackson, because he kept it tight and simple and didn't roll around the tom-toms unless it was necessary—but he was always locked into the groove.

"In Jamaican music my earliest influence was Lloyd Nibbs, of the Skatalites. I learned and listened as a boy during the ska and rock steady eras. One of my first actual recording dates was on an Ansell Collins record, when the style was already reggae with the 'one drop' on the backbeat, you know.

"I listen to r&b, reggae, pop rock, new wave—just a lot of records always. My favorite drummers today are Steve Gadd, Earl Young [of MFSB, Philly soul studio fame], Charlie Watts, Aynsley Dunbar, all kinds of different stylists.

"Another example of how I mix up styles a little bit is the version of the old Temptations we did, 'Don't Look Back,' with Peter Tosh and Mick Jagger. I used a rhythm on the drums that comes out of the Pocomania church services in Jamaica (begins slapping out a double-time pattern on his legs while singing 'Oh Jesus save me, I'm under the rock. . . .') It's a gospel thing that's particular to that church, and I used a similar beat on the tune 'Youth of Eglinton,' with Black Uhuru.

"One of the more recent changes I think we made on Jamaican music was in the late '70s, when everybody was doing four beats to the bar on the bass drum, working around that kind of disco-fied pattern. On a couple of very popular Dennis Brown albums during that period, and especially 'Love and Devotion' by Jimmy Riley, we did like a slowed-down Motown/Stax kind of beat (slaps a rock-ish half-time beat on his thighs), but still keeping the backbeat happening on the guitar chord. That shook things up down in Jamaica a bit."

—*Crispin Cioe*

Robbie in session.

135

11

The Wrathful Madonna

Imagine the resplendent rage of a pieta unshackled by grief and pity; a lioness finally let loose to avenge the lamb. Imagine the Tibetan **shaktis,** those metaphorical extensions of India's female saints (the **yoginis** with red matted hair and bodies anointed with ash) who identify with the feminine aspect of divinity because they know that the female is the power of the male. And imagine the female members of certain ascetic communities like the Essenes, about whom the historian Josephus noted that childbearing was considered among the holiest of devotions.

The Rastafarian woman is an enigma to many reggae fans who have only been exposed to the rampant Rasta lions who strut onstage with an organic banner of dreadlocks to proclaim the patriarchal prerogative. **Carol Cooper** introduces us to two of the priestesses in muslin who lead the female element to the forefront of reggae: Marcia Griffiths and Sandra "Puma" Jones—a madonna and a warrioress, mothers both, blending the family unit with the power of music.

Two Women in Reggae

"Hear, O ye kings; give ear, O ye princes;
I, even I, will sing unto the Lord;
I will sing praise to the Lord God of Israel."

Deborah's Song, *Judges* 5:3

Tuff Gong Records, Jamaica's only Rasta-owned-and-run 24-track studio, was commandeered by Rita Marley after her husband's death. An increasing number of women and children are being recorded there, encouraged to express a Rasta-informed reality.

Pauline Perry, once wife to producer Lee "Scratch" Perry, is now in New York trying her hand at freelance producing with singers Althea and Donna. And Sonia Pottinger, another who had married into an interest in the recording business, took over the old Treasure Isle studios in Kingston and made them her own, creating the new label, Hi Note. It was Sonia Pottinger who released Marcia Griffiths' third solo LP *Steppin',* which stands alongside Judy Mowatt's *Black Woman* and Rita Marley's *Who Feels It Knows It* as a masterful piece of musicianship and an excellent defense of the Rasta ethos as it applies to women.

On the day of our interview, Marcia Griffiths is packing to return to Jamaica, having just delivered her third son, Marcus. In a major departure from both her own good judgement and Rasta protocol, Marcia had spent the bulk of this latest pregnancy on tour with Bob Marley and the Wailers.

Marcia Griffiths is one-third of the I-Threes, who through their work with the Wailers are perhaps the best-known female singers in reggae music. That spring, summer and fall (1980) they had toured Zimbabwe, Europe, then America. Had the American tour not been cut short by Marley's collapse and subsequent death, Marcia was prepared to rejoin the band by winter's end

Rita Marley at work, 1982.

Opposite: **sister Judy Mowatt**

Sonia Pottinger, and (right) I-Threes, 1981.

Judy Mowatt, 1981.

The great Marcia Griffiths.

when the Wailers planned to hit Latin America.

With the somber possibility of Marley's death then hovering over the conversation, we discussed the development of the woman singer in Jamaican pop music, Marcia's own attitudes toward a solo career, and the tricky proposition of the musician as moral messenger.

"Well, this is a gift you get from God, whether you are a singer or a player of instruments," she began. "But it takes time for you to find out what your purpose is, and to develop on that." Marcia is a tall, big-boned and pretty woman, the color of cafe au lait, her hair dreadlocked and covered as a matter of faith. She started singing in school and in church, much like her American soul idols, and was "discovered" by one of the Blues Busters, a brilliant Jamaican soul duo who once toured the States with Sam Cooke. They decided that they had to have her sing on a TV show they were doing, and pulled the necessary strings to arrange it.

"It was 1964, and I sang Carla Thomas's 'No Time to Lose.' From then on, things started to happen for me. I was never just a back-up singer . . . until Bob Marley." Indeed, Marcia's story is quite different from that of most young Jamaican girls who aspired to a singing career at that time. Most never got more than one 45 beyond the casting couch of lecherous and opportunistic producers.

Griffiths, like most Jamaican artists in the '60s, started out on the Studio One label with Coxsone Dodd. He released a string of successful singles for her, mostly covers of American soul ballads and blues. She listened to Aretha, Dionne Warwick and Gloria Lynn, admiring most the lush Broadway production values of the early Warwick hits. There were always live performances, and many were double bills where a foreign artist would be supported by local Jamaican talent.

In those days, the only solo female acts were Hortense Ellis and Marcia Griffiths; so if a top Motown or Memphis soul act came to play Mobay, either Hortense or Marcia would be invited —and if it were Marcia then you could count on

Rita and Judy being there to sing backgrounds. "They used to do back-up for *me*," Griffiths remembered. "In Jamaica they used to sing harmony for me and then, at a certain stage in the show, we would all get together and do a song and everybody would say we sounded like the Sweet Inspirations."

But it was when Marcia teamed up with a gentleman named Bob Andy that she achieved her greatest renown. Together they recorded an album for producer Harry J called *Young, Gifted and Black* that was picked up in 1969 by Trojan records in London. Its success sent the duo to the top of the British charts and prompted them to spend the next three years touring the major cities of Europe. "All the places I've been now with the Wailers," she smiles, "they were not new to me."

European producers were intrigued by Marcia's sound (you must remember that Berry Gordy had by this time made the Motown Sound an international icon) and were always asking her to record a few tunes for them. She did do two singles in German for a producer in Berlin,

exulting in the fact that there she finally had access to a Warwick-type backing track: horns, strings, and chorale. But bad management and her own inexperience cheated her of the best of the opportunities that came her way—including a shot at a Motown distribution contract.

"Harry J was our producer and manager then. I don't know why he didn't hire someone who knew more about management to handle that side of the business, except that he wanted all the money for himself. *Young, Gifted and Black* was such a big record that all of a sudden a lot of people came on the scene wanting a piece of us. We lost a major contract with CBS because people were falsely representing us; Trojan stopped it because they claimed we were contracted to *them*, which was a lie. And when some people from Motown wanted a record from us, or even redistribution on *Young, Gifted and Black*, the people at Trojan wanted so much money for it that the deal fell through. And to this day we have never received a penny in royalties for *Young, Gifted and Black* or the one-shot single 'Pied Piper.' But if you go to London today you'll see them in the stores, still selling."

Disillusioned but not broken, Marcia returned to Jamaica and continued recording, yet with little or no creative control. A solo album released by Federal Records in '72 was called *Sweet Bitter Love,* and it embarrasses Marcia because she let the producer, Lloyd Charmers, choose every cut whether she related to the material or not. She was beginning to develop that consciousness that was springing out of Rasta, which insisted that a singer sing her own song—or failing that, only express those sentiments that revealed the most personal of truths and aspirations.

Marcia had allowed Bob Andy to write material for her, and their intimacy had fostered that kind of professional trust. But in 1975 she entered a new phase in her career, together with her erstwhile partners, Rita and Judy. Although each continued to record as solo artists, they willingly amalgamated into the top-ranking Wailers to become the feminine aspect of Bob

Marley's imagination—the I-Threes.

Working with Marley, Marcia's own song-writing talents began to unfold, with Rasta sentiments as a major inspiration. Her roots were in gospel, so it was not long before the incorporation of African elements transformed her semi-Catholic fundamentalism into a parallel version (*not* an exact version) of Marley's apocalyptic mysticism. When she describes the creation of her tune, "Steppin' Out of Babylon," she recalls a friend having given the master rhythm to her, and her instinctively feeling the nascent song as *her* song. They molded it a bit, then she took it home on a cassette to muse over melody and words. Finally, thinking the rhythm "too political, too militant" for a woman's delivery, she took it to another songwriter: Bob Marley.

"Well, he liked the rhythm, and he danced to it . . . but, maybe the time was too short for him to come up with lyrics. But in the end, I felt that it was purposely left up to me. The melody and lyrics came almost all of a piece one day after I had been reasoning with a sister, telling her

that Marley is gone (the I-Threes were, of course, *his* three), is in doubt. Each of these three survivors of the debacles of the '60s have solo conceptions and solo careers, solo *ministries*, if you will. "When we're working with Bob," Marcia says, speaking as much of all the individual Wailers as the I-Threes, "we all know he is the main one out there and we have to work it out so that the harmonies suit everyone. But if it's a case of Judy or me or Rita leading on a song, conflicts arise. Maybe I'd have to take a harmony that didn't suit my range, or we'd have to compete over the most agreeable second part."

When asked about the latitude Bob allowed them in the studio to arrange harmonies on his work, Marcia admits that they were often asked for their input. "But even after he'd said 'go ahead and arrange this tune,' he had so many ideas it was hard for him to just sit there and let us do it. But we didn't mind it, because the things that would come to him, the things he heard, were always very nice and very unusual."

If Marcia Griffiths represents the first generation reggae women, Puma Jones is the prototype of the new breed. Whereas Marcia grew alongside Bob Marley almost as a sister to that trailblazer, Puma can be considered a spiritual daughter, one of the many who have internalized the Rasta message and have chosen the Marley method of getting it across. Sandra "Puma" Jones, dreadlocked and the color of a tea rose, is a remarkable testimony to the international appeal of Rastafari as a grass-roots movement of revolt and reform, even as the Black Muslims of the early 1960s.

Puma was born in South Carolina and raised in New York's Harlem. She studied social work, and received her master's from Columbia University. She briefly visited both Haiti and West Africa, and tried her hand as a community news researcher for black television. But she was quickly disillusioned by the bureaucracy and hypocrisy of the corporate machinery. So, hearing of the social reforms being made under "Democratic Socialism" in Manley's Jamaica, she

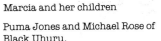

Marcia and her children

Puma Jones and Michael Rose of Black Uhuru.

about many of the problems I had been through and was still having. It was she who suggested that I had expressed these things so well, that I should put them on paper and to music.

"I was saying, that 'even though I've suffered so many injustices, it doesn't really bother me because I know there is another world for me.' The chorus 'steppin' out of Babylon' is not necessarily a movement in the physical. It means rather that you are moving out of corruption and into a state of greater purity than what you might be experiencing in daily life. Babylon can be either a situation or a system, but it is a hell to anyone who knows of love, and light and warmth. So we want to step from a lower life into a higher one, and it's not just a physical step, but an inner evolution."

The apotheosis of the I-Threes into a harmony trio of international stature, particularly now

So Bob's influence continues to pervade the progression of his protégés, even if they seek to work alone rather than in the complex configurations in which he liked to place them. The last time the I-Threes performed was August 1981 in Montego Bay. The government-sponsored Sun-splash IV festival offered one of its four nights as "Tuff Gong Night," to celebrate the artists and the artistry spawned by Bob Marley's vision.

The I-Threes were only one of the vocal groups who fronted the Wailers, performing as they had during 30-plus dates on the European tour as a separate entity, singing their own compositions. Spartan women warriors chanting up the spirit of a fallen comrade, the teacher/the leader/ the priest. We are the Queens of Rasta-fari, these proud businesswomen always seem to say: we are mothers, we are black . . .

emigrated there in 1977 and immediately sought government employment as a social worker in one of his self-help housing schemes.

Jones spent a year helping to set up the very handsome housing projects called Nannyville before she began to uncover the problems in socialist paradise. She observed the resentments nursed by surrounding shanty communities (primarily Back Bush and Mountainside) because these working poor had supported the opposing political party. Puma began writing memo after memo to her project supervisors, warning them to disseminate some of the goods and services being invested in Nannyville to the adjacent settlements, or come election time Nannyville would become a grudge-battlefield when the guns were handed out to bully certain votes from the sufferers.

As a result of this sane advice, Jones's work

Carlene Davis: she could become one of Jamaica's most important singers if she learns to sing reggae.

contract was not renewed the next year, and she found herself having to seek another means of livelihood. The Rasta movements—there were several—were becoming stronger and stronger at this time; partly because Marley had moved back to Kingston to set up his studio, and partly because reggae music was beginning to trickle-down enough money to finance nonsectarian development among the poorer classes.

Puma began performing with Ras Michael and

Sandra "Puma" Jones, MSW.

the Sons of Negus, and through recording, working and performing, she soon became familiar enough with the Rastafarian religious tradition to adopt it as her own. The change in people and their institutions that Puma witnessed under Rasta discipline were far more impressive than those she had witnessed in the

name of liberal legislation or social science. Thus was a very outspoken and independent Western woman convinced toward values that her peers had long ago given up.

"A woman's strength is perfected more through the support that she provides for her man and family." Puma is holding her first son Jah Live as we talk, and her husband Ras Joel has gone to be busy in the next room. "The man has a very steep tradition to trod, and he has a lot to learn. A woman must be a man's strength in this instance, not weakness." She pauses a moment and her gaze unveils just a tinge of reflective contempt. "It is a lion and a *lioness,* not a lion and a monkey."

Puma is most certainly the lioness, serving as a guiding light for more than one reggae lion. Derrick Simpson and Michael Rose invited Puma to join Black Uhuru as they were beginning to develop a reputation under the musical tutelage of producers Sly Dunbar and Robbie Shakespeare. The album the new trio released in 1979 catapulted Black Uhuru into an Island Records contract, to be groomed as successors to the Wailers' meteoric rise to fame.

It was Derrick Simpson who first thought that the addition of a unique female soprano like Puma's would revolutionize their sound; but

more importantly, the developing sensibility of songwriter Rose was ripe for the introduction of American sass and savvy that Puma's broad experience provided. The trio sent each single pulled from the *Showcase* album up the local and British charts: "Shine Eye Girl" (an injunction against cosmetics and flirts); "Abortion" (cautionary and disapproving); and "Guess Who's Coming to Dinner" (hilariously tongue-in-cheek).

The personality of the group may be stated by lead singer Michael Rose, but it is defined by Puma Jones. "In the confusion of Babylon it's easy to forget who you are, the *perfection* of who you really are," Puma begins in her customary soft Rasta patois. "Repatriation is a must, but it is the process of *mental* repatriation that must come first. A reassertion of knowledge, wisdom and understanding. We believe that God is in Man, and that I, my spirit and individuality comes from Creation, and that having existed from then, it can never die. Americans, being surrounded by technology and manufactured goods, lose touch with life . . . with what living can be at its best. When I see a Rasta man, his Queen, and his children, *that* is life to me, not credit cards, not the 9-to-5 grind where you exchange your *time* for money.

"People like that, people who don't live with a consciousness of their nature and history from *time beginning to time end,* more than 6,000 years, are slaves. They cannot conceive of a King of Kings, or a Lord of Lords. Nor could they recognize him. Rastafari is God, and the life plan is far broader than we have been allowed to see it. But all the information is available, in libraries and such, no matter how it's been hidden and scattered. It's up to the individual to seek it."

The three albums that Puma has thus far released with Black Uhuru, *Showcase, Sinsemilla,* and the most recent, *Red,* show an interesting development as to group politics. *Showcase* is by far the most even; showing off vocalist and musicians to equal benefit, varying rhythms from the somber "General Penitentiary" to the pop rockish "Natural Reggae Beat." *Sinsemilla* gives far more emphasis to Sly & Robbie's rhythm section, and Michael Rose's vocals seem to be mixed higher on the key tracks so that the harmonies are less clear than they were on *Showcase.* The single pulled from *Sinsemilla* was surprisingly, a roller disco hit titled "The Whole World is Africa."

Red, an album full of lovely, moody songs with quirky, tintinnabulary percussion and haunting melodies, restores the evenness of *Showcase,* and also offers us the first lyrical evidence that Michael Rose has been profoundly influenced by his comrade Puma Jones. The songs "Puff She Puff" and "Sistren" are comments on that ever touchy subject, relations between black men and women. The former impacts like overheard conversation; the man has no work thus no money, and the woman chafes at a relationship of constant want and little material satisfaction. Fortunately, we are given a male protagonist with little doubt about what he wants out of life, and chief among these is dignity. So he chides his shrewish companion instead of leaving her or eating her, asking her not to give up the ideals their love is founded upon, just because conditions are difficult for the moment.

"Sistren," on the other hand, serves a larger narrative purpose. On the surface it is a moralistic parable extolling the virtues of the country girl over city women. Taken to its allegorical limits, it expands to explain what Rasta offers a woman in compensation for material poverty, and then warns the more crude and dull-witted of men not to abuse the fundamental strengths and virtues of women, for only by mutual respect and support can they surmount their oppression.

Because Rasta, like the Black Muslims, grew out of a ghetto culture and ghetto desperation, its advocates, both male and female, tend to have an inner resiliency and a shrewd survival instinct that must never be underestimated when judging the movement's ability to develop and protect itself. That Rasta is a religion that does not cripple itself by adherence to any central leadership automatically gives it an edge on the Muslims, who were maimed upon Malcolm X's assassination and blinded upon the death of Elijah Muhammed. Like the Quakers, the Rastas believe that each man has no master but God. And like the Akan market women, the Rasta woman believes in her ability to make the family unit an autonomous economic cadre, with extensions that only strengthen the whole.

Puma Jones now lives fairly comfortably in Jamaica, with her husband, two babies and the four children she's adopted from his first marriage. She delivered her second son (Uhuru Sasa—Freedom Now) while on location for Dickie Jobson's film *Countryman.* In the hospital one day, back on the set the next. Radiant.

The gift both Marcia and Puma have most obviously taken from Rasta is a comfort within biological function and social responsibility that many an ardent feminist might envy. Puma, Marcia, Rita, and Judy's motherhood has been incorporated into their careers with an ease that belies the Western and proto-Western harping about children destroying a woman's independence. And the aggressive sense of self-as-an-evolving-perfection is doing more to heal rifts between men and women than many a counselor or encounter group.

Cooperation is the key, a key that Puma puts into practice by allowing her husband to write material for her rather than asserting her own writing skills—in part because she is curious to see herself in his mirror, to know what they, in tandem, are evolving to be.

This is the woman in reggae today, the priestess in muslin, a madonna and a warrioress on the home front of human relations.

—*Carol Cooper (1981)*

Sheila Hylton

Top left: Nadine Sutherland, a favorite of Bob Marley's, recorded for his Tuff Gong label. Many consider Nadine an integral part of reggae's future.

Center: June Lodge, who had a big hit with "Someone Loves You Honey."

141

12

Jamaican Singers In the Eighties

It's an interesting undergrowth: **rockers and dubbers** jostle with the country-and-western stylists and balladeers. A sometimes locksed lyricist (Ernie Smith) croons quasi-traditional hymns: a dread (Gregory Isaacs) clad in a color-coordinated three-piece suit sings '60s-style love songs; virtual paeans to macho supremacy (by Eddie Fitzroy or Barrington Levy) are monster hits; Bunny Wailer, one of the most overtly militant members of the original Wailers, the creator of the classic **Blackheart Man**, releases a rapper.

The irony of the Jamaican singer today is that while he/she (excepting the few superstars) is still at the mercy of a manipulative and mercenary local recording industry, he/she nevertheless remains the conscience of the nation, the voice of Jamaica, responsible for part of the culture's artistic life, its love songs, social commentary, even its national identity.

What follows are various writers' conversations with some of reggae's leading voices.

A Meditation

Jamaica, for its size, must contain one of the biggest external audiences for US country and western music; a country where Pat Boone, Kris Kristofferson or, best of all, the "late great" Jim Reeves can still be firm Sunday-morning favorites with large segments of the mid- and downtown Saturday night session-goers; where the minister of culture and a leading light of the Private Sector Organization of Jamaica can, within

weeks of each other, make calls for some *balance* between the amount of reggae and the amount of classical music given airplay; where the soft-soul meanderings of Teddy Prendergrass or the Manhattans draw audiences that reggae performers only dream of; where the former prime minister released a single during his 1972 election campaign; where the current prime minister was once a record producer; where Bob Marley rarely ever made it to the top of the charts.

For quite a few Jamaicans blessed with the luxury of hindsight, Jamaica's golden era of

Delroy Wilson

Opposite: Dennis Brown

143

music occurred in the '60s: it was the period that saw the peaking and decline of the sound systems and the rise of the recording artiste; it brought into prominence the likes of Derrick Morgan, Prince Buster, Millie Small, Jimmy Cliff and the Maytals, some of whom formed the first wave of internationalisation of Jamaican music. It was the period when the heavenly harmonies of the Paragons and Heptones triumphed over the scores of homegrown "-tones" and "-dians"

Pablo Moses

Edi Fitzroy

Tony Tuff

that emerged marching to the Motown shoo-wap; a period of consolidation, the finding of a range of Jamaican voices and the evolution of the appropriate musical carriage.

By the end of the '70s, very few of these artistes or groups were of major significance. Out of the earlier groups had come such artistes as John Holt, Bob Andy, Peter Tosh, Bunny Wailer, Leroy Sibbles. Some found it difficult to adapt to the new demands, others achieved greater prominence than ever before. Some of the old stalwarts, like Jackie Edwards, Derrick Morgan, Alton Ellis, Owen Gray, migrated to other shores and were rarely, if ever, heard from again locally. Others, like Joe Higgs and Delroy Wilson, master stylists, remained plugging away, but never quite managing to capture the fame and fortune they deserved.

None of the women fared particularly well. Millie Small never outlived ska. Hortense Ellis carried the flag bravely for years but faded inevitably. For the most part, the few that surfaced in the '60s were one-shot artistes. And, for the most part, the '70s were ruled by three individuals that neither separately (as Marcia Griffiths, Judy Mowatt and Rita Marley) nor collectively (as the I-Threes) were to become major forces in Jamaican music.

Most of the earlier exponents of Jamaican popular music had the same concerns as did their North American counterparts, which was only logical as much of what emerged in Jamaica were cover versions of continental hits. The darling-come-back and super-lover themes were but a few of the many that were flogged over and over. Beginning in the late '60s, however, more and more of the singers began discovering their Blackness and Rastafari and logically began

paying more attention in their lyrics to the plight of the dispossessed.

Thus the Wailers. And thus, too, the alliance that many artistes formed with the expressed concern of the People's National Party during the period leading up to the 1972 Jamaican general elections. The PNP Musical Bandwagon attracted some of the leading musicians of the time. Delroy Wilson's "Better Must Come" and Junior Byles' "Beat Down Babylon" became virtual theme songs of those identifying themselves as Sufferers. Max Romeo's "Let the Power Fall On I" and Clancy Eccles' "Rod Of Correction" conveyed the message that the new Jamaica would recognise and pay attention to the oppression of the poor; a belief that in the Camelot of 1973 made the euphoric "Hail The Man" by Ken Lazarus one of the year's most popular tunes.

Despite the images of protest and black affirmation that typify reggae music for many, much of Jamaican popular music is as innocuous and as silly as popular music anywhere else. Such classics of commentary as Joe Higgs' "Sons of Garvey," Bob Andy's "Fire Burning," Max Romeo's "War Inna Babylon," Bunny Wailer's "Battering Down Sentence," Alton Ellis' "Lord Deliver Us," Pablo Moses' "We Should be in Angola," assume extra dimension because of the barrenness of the surrounding landscape. The social questioning that happened during the Manley era provided fertile ground for artistic exploration, but few artistes managed to make the creative transformation, to imbue the cliches and truisms with art. Here, by and large, the groups—Wailers, Diamonds, Burning Spear, Culture, etc.—had more success, although most of

these groups were essentially backups for a dominating, creative, vocal personality.

The biggest names locally, as the decade drew to a close, were the deejays: Ranger, Dillinger, Lui Lepke, Michigan and Smiley; and such love-song specialists as Gregory Isaacs and Dennis Brown. The latter two, perhaps representing the nearest reggae artistes have come to being teen idols, earn, on appearing on stage in their ever-present three-piece suits, the ultimate Jamaican audience accolade that the '80s has ushered in, bloodcurdling screams of **"murderer!!!"**

With the coming of the '80s, a number of new or unfamiliar faces have appeared. Tony Tuff, Eddie Fitzroy and Barrington Levy began topping local charts with yard-style (if chauvinistic) reggae. Some of the deejays started singing, and the top women singers remained Marcia, Judy and Rita. The new faces—J.C. Lodge, Susan Cadogan, et al—remained cover-version girls.

—*Trevor Fearon*

Gregory Isaacs— The Cool Ruler

Few reggae fans would argue that these days the clearest singing and most cogent songwriting in reggae is coming from Gregory Isaacs. A veteran of a decade on the scene, dozens of great singles (from his first "Another Heartbreak" to his recent spinetingler "Top Ten") and several extra-classic albums, Gregory wears his mantle of reggae stardom as if he were born into it. He's the undisputed king of Chancery Lane (also known as "Chancy Lane" and "Idlers' Rest"), the heart of Kingston's downtown reggae scene and, by extension, the rest of the reggae world as well.

What makes Gregory so unique is the sheer Africanness of his singing voice, and the extremely sharp and sensitively plaintive nature of his lyrics. As far as his singing goes, Gregory constructs melodic lines from a monotonal African scale in which he feels most comfortable and from which he rarely ever deviates. Gregory's singing has a sensual, Antarctic cool to it; the effect of much of his music is that of an understated but definitely psychoactive drone, with barely a hook thrown in to kick his audience in and out of trance.

Burning softly in whatever groove his invariably great band lays out for him, Gregory's singing decoys and trips the listener over and over again with the same irresistible lures every time. In Jamaica, they call him the Cool Ruler. And he is.

Mr. Isaacs' lyrics are also something of a revelation. He is certainly the only important reggae star to sing more frequently about the joys of going steady than about downpression and acute sufferation. Yet his portraits of ghetto life and the prison yard glare with an almost photorealistic surge. Songs such as "Poor Natty," "Poor and Clean" and "Loving Pauper" are saintly, dignified laments that vicariously shame many listeners to the point of tears.

When Gregory takes up protest, it is either poignantly personal (*So many years I've been slaving in your factory/And I've never had a chance to talk with the boss*) or tormented and starkly visionary: *When there was no water to water the crops/I cried and I cried and used my teardrops*. Gregory combines such imagery with the merest whisper of melody, sometimes echoed with haunting, calypso-tinged horns. The general effect is a sense of modest grace, of right livelihood, of a gently world-shaking dynamic at work.

A quick revue of Gregory's career shows how a Jamaican singer makes his way to the top via a complex labyrinth of Jamaican and Anglo-Jamaican producers. Gregory started recording with Rupie Edwards in 1973 and, dissatisfied, went on to Prince Buster. The record "Dancing Floor" sold well, but Gregory moved on to team up with Errol Dunkley to form their own label,

African Museum. By 1974 they had released "My Only Lover," four singles, and at the same time Gregory recorded for Lloyd F. Campbell, Pat Kelly, Roydale Anderson and even Rupie Edwards again.

Also in 1974, Gregory recorded for Alvin Ranglin's GG Productions, scoring in Jamaica with "Innocent People Cry" and in England on Trojan's Attack label with "Love Is Overdue." Ranglin also produced his first album, *In Person*, recorded at Treasure Isle studio. In 1975 Gregory recorded for Winston Niney Holiness, Lloyd Campbell and Prince Tony. He also began producing himself with some success.

In 1976 Gregory continued his rounds of the various producers. But Gregory really enhanced his burgeoning reputation that year with his own productions (aided by Peter Weston and Lee Perry), and, in England, Trojan brought out a singles compilation album, *All I Have Is Love*.

By 1977 Gregory was releasing self-produced singles on various labels. A third album, *Extra Classic*, was manufactured in Canada by the

now up to Gregory to follow this sound out into the world as a stage artist.

The rumors had been swimming around New York like barracuda for two weeks prior to Gregory Isaacs' much-anticipated show at the Savoy Theater on November 1, 1981. The word was that Gregory had been shot or been shot at on the streets of Brooklyn. In any case, Gregory was alive, immersed somewhere in the heart of the Jamaican community in Brooklyn where, as in Jamaica, there are no facts and rumors are hard to check. The word was also that the show would go on, and it did.

In fact, it was one of the best concerts I've ever seen. Gregory was touring with Bingy Bunny's Roots Radics band, a downtown outfit of primal reggae strength that mercifully dispenses with the dreaded acid rock lead guitar usually obligatory for the touring reggae band, and so essentially out of place.

After guitarist Bingy does one of his tunes and the Radics run through an overture medley of Gregory's all-time chart-toppers, Gregory himself

music washes over the adoring crowd. Songs like "Sunday Morning" and "Front Door" draw squeals from the little sisters, and when was the last time anyone heard squeals at a reggae show? Gregory kept his hat on, stroked his forked black beard, and didn't say much except to reel off the hits.

Gregory's concessions to showmanship are subtle pelvic movements (carefully monitored by the young dancing girls up front) and a funny medley of reggae impressions: "And if my likkle brother Dennis Brown were here tonight, he'd go something like this . . . And if my big brother Bunny Wailer were here tonight, he might sing it something like this . . ."

The show was subdued, reserved, brilliant. It had that kind of ringing reggae clarity that chimes in the ears for days afterwards. Despite the odd song of protest, the message of the music was undeniably *blue,* in the mystical sense. The feelings Gregory explores, quite like the blues musician Robert Johnson before him, are those of loneliness, rejection and loss.

Freddie MacGregor, an important singer on the Jamaican scene since he became a very youthful member of the Clarendonians in the mid-'60s.

Gregory Isaacs, Boston 1980: "And if I don't get my desire/I'll set your plantations on fire . . ."

We ran into Gregory again a few months later, in the back room of the African Museum Record Shop, Chancery Lane, and asked him what he thought of the label "Lovers Rock."

"I don't think of it. Music just music, and mek reggae music, seen? It's a message that's recognized worldwide.

"Because I personally will not deal with politics, not voting, not thinking about politician. And I am not a man who has a mind to use the name of Jah to sell record to make my living. Yet I am a servant of Jah and a man who regard Africa as my home. As a writer I write not only of me personally but of my friends' situations and things that I might hear or read about. Seen?

"My lyrics are about two kinds of experience, universal experience and individual experience.

"All nations abandon segregation and deal with one love for all mankind, whether black or white. All this war going on in the world, only one thing can conquer this war. Nuh gun and bayonet kyaan do it. *Only love can win this war."*

—*Stephen Davis*

Jamaican Micron label and distributed by an English label called Conflict. Recording for Dennis Brown in 1978, Gregory came up with one of his biggest hits, "Mr. Know-It-All," which was followed by a bewildering series of albums. Deb Records brought out *Mr. Isaacs* while GG came up with *Best Of.* In quick succession Virgin Front Line brought out *Cool Ruler* and *Soon Forward.* Another compilation of early songs recorded for Rupie Edwards also appeared as *For Everyone*, while Sly & Robbie's Taxi label released a potpourri of fresh and stale material as *Showcase*.

Finally, by 1980, Gregory consolidated his position. The music on albums like *Lonely Lover* and *More Gregory* was released on the African Museum label in Jamaica, on the PRE label in England, and on Island Records' Mango label in the US. Best of all, the music itself had become among the most rich and vital to be exported from Jamaica to the rest of the world. It was

struts out in time to "The Border," resplendent in white suit, open-necked black shirt, gold chain and medallion. As he approaches center stage with a smile, one can feel a kind of collective swoon or rush or thrill pass through the female members of the audience. In his artfully laconic way, Gregory is so beatific on stage as to be almost pornographic, and during pregnant vocal pauses in his songs one can hear three-quarters of the audience sigh and coo with pleasure.

If someone shot him, it wasn't showing tonight. Perhaps, considering the singer's widespread reputation as a tough customer, it was just a warning shot. Not many of those to be had in Brooklyn.

Soon everybody is dancing in the dark theater. Jamaican culture has taken over 47th Street. Everybody is stoned and the waitresses are spilling the drinks. Gregory's sad soulful

The King of Lovers Rock

If you asked Bob Marley the name of his favorite singer, after some hesitation he would usually say Dennis Brown. Dennis was born in 1957, and has been one of Jamaica's premier singers since his discovery at the age of ten by a group called the Falcons. Two years later, Coxsone produced Dennis's cover of Curtis Mayfield's "No Man Is an Island," which would be the first of a long string of hits, most of them Joe Gibbs productions.

But Dennis was mainly a hardworking musician on the Jamaican stage show circuit, and

Dennis Brown

Winston Rodney, St. Ann's Bay 1982.

Ras Karbi, a good singer featured in the dismal, short-run Broadway musical, **Reggae.**

he grew up singing with the best road bands Jamaica produced—Soul Syndicate, Now Generation, Skin, Flesh and Bone.

In recent years, Dennis has been producing his own albums (*Wolves and Leopards, Words of Wisdom, Joseph's Coat of Many Colors*) which artfully mingle Jah hymns and hard social commentary with Dennis's chief stock-in-trade—mellifluous lovers rock. Dennis is also a mean keyboard player, as the languid organ riffs on his records attest. Most importantly, he's a likeable, spiritual man who emerged from the Kingstonian reggae wars of the '70s as one of the most popular singers in Jamaica.

His first record was a song called "Love Grows" which wasn't released until after the second record he made for Coxsone, "No Man Is An Island." Dennis kept making records and doing backup harmonies for others like Alton Ellis and Larry Marshall.

Q: *What was it like to record in the Coxsone studios in the early days? You were very young when you first went in. Were you really nervous, or did you have a lot of confidence?*

Dennis Brown: I had a lot of confidence for the main reason that I was established as a Boy Wonder then, and like I used to have a lot of people who loved to hear me sing. Not only with the musicians, but with other artists like Ken Boothe and Delroy Wilson, and all the others, like we *groove.*.

Just went right in and just recorded songs and listened them, and if there were any mistakes, then we would correct them on one take or two take. Usually, first I would run down the song, then I would just take one take, and after that I wouldn't need another one.

I wasn't thinking of competing with any artist as such. I was more thinking of being among them, and sharing thoughts with them; like sharing views, ideas, etc. To be with them was so much that . . . you find that most artists who come in the business and try to compete against other artists never last long, because they exalt themselves too much, because when one thinks their feet are getting too big for their shoes, you find that 90 percent of the people don't really dig that artist because he's trying to hang his hat where he can't reach.

What was it like literally growing up in a band?

I used to enjoy singing with the bands of course, it was like exercise for my voice, but it was bleaching doing so many gigs. I didn't get enough rest going out weekends and sometimes I not reach home till breakfast next morning. Bleaching, yeah. Make me pale and tired, just like bleaching your clothes. See I was still in school then. Officially! I did well at school but I don't know how, it was such a rough. Like we'd have a tour round the island, every night doing a show with around a dozen acts, and I would often come in from the country and still have to go to school, wasted. So it was heavy. I don't know how I cope with that at all. And sometimes I'd skip a whole term, just keep on singing. This was when I was sixteen coming up seventeen and my parents wanted me to forget

this nonsense, further my education and become an accountant, a doctor, something they could look up to. But I didn't see that road, I mean my road was just to deal with music, strictly music.

How did you write your songs?

I was born in February, which means I'm from Joseph's tribe, one of the twelve tribes of Israel. And the purpose a Joseph comes to earth is to deliver people, for Joseph was the one who saved the children of Israel when they were in bondage in Egypt in the days of King Pharoah. He was the one who could really interpret Pharoah's dreams, the visions he used to have, and in so doing he saved the people from famine. Joseph got that power through the same Jesus I deal with now.

When I write a song I try to follow Joseph's way—deliverance through vision from all—true vibration. I want to be a shepherd in my work, teaching and learning, really singing so much. I have to get that feel that I can see something and say yes! I must write about this. But to just sit down and churn out a song, no. Confusion! Confusion confuse, can't pick up the lyrics. Mark, you can pick up some lyrics, like dog-ends in the street, but that would be an everyday thing and you don't want such. You want something new, something the people can relate to and, hopefully, profit from. I don't want to just sing it and not live it. I must live it. If I can sing songs that people can watch me living, then they can take my work.

—*Roger Steffens & Chris May*

I Jah Man Levi

The music of I Jah Man is the closest thing reggae has to so-called New Age music. Layered, atmospheric, spatial, spiritual, I Jah Man reaches for different peaks than other reggae artists, finding his trance in poetry and an almost orchestral sound rather than in the usual ticking meter of classical reggae. Although I Jah Man is a gentle and questing man, he has done time in prison, and his persuasive power is legendary. He is rumored to be the only artist who has ever talked Chris Blackwell into renewing his contract. We found him sitting in the shade, meditating with a draw, at Island's green mansions on West Kings House Road, Kingston.

Q: *I Jah Man, could you tell us your legal name?*

I Jah Man: Trevor Sutherland yunno, in western direction. Spiritually, my name is Serfi Selassie, the sword of the Trinity as I've stated on the first album *Hail HIM,* and as an artist I call myself I Jah Man Levi.

Have you spent your whole life in Jamaica?

Well, I leave Jamaica in 1963 and went to England. Yes, I emigrate to England with my mom an my dad, my sisters an myself. So all my experience musically, spiritually, physically as a man I must say I create all dat in London, England, because obviously it's the place I was. But during my time in England, or should I say Europe, I'm still doing that music because that's where my education of music started and I travel many countries—Germany—Europe all over.

I Jah Man's sound is a slightly different sound, a little bit more complex than what one usually associates with the Jamaican or the "reggae" sound. In my own ear, it sounds a little bit almost orchestral; there's a lot of things happening in the music, the beat is slightly different, you have your own very singular sound that belongs only to I Jah Man and no one else. Would you attribute that to your having been brought up in England as opposed to Jamaica?

Yes, most of my spiritual/physical growth take place in England, cos you're growin' up from a child to manhood. But, my fullness of creativity after knowin' myself as a man going through tribulation, knowin' good an bad, even do sentence in prison, and as prophecy said everyone must make a mistake cos through your mistakes you learn. I mek my mistakes and I feel de Earth had done me wrong as a individual an de only way I could rebonks back or tek back revenge in de Earth, not to destroy de Earth (no, cos I can't destroy de Earth) is to sing and de right way to sing is to sing de way you feel. And I can only sing of my feelings of my experience, what I been through.

So, when I write, I write of my experience; when I pray, I pray of my experiences because there was a time when I never used to be prayin'. It's just a spiritual ting. It have nothing to do wit physical.

What about your composing? The I Jah Man sound is a very beautiful, very ethereal sound.

I'd like to say the I Jah Man that you hear now—well, I can speak from my behalf—that the I Jah Man you hearin' on record is also new to me as I Jah Man. Cos the I Jah Man dat I know myself is an artist who can sit down with his guitar, as an individual and entertain millions. That's the real I Jah Man but until dat is done for the world to see, that is yet to come.

Do you feel that you as an artist reinvent yourself every time you make a recording or compose a new song? In other words, I'm very intrigued by the fact that you say that it's a new I Jah Man every time you do a new album.

Of course he have to re-invent himself, because what you hearin' in him as a individual, it express itself probably in a thousand vibes. But you never understand a fullness of vibes unless it go down on tape by working physically, by, yunno, studio wise and den gettin dat *feedback,* like dat rebonks back from you. Like you say "I Jah Man das great music I *feel* it"—I get a rebonks, like right now my head swell, ah say ah know, is the *spirit,* you know is a *rebonks.*

Your audience has only a vague awareness that you spent any time in prison. Would you tell us what that was like? Many artists say that prison had a beneficial effect on them.

He who feels it knows—I've been through it and there's nothing I could do about it. All I can say, I'm rejoicing now because, through prison, it mek me a brand new man. You know? Selassie I.

What are you working on now, another album, another set of songs?

Well, what am I doing now? (laughs) There's a lot of things I'm doing now. My God, physically and spiritually. For instance, I should be getting married in June (laughs again) so that's one good mark, Selassie I. Creatively, listen man, I got too much music; I don't think I can *live out* that much music I've written, I don't think I can live it out in flesh fe sing it, but I'm gonna try to do my best with the help of who is defendin' it.

What musicians do you like to work with the most?

I like to use the best, for instance—you want me to call all of dem names? It's a list! I'd love to . . . Robbie Shakespeare on bass, and if he's not available I like to use Val Douglas. And you have Sly [Dunbar on drums]; if he's not available, Mikey Boo. You got Bo Pee on guitar if you're in Jamaica, you got the great Willie Lindo [on guitar], you got me, of course, I Jah Man not too bad but still doing my thing . . . you got Wire on organ, he's terrific, Ansel Collins [on keyboards]. In London you got my favorite guitarist Johnny Copiah. He's in London an he doesn't know this, but anywhere I'm workin, I'm goin for him. He played de guitar on "Jah Heavy Load." On congas, obviously you got Ras Michael and the Sons Of Negus.

Do you like to have that classic Rastafarian sound of the akete drums?

Yes, because de drums is a thing that speaks, and don't forget in the beginnin' of time before any instrument the first sounds was voice and then drums. So drums are very powerful. And bass I would like to give this respect—on my last album *Are We A Warrior* there wasn't much credit there on the album for such great artists as Eric Gayle on guitar on "Two Sides Of Love." But I give respect for whatever I want to do or what musician I choose. Chris Blackwell let me go in and do what I wanna do, give thanks for that. I don't get full one-thousand-percent freedom, but it's getting better and better all the time.

—Stephen Davis & Peter Simon

I Jah Man Levi.

"And of Levi he said, Let thy Thummin and thy Urim be with thy holy one, whom thou didst prove at Massah, and with whom thou didst strive at the waters of Meribah;

Who said unto his father and to his mother, I have not seen him; neither did he acknowledge his brethren nor knew his own children: for they have observed thy word, and kept thy covenant.

They shall teach Jacob thy judgements, and Israel thy law: they shall put incense before thee, and whole burnt sacrifices upon thine altar.

Bless, Lord, his substance, and accept the work of his hands: smite through the loins of them that hate him, that they rise not again.

—Deuteronomy 33, 8-11

A Good Smoke with Peter Tosh

Jamaicans look to Peter Tosh for uncompromising Rastafarian preaching and for moral authority undented by the lead-tipped clubs of the police. Wherever he goes in this world, Tosh brings that righteous aura along with him. At some concerts, steel manacles hang from Peter's left wrist, symbolic of the social chains that bind a suffering people back home. In Toronto, a reviewer said that watching a Peter Tosh show was like staring the entire black race dead in the face.

After leaving the Wailers in 1974, Tosh recorded the pro-ganja anthem "Legalize It" and the anti-cop polemic "Mark of the Beast," as well

Peter Tosh: "Legalize it, and I'll advertise it. . ."

as two crucial albums in the development of reggae from local ricky-tick into a planetary sound, *Legalize It* and the stinging, epochal *Equal Rights*. But the turning point in his career was the so-called "Peace Concert" held in Kingston in 1978, at which Jamaica's top reggae groups had agreed to perform.

Among those attending the show were members of Jamaica's political elite—Prime Minister Michael Manley and his cabinet, the opposition leaders, and most of Jamaica's parliament and judiciary. Tosh sauntered onstage with a ganja cigar in his beak and proceeded to lecture his captive audience for 45 minutes on the evils of oppression, neocolonialism, and the "shitstem." Pointing a long black finger at Manley, Tosh harangued the prime minister on the sufferings of a poor people deprived of

human rights and legal marijuana. The crowd of ordinary Jamaicans in the audience, assembled in the bleachers, cheered themselves hoarse. Tosh and the band then lit into a stinging set that ended pointedly with "Legalize It."

Mick Jagger of the Rolling Stones happened to be at the Peace Concert and witnessed Tosh's dread-brilliant folk essay on political economy that day, and then the spellbinding music that Tosh and band, propelled by Sly & Robbie, put forth afterward. "I don't want no *peace*. I want *equal rights and justice*." Perhaps Jagger also got that eerie, impossible-to-resist feeling of staring the entire black race dead in the face.

Signed to the Rolling Stones' label, Tosh, Sly and Robbie recorded three important albums (*Bush Doctor, Mystic Man, Wanted Dread or Alive*) that showcased updated versions of Tosh classics ("Soon Come," "I'm the Toughest") and new avant-garde reggae ideas like "Buck-in-Hamm Palace" and "Oh Bumba Klaat." With the Stones' support, Tosh retained his place as one of the premier reggae singers of his generation.

This interview took place in a hotel in Cambridge, Mass., during the first Word Sound and Power tour in 1979. In the corner of the room Tosh's omnipresent "Inicycle" leaned against the wall. Tosh rides the tall unicycle everywhere—backstage, while visiting radio stations, down long hotel corridors at four in the morning. The Inicycle has been all over the world with Tosh and seems emblematic of its owner's stance in a dangerous world: precarious yet balanced, eccentric, uniquely upright. During the interview Winston Hubert MacIntosh manhandled and drew upon an impressive cone-shaped spliff. *SSSSwwwwwwwfffffttttttt!!!!*

Q: *It must be difficult for a touring reggae band to maintain its herb supply.*

Peter Tosh: Well, herb is all over America, mon. You don't have to bring no herb here

anymore. *Ssssswwwwwffffttt*. Ahhh.

Is it as good as what you find in Jamaica?

No way. Psychologically, you just have to pretend that it is good— pretend that you smoking the best draw—till you reach home, where the best is.

As a connoisseur of herb, what do you prefer?

Well, Thai stick not bad. And the Colombian now, the quality varies, but the other day I get a draw of Colombian in Milwaukee. *Exclusive!! Ssssswwwwwffffttt*.

Milwaukee?

Yes mon. And Milwaukee is a place where you don't get herb, but I get herb. Yeah mon. Great draw! Was a brother brought it for me. And I also like a thing called Maui wowee. Yeah mon.

In many of your songs, you call for legalizing marijuana. But there's a theory that if Jamaica legalized it, the country would be transformed into an outlaw agronomy operating under United Nations sanctions . . .

Bullshit! (*kissing his teeth bitterly*). Nine out of ten people in Jamaica smoke herb. Everyone an outlaw.

No, I mean the United Nations has these antidope statutes . . .

United Nations bullshit! (*furious*). Me no wanna hear that argument there. Who are them who take counsel against I&I, to see that I&I are separated from I&I culture? He who created the earth created herb for the use of man, seen? If herb was growing in the blood-clot United Nations, you think Jamaica could go tell United Nations what to do? So how come the *bumba ras clot* United Nations dare to come and tell us what to do? Fuck the United Nations! My Father grow herb, and if my Father know what is right would have made herb growing in the United blood-clot Nations, not just in Jamaica for I&I who praise him continually.

Why do Jamaican politicians pay so much attention to the music?

Well, dem have to listen to what the people say to know the people's view. Reggae is telling them what's on the people's mind, seen? 'Cause the singers and players of instruments are the prophets of the earth in this time. It was written: Jah say, "I call upon the singers and players of instruments to tell the word and wake up the slumbering mentality of the people." Seen?

What about your political speech at the Peace Concert?

I devoted my time and my energy to making a speech, because sitting before me I saw the prime minister and the whole establishment approximately. So it seemed the right time to say what I had to say as a representative of the people, because irrespective of the way I would like to live, I still must live within the shitstem. I've become a victim of the shitstem so many times.

What happened to you after the speech?

Three months later, yes, yes, yes! I was waiting for a rehearsal outside Aquarius Studio on Half Way Tree [a main Kingston avenue], waiting for two of my musicians, and I had a little piece of roach in my hand. A guy come up to me in plain clothes and grab the roach out of my hand. So I say him, wha' happen? He didn't say nothing, so I grab the roach back from him and he start to punch me up. I say again, wha' happen, and he say I must go *dung so* ["downtown" in police jargon]. I say, *dung so?* Which way you call *dung so?* That's when I realized this was a police attitude, so I opened the roach and blew out the contents. Well, him didn't like that and him start to grab at me aggressively now—my waist, my shoulder, grabbing me and tearing off my clothes and things. Then other police come and push their guns in my face and try brute force on me.

Did they know who you were?

No, I don't know. But you don't have to know a man to treat him the way he should be treated. But because I am humble and don't wear a jacket and tie and drive a big Lincoln Continental or Mercedes-Benz, I don't look exclusively different from the rest. I look like the people, seen? To them police, here's just another Rasta to kill.

Dem took out dem blood-clot gun and mosh it against my face and fuckery like that. They take me to their station, and one police start to level a terrible blow at I, and I duck and he hit the police behind me, bring blood to his face, then dem all over me! *Bumba clot!* My appearance to them in the police station is like a criminal, because according to the shitstem, if a youth is a *dreadlock,* he's a criminal, seen? Guilty until proven innocent.

Now eight-to-ten guys gang my head with batons and weapons of destruction. They close the door, chase away the people and gang my head with batons for an hour and a half until my hand break trying to fend off the blows. I run to the window and they beat me back with blows. I run to the door and they beat me back with blows. Later I found out these guys' intentions was to kill me, right? What I had to do was play dead by just lying low. Passive resistance. And I hear them say, yes, he's dead. But I survived them, by intellect. Yes I.

Why'd they pick on you?

It was because of my militant act within the society, because I speak out against repression and the shitstem, seen? Yes mon! I know it's a direct connection. I've been threatened before in Jamaica many times. Once, at the airport in Kingston, the superintendent of customs drew his gun and said he had wanted to kill me for years.

Why are militant artists such a threat to Jamaica?

Because their words are corruption, and where there's corruption, there must be an eruption. Ya no see? Politricks! Politician been promising the most good but doing the most dangerous evil. And all the people get is promises. A generation come, and a generation go, and nothing is accomplished.

What about your relationship with the Stones?

Well, even their name alone is a great input. I see it as a blessing, seen? One of my Father's blessings, because of I determination to spread the word. Finding Mick and Keith to spread the word and deal with the music—knowing they not only are interested in the music, but love and respect the music—is great, great blessing.

Is there an affinity between reggae's outlaw roots and the Stones' outlaw image?

Well, I see it and know it, so because I see and I know, who feels it knows it. Yeah mon!

Why did you and Mick choose to showcase an old Motown song, "Don't Look Back," in your Bush Doctor *album, instead of one of your more militant songs?*

Well, that is a psychological procedure, because I am a scientist, seen? 'Cause I'm a mon who has studied human psychology and knows what two-thirds of the world loves, seen? If you're trying to get across to two-thirds of the world, you proceed psychologically by giving them what they want. After they dance to what they want, they must listen to what you've got next, seen? And also I like the title, "Don't Look Back," because I don't intend to.

Why does preaching play such a strong role in reggae, especially in your *music?*

Well, mon, that is coming from my Father's message chamber, seen? I preach, yes mon, but I do not judge. No man is here to look upon what another man is doing. Judge not, lest ye be judged. I say, make sure your doings are right, so that when the payday comes around, what you get in your envelope will be satisfactory. Ya no seen?

Why have so many cultural explosions —reggae, Rastas, dope—come from Jamaica?

Because we are the prophets of this Earth. We are they who were executed by Alexander the blood-clot Great and those great pirates who used to go round and chop off the saints' heads. All these things are revealed between the lines through the Third Eye. I&I see ourselves as the reincarnated souls of those carried off into slavery.

Are you surprised by the dramatic acceptance of reggae over the last few years?

It was prophesied, my brother. Only fools are surprised at the manifestations of prophecy. Seen? Only those who cannot see between the lines will be surprised.

What about the future of reggae?

Yes mon. Fifteen years from now, there will be a different dispensation of time. The shitstem will no longer be. All the places that are built upon corruption shall be torn down and shall be no more upon the face of creation. Yes mon! Five years from now will be a different age. Five years from blood-clot now will be totally different. No wicked left on the Earth. By 1983 Africa will be free.

—Stephen Davis

Mick Jagger and Peter Tosh: "You got to walk and don't look back..."

149

Jimmy Cliff

Jimmy Cliff was born James Chambers in 1948, the son of a tailor who lived in Somerton, St. James. By the age of 14 he had migrated to Kingston and recorded his first song, "Daisy Got Me Crazy." The year was 1962, the ska craze was in full tilt, and James Chambers apotheosized into Jimmy Cliff, teenage ska star. His producer, Count Boysie, paid him one shilling to do the song.

One evening, passing by Beverley's, a downtown Kingston emporium that sold ice cream and records, Cliff decided to perform a spontaneous audition for the three Chinese brothers who

career. On a tour of Brazil he wrote "Wonderful World, Beautiful People," which was a worldwide hit.

In 1969 he recorded "Vietnam," which Bob Dylan called "the best protest song ever written." The following year produced the sensational songs featured in *The Harder They Come*. Cliff's blistering performance in the primal reggae film effectively turned his career into a legend; in the ten years since the film, he has worked all over the world and experimented with a myriad of styles and beliefs.

Enormously popular in Africa, Cliff and his crack band, Oneness, are constant sell-outs in venues as disparate as Cameroon, South Africa, and Nigeria. The concerts, whether in Africa or Europe, aren't much different from those in New York or San Francisco. By the end of the show, the audiences are juking in the aisles as one of reggae's greatest voices soars on into the smokey night air.

Q: *In* The Harder They Come, *you wore a shirt*

black, as a black star. But y'see, white is purity still, it represents purity. It's not really the color now, but how many points you use in a star. A five-pointed star represents man's five senses still. But the six-pointed star is more representative of I now as a black man from the tribes of Ishmael and Israel, y'see. That's why we used it in the film.

You were in South Africa this year to do some shows, and this sparked a controversy concerning whether it was ethical for a reggae musician to perform under conditions of apartheid. Any comment?

Matter of fact, I wanted that it should have been a bigger controversy. I wanted to get people thinking more about it.

Where did you write "Many Rivers To Cross"?

In Jamaica. But that was the same period of time when I came back to Jamaica after four years, before the movie, dissatisfied with myself for not accomplishing what I went to England to accomplish. And so that's when I wrote "Many Rivers to Cross." Like the white cliffs of Dover,

Well they tell me of a pie
up in the sky
Waiting for me when I die
But between the day you're born
and when you die
They never seem to hear
even your cry
So as sure as the sun will shine
I'm gonna get my share now,
what's mine
And then the harder they come
The harder they fall
One and all

—Jimmy Cliff,
"The Harder They Come"

150

owned the store. He improvised a little tune called "Dearest Beverley," which convinced one of the brothers, Leslie Kong, to go into the record business. The first record they did was "Hurrican Hattie" ("If you mess with me/I'll tear you up like a hurricane"), and it was an immediate smash. Jimmy Cliff was, at fifteen, a celebrity, and Kong found himself at the top of the Jamaican music industry.

Cliff continued to churn out hits ("King of Kings," "Miss Jamaica") and toured the Caribbean with ska package shows. In 1964 he played the New York World's Fair, backed by Byron Lee and the Dragonaires. After that, Cliff moved to England to seek fame and fortune, returning to Jamaica in the late '60s to resume his recording

with a yellow six-pointed star for the crucial recording-session scene. In concert over the past five years you've been wearing a white five-pointed star. But lately you've been wearing a yellow six-pointed star again. Is the symbolism significant?

Jimmy Cliff: The six-pointed star represents two tribes, Israel and Ishmael. When you read the Bible, these are the two most important tribes, and I am descended from both of these. I be of the seed of Adam.

So why did you switch to the white star after The Harder They Come?

Well, the color doesn't make much difference now, y'see, because the gold star that I wear tonight—our flag is red, green and gold . . . and

we used to go across with my little van and take the ferry down in Dover and go across to France or Germany and work for nothing. That's "Many Rivers to Cross."

Was "the Harder They Come" in existence before the movie, or did you write it for the title of the movie?

I wrote it for the movie. How it came about, they started out calling the film "Rhygin" till, after Perry [Henzell] met me, he started calling it "Hard Road to Travel" which is another one of my songs. Originally what I got on script was something different from what you see on screen now. Cuz he would say like, "How would you do that, Jimmy?" and I just *do* it, you know. Cuz it something that I'd *lived*. So they decided the film still need a title song. They had some songs which he thought he was going to use in it, like "Johnny Too Bad," "Rivers of Babylon," "Draw Your Brakes," "Sitting in Limbo," "Many Rivers to Cross." But he still think he needed a title song to fit the character, so I wrote the song.

"Sitting in Limbo." Do you remember when you wrote that song?

"Sitting in Limbo" I wrote when I was in South America second time, 1970. I went to South America 1968 and 1970. It was 1970 that I wrote "Sitting in Limbo." I had the idea for the song before I left England and I went to South America and I developed it from there.

The feeling of being in Limbo was from Jamaica. The movie started 1970—*The Harder They Come*—and it was at the time I felt that feeling. I'd been in England for four years, and came back to Jamaica, not making it in England, you know. Like I leave to make it. Came back to Jamaica, and lost the popularity that I had. People even start thinking I'm a foreigner now.

Can you define reggae music?

Yeah, reggae music is the cry of the people, that's what it is. What is this cry? It was a cry for recognition, identity, respect, love, justice. This cry was born out of the spirit, after the backlash of the slave had finished. It was the same thing that Rastafari was born out of. We had to take up the Bible and read it, and see where we identify in it, because it was written for us to see ourselves in it.

Of all the people who wear the title of "reggae star," you wear that title most uncomfortably. Why?

Because you see, you can't limit me to reggae. Because my concept of reggae is universal, the whole entire planet; the *whole entire universe* I deal with when I think of reggae. Because reggae, now, is a combination: any form of music, I can take anything, so anything can come to into reggae, that's the uniqueness of it, it's dancing and it's listening. And it's the music that the Bible speak of, that will be the music in the last days, that the singers and players of instruments will carry. This is the music. And

that's why it can't die. It's not a fad that going to blow up, and tomorrow you don't hear about it. It moves with the time, and we always dealing with what's happening now, pointing a finger at Babylon.

Your interest in Islam was cause for much comment in Jamaica.

Well, see now, my religion is Divine Culture, but I believe in all the prophets that came with the same message from the one divine supreme Being. So therefore, is only One Truth you have, and one Divine supreme being. So I believe in the principles and everything that Prophet Mohammed came with, like I believe in what Jesus came with, like I believe in what Moses came with, *all* the prophets. My religion is Divine Culture.

—Roger Steffens & Stephen Davis.

Jacob Miller, before his passing in 1980, was widely regarded as one of the most promising singers in Jamaica. Backed by the Inner Circle band, Miller was looking forward to a world tour with the Wailers when he died.

Max Romeo's career began with his monumental hit "Wet Dream" in 1968, which reportedly sold millions of records in England. During the early '70s Max recorded important songs associated with the rise of Jamaican socialism ("Let the Power Fall"), and in 1975 wrote and recorded for producer Lee Perry the devastating "War Inna Babylon," which was immediately banned by a worried government and is still hailed as one of the most brilliant records in reggae history. One of Jamaica's best songwriters, Max and his family relocated in New York in the late '70s, where a collaboration with Rolling Stones guitarist Keith Richard yielded an interesting new direction for this greatest of Rasta crooners.

Singer Jimmy Riley used to be part of a classic rock steady duo (variously called the Uniques and the Techniques) with the late and legendary singer Slim Smith. Still an important voice, Riley is best known for "Tell the Youth the Truth."

Page 152:

The Clash, looking wary in Belfast, scene of the longest-running white riot.

Reggae International

TOO
MUCH
PRESSURE

13

Black Albion

Jamaican music came of age in England in
many ways, and despite the contradictions inherent in the colony-
mother country relationship between
Jamaica and England, London was
where the first two generations of
reggae masters came to make their
stand after achieving local success in
Kingston. In those days, London was
an imperial capital, the natural arena
in which a West Indian star could polish his act and
break into planetary show-biz. For some musicians,
like Jimmy Cliff and the three Wailers, the strategy
worked. For others, the adventure ended on the
assembly lines of Midlands factories. Eventually,
a triumphant new generation of British-raised reggae
musicians took on a culture imported from Jamaica
and remade it in their own image—hip, haard, and
cosmopolitan. In this section **Chris May,** the editor of
London's respected **Black Music & Jazz Review,** provides
some background to British reggae , and profiles
several of his personal heroes.

Then sub-culturist **Dick Hebdige** dissects the important, short-lived 2 tone movement, in which white
and black Britons harnessed the jumping power of ska
and turned it into a fierce, integrationist form of proto-
reggae whose effects are still being felt today. Steel
Pulse was the first British reggae band to make an
impact outside of England, and **Peter Simon** talks with
head Pulse David Hinds.

A History of British Reggae

The story of Jamaican music in Britain is the
story of various Jamaican-born styles—notably
ska, rock steady and rockers—transported to an
alien culture and there gradually shedding their
their Caribbean mores and finding a distinct and
individual geographic identity. Like the socio-
economic struggles of the people who have made
the music, strangers in a strange land, the process has been a long and difficult one. Through
the '50s, the '60s and much of the '70s the
music and its audience suffered cultural es-
trangement and, comparing themselves to their
Jamaican cousins, a debilitating sense of inferior-
ity. As a result, what they manifested was not a
conscious or even unconscious desire for esthet-
ic independence, but instead a quite deliberate
effort to hear, copy and master Jamaican initia-
tives. To generalise, up until the mid-'70s the
prevailing mood amongst British-based artists
was one of we-can-do-it-as-well-as-you rather
than we-can-do-something-*different*-from-you.

By 1981, the poor-relations complex had largely
disappeared—taking along its several injurious
ramifications—and Britain can now boast a body
of artists whose work not only stands favourable
comparison with anything coming out of the
Kingston studios but which is also wholly
unique. In the vanguard of this new movement
are artists like Linton Kwesi Johnson, Aswad,
Dennis Bovell and George Oban. LKJ is the one
who has so far made the greatest international
impression, through his vocal albums *Dread
Beat An' Blood, Forces Of Victory* and *Bass
Culture.* But it can't be long before his colleagues
make a similarly substantial impact overseas.
Aswad, Britain's pre-eminent self-contained
band, forwarded the astounding local-militant
"Warrior Charge" single in 1980, followed in
1981 by the the equally exquisite thunderer
"Finger Gun Style" and their fourth album, *New*

Linton Kwesi Johnson and John
Cooper Clarke.

Opposite: South London, 1981.

Chapter. Dennis Bovell, after acting as the mainstay of the Matumbi band since its inception in 1972, left the group in 1981 to pursue a solo artist/producer career, and has already surfaced with one stunning aberrant reggae double album, *Brain Damage.* George Oban, Aswad's original bass player, now leads a studio band called Motion, whose eponymous debut album (again 1981), has taken homegrown into a previously uncharted, and swingingly assured, jazz/Latin fusion vector. If any one year goes down in the history books as the year British reggae finally came of age, then 1981 it will have to be.

Jamaican Music in Britain: 1950s to Mid-1970s

"Unlike most other European countries, post-war Britain was in the position to turn to an alternative and comparatively uncompetitive source of labour in its colonies and ex-colonies in Asia and the Caribbean. Colonialism had already under-developed these countries and thrown up a reserve army of labour which now waited in readiness to serve the needs of the metropolitan economy. And it was to these vast and cheap resources of labour that Britain turned in the 1950s." (A. Sivanandan, "Race And Class," London 1976).

To tell the story of the Caribbean emigrants to Britain since World War II would, of course, require a book to itself. But some awareness of their exodus, its motivations and extent, is necessary: for without the British state's active encouragement (in which 'the streets are paved with gold/come to the Mother Country/we love you' myth figured large) far smaller numbers of emigrants would likely have come to Britain. And without them, homegrown reggae, in its present stage of development at least, would not have emerged.

Suffice to note, then, that the '50s and '60s saw continual and substantial Caribbean emigration to The Mother Country. Precise statistics have never been compiled (or, perhaps, are just un-published), but London's Institute of Race Relations has estimated that between 1955 and 1962 there were 301,540 emigrants from the Caribbean, of whom 178,270 came from Jamaica.

Once here, like migrants the world over, the new arrivals were promptly pushed into the worst-paid, least attractive job opportunities and housed in metropolitan slum areas. They performed the menial labor white Britons no longer aspired to.

It was these conditions which accelerated the early growth of Britain's ex-Jamaica music business. For the worse the conditions the greater the incentive, the need, to find sustenance in the culture left behind. Drinking/social clubs (usually illegal) sprang up in all West Indian ghetto areas and the music they provided came from home.

The next step was the formation of locally-based record labels, to cater to Jamaican club and family social life. The first such label was Melodisc, founded in 1946 to import American jazz, but by the late '50s increasingly concerned with importing Jamaican covers of American r&b (notably the efforts of bandleader Byron Lee). As

Jamaican producers increasingly turned to making their own indigenous music, nascent ska, Melodisc imported that too.

Other labels grew up and followed Melodisc's pattern. The early '60s saw the formation of Sonny Roberts' Planitone label (now evolved into Orbitone), and in 1962 Chris Blackwell traveled to London to check out the feasibility of setting up a branch of his Island label in Britain. In 1968, Trojan was set up, and—with Island—quickly established a dominant position in the rapidly expanding industry.

The first British indies, these labels soon grasped the financial implications of releasing their own local productions, as opposed to merely distributing Jamaican records. And they found no shortage of talented musicians eager to record. The Caribbean migrants included many singers who believed, usually erroneously, that they would make their fortune once arrived in Britain. The Aces, Winston Curtis, Errol Dunkley, Alton Ellis, Desmond Dekker, Laurel Aitken, Junior English, Sharon Forrester, Owen Gray, Louisa Mark, Gene Rondo, Roy Shirley and Nicky Thomas were among the many who came to Britain in the late '60s/early '70s. Some stayed a few years before going home disillusioned. Some remain in Britain today. Almost all enjoyed sizeable ethnic chart successes. But today, of the artists mentioned above, only Errol Dunkley has managed to create a relatively secure and well-paying career, and then only after many years of hardship.

But, by the mid-'70s, a new generation of musicians had surfaced. Many of them were born in England, and of the remainder most had left Jamaica in early childhood. The socio-cultural background of this new wave was as much British-informed as it was Jamaican; often, indeed, more so. The youths didn't hanker after Jamaica to the degree of their parents. (They didn't hanker after Britain either in the main, as Rasta turned their heads increasingly towards Africa. But that's another story, which we'll come to later.)

Above all, the new musicians were *confident.* They were fed up with being told, in the streets and on the stage, that they couldn't hold a candle

to the Kingston stars. So they set about proving their worth; as much from self-pride as a conscious unilateral declaration of independence. Dozens of short-lived and frequently interdependent bands and solo artists stepped forward in the early/mid-'70s: Matumbi, Aswad, Black Slate, Delroy Washington & I-Sus, the Cimarons, the Blackstones (one of homegrown's rare, and excellent, vocal trios), Tradition, Misty, Steel Pulse, the Sons Of Jah, Dambala, Brimstone, Movement, the Undivided, I Jah Man Levi, Capi-

tal Letters and the Regulars.

Black Slate, who've since had a chequered history, from which they're only now returning to a position of musical strength, were perhaps the most initially promising of the new wave. And certainly the most overtly British. The band's 1976 single "Sticks Man" (since re-released at least four times in Britain alone), was —with Delroy Washington's "Streets Of Ladbroke Grove"—the first profound reggae expression of the black British experience. (It dealt with, and damned the causes for, the internecine petty crime debasing ghetto street life.)

In an interview with Slate shortly after the release of "Sticks Man," I asked lead vocalist Keith Drummond why he thought the British socio-cultural perspective had begun to make itself felt in local reggae music.

"Well, you spend all your life in this country and of course you don't know certain things about Jamaica. In my own case, over half my life has been spent in Britain. So when you combine those two experiences together, half from here and half from Jamaica, you obviously don't have the same feel as they have over there.

"A lot of UK-based bands did try to just copy the rhythms and so on of Jamaican reggae, but they're learning from their mistake. By copying you don't ever learn what you can really do. Now it's dawning on more and more bands that they're wasting their talent just going with the sound you hear from Jamaica. Better go with the present feel you've got in this country. You don't know what they're going through in Jamaica, you can only read about it secondhand. So sing

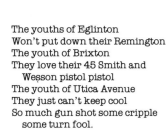

Black Slate

The youths of Eglinton
Won't put down their Remington
The youth of Brixton
They love their 45 Smith and
  Wesson pistol pistol
The youth of Utica Avenue
They just can't keep cool
So much gun shot some cripple
  some turn fool.

—"Youth of Englinton,"
Michael Rose.

about the sufferation you're going through here.

"The sufferation in Jamaica, I think, depends on who's in power at any one time. In this country, it doesn't matter who's in power—if you're black you're going to go through sufferation. They say you can't make reggae unless you're a sufferer. Well, it's not just the Jamaicans who suffer. We suffer too, and now we're singing about our own condition."

Coincident with the upsurge in homegrown talent came the mid-'70s label boom. A new generation of youth-run indie labels sprang up which both fed off and helped forward the new artists. The initial reason for the label explosion was in the main the 1975 crash of the Trojan empire: its demise (temporary, but from which it has never fully recovered) opened massive entrepreneurial opportunities for ambitious new labels (often, incidentally, set up by youthful ex-Trojan employees). Virgin Records, an English rock label, attempted to fill the gap but was met by considerable—and considerably better informed—competition. Of the many labels who sprang up around the time of the Trojan crash, the pace-setters were Groove Music, Hawkeye, Cha Cha, D-Roy, Vulcan, Klik, Burning Sounds, Manic, Ballistic and Venture. Some still prosper, some have fallen victim to the depressed British economy which has hit black businesses hardest.

More recently, some of the economic malaise gripping homegrown reggae has been somewhat lightened by the burgeoning popularity of Lovers Rock, a Jamaican form which has been integrated into the popular love music of British artists, notably from the female side. A host of solo artists and harmony groups—Cassandra, Sonia, Marie Pierre, 15–16–17, Black Harmony, Jean Adebambo, Carroll Thompson, Janet Kay, Mellow Rose—have sprung up, selling quantities of records unprecedented in the history of the black British record scene.

Homegrown Today

Rico: Keeping the Flame Alive

One could argue the semantic toss of whether trombonist Rico Rodriguez is a homegrown or Jamaican artist up until the coming of Armageddon. Certainly Rico was born in Jamaica and certainly his musical roots and contemporary mores are Jamaican, or more precisely Rastafarian. But Rico is widely regarded as a British artist because (a) he's lived and worked here since 1961, with only a few breathers back home; (b) he's been a continual source of local inspiration during all of that time; (c) he's given the deeper-roots stamp to much of the recent 2 tone music, itself a peculiarly British phenomenon.

Born in 1934 in Kingston 2, Rico is a graduate of the famed Alpha Boys School, a Catholic outfit which placed an unusual emphasis on musical education. (Other luminaries of Alpha include Don Drummond, Dizzy Moore, Lester Stirling and Roland Alphonso.) But Rico's most lasting influence was the period he and Drummond spent living in Jamaica's Wareika Hills (1958 to 1961), studying and playing with the music-dominated Rasta community presided over by Count Ossie and his Mystic Revelation Of Ras Tafari.

In 1961, sick of the police and straight society and fed up with being ripped off by Jamaican producers, Rico came to London and spent much of the '60s on assembly lines. Between 1972 and 1976 he was a leading light of the Undivided,

originally a backing group for Gene Rondo but from 1974 (with the release of the *Listen To The World* album) a self-contained outfit which did much to bring authentic reggae to British audiences through extensive road work.

Rico's first fifteen years in Britain were financially grim ones, and it wasn't until he signed to Island in the mid-'70s and recorded *Man From Wareika* (1976), that Rico's career began to look up. Since then of course he's civilized the music of the Specials and continued to record his own blistering Jah-jazz music. His latest album, *That Man Is Forward* (1981), is amongst the finest, most muscularly sophisticated reggae music ever recorded.

Rico is far from rich today, though he's more comfortable than he's ever been before. A genuinely supertalented musician, he remains remarkably free of the rancour one might expect from an artist of his stature, frequently ignored by the record business in favour of less talented but more easily marketable white artists.

"Over the years I've struggled, suffered, I've

developed a lot of patience I would say. You *can* feel vicious, but over the years you build a resilience and you conquer it. Even though, at times, it's like *we* do the hard work and *they* reap the benefit.

"In the middle '60s I used to do shift work at Dagenham [Britain's equivalent to Motor City]. And that was hard. You come home so tired you cannot practise. Sometimes I'd say to myself 'what are you *doing* here?' And people would say the same to me.

"But I feel strong now, not weak like I used to. I used to think about running back to Jamaica in desperation. But since the Specials, things have been better. Everyone in the band says I'm looking better, playing better. And they like me better too!"

Aswad: Rocking in the Belly of the Monster

Formed in 1975, in the Ladbroke Grove (Notting Hill) area of West London, by bassist George Oban, guitarist Brinsley Forde and drummer Angus Gaye, Aswad is the youngest of the

Aswad, in the streets of London.

Rico Rodriguez and band

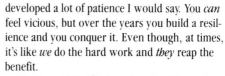

157

homegrown bands to have emerged from the mid-'70s school. Both in terms of their ages and in terms of history: Matumbi, the Cimarons and Black Slate all predate them. Perhaps that's one of the reasons behind the group's pre-eminent position amongst homegrown outfits: less a part of what went on before the emergence of homegrown, more youthfully rebellious in every way. For the heart of Aswad's strength lies in rebelliousness: from a down-the-line Rasta collective who deny they're political (in Eurocentric terms), their records rail against social injustice in Britain/Babylon, with the police a frequent target of their acid attacks.

Aswad have had several personnel changes, but the current and seemingly stable line-up is Gaye, Forde, bassist Tony Gad (a.k.a. Tony Robinson, originally keyboardist for the band, taking over the bass role when George Oban split in late 1979/early 1980) and percussionist Levi. They've released four albums—*Aswad* (1976), *Hulet* (1979), *Showcase* (a 1981 singles compilation) and *New Chapter* (1981).

Aswad's 1970s releases, though strong, never fully captured the potential of the band, and it wasn't until 1980's "Warrior Charge" single and two subsequent albums that they've really cracked the vinyl side of their work. Their recent single "Finger Gun Style" and album *New Chapter* have unquestionably established them as the hardest, most outspoken homegrown roots Rasta band yet to emerge, a position they seem in little danger of losing in the foreseeable future.

One of the beauties of Aswad's music is that, unlike some staunchly Rastafarian bands, they aren't afraid to experiment with reggae. Their lyrics may often be full of biblical imagery but there's no ostrich-like fundamentalism about their gestalt.

"That doesn't stop anything at all," Brinsley Forde says. "Cos we're musicians first of all, although we're playing reggae music. We're musicians and we want to improve. And any sound we hear that will suit our reggae music, we put it in. Is what we like to do. And that improves reggae music see, just like you find jazz improved.

"You don't find the same attitude with musicians in Jamaica, not really. But you see, it's like, they're the *root*. Reggae's like a plant, and you have the root, and you have the flower. In Jamaica they have new things in the music as well, plenty new things, but it's different new things than we could use here. We each have certain ideas about what goes where, but is the the same thing, both sides are improving."

Dennis Bovell: Mutant-Reggae Maestro

Not long ago, Dennis Bovell, co-founder of Matumbi back in 1972, handed me a copy of his new solo album—*Brain Damage*—and told me he was no longer working with the group and that he hoped *Brain Damage* would fry a few crania.

Had anyone but Dennis been behind it, *Brain Damage* would probably qualify as the most outrageous example of ill-advised conceit yet produced by an industry already notorious for its galloping egos. For not only did Dennis write and produce the set, a double to boot, he also mixed it, arranged it, sang on it and played most of the instruments (from drums to guitar to bass to synths to piano to violin to organ). And if that's not involvement enough, the entire project was conceived and executed in Dennis' own Studio 80 in South London. *Brain Damage,* to put it mildly, is a solo album.

But what's all this frying of the crania? Well, there *are* some classic homegrown tracks on the set, but there's also a hefty proportion of mutant/aberrant reggae: calypso-tinged, rock 'n' roll-tinged (the Matumbi evergreen "After Tonight" gets that treatment), boogie-tinged, mutant disco-tinged and . . . you get the picture? It struck me that Dennis was deliberately courting the condemnation of The Roots Kangaroo Court with *Brain Damage.* Indeed he was, he said; he deliberately went out of his way in the making of the album to incense Britain's reggae purists.

"I did that to 'After Tonight' to really fuck their heads. That's why there are a couple of straightahead roots tracks just before it. Get them in a fundamentalist frame of mind and then zap them. Too many reggae listeners are too set in their ways, their brains have ossified. So maybe, by shaking them out of their stupor, I'll get a little more fresh air blowing through the scene. Which it certainly needs."

Alongside his newly established mutant-reggae track record, Dennis of course has an even longer one in straightahead reggae. He's been involved with most of LKJ's productions. Merely the tip of the iceberg as Dennis says, and he's not bluffing, "I looked in the reggae top twenty once and I found that I had worked on eighteen out of the twenty entries."

Don't get the idea that Dennis Bovell is one swellhead though. He's a supremely relaxed person, and well open to criticism. It's simply that he does know his talent. He does feel hampered by straightahead reggae, despite his love for it. And out of this love-hate relationship a new chapter in British reggae will assuredly emerge. *Brain Damage* is merely the first page.

George Oban: The Man Behind the Motion

Like Dennis Bovell, George Oban is an ex-founder member of one of Britain's foremost reggae bands (he was the original bass player with Aswad, and played with the group from its birth in 1975 until early 1980). And also like Dennis, George is setting about revolutionising Anglo-reggae music. In July 1981, after nearly eighteen months off the scene, George surfaced with his *Motion* album. Aberrant reggae of a different sort: where Dennis favours head-on collisions between different styles (which nonetheless mesh perfectly), George has gone for a subtler, more multi-level approach. *Motion* fused reggae bass-and-drum charts with subtle paradigms of jazz/Latin/funk.

Equally surprising, given the aforementioned Roots Kangaroo Court, Judge Puerilist In Session, was the uniformly ecstatic response with which

Oban's experiment was received in UK reggae circles.

George was pretty surprised too. The reason he left Aswad was, how shall we put it? . . . not the usual "musical differences" smoke screen beloved of press agents. There was no smoke screen, there really *were* musical differences. In 1978/9, when George attempted to inject some of his idiosyncratic vision into Aswad, the band (to put it bluntly) kicked him out.

Which was reasonable enough, and happily the rift has long since been mended (Angus Gaye and Tony Gad both guest on *Motion*). Nevertheless, George confidently expected the album to get a beating amidst accusations of betraying his roots.

That he didn't receive same says much for the future of British homegrown: openmindedness is a necessary prerequisite for successful evolution. How, if at all, does George approach the vexing debate over the definition of roots?

"To take it right back, I was born in Britain. And as I never even visited Jamaica until 1971 my musical roots, if you like, were primarily people like the Beatles and the Beach Boys—the sort of records we'd bring into the school lunch time disco sessions. I'm talking about London in the mid-'60s now. The first reggae I can remember hearing was in 1968, 1969, when a mate brought some record or other round.

"So my earliest roots were split between a lot of rock, some reggae, and the Pentecostal gospel music I played guitar for in a church up Kensal Rise [a northwest London ghetto-cum-suburb] as a youth. Later on of course I got heavily into jazz, after listening to Return To Forever and them.

"When I was ejected from Aswad there was all sorts of emotional things being said, which hit me hard, but I and them was young still. But I mean, what *is* roots? Music is shapeless, colourless.

"And when you trace it right back, Jamaican music, you find, is based on American roots, as well as the African heritage. So, in reality, every person's roots is different."

—*Chris May*

George Oban, forging new Anglo-Jamaican sounds . . . .

Professor Bovell in uniform.

Ska Tissue: The Rise and Fall of 2 Tone

"All Indians must dance, every-where, keep on dancing. Pretty soon in next spring, Great Spirit come . . . All dead Indians come back and live again. They all be strong just like young men, be young again . . ."

Wavoka, leader of the Sioux Ghost Dance religion of the 1880s.

One cold night in Birmingham in 1978, I met Jerry Dammers, keyboard player with Special AKA, then the Coventry Automatics, later still the Specials, at the flat of the group's third manager, Mike "Shoop" Horseman. Crouching on the floor over his sketch pad, Dammers, the man who masterminded 2 Tone, looked up from a doodle he'd just completed of a pair of shoes next to the photo of Peter Tosh in his early Wailing Wailers days; the photo which, in negative, was going to be the 2 Tone trademark. Dammers looked up and said:

"What I need now is *loafers*. A pair of loafers just to top it off." Loafers . . . black slip-ons with a leather tassle across the front, cut low under the ankle with a thick, heavy sole. These talismanic black objects, summoned up like dead relations at a seance, were lumbering back from the past and into the late '70s where they would stand for Jerry Dammers, as another sign of 2 Tone, and later still, as the logo for the 2 Tone film. These were the shoes the skinheads used to wear back in 1969 on ska nights down at the city-centre clubs with their tonic mohair suits—the "two-tone" suits which changed colour depending on how the light caught them. Now these things were to be worn again, brought back to life along with the cheap, choppy music, the "nutty" dance moves, the sta-prest trousers, the white socks, the Fred Perry sports shirts, the pork-pie hats (a.k.a "stingy brims" or "blue-beats"). The shoes were just one brick in the edifice, a telling symbol in the Dammers 2 Tone Dream.

Dammers knew that if he got the

details right—the things that the persnickety young punters noticed —he might be able to swing the whole package. And the package, in this case, consisted not only of an image and a sound but also of an attitude, a posture, amongst other things, on race.

When looking at 2 tone, the point to remember is not that it was, as some rock and reggae purists have suggested, a "media-created hype" (less "authentic" than the original '60s ska movement), nor that the music produced by the groups (the Specials, The Selecter, Madness, The [English] Beat, the Body Snatchers, UB40, and the Swinging Cats), which gathered beneath the 2 Tone

banner during its brief and highly-publicised career ripped off the originals, the neglected makers of the black Jamaican musical tradition: Don Drummond and the Skatalites, Prince Buster, Laurel Aitken and the rest. After all, the 2 tone groups hardly concealed their dependence on the first ska phase. Even the names of the 2 tone bands carried their histories on their sleeves. The Specials took their name from the "special" one-off recordings made for the early sound systems in the days of Duke Reid; and Madness lifted their title from the Prince Buster hit which did the rounds of the British mod dance halls in 1965.

Instead what's important about

2 tone is that Jerry Dammers realised that when dealing with the popular music industry, the important issues for the artist have less to do with staying "honest" and "authentic" and refusing to "sell out" than with grabbing and retaining control of the product at every stage and in all its forms. What he saw was that artists should be concerned not just with writing songs and getting them performed and recorded, but with keeping maximum control over every aspect of production: over record mixes, release dates, label and cover design, promotion, marketing, retail distribution and . . . image. If you could get that kind of control, then you might be able to say something worth saying in the accent and the manner of your choice. But what

Top: Jerry Dammers of the Specials. No teeth.

The Beat. In America the group is called the English Beat. "Hands off, she's mine!!"

he or anybody else in 1978 could not have predicted was the speed and the scale on which the 2 Tone Dream was to take off . . .

Rough Trade, Smooth Deal

Within a year, the Specials had borrowed £700 from a local entrepreneur and used it to record a tribute to Prince Buster's "Al Capone" called "Gangster." Rough Trade, the London-based independent label with its roots firmly in "alternative" punk, agreed to handle distribution. The B-side was was an instrumental track called "The Selecter," recorded by Neol

159

BAD MANNERS
THE beat
THE BODYSNATCHERS
MADNESS
THE SELECTER
THE SPECIALS

Madness on stage. Ska meets low British comedy.

Selecter's A-team in Boston, 1980. The original band dazzled with impossibly hot performances, but couldn't sustain itself within the amorphous, shifting contexts of 2 Tone ideology.

Davies and John Bradbury, the drummer with the Specials. Rough Trade pressed 5,000 copies, which were then encased in a snazzy, black-and-white check sleeve designed by Dammers himself. (The b/w check introduced two major themes which were to dominate early 2 Tone output: '60s revivalism (Op Art?) and—more obscurely—the multi-racial ideal: black and white adjacent yet separate, different but connected like the squares on a chessboard).

The record achieved cult status in England within days of its release. It was well received by the music press and by deejay John Peel, the BBC's own alternative taste-maker. Soon, Elvis Costello and Ian Dury were showing conspicuous interest. The Specials, "Gangster" and 2 Tone were so immediately successful that the group was able to negotiate an unprecedented deal with Chrysalis. The Specials and the newly formed Selecter were made directors of 2 Tone, issued a relatively substantial budget, and given a guarantee by Chrysalis that they would release a minimum of six singles a year, singles chosen exclusively by 2 Tone directors. This was a virtual coup, and it opened the way for The Beat to secure a similar deal with Arista in late 1979, setting up their own label, Go Feet.[1]

This shift in the relationship between young recording artists and their record companies had been precipitated largely by the crisis in confidence which permeated the industry in the wake of

punk. (How the hell do you tell good music from bad after the Sex Pistols?) But it opened up the way for more flexible, less cautious signing and management policies. It allowed for more speedy turnover of product and more fluent contact with the young, fickle audience. Incidentally, it accelerated the process whereby new "street" styles and sounds get generated, removing the obstacles and checks which would normally slow down the industry's response to demand. The responsibility for making profits had begun to devolve onto the narrow shoulders of the artists themselves.

Within a matter of months, Dammers and the Specials had stormed the citadel. By the end of 1979, 2 Tone music was beginning to figure heavily in the British charts. One edition of BBC TV's *Top of the Pops* in November featured no less than three new 2 Tone singles: the Specials' "A Message To You Rudy," "One Step Beyond" by Madness and The Selecter's "On My Radio." The ideals and objectives formed in the frustrating years of provincial anonymity were now, on the face of it, realisable. Dammers' vision of the future was about to have its day.

A Documentary Vision

The Dammers Dream had been shot in black and white. It had originally consisted of a fusion of rock and reggae. When, in 1977, Horace Panter (Sir Horace Gentleman), Lynval Golding and Jerry

Dammers together formed the Coventry Automatics, they sought to reflect the multi-racial composition of the group in its music by combining punk and heavy reggae. But as Jerry puts it, when they played the local clubs: "The two tended to stay separate. Audiences used to be dancing, then they'd pogo, then they'd give up."[2] They were forced to turn back to ska and bluebeat, back to a less separatist form of Jamaican music than "ethnic" roots reggae.

Other local groups were moving in a similar direction. Neol Davies, founder of The Selecter, began playing bass with a soul-reggae outfit called Chapter 5 in the mid-'70s, whilst Dave Wakely, guitarist with The Beat, set out some years later, in his own words,[3] to mix punk's "high

energy" with the "fluid movement" of dub. And Ranking Roger, the group's black front-man and toaster, crossed all the categories: he began (with orange hair) as the drummer in a Birmingham-based punk band called the Dum Dum Boys and toasted with the multi-racial reggae band UB40 before opting for the more eclectic sound of The Beat, which draws on rhythms rooted in jazz, West African and Afro-Cuban forms as well as in rock, ska and reggae. The Specials, then, were not the only local group to synthesise black and white expression, black and white experience . . . but they were the first to make a really convincing *popular* mix. They were the first to keep the crowd on its feet and dancing throughout an entire set.

Knees Up Mother Brown with Coconuts

Behind the fusion of rock and reggae lay the hope that the humour, wit and style of working-class kids from Britain's black and white communities could find a common voice in 2 tone; that a new, hybrid cultural identity could emerge along with the new music. This larger message was usually left implicit. There was nothing solemn or evangelical about 2 tone. It

[1] The first record (excluding their own output) which The Beat brought out on Go Feet was Cedric Myton's **Heart of the Congos**, previously available in Britain only as an import.
[2] from **The 2 Tone Book for Rude Boys** by Miles (Omnibus Press, 1981).
[3] Ibid.

ere sublimated, as in reggae, to the rhythms. And the rhythms were what pulled the crowds in. Fast and jumpy, they provided the perfect complement for that nervous, wiry kind of dancing idealised by every English inner-city subculture from the original teds of the '50s through the mods, rudies and skinheads of the '60s to the Northern Soul fans ten years later. The ideal inner city dance is a very English affair. Manic yet restrained, it bears little relation to the free-form stuff favoured on the college circuit in the States. (Dave "Shuffle" Steele, guitarist with The Beat, was unimpressed by the dancing he saw during the group's first US tour: "They were all so floppy and out of time," he said. "Actually, they're easily the worst dancers we've found yet.") The inner city stomp, on the other hand, is improvisation within a tight structure. It's graceful but the grace is always "under pressure," Fred Astaire on leapers.[7] And just as, in the '30s, Astaire's syncopated tap routines had drawn heavily on negro jazz dancing traditions, so the modern English stomp has its roots in the black West Indies, in backyard Kingston blues parties. 2 tone made these roots visible. As the sun sets on the British Commonwealth, 2 tone braided musical strands from England, America and the old Caribbean colonies, and turned the wake into a carnival. They gave us the Ghost Dance of the British Empire, played out at the moving point where the pre-War Lambeth Walk meets Peter Tosh's Steppin' Razor: culture-clash converted into fun—Knees Up Mother Brown with coconuts.

moved, since 1977, into the worst recession since the war. Punk's gloomiest prophecies were realised by a Conservative government pledged to a monetarist policy of massive spending cuts and the systematic demanning of British industry. By 1980, for thousands of British school-leavers, there really was "no future:" no work, no likelihood of finding work, minimal welfare, and the heightened possibility of nuclear war in Europe. In purely political terms, "No Future,"[8] the Sex Pistols' sonic assassination of the Queen, monarchism and "good musicianship," was beginning to sound transparently contrived, almost quaint, rently literary when laid alongside The Beat's straightforward plea to the current Prime Minister, Mrs. Thatcher, to "for God's sake, stand down, Margaret."[9]

Concrete Jungle

2 tone grew out of punk, and there were links between the two movements. Punk and 2 tone both cultivated the romance of the Street (an important mythical site in the geography of rock, at least since *West Side Story.*) The lyrics and the looks of both punk and 2 tone referred more or less directly to what Peter York has called the "1958 council estate teenage greaseball" cluster.[10] They both sought to break the Atlantic connection; both were moved by a desire to tap British experience and to shake off the traditional dependency of British rock on American styles and motifs.

2 tone music was ska at 78 rpm, sung with a nasal English accent, and many of the groups spiced things up with a distinctively British sense of humour which derived from the old music halls and which blended in neatly with the ska tradition of boasting, self-mockery and bad-mouthing developed in Jamaica by men like Buster and Duke Reid. Madness, in particular, play it for the laughs. Their line-up includes an Irish-Cockney giant called Chas Smash who, in dark glasses, with a stingy-brim tilted to his eyebrows, performs odd, robotic dances. The top half of his body is as stiff as a board, all the movement taking place below the knees. Madness on occasion wear Turkish fezes (an obscure and rather ancient British joke kept alive by the stand-up comedian Tommy Cooper, but which goes back at least to the pre-War period).

It's hardly surprising, then, that the 2 tone groups refused to pronounce the "correct," "responsible" line on race. Instead they built on what was already there, and, in

the West Midlands at least, there was plenty. The Coventry and Birmingham music scene is in some ways unique in Britain. The rock and reggae communities have never been as segregated there as in London; in pubs in the predominantly black areas of Birmingham's Balsall Heath and Handsworth, it's not unusual to see black and white musicians of all ages jamming together. Birmingham must be one of the only places left in Britain where it's still possible for a white man to get into a shebeen without wearing a blue uniform and kicking the door down.

So, because a casual basis for exchange existed in the area, the rhetoric of anti-racism could generally be dropped. At the simplest level, the 2 tone bands visibly and audibly demonstrated that racial harmony was a possibility in Britain, at least among disaffected youth. Ranking Roger explained his position on anti-racism in 1981: "we don't have to say to people,

ed an alternative to the well-intentioned polemics of some of the more highly educated punk groups, who tended to top the bill at many of the early Rock Against Racism gigs.[4]

Dammers and the rest had sensed that there was a growing reaction on the part of the working-class rock audience against "message music," a movement away from sixth-form Brecht and crudely anti-Establishment lyrics. The 2 tone bands were more interested in harmonising the form and the sense, so that, without being obtrusive, the multiracial message could be *inferred* by the sound and the lyrics, rather than a political programme. Instead of imposing an alien, moralising discourse on a popular form (alien at least to their working-class constituency), bands like the Specials worked in and on the popular, steered clear of the new avant gardes, and stayed firmly within the "classical" definitions of '50s and early '60s rock and pop: that this was music for Saturday nights, something to dance to, to *use*.

The politics were there but they

They were giving shape to a sensibility rather than a political programme. Instead of imposing an alien, moralising discourse on a popular form (alien at least to their working-class constituency), bands like the Specials worked in and on the popular, steered clear of the new avant gardes, and stayed firmly within the "classical" definitions of '50s and early '60s rock and pop: that this was music for Saturday nights, something to dance to, to *use*.

The politics were there but they

This didn't stop the bands from making serious statements, but the 2 tone strategy differed fundamentally from punk's. The Specials, The Selecter and the rest had gone beyond the arch, self-conscious nihilism of the Sex Pistols and the angry rhetoric of the Clash. The political objectives of 2 tone were more modest: unemployment, the police, and authoritarian Government. The targets were more clearly defined. This shift in strategy was a consequence of larger social and economic pressures. Britain itself had

[4] Formed in 1976, Rock Against Racism was set up by people working in and around the rock industry to combat racism.

[5] A similar submerged politics operated within 2 tone on the gender front. The Body Snatchers was an all-girl ska/reggae band formed by Nicky Singer, the rhythm guitarist. Probably the most significant contribution in this respect was made by Pauline Black, vocalist with The Selecter. Dressed in a sharp suit and a bluebeat hat, she looked as "rough and tough" as any rude boy and provided a role model which contrasted with the image of dignified but passive womanhood enshrined in roots reggae where Rastafarianism still holds patriarchal sway. Pauline Black broke with the stereotype presented by groups like Bob Marley's backing singers, the regal but ultra-feminine I-Threes.

[6] from **The Beat Twist and Crawl** by Malu Halasa (Eel Pie Publishing, 1981).

[7] "Leapers" – English subcultural slang for amphetamines.

[8] also known as "God Save the Queen" (1977).

[9] "Stand down Margaret," The Beat (Arista, 1980).

[10] Peter York, **Style Wars** (Sidgwick & Jackson, 1980).

Skinhead on the go, Fulham Road, London.

The Dream is Over . . .

As things got worse in Britain, and worse still for the black community, who are subject not only to a higher unemployment rate but to increasingly vicious, unprovoked attacks from racists, many 2 Tone groups began to adopt a more open, less hipsterish stand on the issue. In June, 1981, the Specials organised a Peaceful Protest Against Racism at Butts Athletic Stadium in the Earlsdon district of Coventry in response to an earlier violent protest against the local Asian community—the fatal stabbing in April in the city-centre in broad daylight of a 20-year-old boy called Satnam Singh Gill.

he's black and I'm white, or I'm black and he's white. We don't say that between songs. I mean, people can see for themselves. If they can't they must be blind or something, because black and white are there. They're playing together and loving every minute of it . . . that's just love and unity.[11]

However, in this respect, some 2 tone fans were both blind and alienated, and tended to steer clear of "love and unity." Even at the earliest ska revival gigs, there were fascist contingents amongst the fans: young white supporters of the far-right National Front and British Movement parties. Throughout 1979 and 1980, there were reports in the music press of skinheads chanting "Sieg Heil" at Madness concerts. (Madness, the only London ska group, are also the only all-white 2 tone group. They are signed, in fact, to Stiff Records). Some far-right rudies referred to the Specials as the Specials Plus Two (a symbolic excision of Neville Staples and Lynval Golding, the two original black Specials, subsequently joined on tour by the veteran ska trombonist, Rico Rodriguez.)

By 1981, the Dream, buckling under "too much pressure," was in danger of falling to pieces. The original 2 Tone roster had split up the early days, when the final mix for The Beat's first (and only) 2 Tone single "Tears of a Clown" had been decided by a ballot amongst all the 2 Tone groups, had become dissipated as the commercial and administrative problems of running the expanding 2 Tone empire began to assert themselves. The Dream went down under the combined weight of intensive tabloid interest, continuous exposure in the music press and a flood of cheap and nasty spin-offs churned out by outsiders: 2 Tone badges, scarves and ties; Specials T-shirts, Selecter socks and Madness tupperware. (The concessions had proved more slippery than Dammers had imagined.) Eventually, he had to face up to the fact that 2 Tone had grown beyond his good intentions. Every 2 Tone move was monitored, analysed, assessed as a possible trend. "It's become a monster," Dammers confided to one reporter, "Frankenstein's monster." Finally, he cracked, suffering a breakdown at the mixing desk as he helped produce the soundtrack for *Dance Crazy*, the film of the movement he'd created. "I dunno how to describe it," he said later, "but I just went to pieces. I haven't had a week off in the past two years. I've been living out of a suitcase like some sort of tramp. . . ."[12]

The Selecter finally broke away at the end of 1980, and by then the music had long outgrown its origins in ska. By the time the second album, *More Specials*, was released in June 1980, Dammers had moved from "Long Shot Kick the Bucket" into muzak. Former certainties had already been eroded and discarded along with the self-conscious populism of the early 2 Tone output. This had all been displaced by that impatience with the settled and the given, that restless urge to violate existing musical categories and audience expectations which has marked most forms of British rock and reggae at least since punk and 1976.

In the autumn of 1981 at a concert in Cambridge towards the end of the last British tour the Specials were to give, Dammers and Terry Hall, the lead singer, were arrested for "behaviour likely to cause a breach of the peace" when they tried to prevent the crowd from fighting and throwing cans at each other and the stage. They were later found guilty of "inciting violence" and fined £1,000. ("This isn't a town, it's a trained-dog act," muttered Dammers to reporters. The inevitable rumours of a split began to circulate and in late November they were confirmed. Terry Hall, Neville Staples and Lynval Golding had left to form the Fun Boy 3 and were about to release a record entitled *The Lunatics (Have Taken Over the Asylum)*. Dammers was reported to be thinking about reforming Special AKA and returning to the original project of opening a studio in Coventry to serve as a launching-pad for local talent. And meanwhile, The Beat are making records about the Bomb.

Ska has been laid to rest again. Meanwhile a new generation of nostalgics is being born—a generation hooked on early 2 tone tapes who will look back fondly to the time when 2 tone ruled the airwaves and more especially to the moment in July 1981 when it all seemed to crystallise, the moment when, with Britain facing its greatest social and economic crisis since the '30s, black and white youths clashed with the police in the decaying inner rings of the country's larger cities. As the riots flared in Toxteth, Manchester, Liverpool and London, in Birmingham and Coventry and Wolverhampton, the BBC played the week's National Anthem, the people's choice, the British number one, the Specials doing "Ghost Town:"

This town is coming like a ghost town
Why must the youth fight amongst themselves?
Government leaving youth on the shelf.
This town is coming like a ghost town
No job to be found in this country

Anti-Nazi rally in London. Despite an affection for fascistic style, most punkers were dead against the Nazis.

Postscript

We're gonna have a party
It's a punky reggae party.
The Wailers will be there.
The Jam, the Damned, the Clash.

Rejected by society, treated with impunity, protected by their dignity.

Bob Marley, "Punky Reggae Party," 1977

On the night of January 7, 1982 at a club in Coventry called Shades, former Special Lynval Golding was attacked without provocation by a gang of white youths and subjected to an assault of such ferocity that the wounds to his face and throat alone were to require 28 stitches. Hospital sources reveal that his eyesight may be permanently impaired. The next day Golding released a statement urging his fans not to retaliate:

"My music is about peace, and I'm sure the guys who did this to me will feel sorry for what they did, because I'm a guy who wants to live in peace with people . . . It's funny, you know, because I've never thrown a blow at anyone."

The party's over, Marley's punky reggae party. And Marley's dead. We've come a long way in our loafers since the lights went out.

—Dick Hebdige

11 from Halasa (op cit, 1981)
12 from Miles (op cit, 1981)

Linton in London

Some of the strongest and most direct verse being written in English today is coming from a young black British poet. Linton Kwesi Johnson sets his militant and utterly penetrating verse to some of the hardest reggae-derived backing music imaginable, a subtle instrumental force that propels Linton's steppin'-razor poems with a fiery and stark beauty, relentlessly urban, like the wet nighttime streets of southeast London.

This new poet first came to international attention with his *Forces of Victory* album, which put him dancing on the cutting edge of avant-poesy. A more recent record, *Bass Culture*, speaks even more in its imagery to the dreary and dangerous conditions in which black Britons are made to live. But any careful listener can tell, just by his serious monotone, that Linton is reaping a cultural whirlwind. Rarely has poetry taken on such astute and aggressive front-line characteristics as has Linton's. And unlike most prophetic poets, Linton lived to see some of his darker political visions come true in the street rebellions that exploded across urban Britain in the spring and long hot summer of 1981.

Inglan is a Bitch

Linton Kwesi Johnson: I was born in a small country town called Chappleton, in the rural parish of Clarendon, in Jamaica in 1952. I come from a very poor, peasant, subsistence-farming background. Country people. I came to England at the age of eleven, and grew up in the black neighborhood of Brixton, and went to secondary school here.

Q: *When did you start to write?*

I began to write around 1970. I was in the Black Panther movement at the time, nothing to do with the Black Panthers in America, but part of the black movement of the '60s and early '70s who were largely inspired by what blacks were doing in America for themselves.

How was it different in England?

The difference was that we weren't connected organizationally. But we were organizing around similar issues—police brutality, housing, education, and so on. Unlike the Americans, we had no arms whatsoever, we didn't take that military line. Of course, there was a different situation. Our members weren't being murdered and gunned down like they were in America. They were simply being beaten and put into prison.

So, in the Panthers I came across *The Souls of the Black Folk,* W.E.B. Dubois' classic book about the post-emancipation experiences of blacks in America, which moved me to the extent that I began to write poetry. And that's how I began.

When did you begin to publish?

1973. Firstly in *Race Today* and then bits and pieces here and there. Then my first book of poems, *Voices of the Living and the Dead,* came out in 1974, followed by *Dread Beat and Blood* in 1975. And I have another publication coming from the printers any day now called *Inglan is a Bitch.*

A time came in the writing of my poetry where I couldn't properly express the kind of experiences I wanted to express within the English language. 'Cause one wanted to talk about the Caribbean or the black experience in Britain and it was only natural for me to do so in the everyday language of the people. And of course working within the tradition of West Indian dialects—oral languages—meant that I was working in a poetic tradition in which music is integral. All oral poetry has a musical base, a rhythmic base.

And I was very influenced by what the dub lyricists were doing, people like Big Youth and I. Roy, and earlier on U. Roy. I had a workshop called Rasta Love, a group of Rasta drummers and poets, and we used to go out and do things in libraries and colleges and youth centers, in a workshop setting. That was the beginning of my musical involvement.

Since 1972 I've been involved in studying reggae music, its roots, its background and so on, as a hobby. And that was another musical input into my work. And then when I began to write my lines, they always came with a bass line, in semi-melodic fashion. . . .

How did you get hooked up with Island Records, which gave you more of an international base?

Island did *not* give me an international base from which to operate. The fact that I'm a black person from the Caribbean who lives in Britain means that I *have* an international base. Y'know? I only went to Island because they offered me a better deal than Virgin did for subsequent recordings.

But now I've decided not to

make any more records for a while. I don't feel that one should keep churning out record after record like that. I see many people doing that, and I think in the long run it does more damage than good to the artist. It's one thing to chase money, but it's another thing if you're serious about what you're doing, and you want to do it with some sincerity, and you have some criteria about craft and meaning and so on. . . So you don't just churn them out, y'know?

Some of your best material deals with the troubles blacks in Britain have with the police, but it seems to speak to a much wider black experience. In particular you attack the so-called "Sus" law, which allows the police to collar young blacks on the merest suspicion. Have you ever been sussed?

Me? I have never been sussed. I have been beaten up by the police, I've been framed by the police, I've been harrassed in the street by the police and been intimidated, but I've never been done for Sus. I've been done for assault, but never for Sus. That poem ["Sonny's Lettah"] isn't based on a personal experience; it's a dramatic portrayal

of a general experience, a collection of experiences, trying to bring home the reality of that issue in the most dramatic way I was able to.

Your record Forces of Victory *seemed to be a cycle of poems directed as a response to the emergence of the fascistic and racist National Front as a street entity in England . . .*

No. No no no. We wouldn't ever ever. . . I myself and the people I work with politically would never do anything as a reaction to the National Front. Y'know, it tends to make them out to be more important than they actually are. They're an insignificant fascist group in Britain. They have no real mass base as such. They have no big following. They have no power. They just a kind of an extension of the police force, if you like. They take care of those kinds of terrorist activities that the police couldn't so easily get away with. Like petrol bombings of people's shops and all that kind of thing. Killing people on the street like the Asians that were killed last year. The police turn a blind eye.

Actually, the title *Forces of Victory* was a celebration of the Carnival masque that we had played the year before, in '78. Every year we have a carnival in London, at Notting Hill, where we celebrate the freedom of the streets, to express ourselves in song and dance and masquerade. Each band has its own theme, and our theme was the Forces of Victory, liberation struggles of

Linton at the old **Race Today** office, with editor Darcus Howe.

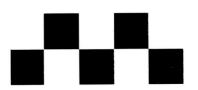

colonial peoples throughout the world. And the victory of the progressive forces within the Carnival movement in Britain against the State, which was trying to destroy the movement. And against the opportunists within the movement who were trying to use it to further their own ends.

One of your most interesting lyrics is called "Black Petty Booshwah."

It speaks to the emerging black middle class in Britain, and we'd have to say black petit bourgeois, because they are not a middle class in the historical sense of the middle class in Europe. They're by and large educated or semi-literate blacks who have middle-class aspirations, who don't believe that the black working class will never be able to extricate itself from the colonial conditions under which we live in Britain. This class seizes an interest for itself, in being able to make a living out of those very conditions, as mediators for the State between blacks and the State itself.

Mek We Let Go Religion

People who love reggae pay very close attention to your lyrics, especially in Jamaica. In "Reality Poem" there's a couplet— "This is the age of Decision/Mek we let go religion"—that has been interpreted by some as a challenge to the power and attracton that Rastafarian religion has, especially for young people. Is that reading too much into it?

That is not reading anything into it at all; it's close, but not close enough. Its a general comment on the fact that people are tending to seek all avenues of escape from the harsh and ugly realities of a colonial existence, whether it be in Britain, the Mother Country, or in Jamaica where people are still living under neo-colonial conditions (whether the party in power calls itself democratic socialist or not).

But people are looking for ways of escaping, whether it be through Jah Rastafari—going back to Africa —through Pentecostal churches, through alcohol, through drugs or whatever, through style and dressing smart and being slick and being hip. So this poem simply makes a plea for people not to seek ways of escaping from reality, but to confront realities face-on and try to transform them.

What is happening in England is

that a lot of youths are calling themselves Rastas without knowing the implications of what they're saying and what it means to be a Rasta. They become Rastas not in the way people became Rastas in Jamaica from the '30s to the '50s even, but they become Rastas in the same way that European kids became hippies as a consequence of listening to rock music and being moved by the message of rock. Its just superficial, y'know?

Rasta has become the ideology of reggae music. It's very misleading.

Do you think that's unfortunate?

I think its unfortunate, yes, because it acts as a barrier to innovations in the music. Many singers are falling into the Rasta trap. You see it right here in England, y'know. One of the best reggae bands in Britain is called Aswad; they play excellent music and can sing and so on, but their lyrics don't really express any reality. It's a trap we're all slow to move out of, even though we're no longer trying to ape what is being done in Jamaica musically.

But I want to make it quite clear: I'm not anti-Rasta. I think there are many things within the Rasta movement which are positive. And there are some negatives, too. I believe it's a dynamic movement, with many different tendencies and ideological variations of it and so on. I believe it has some role to play. But I don't believe it has any political relevance whatsoever.

What about poetry? What are you reading lately?

Poetry? The two haardest poets in Jamaica right now are friends of mine: Michael Smith, who has written the most remarkable poem to come out of Jamaica for fifty years called "Me Can't Believe It." And Oku Onuora, who was formerly called Orlando Wong, writes some very haard—what he calls "dub poetry" but what I called prefer to call reggae poetry. He's made a record recently called *Reflections in Red* that is really powerful. It's a comment upon the abortive peace truce that was tried between the rival gunmen in Jamaica. He made a comment in the poem that there could be no peace until there was equal rights and justice, and obviously he was right because the peace truce was a joke. There was something like sixty killings a month.

There are several British reggae groups on the scene at present.

Have they managed to add anything new to the music?

Yes, they have. We are talking about groups like Aswad, Matumbi, Steel Pulse, Tradition, Black Slate, Movement, Misty and a host of others. There are some individual singers like Janet Kay, Sonia Cassandra and other talented artists. These have brought a new feel to bear on the music. Feel is very difficult to define, because it is emotive, it is abstract. What I am trying to say is that the kind of reggae that we produce here in Britain is informed by different tensions. The tempo of life is different. Those who make records in Britain for the most part are either born or grew up here. They have therefore been exposed to a much wider variety of international sounds, and must have been influenced by them, even though many would not admit it. In turn, we have influenced, from time, popular, metropolitan music and continue to do so today.

Turning to your own music, you appear to have incorporated several strands of Caribbean music into your work. Could you describe them?

Folk forms, religious forms, calypso, soul, jazz just come out in my poetry, really. "Forces of Victory," for example was a poem which celebrated the theme which Race Today Renegades played at Carnival 1978. It was simply a celebration of our theme. It was informed by calypso beats and rhythms. Most reviewers missed the fact that it was informed by that. The same goes for the poem, "Man Free," about Darcus Howe. Between the lines of "Darcus Outta Jail" and "Race Today Cannot Fail" is the beat of a steel band. That is what I heard.

"Inglan is a Bitch" is a ballad. "Lorraine" is informed by soul. It

is the mood of the poem, the atmosphere and the feel I am trying to invoke, which recall certain traditions.

You have recently launched the LKJ record label. What do you hope to achieve?

I have very modest hopes for it, really. I am trying to make an independent intervention as an artist who is making records and believes he has something to contribute towards the development of reggae music in Britain. I aim to show by example what it is possible for artists to do by their own efforts, however small the impact. How the music is developing stylistically, and so on. I hope it will reach the stage where it is self-sufficient. In other words, that it can pay for itself. Then I may be able to give a lot of the young artists the opportunity to make at least one record for themselves.

You have a great guitarist playing with you . . .

His name is John Kaipye; he's of African and Irish parents, born in this country, a first-class guitarist who's been around for years! He's the best black guitarist we have in Britain, and he works very closely with Dennis Bovell of Matumbi. He plays flamenco. He has jazz leanings, blues leanings, reggae . . . He's a man with the capacity to experiment, and work in different styles. When we go to the studio to work, apart from various things like chords and so on, you don't tell him what to play; you just leave him alone and he plays.

Why don't you perform your material with your band?

Because, basically, I never ever perform with a band, and don't intend to. Because I'm not a reggae artist in the sense of a group like Toots and the Maytals or Bob Marley and the Wailers or Steel Pulse . . . I'm a poet, and I think that poetry should stand on its own, and has enough strength and musicality to stand on its own. Since I've made records, I have to obviously make some compromise to musical audiences who want to see or hear me perform. And what I do in those cases is perform to taped backing music, and I just perform the lyrics or the words over the music with some dancers on stage that try to mime and skank to the rhythms.

So you don't consider yourself a professional musician.

Definitely not. I'm a poet. Period.

—*Stephen Davis*

Oku Onuora

Oku and Linton Johnson, Brixton.

Steel Pulse

Steel Pulse from Handsworth, Birmingham, was the first of the British reggae bands to make any impact outside of England. When Steel Pulse first put on white sheets and sang of the horrors of the Ku Klux Klan, the whole reggae world pricked up its ears and *heard.* These days, Steel Pulse ranks with Third World as one of the slickest, most professional touring reggae bands around. Peter Simon caught up with lead Pulse David Hinds one afternoon in New York . . .

Q: *Where are you from?*

David Hines: I was born and raised in England, Birmingham.

Is that true of all the members of the group?

Fonso and Selwin were born in England as well. Basil and Ronnie were born in Jamaica. Steve was born in Nevis.

What is the story of Steel Pulse?

Well the history starts when . . . like with Basil, who's been playing acoustic guitar probably a few years before. The last year at school, I was about 17 at the time, me and Basil. The rest of the guys, them left school to colleges and work like Ronnie. And Selwin, went to the same school as those. It was a secondary school. During that stay there, Basil did suggest that we form a group, and I took an interest and learned to play the guitar. I never had any idea that I'd end up as a musician. I thought I was gonna be something like a fireman or a draftsman or even something like a fine artist, 'cause that's what I went on to, a fine arts college. And at the time, me and Basil did go on to a college and were learning to play the guitar, and Ronnie decided to come in on it and was taught on the bass, and Selwin pick up on keyboards, and we decide to rehearse like once a week on Sundays 'cause it was the only spare time that all of us had.

How long ago was this?

This was about 1974. We were all learning to play at those times, and we had our first gig as a band, decide to go on stage in a pub in Handsworth area called Crampton. Fonso and Steve weren't with the band as yet. It was Basil's brother and another member of the band. Our first concert was every Friday night at the Crampton, and we was only getting something like equivalent to $40 after playing several hours, but we didn't mind doing that. We had to take the equipment in a small mini-van; I don't think you got any car in America small as the van what we used to carry the equipment in. We used to have to make about 45 trips from our houses with the equipment. We couldn't afford to miss one night because we needed that money to get more equipment and get a better sound. That's how dedicated we was, y'know. Two night club owners were coming down to the pub and watching us. It was like their way of having an audition. And they took us up and decide to make us play in their clubs in the Handsworth area. We were doing cover versions that pertained to what we're still dealing with today.

For example?

Like Burning Spear, "Do You Remember Ol' Marcus Garvey," "Slavery Days," a lot of Marley's music as well, like "Jah Live." A lot of people didn't want to know about Rastaman music and things. So we were banned from clubs. They just didn't want to have us at their clubs anymore. We had to be sticking around, waiting for like once a month for concerts and things. And then the punk scene come in. And the punks, as you know it, were picking up reggae music, what the system was rejecting. The top punk bands had a tendency to have reggae bands supporting them, and we went down to sort of a monkey-looking club called the Vortex and so we had our first recognized London gig and the audience was all white, 'cause no blacks didn't really come to punk concerts. The punks used to spit, that was their way of showing that they appreciate your music. Throwing beer mugs and beer bottles around the place. That's their way of saying that they're in the groove of your music.

Were you in England during the 1981 riots in Brixton and elsewhere, or were you touring?

I was on tour, that's my witness. One expects those kind of things. When I check back its kind of ironic to know that it was a year ago, the same month of April that a riot took place in Bristol over a lot of police harassment once again. The blacks and other groups of people, probably white sympathizers, probably couldn't take no more of that and decided to revolt. The same thing happen in Brixton and to tell you the truth, its possible that it can happen in other places in England as long as those kind of law and things are still manipulative.

In your music, there's a lot of racial commentary and political oppression being discussed, and yet your audiences are mostly white people. I'm wondering how you feel the white people respond; are they basically compassionate and understanding? Do you get any particular response from white people?

It varies throughout the country, throughout the United States, it varies. There's a lot of white people on the east side, they'll come to concerts, they'll know what's happening in the songs, they're familiar with the words we're saying and as a result, they want to take part in what we're getting involved in too. Probably on the west side or even down south, the whites, they find out that they like what they come to see because we're not only dealing with . . . a lot of people have a tendency to come to a Steel Pulse concert out of mere curiosity. A lot of people probably bear in mind what we're saying, but they're not really that responsive to what we're saying. They probably get more involved in the actual musical side of it. But that is OK, because I'm not a politician and really, I want everybody to bear in mind that Steel Pulse are musicians, just speaking the truth.

I compare your music to Third World in Jamaica. Do you see what I mean by that at all? There's a certain, I wouldn't say commercial, but real slick and tight and professional quality to your music, similar to theirs.

We know that we're going to come across a lot of people who are gonna want to see if the reggae musicians can really play what they do on the records. A lot of people used to have a tendency of saying that it's half studio work, they can't really perform certain things on stage. What Steel Pulse is here to say is that our music is *hard.*

—Peter Simon

Steel Pulse, from Handsworth, Birmingham.

Lead Pulse David Hinds

14

White Reggae

Rolling Stones, Blondie, Eric Clapton, Police, Clash, even Bob Dylan—rock & roll in the '80s has been thriving in part by adopting to the planetary shock wave of reggae music. From the original pioneer pop stars dabbling in tinny Kingston studios, through the glorious punky-reggae party of the 1977/78 new wave, to Blondie's popsy rockers chart success, white reggae has almost always been interesting and heartfelt, a new channel for the no-future generation raised on various boring and worn-out cultural models. Today, more than ever, white reggae is becoming ubiquitous. Doubters have only to consult their radios. White reggae and its various cosmodemonic implications are here dissected by writer/musician **Lenny Kaye,** an early literary celebrant of rock culture who went on to play guitar for the Patti Smith Group and is currently fronting his own band. He writes with the authority of an early participant in the great white reggae experiment.

On Guard, Babylon!

Within all music is the spirit of travel. Crossing continents, touching foreign shores, a people's need is seen through a beholder's eye. "White" Euro-American reggae tells us more of its own impulses when it chooses cultural ingredients from the Jamaican-African stew than the original "black" reggae itself. The mix is complicated because reggae itself has borrowed from both black and white forms (like Gulf Coast rock and roll), and further twisted by the colonial nature of the relationship, questions not only steeped in centuries of ancestral struggle but actually a large part of the emotive force behind reggae itself, a reason for being.

The classic duality: light vs. dark, white vs. black. Yet far from confrontation, the give-and-take between white and black reggae has been an intermingling on several different levels, a backscratching coexistence based on mutual favor: as the international popular music community encompasses reggae, so reggae can become a part of that community.

Does this mean that reggae's internal force must be diluted for it to reach a wider audience? Perhaps, but I prefer to see it as adaption and mutation, the spread of a music's mores as it becomes universal, reaching beyond an exclusivity of race and religion. It matters not who drinks water drawn from the same well.

Lenny Kaye in the days of **Radio Ethiopia**, 1976.

Opposite: U. Roy and Johnny Rotten, Hellshire, Jamaica 1978.

Steps to Reunion

To speak in the broadest of generalities, white music has generally relied on black music to set its rhythmic impulses, as well as express an adversary position vis-a-vis the cultural mainstream. In the 1950s, heavy black r&b jump and blues bands helped put drums on the stage of the Grand Ole Opry to birth the squalling baby of rock and roll. In the 1960s, a blues rediscovery (introduced to America via the odd transatlantic cable of the English Invasion) plus a sharp dose

Eric Clapton covered "I Shot the Sheriff" and boosted Bob Marley's career.

Paul Simon in 1972: "Mother and Child Reunion" was recorded in Kingston the previous year.

Peter Tosh takes the mike to sing "Get Up Stand Up" at a Wailers show in Los Angeles, 1978.

of Soul (Motown or Stax) provided the primal ingredients.

The Caribbean-based light ska and rock steady that was Jamaica's stock in trade during these years was all too "ethnic" to make more than a fleeting impression on the white audience. Keyed by the bounce and brightness of a Beatles' "O-bla-di O-bla-da" or Mungo Jerry's "In The Summertime," the sound was regarded as little more than ethnic novelty. Even Desmond Dekker's surprise 1969 crossover hit "Israelites" found its biblical weight subdued as it moved internationally, serving more as a succinct calling card for pioneer producer Leslie Kong than it did as an opening salvo for Jamaican music.

Paul Simon, in his 1971 "Mother And Child Reunion," was the first to attempt to move past the lush tropical imagery that this budding music seemed to suggest to outside ears. It is to Simon's credit that, as a foreigner, he captured a particularly Jamaican mood as well as an immediate theme for his song. Recorded in Kingston's Dynamic Sounds Studios under Kong's supervision, the bubbling musical undercurrent was integral to "Mother And Child" 's lyrical yearning. Simon had looked beneath the smiling surface of Jamaican music, and pellucidar-like, found another world.

Meanwhile, that didn't mean you couldn't dance to it. England in 1968 was treated to the sight of white skinheads moon-stomping down to the sounds of freshly imported ska, spilling over from the immigrant West Indian population it was meant to serve.

Familiarity with Jamaican folkways did not extend to America, where musical tastes seemed to lump everything from beneath its southern border as the latest Latin dance craze. Cha-cha, rhumba, calypso, bossa nova . . . all the same, *verdad?* But reggae was more than a rhythmic variant or an incomprehensible foreign-language jumble; it was a very American product, complete with "hit" singles and a singing style carried intact from such as the Moonglows and Sam Cooke.

There was little understanding of the soul of the music, however, the social set and setting which might bring reggae into sharper focus. Guided more by sense of feel than actual knowledge, powerhouse American rockers like the J. Geils Band experimented with the rhythmic components of the sound, scoring a 1973 breakthrough when they harnessed the chugging thrust of reggae to a standard blues rave-up in "Give It To Me." It was a start. Earlier black pop singer Johnny Nash weathered a dry spell in his career by spending a great deal of time in Kingston, returning to the US with the hope-after-hope message of "I Can See Clearly Now," following it with Bob Marley's first US hit as a writer, "Stir It Up."

Reprises in Limbo

When reggae's breakthrough into public awareness finally came for America, it arrived not just as music but as a film. Perry Henzell's *The Harder They Come,* with its accompanying soundtrack, proved an introductory tour de force. Now the music could be seen as it was lived (albeit romantically) on the streets of Kingston.

But it was Bob Marley's pop instincts that caught fire first. Eric Clapton notched a hit with a relaxed cover version of "I Shot The Sheriff" that was architecturally correct if undramatic. Other blues scholastics like the Rolling Stones attempted their own reggae incursions, the ska step of "Luxuries" and a reprise of festival-winner Eric Donaldson's "Cherry Oh Baby." On

the whole, though, the results were more well-intentioned than successful, a Caribbean vacation taken with one eye on the phrase book.

In America, cover versions were rife, typified by Three Dog Night's homogenized repackage of Greyhound's "Black And White," complete with children's chorus. The Shakers, one of the first white all-reggae groups, sounded more like earnest folk musicians on their album *Yankee Reggae.* The sole bright spot, from a most unexpected quarter, was *Escape From Babylon,* a courageous, stunning album by Martha Velez that made no apologies for transcending its racial barriers. Produced by Bob Marley, guided by the free flight of Velez's "Wild Bird," its most inspirational track, Velez's throaty voice rode the nooks and crannies of the Wailers rhythm section with startling ease.

In 1976, the underground revolt that had long been boiling in rock and roll finally spilled over into public attention. Christened punk, later (and broader) new wave, it was more a cyclic regeneration of the form than a complete overhaul; but given an initial underdog position, it quickly searched for musical allies. Black-oriented sound (BOSS), a usually reliable source of reinforcement, was in enemy hands (or so the "Disco Sucks" legions thought before the advent of dance oriented rock), and in casting about for possible alternate energies, punk came upon a reggae newly revitalized and revivalized.

Star-crossed, they were meant for each other. Rock and roll, rejecting increasing absorption into the mainstream, identified with Reggae's cry for confrontation, its use of the music as political and social tool. Reggae, for its part, had taken a hard-line stance in hopes of solidifying its own identity, a Third-World art rising to challenge the First World and declaring its independence.

Both musics had reached a peak of militancy at the same moment. Thus magnetized, they began to move irresistibly toward one another, bartering and bargaining in pragmatic trade.

The most political of the English punk bands, the Clash, were among the first to raise a banner of solidarity with reggae. Bassist Paul Simonon often claimed to have learned his instrument from playing along to reggae records, and singer-lyricist Joe Strummer's apocalyptic fascination with urban terror found fertile nourishment in Jamaican song. Indeed, the group's debut hit, "White Riot," was based on a seminal

event in both punk and reggae mythology, the racially based disturbances in London's Notting Hill during late summer of 1976. Aligning themselves within a music of protest and exile, each faction saw in the riot a tangible example of their dispute with the British mainstream, and in such outward stylistic objections as hair (the punk spikes and the dread's curls), stigmatic clothing (the symbolic dog collars and chains of slavery), and moral stance (punk's deliberate flouting of convention matched by Rastafarianism's strict dietary and other codes), made manifest their alienation.

The Clash have persevered, aware of their predicament but instead choosing to utilize it as the backbone of their art, constructing an ethos based on political opposition. In the tradition of Woody Guthrie, Pete Seeger, or especially Phil Ochs, they write from the headlines of today's papers; for reggae, this has meant a socially aware dub that is unafraid to explore the very bottom of bass frequencies as it moves to a skittish high end, backed by an advisory association with Mikey Dread, a slick master Jamaican disc jockey with innate show-biz appeal.

"Ain't It Strange"

Real-life America, however, seemed less real and more comfortable. The '60s had delivered a '70s filled with individual promise (witness the Me Decade), yet anyone could sense the decay beneath the surface. The crisis was more spiritual than political, or so it seemed in the art-aligned rock world which ground the mid-'70s new wave. In New York, a series of literate, conceptual bands with strong ties to other mediums (film, poetry, painting) sprang up, based around the Bowery bar CBGB and the venerable Max's Kansas City. Reggae appeared early as a "legitimate" music on this scene (Bob Marley opened for Bruce Springsteen one night at Max's, for example), and as it grew more familiar, became a factor in some of the bands' repertoires.

The Patti Smith Group, more than most, found a great deal of sympathetic vibration in reggae music, and as a member of that band, I was able to observe (and often help implement) the changing face reggae presented toward us and the uses we in turn made of it.

If the new wave struggle in America was meant to be carried on the aesthetic level, this

didn't make it any easier. The Patti Smith Group, the other bands, and the thousands of kids who seemed to see in our early tours a tangible harbinger of progress felt a sense of kinship that bound us in spirit to reggae's lyrical declarations of war. In *Radio Ethiopia,*, PSG's second album, we chose the hypocrisy of FM radio as our symbolic battleground, the betrayal of a rock and roll dream, and pledged to resurrect all in a station dedicated to the concept of freedom: the voice of Selassie's land, descended from Solomon and Sheba, the cradle of man and the last port of call for Rimbaud.

It was in "Ain't It Strange," however, the album's only piece written in straight reggae form, that Patti truly chose to confront her desire's object. A song about the whirl of religious experience, Rastafarian in consciousness if not in actuality, it played out on the stage the sensuality and fear of such a mating, a ritual that grew ever more ornate as the tour continued. Wrestling with the devil, it pitted good against bad, each shading one to the other in a kind of mad dance. Tappa Zukie, introduced to the band by black filmmaker-disc jockey Don Letts (an integral matchmaker between early punk and reggae), performed the song with us at London's Hammersmith Odeon, calling on Patti to "repent." "I won't," she thundered back, daring her Lord to "make a move," challenging the peak.

One night in January 1977, our record and New Year's live broadcast banned from New York's flagship station ("You can't say fuck in Radio Free America" wrote Patti in a broadside), she tossed the gauntlet to a frenzied Tampa, Florida, audience. The music dizzied, tilting the stage; reaching for the microphone, she tumbled back-of-the-head-first to the hard cement floor, fracturing two vertebrae in her neck. "Hand of God, I feel the finger . . . ."

"Ain't It Strange" proved to be a turning point. Thereafter, Patti would move toward reconciliation, a music of the knowing rather than the unknown, conversion as choice rather than surrender.

Between Forms

The year of the Two Sevens Clash had arrived, bringing with it an aquarian promise of new wave's eventual triumph. Bob Marley bestowed his blessing and awareness with "Punky Reggae Party," and the broad musical coalition that resulted mixed reggae and rock in increasingly sophisticated ways.

Elvis Costello took the taut suspense of a reggae rhythm guitar to build the Dashiell Hammett scenarios of "Watching the Detectives," each word clipped and punctuated. Bob Dylan, perhaps as a foretaste of his gospel conversion, added reggae rhythms to "Don't Think Twice," having the opposite effect. British bands like the Members ("Off Shore Banking Business") and the Ruts ("Babylon's Burning") constructed their own recipes utilizing the two forms.

Experimentally, the open-ended *mixage* that was rub-a-dub influenced many of rock's more avant-garde elements. The Sex Pistols had never exhibited Johnny Rotten's professed love for

The Sex Pistols weren't really associated with reggae, but singer John Lydon's next group was an attempt to fuse dub music and punk style. It failed.

The Police—Sting, Stewart Copeland, Andy Summers.

reggae, but his new incarnation as John Lydon, guiding light of Public Image Ltd., found this fascination become quickly paramount. Recognizing that given a constant beat, nearly anything can be layered over it and sound "right" (an important mechanism of most dub music, even to the actual removal of the rhythm), PIL (particularly on *Metal Box*) created a music of seeming chaos, tied together by the omnipresent rumble of Jah Wobble's bass and an endless succession of drummers.

Similarly, the Slits found in reggae a pathway from accepted Western logic, "going native" by following a line of primitivism that is reggae's Jamaican heritage. Though Ari Upp liked to talk in Jamaican slang, the group's real reggae link was the choppy effectiveness of their sing-song chords, the tribal masks they would wear in "Typical Girls," their insistence that "silence is a riddim too." There were other radical uses as well: Nina Hagen's harsh "African Reggae" brought to mind the 1936 German Olympics,

Smitty

Patti Smith and Winston Rodney.

while in France Serge Gainsbourg with Sly & Robbie turned the sacrosanct "Marseillaise" into a French reggae anthem, provoking numerous death threats.

Rock Against Racism, the only political movement of note thrown up by the new wave, was still little more than a rallying cry, but in England in the late '70s, it seemed as if a multi-racial music might actually become reality. The 2 tone (black and white) groups, operating from their own well-organized headquarters in Coventry and Birmingham, suddenly struck the fancy of Europe (and later America) with a brisk combine of older ska and younger rock. Like r&b party bands, they suddenly showed that not all Anglo-Jamaican music had to be solemn and prayer-like, and they tapped a responsive good-time chord in their audience.

The Police polished the mixture to a high sheen, combining blonde-on-blonde looks and hooks with an intelligent regard for the strengths of each music, the reggae use of rhythmic space with the nigh-limitless energy of rock. In the hit that introduced them to the world, "Roxanne," their reggae seemed to move backwards, a reverse suddenly shifting forward when it came time to drive the chorus home.

Reggae was, at last, a familiar part of the language of popular music, a vocabulary to be utilized and drawn upon as much as any other structural device. By softening its political content and boosting its pop ingredients ("Reggae May Finally Make US Dent" blurbed *Billboard* in January 1980), the tide had turned in terms of white appreciation. For Blondie, this might have been paraphrased "The Tide Is High." Remaking an old Paragons hit intact, Blondie mounted a planetwide number one in the grand tradition of marketplace pop. There had been other reggae-inflected smashes—10cc's "Dread-lock Holiday" noted "I don't like cricket/I love

it!" while the familiar scratch guitar and whisking hi-hat rebounded around the track—but none so widespread or infectious.

It would be nice to say that this cultural exchange worked both ways. Only in black music does it seem as if some compromise might be struck, and even there, layers of suspicion and interracial rivalry have to be resolved if progress is to be made. High fashion model Grace Jones went *nouveau* wave with the

rhythm section of Sly Dunbar and Robbie Shakespeare, while rude girl Sheila Hylton (herself a former beauty queen) returned the favor by doing the same with the Police's "The Bed's Too Big Without You." Even Miles Davis's new band plays reggae.

Stevie Wonder, who sometimes seems as if he

is black music, made the most recent advances when he sinuously heaved the two musics together in a well-named "Master Blaster," a solid wall of reggae and r&b that did much to break the unspoken Jamaican barrier in the US black community. His proposed tour with Bob Marley and the Wailers might have clinched the issue, especially coming after Marley's own first black hit, "Could You Be Loved," but Bob's untimely passing placed that question within the might-have-beens of immortality.

Marley's figure overshadows any discussion of musical communication between cultures. A unique presence, he embodied a marrow that is simultaneously at the core of each race. His roots were both African (realized most highly on the flag-draped *Survival* album) and in his adopted western hemisphere, an acknowledgement of place that resulted in a music truly all things to all people.

Hybrid Prophecies

They are always black, sent across the cultural chasm to teach the thudding heart; the white understands it, and sends back that under-standing, and again, until where one stops and the other begins is merely an arbitrary line set in an endless flow, the concept of time. Little Richard, Chuck Berry, and Jimi Hendrix, talking shop with Elvis, the Beatles, David Bowie. Miles Davis meets Hank Williams. Down the long line of history, each no more or less important, a Jamaican singing trio trying to learn the words of a Hot 100 hit, an American rock band dropping into "Satta Amassagana" during the course of a Saturday night set.

In Don Letts' film on the early days of punk, *The Punk Rock Movie,* there is a precious scene showing a long-haired dread attempting to teach the basics of reggae drumming to an attentive white band, Alternative TV. The earnest concen-tration of all the participants, the desire to experience the world of the other, even on such an abstract level as music, is the umbilical cord which ultimately binds reggae to its white neighbors. —*Lenny Kaye*

Grace Jones

Right: The Blue Riddem Band mashed down Reggae Sunsplash '82 with a sunrise set of murder-ous ska tunes and perfectly recre-ated Studio One riddims. 25,000 Jamaicans got up and rocked.

Hardcore reggae fan Keith Richard with Robbie Shakespeare.

Ten Minutes with Sting

Born Gordon Sumner 29 years ago in northern England, Sting taught school and played jazz bass in local bars until tapped for a London punk group by American drummer Stewart Copeland, the son of a CIA agent—hence the band's name. Copeland and Sting were joined by guitarist Andy Summers, a rock vet in his late thirties known as one of the best guitars in the UK. The group took off on the coat-tails of Sting's love song to a young whore, "Roxanne," an unexpected hit worldwide. In concert the Police proved to be electrifying. Sting sings in front of the extended chording of Summers and the crackling white reggae drumming that Stewart Copeland provides. Dancing and swaying in place, Sting projects a hip intelligence and persona that hasn't gone unnoticed by filmmakers. His portrayal of the main mod in *Quadrophenia* was incredibly strong.

We interviewed Sting backstage after a recent gig. Drenched in perspiration and sipping a beer after a knockout performance, Sting turned out to be an ardent conversationalist, speaking with more than a trace of English north country burr.

Q: *How did the Police come to be the top white reggae band?*

Sting: Reggae has been a part of British sub-culture for the past thirty years, since there's been a large West Indian community in England, so it's not as if reggae just suddenly appeared fresh from Jamaica. It's always been *there*, and its been in the British top twenty. Ever since Millie Small did "My Boy Lollipop."

As far as me as a musician, my interest in playing it was fairly recent. Ahhh, I think it was probably Bob Marley who was the touchstone between my interest in black American music and jazz. Then I found in reggae an interest that was bass-oriented; reggae is bass music, where the bass takes a leading role, a very dominating role, which obviously appealed to me, a bass player.

And Marley's singing had a great effect on me, a very great effect on me. So I would cite old Bob as a major influence on the Police, as musicians—just as James Brown had been for the previous ten years.

Were any other reggae musicians as influential on you?

No, not as essentially. In fact, once we had the basic input, we tended to forget about reggae, and forgot about the ethnic Jamaican roots. Now we don't hear too much, apart from the odd Burning Spear album . . . because we've already assimilated it into our own style, our own *whiteness,* so that we now have a hybrid that has little to do with reggae.

In the beginning you could see that we jumped around a lot. Take "Roxanne:" we played standard white rock and eight bars later we'd play very formal reggae. What we've done over three albums is to assimilate both, so in a song like "Don't Stand So Close To Me," you have both influences, but quite subtly blended.

So we're not playing either. We're playing something else. I think that's quite unique.

What do you think of the other new wave attempts at white reggae?

I applaud their interest, because it's a great rhythmic area that hasn't been explored to death, like a lot of other rhythmic areas, the backbeat. And they all do it to varying degrees of efficiency, of course, y'know. A lot of groups use it as a political stance. Just by the association of playing reggae, it means they're in line with the Third World and the politics of the Left. *That* I'm not particularly interested in. I'm interested in the music.

Music crosses barriers, and reggae music crosses a barrier for me.

What about the 2 tone bands, like Specials and The Selecter?

They're all very valid, very enjoyable, as long as they don't stop there. And the Specials didn't. In fact they surprised me greatly by going and developing something that is totally their own. Their first album was very ska, very traditionalist, but the second album is . . . somewhere else. You can see where it's coming from, but it's going to a different place, and that is very, very laudable.

But I don't want to decribe what they're doing, or even what the Police are doing, because it's putting a wall or a boundary around music, and the whole thing I'm against is boundaries in music. Because I think that's what's wrong with American music at the moment. You open Billboard, and you see a page dedicated to black music, to disco music, country music, Latin music, white music . . . these are very very rigid boundary lines. When there's little crossover you get stagnation, and stagnation is what's happening in America. American music is dead on its feet.

English music on the other hand . . . there's only one radio station in England, Radio One, and the programming is very catholic. So one minute you're listening to reggae, the next minute you're hearing country . . . I mean, it might be noxious to some people but there *is* a link, there *is* crossover, you hear all different kinds and that's what we need. I mean, we *need* to hear Emmylou Harris, heh heh, it's *important* to hear different kinds of music. In America, what the radio is really all about is selling soap powder, innit?

So where do the Police fit in all this?

There are a number of forces at work, the strongest being commercialism. I'm interested in playing to a lot of people, and that obviously tailors the music. The fact is that the music we're making coincides by accident with what is commercial right now. It's very fickle though; in three months or three years that could change drastically. What we enjoy could be totally out on a limb.

But at the moment I'm enjoying the power, enjoying the music we're making, selling a lot of records. That's important to me, I'm not gonna deny it.

—Peter Simon & Stephen Davis

Sting . . . many are called, but few are chosen.

Hide my face in my hands
Shame wells in my throat
Our comfortable existence
is reduced to a shallow,
   meaningless party
Seems that once some innocent
   dies
All we can offer them is a page
   from a magazine
Too many cameras and not
   enough food
This is what we've seen
Driven to tears . . .

—Sting

One half of Steel Pulse with two thirds of the Police.

171

15

The Battle for Jamaica

The struggle for control of modern Jamaica began in 1938, when a series of bloody strikes on sugar plantations coalesced into the Jamaican trade union movement. For the previous 400 years, Jamaica had been run less as a colony and more as a huge agricultural factory by a small Anglo-Scottish plantocracy who kept their African slaves and their descendents in perpetual penury. But from the labor struggles of 1938 emerged Jamaica's first union and a flamboyant, revolver-toting politician named Alexander Busta-mante, who would dominate Jamaican political life for the next thirty years as leader of the Jamaica Labour Party (JLP). The same year also saw the founding of Jamaica's other political party, the socialist Peoples National Party (PNP), by Bustamante's more cerebral cousin, Norman Washington Manley.

In this chapter, **Stephen Davis** briefly examines the background to the battle for Jamaica in the late '70s and talks with the candid leader of a new force in the Caribbean, Prime Minister Edward Seaga.

A Voice in the Workplace

By 1962, when Jamaica gained its independence from the longest colonial administration in English history, the rivalry between the JLP and PNP for control of the island had hardened into rigid territorial distinctions, especially in Kingston. The two parties had developed their own finely honed code of subtropical justice, apart from British colonial law. Most arguments were settled out of court, at night, in the alleys of western Kingston's notorious slum districts. Entire neighborhoods and their populations came under the personal rule of party bosses and their henchmen.

Today one speaks of sections of Kingston "controlled" by this cabinet minister or that gunman. Housing, jobs, food—the very ability to live in the city—are dominated by this system, one that engenders fierce political loyalty and utterly brutal violence in the poorer neighborhoods, the roots of the gunplay that has plagued the Jamaican capital for the past five years.

The JLP governed Jamaica rather sleepily for the decade after independence, buoyed by the general economic boom the West enjoyed during the '60s. Jamaica was the kind of tranquil paradise where retired British civil servants, like the late Ian Fleming, could retire on their pensions and write suspense novels. But by 1972, the mass of Jamaicans, especially the teeming poor, were ready for a change. They found that change in Michael Manley, the son of the founder of the PNP.

Michael Manley might have been ideal for Jamaica in the '70s. Born in 1925, he served in the Canadian Air Force during WWII, and later studied at the London School of Economics under the great Fabian socialist Harold Laski. Back home in Jamaica, he worked as a labor

Norman Washington Manley, founder of the Peoples National Party.

Alexander Bustamante, founder of the Jamaica Labour Party.

organizer and journalist, eventually writing on the problems of emerging nations for journals like *Foreign Affairs* and *The Nation.* Manley's political autobiography, *A Voice in the Workplace,* is considered one of the most interesting books ever written on trade unions in the Caribbean.

Articulate and charismatic, outraged at the pathetic gap between rich and poor in Jamaica, Michael Manley was considered a savior by Jamaicans in 1972. Some years earlier, he had invited Ethiopian Emperor Haile Selassie —revered as the living god by Jamaica's estimated 80,000 Rastafarian brethren—to Jamaica for a state visit. During his stay, the emperor presented Manley with an imperial scepter as a personal gift. In the eyes of the Rastas and many Jamaicans, this gift bestowed on Manley a powerful moral authority; when Manley took his socialist campaign into the countryside and brandished this "rod of correction" (as he called it), people would prostrate themselves with awe. They called Manley "Joshua" then, for he would

Michael Manley on JBC, and with his supporters, 1980.

"an de beat wel red/an de scence wel dred/and de man dem a loot an shoot/and de fia a bun/and de blud a run/an some people doa' kno weh fi tun/an de politician a preach/an de preacha a pray/but tings a get worse day afta day/an den from de eas' an de wes'/an de nart an de sout'/a shot peace! an de man dem from Reama an jungle a bungle/a dance an a prance/to some heavy reggae ridim/an de beat wel red/an de scene we dred/an de man dem a loot an shoot/an fi a lang time/de man peta waila wailin in de wildaness:/dere can be no peace no peace/until until/dere's equal rites/equal rites an/Justice-tice-tice-tice/an de likkle dutty bagabone a bubble/to a heavy hip/notic survival ridim/an im madda wid har han pon har jaw/a sing a sad sad song a redemshan/an im bredda from de crack a dawn/a dance a dance wid death/tru de bluddie black asfalt streets a de city/without any pity/an de people dem a wail:/free Michael Bernard/down with capitalism/it's ritten on de wall/babilan Kingdom mus fall/natty dred bawl:/dere can be no peace no peace/until until/dere's equal rites/equal rites an/Justice-tice-tice-tice-tice."

—"Reflection in Red"
©Oku Nagba Ozala Onuora

lead them now as his father Norman, like Moses, had once led them out of colonial bondage.

Elected in 1972, Michael Manley replaced the JLP bureaucracy with his socialist cadres and set about changing some of the deeply engrained assumptions about life in Jamaica. The Jamaican mercantile middle class—Chinese, Lebanese, Jews—which had known semi-official protection for hundreds of years, suddenly were on their own, subject to the same custom duties and currency restrictions as everyone else. Since the 1972 expulsion of the Asian community from Uganda was still fresh in everyone's mind, the Jamaican middle class panicked and started to flee. A contemporary joke had it that Michael Manley called up the leading Chinese businessman, Mr. Chin Loy, one morning to ask why so many Chinese were leaving Jamaica, taking their money and resources with them. Mr. Chin Loy told the prime minister to call him later in the day for his report. When Michael called back, Chin Loy's secretary told him that Chin Loy and family had moved to Coral Gables that

afternoon.

But for the majority of Jamaicans, the black disenfranchised poor who make up 95 percent of the island's two million people, Michael Manley looked like a godsend. "If our socialist programs are allowed to mature," one Manley supporter told me back in 1972, "Jamaica could finally become a paradise for Jamaicans, not just for the tourists." Clearly, a country with as fierce a national spirit as Jamaica had been run as a banana republic for far too long.

Michael Manley didn't really begin to bother anybody outside Jamaica until, not long after his election, he asserted his independence from American dominion in the Caribbean by cementing a friendship with Fidel Castro (Jamaica is just 90 miles south of Cuba), bringing in Cuban advisors and technicians to build schools and to staff the island's chronically undermanned hospitals and clinics. The Cuban connection not only worried American governments from Nixon to Carter, but infuriated Manley's opposition at home and provoked years of shrill charges of Manley's communist leanings and latent totalitarian tendencies.

But Manley's problems began in earnest with the Arab oil embargo and subsequent price hikes of 1974. (Ironic, given Manley's ideas of solidarity with the Third World). Depleted by oil expenditures and aided by the flight of business capital to the US and Canada, Jamaica's foreign reserves began to dwindle dramatically. To compensate, Manley increased the bauxite levy, the price North American firms like Reynolds and Alcan pay to dig up and export Jamaica's vast bauxite reserves, the red minerally earth that is the raw material of aluminum. But the increase was a drop in the bucket compared to the price of oil, and without money to spend, and with severely limited international credit, a small nation like Jamaica couldn't import the necessities of life. For the first time, there began to be shortages in Jamaica; first cooking oil, then rice, then soap, then everything.

In 1976, when the International Monetary Fund convened in Kingston for its annual meeting, the city's starving ghetto blew up, carefully timed to embarrass Manley just as world attention was focused on Jamaica. As anti-Manley labor strikes became common, shortages of food became severe. Since 1976 was an election year, the Manley forces—mindful of what had happened to Marxist president Salvatore Allende in Chile two years before—began to cry "Destabilization." Because of Manley's socialism, because he was close to Castro, it was whispered that American interests were doing to Manley what had been done to Allende. Jamaican opposition leader Edward Seaga, now head of the JLP, began to appear in Jamaica's virulent street graffitti as "CIAga."

But in spite of Manley's problems, the 1976 election was not even close. Campaigning for Manley, Bob Marley and his family were the victims of an assassination attempt that cast sympathy toward Manley. When the vote was tallied, Manley and Jamaican socialism were given a broad vote of confidence for another five years.

Michael Manley's strong cards in these years

were his energy, his visionary idealism, his skillful use of charismatic rhetoric, and Jamaica's emerging position as a world cultural leader via reggae music and the attractive spiritual nationality of Rastafarianism. Despite all this, Jamaica turned sour in the late '70s. As the IMF demanded increasingly grim spending curbs as a condition for further loans to Jamaica, life for the great Jamaican people got meaner. Food became scarce, expensive, and difficult to buy. In interviews from this period, Bob Marley, Jamaica's most eloquent and widely heard common voice, used to emphasize to reporters that Jamaica was a place where everyday people were in severe competition with each other, *just to eat*. Nothing seemed to work in Jamaica anymore, and today Jamaicans say that if it hadn't been for the illicit but widely lucrative ganja trade, with its influx of millions of dollars a year, Jamaican society might just have blown away with the first tropical storm of the 1980 season.

Early in 1980, then, Michael Manley called an election. The issues were outwardly simple: either more socialist transformation of Jamaica under Michael Manley, or a return to a pro-US, private-enterprise economy under Edward Seaga. So great were the tensions that thousands of Jamaicans left the island for the duration of the election, fearing either a military *coup d'état* or at the least, civil insurrection.

They were not far off the mark. In Jamaica, the 1980 elections will long be remembered as the worst in a long series of bloody ballots. By July, street warfare between the two parties had killed 400 people, almost all in Kingston. Goon squads of young gunmen roamed the ghettos, attacking opposing neighborhoods with M-16 rifles and Belgian .9 mm sten guns. The Jamaican police with .38 service revolvers were heavily outgunned and tended to stay out of sight. In the western Kingston slums it got really bad, with old women shot in their beds and children butchered with machetes. Tribal warfare. In the notorious Gold Street Massacre, a JLP dance was savaged by para-military troops who landed at the waterfront dance site in rubber rafts. In the crossfire, a dozen teenagers died. Later in the campaign a PNP cabinet minister was shot to death when his car strayed into the wrong neighborhood. Political rallies were routinely fired upon, as were both Michael Manley and Edward Seaga, during the course of the campaign.

By Election Day at the end of October, the death toll hovered near 700, and Jamaica was an armed camp. Military units set up roadblocks to intercept weapons, but many Jamaicans interpreted it as a coup on behalf of Manley in the face of obvious electoral defeat. In a famous AP photo reprinted around the world, Seaga is seen sprinting between bullets as his bodyguards lay down a withering covering fire. Ballot boxes were stolen, voters were intimidated by gunmen, and election officials were pinned in their homes by gunfire.

When the dust had settled and the blood had dried, Michael Manley's social activism had lost to the realities of national survival in the '80s. Edward Seaga had won the battle for Jamaica. The people hailed him as "Financial Wizard" and

"Cultural Leader" with the same traditional Jamaican optimism that they had once hailed their "Joshua," Michael Manley.

"Deliverance"

When Edward Seaga assumed the leadership of Jamaica late in 1980, his campaign slogan had been "Deliverance." The Tourist Board immediately adopted the slogan "Smiling Again." And

anyone who travels there can see that there *is* a new spirit, a new breeze in Jamaica these days, after years of brain-drain and psychic doldrums. Slowly, skilled Jamaicans who had fled the hard

times of socialism began to trickle home, some almost sheepishly saying that they just couldn't find the easy lifestyle anywhere else. When he took power, Seaga kept the post of Finance Minister for himself, and put some of his vaunted economic acumen (and his contacts with such New Right think-tanks as the American Enterprise Institute) to work. Crucial negotiations with the IMF, broken off by Michael Manley due to the Fund's draconian curbs on Jamaican social spending, were renewed by the new prime minister, and loans were renegotiated.

Seaga was the first head of state to confer with Ronald Reagan after the latter's inauguration, proposing a sort of mini-Marshall Plan to revitalize the Caribbean and protect the region from communism. And, indeed, Jamaica now is seen by US interests as a test case for the success of capitalist policy (after eight years of socialism's perceived mismanagement) in the Third World. No less an American corporate commander than David Rockefeller has stepped out of retirement to chair a group of high-power businessmen dedicated to promoting American investment in Jamaica, restoring stability, and keeping Fidel Castro in Havana. It should be noted that Jamaica is also developing strong economic ties with West Germany, Norway, Mexico and Venezuela.

Scenes from the 1980 Jamaican general elections:

From where does pain come
 to us?
From where does he come?
He had been the brother of our
 visions
from time immemorial
And the guide of our rhymes

—Nazik al Mal'-ika

Edward Seaga

Edward Seaga at home.

Edward Seaga was born in 1930, in Boston, to Jamaican parents of Scottish and Lebanese ancestry. After graduation from Harvard in 1952, Seaga returned to his parents' homeland intending to do anthropological work in the Jamaican hill country. This put Seaga into contact with Jamaica's African religious cults, like the Pocomania revival sect and various groups of Kumina dancers. After recording and annotating an album of the island's cult music for New York's Ethnic Folkways record series, Seaga gradually moved into the Jamaican record business in the late 1950s, recording the music of Jamaica's pre-reggae ska musicians like Byron Lee and the Ska Kings and the singing duo of Higgs & Wilson. As president of West Indian Records, one of the largest firms in the Caribbean, Seaga was eventually lured into politics by JLP boss Bustamante.

For twenty years, Seaga has represented in the Jamaican parliament the same rough and tough Trench Town slum constituency, Tivoli Gardens, arguably one of the worst neighborhoods in the world. His reputation as a financial wizard comes from his stewardship of the economy during his term as finance minister in the JLP governments of the prosperous '60s. Today, Edward Seaga is widely regarded in the Caribbean as one of the region's most capable men, in one of its toughest and most relentless jobs.

Jamaica's new prime minister rarely gives interviews; when he does receive reporters it is usually within the luxurious confines of Jamaica House, the PM's official residence on Hope Road in uptown Kingston. But when Peter Simon and I were in Jamaica to research this book, I arranged to spend an hour with Seaga at his office in the Finance Ministry while he worked feverishly on his government's first budget.

So on a blazing bright morning, we took a cab to the ministry on National Heroes Circle in eastern Kingston. At the ministry, security

was heavy due to Seaga's presence. We were shown to an anteroom outside Seaga's office and sat down to wait. Suddenly the building's halls literally erupted with the sound of running feet. Looking out the window, I saw Edward Seaga, surrounded by jittery bodyguards, jump into a sedan and roar off in the direction of Jamaica House. So much, I thought, for our interview. Just then the door opened, and Seaga's press secretary, looking flushed and shaken, said: "I'm sorry, gentlemen, but we've just

had word that President Reagan has been shot, along with his press secretary."

Then I understood the pale look of panic on Seaga's face as he got into his car. The first head of state to see Reagan, tied to him by policy and destiny, Seaga knew that if Reagan did not survive his wounds, his new government might not either.

But a few days later, things had calmed down a bit, and Seaga's budget was being debated in Parliament. On another crystalline Carib-

bean morning, we drove up to the iron gates of Jamaica House, were scrutinized by policemen carrying sten guns, and were admitted onto the grounds. The house itself is modern, furnished in carved Jamaican antiques. For Edward Seaga, it's an official residence only. He and his wife live further up in the mountains overlooking Kingston.

During the Manley years in Jamaica, Seaga was popularly caricatured as a gun-running right-wing heavy. CIAga, always just on the threshhold of a *coup d'état* on behalf of the old oligarchy. So it's odd to find instead an unprepossessing man of medium build and piercing eyes, seated in a Harvard commemorative chair in a cluttered office darkened against the burning glare of the tropic daytime.

The "Stabilization" of Jamaica

Q: *As we travel around Jamaica, it's impossible not to notice a very positive spirit, as if the old Jamaica was trying to reinvent itself.*
Seaga: Smiling again.

When you took office last year, did you find yourself trying to reinvent government in Jamaica?

No, we've always had what we have today, with the exception of the deterioration that took place during the past five years. Because the first three years [of the Manley government] weren't quite so bad. We've always had a good functioning government apparatus with normal bureaucratic problems, but we also had good spirit in the people, who were motivated by initiative and by enterprise and hope for the future. We had a track record of good performance and a forward-looking country that was *always* ahead of its peers in our category of Third World developing countries, or on a par with the best. All of that deteriorated in the last five years: during that time standards of living dropped in Jamaica by 57 percent. The country's finances were virtually wiped out. The foreign exchange was wiped out and our budgets couldn't be financed. And people lost hope generally. There was no confidence in the future. We were treated to regulation after regulation, restriction after restriction, and it was a government of what you could *not* do rather than a government of what you could do.

Why did the Jamaican people vote so overwhelmingly for Michael

Manley's democratic socialism in 1972 and 1976? Did they know what they were getting?

In '72, they didn't know. They thought they were voting in what they normally do at the end of every two terms of office—a new team whose ideas don't differ that much from the government they succeed, but having more dynamism, a better management team, et cetera. And perhaps some new policies. But they were not prepared for any radical shift. That was the first time.

In 1976, it's really difficult to judge what took place then. We maintain that that election was so rigged that the results were never true ones. And we believe that the real results of 1976 would have been a narrow victory, one way or the other. In which case, the people at that time would have begun to express that dissent. The extent to which that election was so rigged led to electoral reforms between 1976 and 1980, which has given us a system that gave us the fairest election we've ever had.

Why do you think Michael Manley's experiment with socialism was unable to succeed in Jamaica?

Well, what experiment? There was no experiment. There was an attempt to transform Jamaica into a model socialist state. There's nothing experimental about that. There's a copybook formula for that, and we saw all the steps being taken, from 1974 on. That's when we began to warn of the extent to which the society was being geared for a transformation into the Cuban-type model. Some people accepted what we said, but between 1976 and 1980 Jamaicans really woke up. And one of the things that made them wake up was when the Cuban ambassador to Jamaica (Ulysses Estrada) virtually insulted the people of Jamaica, and the Manley government was not able or did not take any steps to declare him *persona non grata*. Since Manley had just declared the American ambassador *persona non grata,* people began to think the Manley government was a mere pawn of the Cuban government.

But what really alarmed us was the party-to-party relationship we saw formed between Manley's Peoples National Party and the Cuban Communist Party. The Cuban delegation to the 1974 PNP conference was headed by the notorious Manuel Pinera Lasado, alias "Barba Roja," who was head of the Americas Department of the

Cuban Communist Party, which is their bureau charged with subversion in the Americas. Prior to that he was head of the DGI, the Cuban intelligence service. That sort of close linkage, where that kind of man becomes your chief delegate to a party convention, was the signal for us to realize that there was a linkage between the two parties.

And we've been proven right on that. That linkage has gone well beyond the Cuban Communist Party to involve the CPSU, the Communist Party of the Soviet Union. You may have noticed that the chairman of the PNP, D.K. Duncan, recently attended the meeting of the Supreme Soviet in Moscow and made very complimentary remarks about the whole communist movement, and about fraternal relations with Jamaica and the Peoples National Party.

How do you respond to allegations that the Manley government was destabilized by Western intelligence and business interests, much in the same manner as the Allende government in Chile?

I would not want to respond. Those charges were made in desperation by a government whose management abilities had collapsed. Any Jamaican can tell you that the Manley government destabilized themselves.

As a young man, you were deeply involved in researching rural Jamaican folk culture. Could you describe some of your work in this area?

After I graduated from Harvard,

I was engaged in a study on the development of the child, partly sponsored by the University of the West Indies. I was interested in the period from pre-birth up to the age of about 15 years. In the course of doing that, I came upon a number of interesting things concerning the spiritual cults in the country, which led me to want to study the cult

groups as well, and I was able to obtain additional financing from the Para-Psychology Foundation. These cult groups are collectively known as Revival Cults, which consist of two types, the Pocomania group and the Zion group. And then there is the Kumina cult group, which is different from the Revival groups in that the latter is Christian-based in its theology, whereas the former is African-based. I studied all three of these cult groups and recorded their music, and have written on all of them to a certain extent.

When I was through with these studies, instead of going on to do my post-graduate work, I became involved in politics, and I was involved with the recording business in Jamaica as well.

It seems a logical connection in Jamaica, going from the recording business to politics. Both involve knowing the people's taste. Do you agree?

Well, both of these things happened to me by accident. I had no intentions of becoming involved in the record business. But having academically recorded folk music in Jamaica, I was constantly being

asked about the sources of the music, and the availability of recordings, and on that basis I decided to make these recordings available, which sort of eased me into the recording business. It was not a plan.

I didn't plan on becoming involved in politics either, but because I had a deep and intro-

spective experience with the folk culture of the country, I found that I was able to see things quite differently from most of the people who were decision-makers in public life, and by being able to shine new light on some of the old problems I came to the attention of the political leadership. And eventually, by consultations and discussions and involvement at that level, I found myself becoming involved with the political life of the country.

The base for both (music and politics) is common; the period of

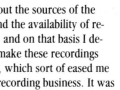

Fewer Jamaica murders

Kingston, Jamaica (AP)—The murder rate in this Caribbean island nation dropped by nearly half in 1981, the Police Information Center said. According to the figures released yesterday, there were 490 murders in 1981 compared with 857 murders in 1980.

Associated Press, February 1982

Never make a politician grant you a favor. They will always want to control you forever.

"Revolution," Bob Marley 1974.

Edward Seaga and family.

Hugh Shearer, Ronald Reagan and Edward Seaga at the Kingston airport, 1982. Shearer, a former prime minister and current foreign minister, has long been involved in the banning of reggae songs he considered inflammatory or subversive. Shearer's latest targets are the toasting and skanking deejays, whose preoccupations with sex and goofiness he considers shameful.

Drying marijuana in the hills of St. Ann. Mr. Shearer, one feels, would not approve.

time that I lived in rural and urban communities studying the folk life of the country was a three-and-a-half-year period. It was an invaluable opportunity to learn about the folk life of the nation, which very few people at decision-making levels have the opportunity of seeing firsthand. It gave me the most intimate possible relationship with the people of Jamaica.

Now that reggae music has achieved almost mainstream cultural proportions in places like northern Europe, West Africa, and to a lesser extent the US, I find it odd that reggae has yet to achieve mainstream cultural status in Jamaica. Why is this?

In the early '60s, when Jamaica developed its first musical idiom—ska music—at that time we had a small market here, and the limited opportunities that go with a small market. So Jamaican musicians began to record in the United Kingdom, selling to Jamaicans living in the United Kingdom. The music was given the name Bluebeat. That music, which was developed in my own constituency [Tivoli Gardens], was *never* known or heard in the middle-income or higher-income areas of Jamaica.

At that time I tried to promote the music—I was the minister of development—and I had a couple of teams sent to the United States to work on this. It gained some small acceptance, and if we had had a pocketful of money to work with, we could have put the music over then, almost twenty years ago. But I think we were able to get enough attention payed to our music and the ska dance-form to start the ball rolling.

When reggae came along five years later, it was able to pick up where the ska promotions had left off, and from where the ska music

itself had left off as a music form. It developed an attractive beat, but most of all it developed a superstar, Bob Marley, along with it. There were earlier people who began to break international ground—Jimmy Cliff, Desmond Dekker, Peter Tosh, the Maytals, and so on—but when Bob Marley came along he was a terrific hit as a performer, and his music happened to coincide with the sort of protest music that was popular in the United States at the time. Hence, the Jamaican musical form became identified not only as a rhythmic music, something that is really meaningful to people.

Why are Jamaicans largely unaware of the impact their culture has had on a worldwide basis?

You must understand that for the last few years we have been closed away from the outside world to a large extent. Prior to that, reggae was just coming on the scene. In the days when we were promoting ska music, Jamaican people knew what Jamaican records were in the popular music listings, the charts of Europe and North America. In the dark years of the Manley government, it was little value to know these things, for the simple reason that people were so consumed with the problems of survival. Music didn't register as something of primary importance. Secondly, Jamaican artists had to seek their own avenues of advancement outside of Jamaica, and most of the artists left Jamaica and set themselves up in bases abroad. Such information about their success that came back to us from abroad was only a fraction of what was really happening.

Winds of Change in the Caribbean

You were the first head of government to see Ronald Reagan after he assumed the presidency of the US, and in that period you made several statements concerning the role of the ganja (marijuana) trade in the present economy of Jamaica. Could you elaborate?

Yes. That came about through a misquotation by AP or UPI, one of the wire services, of a statement I had made in Florida in reply to a similar question in early December. What I indicated was both sides of the story. We have an effective machinery [to control ganja] which is working effectively, but it's rather limited. Last year alone, 88 light aircraft were seized, some 200 people were detained. For a country that does not have a large security force, because it is not in our tradition, it's a very effective operation. On the other hand, there's no question about it, the scale of operations is much bigger than that. And it became much bigger during those dark years, because the economy was depressed to such an extent that people started to become more and more involved in the growth and export of marijuana. While the great bulk of these earnings are never seen in Jamaica —they are lodged in foreign bank accounts by the big dealers—such rub-off as came to the Jamaican economy served to purchase scarce raw materials and other goods and services that the Bank of Jamaica had not dollars to purchase. To that extent it was of some impor-

tance to the Jamaican economy. As we move back to buoyancy, it will become of less and less importance.

So what I was trying to indicate was that there were two sides of it. Some people would tell you that half the factories in Jamaica have been able to stay open because of

ganja during the dark years, and I don't know if I could dispute this. But that still does not deter us from our own position, and that it is an illegal activity, and we treat it as an illegal activity. We indeed treat it more so as an illegal activity than the United States does, because we haven't legalized the use of it, not even in small quantities.

There was some speculation that your remarks might have been paving the way for the decriminalization of marijuana in Jamaica.

No, my remarks were just frank remarks. I'm used to answering questions frankly.

Are you aware that you and your party have been linked to ganja-smuggling and gun-running in Jamaica by anti-CIA groups in the US?

Yes, I'm aware of these things.

The main thing to bear in mind is that they have no evidence, because there is none. Our intelligence indicates the big dealers are not even Jamaican anymore, but mostly foreigners.

Jamaica has narrowly survived a failed socialist revolution, with its democratic system intact. How close did Jamaica come to civil war? Or is "civil war" too strong a term to describe what was happening in Jamaica during the last election?

No, it wasn't a civil war. What really happened was the fact that we had a nine-month period of notice of an election, instead of the normal time of five or six weeks.

Why did that happen?

It happened because Manley could not have continued to hold the country together unless he was able to indicate the date of an election, and an early date. Manley had two more years to run. His term of office would not have been up for another two years *after* the election. But he was not able to hold the country together because it had reached rock bottom. On that basis, he had to give an election date, and it took nine months because a new voters' list was being prepared.

Nobody would have accepted an election based upon the old, fraudulent voters' list. With a nine-month period to run, and with so much at stake—because we were not just voting on a different team of men with the same ideas, we were voting on a totally different ideological system, a totally different development strategy, a totally different perspective of the future—because there was so much at stake, men took *intense positions* that they had never taken before. And people who were never involved in the political life of the country became involved.

So, we didn't come to civil war, but because of the prolonged pre-election period there was a mounting toll of the results of political violence, which when added up looked like a large number, and was a large number (more than 700 dead). If you had put that within the framework of a six-or-eight-week period, it would not have been anything near the proportions of what we had.

Eric Williams died today in Trinidad after 25 years as prime minister. How does that change the Caribbean?

It's got to be changed, because he was one of the last of the major national figures, and the Caribbean is now in the hands of younger men, and fortunately younger men have been able to restore the Caribbean to its vitality and have been able to pick up the dynamism that was evident at the beginning of the movement of Caribbean independence, and have been able to overcome the threat to the traditional Caribbean method of development and the Caribbean way of life that was evident in the '70s. It's a tribute to this group of 32 countries, all of which, except for four, are democratically governed and have proven themselves to be democracies time and time again through changes of government . . . that have made this region not just a centerpiece of popular music—because in the same way you have reggae here, Trinidad has its calypso which is equally exciting—has made this area a centerpiece of democracy which is unequaled in the world.

It is also a testimony of the people who reside in the Caribbean, that they have adapted themselves to the system, and have made it work so brilliantly. So the

Toward a Caribbean Economy

What, then, is in store for the new Jamaica under Edward Seaga?

For one thing, the foreign businessmen are back in Kingston again, talking profits and making deals in the lobbies of the Pegasus and New Kingston hotels. On the streets, the burned-out car wrecks and other detritus of urban civil war are gone. Market shelves, once bare, are now filled with goods. After more than a year in office, the Seaga government is beginning to restore Jamaican life to its old pace.

Naturally, this process has been helped by the infusion of millions of foreign dollars. After making peace with the IMF, Jamaica signed a $698-million loan agreement

flowed into Jamaica. Such proposals should only increase now that Seaga has removed the Cuban bogeyman from the Jamaican landscape, having broken diplomatic relations with Havana in November, 1981. The issue was nominally that Cuba had refused to return Jamaican fugitives wanted for murder, but long-time Jamaica watchers feel that Seaga was finally culminating the JLP's long-running feud with Fidel Castro over the influence he exerted upon Michael Manley during the '70s.

But what of the prospects for Jamaica beyond the immediate future? The clear lesson of recent history is that neither Michael Manley's socialist public spending nor Seaga's free-market philosophy is going to produce any economic miracles in Jamaica, at least as long

Continued from page 71

Important Dates in Reggae History

1978.—One Love Peace Concert held in Kingston.

1980.—Edward Seaga, one time folklorist and record producer, elected prime minister.

1981.—Bob Marley dies in Miami. Severe rioting in black and poor neighborhoods of English cities.

Edward Seaga at Jamaica House, 1981.

Caribbean is now in the hands of young men who have not lost the lesson of the last five decades of Jamaican history, and in fact are determined to protect that heritage, and have succeeded by no less than six elections in 1980, demonstrating the extent to which the modern leadership of the Caribbean has prevailed over those who were adventurers and who were seeking to deviate from its traditions.

with the Fund. Seaga has also renegotiated Jamaica's old loans with a syndicate of twenty-five commercial banks and obtained $71 million in new credits. Foreign aid, including $100 million from the United States and $62 million from Jamaica's oil-rich regional neighbor Venezuela, has also poured in.

As of 1982, Jamaican officials were confident that their fragile economy was on its way to revival. Thanks in part to David Rockefeller's US Business Committee on Jamaica, over 400 investment proposals (worth more than $1 billion and ranging in scope from shrimp farms to cosmetic factories) have

as general recession remains the worldwide economic forecast. Privately, Edward Seaga is reported to have said that given the right conditions, Jamaica could be an incredibly prosperous place, the Hong Kong of the Western Hemisphere. This kind of thinking is a relief to those who not so long ago were fearful that this fruitful green island in the sun, peopled by some of the handsomest, most generous, most energetic people in the world, was on its way to becoming another Haiti.

—Stephen Davis (1981)

179

Reggae International

There are very few cosmic and earth-shattering statements left to make about reggae music. For many people, reggae is simply **it**, everything they've been searching for, a hip culture that thinks and prays and really means something righteous, optimistic, strong and wholesome. Plus you can dance to it so beautifully. Reggae is a philosophy that heals. The mini-trance produced by good roots reggae is Jamaican psychic hygiene for our apocalyptic era.

Most important, the rest of the planet is getting the message. Africa is giving birth to new forms of Afro-reggae, the best of which comes from Senegal. Australian blacks are adopting the sounds and riddims with hard authority, and young Moroccans dance to the sound of Bob Marley. **Stephen Davis** reflects on his experiences in Jamaica and reggae's international appeal, and dispersed throughout this chapter are some reggae epiphanies of **David Silver**, personal encounters and revelations in reggae over the past five years.

Half Way Tree

It's a pleasingly warm Friday night in February in Kingston Jamaica, and the Reggae International team (writers, editors, photographers, art directors, Dread security, drivers, friends and enemies) are happily lounging in a little rum bar near Half Way Tree with a bunch of local musicians, drinking Red Stripe and listening to the weekly Top 30 countdown on the JBC.

The deejay is the legendary Barry Gordon, a droll personality who on Saturday nights broadcasts live from dances in places like Mandeville, giving away quarts of Creamy Corner ice cream to young girls who provide the correct answers to his typically lascivious quizzes. With a wicked chuckle, Barry likes to ask these nymphets if they know, for instance, in which parish the village of Maidstone is located . . .

When we tune in, Barry is just taking the needle off of number 22 for the week, John Holt's "Ghetto Queen." With its salubrious lyric and hard backing by the Roots Radics band, the tune draws appreciative listening from the musicians, even though it's been on the charts and jukeboxes for several months. Next up is number 21, "Ice Cream Love" by Johnny Osborne, also backed by the Radics, with the perfectly lewd chorus of "My love is warmer than a chocolate fudge." (Lately one of the thematic preoccupations of roots reggae, especially in the "slackness" style of the sound-system deejays, is the intricacies and mysteries of the female pudendum.)

As the countdown segues into number 20, LeRoy Smart's version of "She Love It in the Morning," the assembled musicians guffaw and begin to tell LeRoy Smart stories: they say he'll occasionally rob a supermarket between hit singles. They say he's a pickpocket. They say that once LeRoy was so mad at his manager that he followed him all the way to England, beat him up and shot him, and did a couple of years in

Opposite: Rita Marley entertains a massive peace demonstration in Central Park, New York, 1982.

181

Her Majesty's prisons for his trouble. Is this true? They all swear up and down that it is.

Red Stripe beer travels directly from my gullet to my bladder, and I missed whatever was number 19, but number 18 is Gregory Isaacs' monster from the previous year, "Front Door." Typically brilliant Gregory lovers rock with a typically sensitive and evocative lyric and a typically brilliant mesmerizing hook—"But *I*, don't want to be lonely tonight." Everybody in the room sings along.

Mr. Isaacs is widely regarded as the top Jamaican singer of the day, with legions of loyal and adoring fans including this writer. Yet rumors of the singer's dark side abound. They say he administered a beating to another famous singer not long ago over a financial matter, then stuck this musician in the trunk of his car, drove to another location and beat him up some more. They say that nobody on Chancery Lane would speak to Gregory for a month. Is this true? They shrug, and smile sadly. Some say that Jamaica is a place where there are no facts, only rumor and opinion.

The story of this great star's misbehavior causes a flood of evil gossip, all of which is sworn to be gospel. They say that Ripton Hylton, known to the universe as the deejay Eek A Mouse, is in trouble with the police for putting a boulder through the windscreen of producer Junjo's BMW because of this producer's alleged non-payment of any royalties on Eek's big hit "A Wa Do Dem." Then someone pipes up that Big Youth and Trinity were gambling after hours at Joe Gibb's studio when the place was invaded by Trinity's brother, armed to the teeth and looking for revenge for some transgression against him. But Trinity had somehow disappeared, so his brother simply stuck up the place, taking money, watches and chains. Eventually, it is said, Jah Youth got his jewelry back.

Just as some lout was claiming (surely preposterous, I hope) that Niney the Observer's fingers had been chopped off by a villain called Leggo, I went back to the radio. Number 17 was the Pointer Sisters' "Slow Hand." Jamaicans love this kind of slick black Yankee neo-soul.

A disturbance in the saloon caused me to step outside for a moment and miss number 16, but number 15 for the week was deejay Yellow Man skanking on Lerner & Loewe's "I'm Getting Married in the Morning." Yellow Man is an albino, and has spent his life being called "dundus," a derogatory Jamaican term. Now that he's a hot deejay and a star, Yellow Man travels with bodyguards so nobody will call him dundus anymore. Can't really blame him. I like Yellow Man, but personally I prefer Stanley Holloway's original of this particular tune.

Number 14 is another hot deejay, Lone Ranger, doing his hit "Rosemarie." Number 13 is the Commodores' "Oh No." When Barry Gordon breaks for the news, we hear that juke boxes have been taken off the list of prohibited imports. Not surprising, considering Prime Minister Seaga's background in the record business. Some of the musicians are grumbling that since his friend Seaga came to power, Kingston's music biz kingpin Byron Lee has been moving to take over the entire industry, turning his Dynamic

Leroy Smart, master vocalist.
Tristan Palma

Sound complex into the hub of the reggae industry. Dark rumors abound of vandalism of other people's record stampers and other equipment.

Number 12 is Tristan Palma, a talented tuff-faced teenager, singing "I'm Ready." Number 11 is Deniece Williams' "Silly." Number 10 is deejay Ranking Toyan (rated high by those present) singing "Bubble with Me," a skank built on the same "Have You Ever" rhythm used by Yellow Man back on number 15.

Number 9 is Diana Ross and Lionel Ritchie's "Endless Love." The general mood in the bar is dampened by three and a half minutes of desultory cooing, but livelied up with Dennis Brown's wonderful number 8, "Have You Ever Been in Love" on Sly & Robbie's Taxi label. The popping syncopation of the Sly & Robbie battery, turned louder by the barman, seems to lift the tin roof off its beams. The pace is kept hot by number 7,

Jimmy Cliff's sophisticated dance song "Rub A Dub Partner." Rad Bryan is on lead guitar, blasting off the radio with that clean spanking sound obtainable in Jamaica mostly at Dynamic Sound, where this was recorded.

The set is rounded off with number 6, Beres Hammond's torchy ballad "If Only I Knew." During this, I get into an argument over who played the hardest guitar for the Wailers. My chauvinistic suggestions of Al Anderson or Don Kinsey are greeted by laughter and threatening gestures from the Jamaicans, mostly partisans of Chinna Smith or Junior Marvin.

OK, the top five. Everyone listens a bit more carefully. Number 5 is one of the greatest reggae songs of all time, "Top Ten" by Gregory Isaacs. Pure reggae sex. Gregory responds with paternal concern to a young daughter's petitioning to enroll in Prof. Isaacs' college of carnal knowledge. "You may not be in my top ten," Gregory consoles her, "but you're still a student in my class." The backing band, as with most of Greg's music, is Radics. The plaintive horn line echoes the ancient "Peanut Vendor" calypso.

Number 4 is Eddie Fitzroy's "Youth Man Penitentiary" again backed by the Radics, Dwight Pinkney goosing the well-worn studio rhythm with a spectacular lead vamp that propels the song like an Exocet missile.

Number 3 is the Mighty Diamonds' happy ganja chant "Pass the Kouchie," a *tour de force* for Sly & Robbie, Gussie Clarke producing. Nice to see the Mighty Diamonds back on the map.

Number 2 is Michigan and Smiley, currently Jamaica's two reigning deejays, with their monstrous hit "Diseases." A macabre litany of the worst things you can get, the song has somehow touched a raw nerve in Jamaica, where medical treatment is not taken for granted, medicines (especially in the countryside) are rare, where people tend to die or be crippled by dangerous diseases. The horror of Bob Marley's cancer was by no means lost on his countrymen.

Talk in the bar ceases as Barry G slips the JBC's number 1 theme cart into its slot and the nation of Jamaica pauses to hear which song the planet's most discriminating reggae audience has judged to be number one this week. Everyone in Jamaica of course knows that if this world had any justice to it Rita Marley's worldwide smash hymn to sinsemilla, "One Draw," would be perpetual number one in Jamaica for months and months.

But "One Draw" has been banned from the Jamaican airwaves for its humorous and worshipful stance on herb. So instead . . . the number one record this week in Jamaica . . . the very sugary essence of the music Yard has invented and sent out to take over the world . . . *is* . . . Helen Reddy doing "I Can't Say Goodbye to You."

I can't take it. I really should leave that white rum alone.

I stagger out to my rented Toyota Starlet and point it home toward Ruthven Road. On the dashboard radio, RJR is playing Rick James. "Gimme that stuff, that sweet funky stuff!!!"

Toots in Central Park, 1976

On a gorgeous summer's day, Toots and the Maytals outside in Central Park: by the third song, thousands of energetic New Yorkers on their feet dancing, like the Yankees have just won the World Series, as if Toots had been given thousands of keys to the city. Music acting as a loose-limbed, unceremonious healing wave, Toots leaping and crouching, a knockout mixture of Otis Redding and James Cleveland, communal reggae soul, with the chopping, optimistic Maytals bounce behind him. One of those events that your heart wants to go on forever: a true congregation of agreement, everyone knowing that this will make their day, no matter what the particular personal metropolitan anxiety.

Toots simply made us all feel big, sexy, yet humble and quiet inside, just like him and his sound. Sacred moments are never dull; holy entertainers never exhibit a pompous side. They exude ease and untarnished life-love. This is what infects and uplifts an audience.

Toots that day was the best example I have yet seen of the performer as soul guide, moving throngs of urbanites into an exultant territory in themselves. He acted out his natural role as reggae sound shepherd, emblematically directing his dance in front of the flock, enchanting them into group feeling, shouting and singing his modern motored Bible chants until we all broke, surrendered, and felt, even temporarily, the glow of harmonized heart-power. Reggae's special alchemical force again had forced some fast redemption.

Wailers at the Beacon, 1976

The first time I saw Bob Marley and the Wailers in concert was at the Beacon Theatre on the upper west side in New York City. Their records had already totally captivated me, but even so I was shocked by the sheer firepower that the band had on stage. The audience was raving throughout the concert and from my front row seat I was quickly transfixed beyond help by Marley's pure musical grasp. The band's medicine music magic, which existed deep in the silences and spaces of the music as well as the actual sound, brought on a trance-like state, permeated by dread and joy simultaneously. Any kind of pop or rock comparison was futile.

The music was transmitting from another place altogether, and mutated by off-the-street, thought-filled, anxiety-prone, mid-'70s nervous system into a new, welcome sensorium, ready to receive extra-dimensional experience. The audience was highly excited, but never out of control, a state often to be felt at reggae concerts. Marley's gestures and expression were leonine, proud, even arrogant, but there was a constant sense of his humility as he danced under the banner of the Lion of Judah.

Even though this was my first live Wailers concert, I felt right at home, with the same kind of mysterious recognition I felt 13 years before at early Rolling Stones performances in London, the major difference being the designed presence of spiritual vibrations, a strong feeling of connection with Jah, a realization of Godhead. The struggles of the black man are not exactly my individual life-contour in this incarnation, but the universal battle to connect with the underlying Law is. This first Wailers encounter helped me immeasurably to have a clearer, richer, more truly felt sense of the presence of the Divine.

The epiphany was made whole for me by the incredible polarities present: the alien chanting of the massively specific and localized Jamaican sect, the absolutely sincere sense of personal identification with the music and the multi-level sentiments therein.

It was immediately obvious to me that Marley, though just a man, was built around a heart pumping cosmic blood, that this band stood alone on the planet in its closeness to an eternal rhythm. Their wail was mine, their power could inspire all of ours.

Ras Michael on TV

Ras Michael and the Sons of Negus amble into the TV studio and I stop my video-directing babble and walk over to the young, handsome, ancient, dreadful Michael and greet him. Very soon, a sacred (and I use the term with thorough confidence) atmosphere sweeps the steel and glass, slightly military, video studio.

Michael sings and drums and talks and prays and jokes, and the cameras detail the highly visual features of his seemingly countless drummers while pausing here and there on the masterful fingers of the silent, smiling Chinna Smith as he punctuates the band's African/Venusian rhythms with delectable cuts of electric guitar. The banner they hang up behind them creates a final video tableau of impenetrable beauty and power, and as a New York TV person, I feel relief and even pride at electronically grabbing all of this. This TV show is more fundamental and more sacramental than any I ever did.

Visionary television exists after that taping. Ras Michael's utterly singular sound coupled with his shamanistic reach cracks the sterile gestalt of TV and sends me reeling.

—*David Silver*

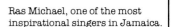

Ras Michael, one of the most inspirational singers in Jamaica.

Freetown, Sierra Leone

On the West Coast of Africa, the rainy season lasts for months, and whole days are spent listening to the tapping of droplets on tin roofs. In Sierra Leone, people like their food spiced extremely hot, and they read newspapers like *We Yone*, published in *krio* (creole), chock-full of grisly stories of alleged child sacrifice by the various tribal and secret societies that compete with each other for the nation's heartbeat.

If we stretch the point, we could even call Sierra Leone a cultural colony of Jamaica. The attentive reader might remember that the rebellious Trelawney Maroons of 1796, who went to war rather than allow a pair of pig thieves to be publicly whipped in Montego Bay, were first deported to Nova Scotia, and then to the new British abolitionist territories in Sierra Leone in 1800. Many of Freetown's best families trace their heritage to the Maroon settlers, and even the semi-benevolent president Siaka Stevens speaks well of Jamaica, although conventional wisdom has him as half Limba, half Sherbro: African all the way.

In Freetown's torrid shanty nightclubs, like Omar Khayyam's, Africans dance the current big dance, the Minimal, as if they were fucking. In other words, they dance like Jamaicans. And what they're dancing to is mostly reggae. Not only the obvious Jamaican exports—Marley, Tosh, Cliff—but to homegrown Sierra Leone West Coast of Africa reggae.

In Africa today, many young bands under the age of thirty are reggae bands, and if you walk down Krootown Road in Freetown on one of these rainy monsoon Monday mornings, you hear reggae blaring out of the scrap-metal speakers of music shops and cane whiskey bars. But it's reggae to an ineffably sweet African touch. In Freetown the local reggae bands are called the Godfathers, the Afro-National Band, the We Yone Band.

Whereas most African rock bands play a fast, pumping, guitar-driven variant of Afro-beat or highlife, African reggae bands tend to play a slow, ticking, carefully studied brand of reggae, sung falsetto in both verse and chorus, with long and utterly hypnotic instrumental patterns between vocal segments. Interestingly, there seems to be very little aping or covering of the obvious Marley and Cliff material. Instead, the African musicians tend to use reggae exclusively as romantic music.

Lyrics usually address a lover, and the rude and rebellious aspect of reggae (Bob Marley excluded) has failed to make much of an impression on African musicians whose musical messages are somewhat constrained by repressive regimes who are tolerant of the insouciance of reggae and calypso only as long as the political

A dub session with Prince Mohammed, Boston, 1981.

message behind that attitude stays safely in the Caribbean. One Jamaican promoter who journeyed to post-independence Zimbabwe to attempt to set up a reggae tour was told flatly by someone in the appropriate ministry that the government didn't want reggae in Zimbabwe now that the war was won.

When Bob Marley's anthem, "Zimbabwe," was released in 1979, Africans recorded at least nine cover versions in music centers like Salisbury, Lagos, Abidjan (Ivory Coast), Accra, Freetown, and Dakar (Senegal). It was no accident that in Zimbabwe, the now-disgraced warlord Edgar Tekere invited Bob Marley and the Wailers to play at the independence ceremony.

The best African reggae we've heard comes from Senegal, specifically a group called Touré Kunda that had a couple of hits in France during 1980, "Africa Lelly" and "Emma." Where most African reggae players attempt to faithfully reproduce reggae time, the Touré brothers mix Africanisms and sweltering vocal acumen with the basic rockers rhythms and Rastafarian religious and philosophical beliefs.

Most Africans believe that Jamaicans don't have much to tell them about Ras Tafari, but Touré Kunda is the best possible example of what one might call a weird transatlantic cross-cultural bounceback. Touré Kunda is also the most accessible African reggae band, at least in the West through the group's Parisian record label. Most African reggae singles are available only on cassettes compiled by local record shops, and the few of these that reach across the ocean are just a trickle of the vast new form of Afro-reggae about to flow out of Mother Africa. Watch and see.

Boston & Sydney

A word about what reggae has done, in a small way, for the city of Boston, Massachusetts. Boston is a very segregated and violent town, where whites and blacks do not mix well. If you took a poor neighborhood from Belfast and a poor neighborhood from Port-au-Prince and put them together with a wealthy neighborhood from South Kensington in the middle, you'd have a close approximation of the social structure of Boston. The point is that the *only* place where young blacks and young whites can mingle freely and unselfconsciously in Boston is

at reggae shows.

The reggae vibration is revolutionary and *physical*, but it isn't violent. Of course someone will suggest I tell this to the unlucky murder victim at a Black Uhuru show in London in late 1981, but that's not the point. Reggae works for Boston and maybe also for Cape Town and Recife as well. Reggae *works*.

And working hard, if last week in Kingston was any indication. As I was coming out of the New Kingston Hotel one day, a neighbor of mine from Massachusetts pulled up in a Datsun which disgorged a bunch of white Rasta musicians and their guitar cases into the hotel. Another white reggae band in Kingston to record. My neighbor was also going to sound system dances with tape recorders and large wads of cash (earned promoting reggae shows in Boston). He was paying deejays for their toasts, intending to release them later on an album, with hopes of making

Soccer Bob

New Year's Day, 1980, at Hope Road, Earl Chin and I are meeting with Bob about several interesting business matters. It is 75 degrees and as we drive into the compound, we see Bob sitting on the stoop of the big house with a few brethren. He greets us and we talk about nothing and everything for a bit. Marley makes me a gargantuan spliff and my mind soon lowers gear and I join the assembled in peaceful sunshading. Smiling and light chatter.

Suddenly, Bob gets up and collects together the soccer players, and I become one of three spectators as two almost complete teams take up the game at the back of the house in the concrete yard, some playing in sneakers, some barefoot. The game is hard-fought.

Bob plays inside right and is a fine player, weaving and darting and dribbling, passing generously and accurately to the other forwards, laying on goals or near-goals for them every time. He does not shoot at goal himself, just passes, passes.

The game goes on in the ganja afternoon for a long time and I see Marley, like a prince off-duty, guide the game, with his cohorts tackling him hard, never pussyfooting. And I settle into my deeper feelings about Marley—a great controller of the ball, a shooting star who does not shoot, a team player despite his obvious authority. His relationship to the game was as his relationship to power itself—a leader, but never a megalomaniac, a shining frontrunner, but never one who had the delusion of the power being truly his own.

Bob's team wins, but the losers are just as happy. His extraordinary royalty is that of the shaman-king, never that of the political monarch. A young lion, Marley, but aware of the place of strong youth, old youth within the permanent citadels of wisdom.

Jahmalla

Cleon Douglas of Jahmalla is a wise, articulate Rasta and a real acclimated Jamaican in the States, understanding Yankee ways while decidedly keeping his head way above any Babylonian life formats. His band's name means "peace" in Swahili. Cleon's daughter's name is Jamillah ("beautiful"), so the name of the group is the masculine form of that.

Jahmalla is an extraordinary band, combining Cleon's mature and rock-hard reggae-sense with the genetically masterful sounds of supreme trickster drummer Noel Alphonso, son of Roland Alphonso, originator of ska and no-kidding Jamaican legend; keyboardist Michael Ranglin, son of another bonafide reggae Olympian, guitarist Ernest Ranglin; bassist Boogsie, one of the great heart-throbs of the music; and Brian Montiro, American funk lead and ambassador of the band to rhythm and blues, rock and roll and Ike Turner-type thrust.

This strong team of players has been galvanising New York audiences for several years now, and every time I see them I am nothing less than shocked at their ability to go from their moving roots original "Israel Train" straight to a Dylan, Doors or Creedence song seamlessly. Their songs emphasize the universality of true reggae practitioners—adventuring everywhere there is fire and spirit, but always with their aloof yet grounded rhythm section pounding and rattling its way through atavistic reggae roots.

As I said, Cleon is a wise singer and person, and his everyday reasoning and demeanour is an epiphany in itself. Watch Jahmalla rise. The '80s will be their time to get global and point up the anti-nationalistic essence of the genuine Rasta artists.

Marley and friends after football in the park, London, 1978.

Jahmalla

Jacob Miller R.I.P.

Two memories, both intense as only the serious jester Jacob would make them. Driving through the New York rain listening to a wonderful tape of some Inner Circle Dutch and German recordings, Jacob accepting our compliments graciously, the music tough, witty and quite unique, better than anything yet on record, implying that Jacob's time was finally coming and another name would be on the rarefied Rasta roster. As we enthuse, Jacob starts to laugh with pleasure, while cursing the slippery city streets, Jacob ready to sit on top of the world, if the world could take the strain.

Cut to Jacob running wildly along the Arrivals corridor at Norman Manley Airport in Kingston to greet me as I arrive coincidentally one time as he was leaving. Ten yards away, he leaps the dividing barrier, completely belying his big frame to land like Pan or Ariel right in front of me. We all laughed; that was the last of him for me. The '80s lost two reggae giants and the original Inner Circle will now always be just that —Jacob's lively thing circulating inside us who knew him, forever zestful, never really lost.

—D.S.

so much money that he could buy a villa in Ocho Rios and never have to hustle again.

And there was Dr. Dread, a record shop owner from Washington DC, who publishes a reggae newsletter and who was in Kingston to record local talent for his shop's custom label. There were people from two enterprising American labels, Nighthawk of St. Louis and Shanachie of New Jersey, who want to be for reggae in the '80s what Island Records was in the '70s. All the major studios are busy. New movies are coming out. Incredibly, reggae seems to be revising and renewing itself on a yearly basis, and not only in Jamaica and the US.

In Sydney, New South Wales, Australia, there's an incredibly vibrant reggae band staffed by black people who used to be called aborigines. No Fixed Address is the group's name, and the music they make is extremely hard, Jamaican-sounding reggae, played so right and tight that pandemonium sometimes attends their gigs. "Black Man's Rights," "Greenhouse Holiday" and "The Vision" are songs so full of reggae authority that they wouldn't be out of place on a Wailers or Culture album.

But not only that. Dub poet Oku Onuora is presently touring Germany to sold-out houses. Record shops in St. Louis, Missouri, can't keep reggae records on the shelves because the demand is so high. Rita Marley's phenomenal "One Draw" is high on the charts in Austria and Singapore. Tappa Zukie records are played at the chicest boîtes in Paris and Antibes. Peter Tosh's shows in Japan have inspired almost religious frenzy in Tokyo and Osaka.

On the day Bob Marley died I was buying vegetables in the market town of Ksar El Kebir in northern Morocco. Ksar El Kebir was a great city with running water and streetlights when London and Paris were muddy villages. Moroccans tend not to check for any form of western music, vastly preferring the odes of the late great Om Kalthoum or the latest pop singer from Cairo or Beirut. But young Moroccans *loved* Bob Marley, the only form of non-Arabic music I ever saw country Moroccans willingly dance to.

That afternoon in Ksar El Kebir, Bob Marley banners in Arabic were strung across the main street, and I ran into a car full of Moroccan teenagers smoking kif and playing "Pimpers Paradise" on the cassette deck of their battered green Renault.

Reggae International, indeed.

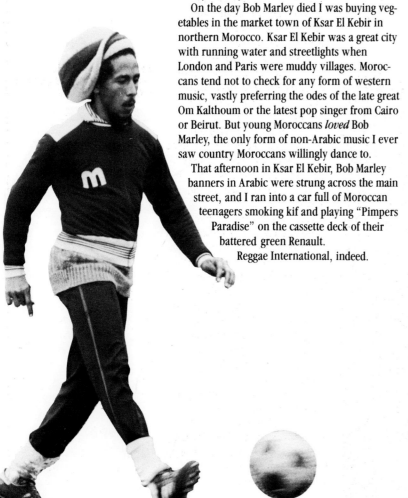

Goodbye Bob Marley

The elegant invitation bore two embossed Lions of Judah. It read:

PSALM 2

How good and how pleasant it is for brethens And sistrens to dwell together in one Inity Give praises unto the Almighty JAH Rastafari

Mrs. Rita Marley and Family requests your presence at their Birthdate Anniversary of the Hon. Robert Nesta Marley OM, our beloved brother and friend.
To be held at Nine Miles, Rhoden Hall, St. Ann, Jamaica WI on the 6th February, 1982, at 5 p.m.

The morning of the 6th dawned bright and clear. At nine a.m., the JBC began broadcasting a long birthday tribute to Bob that had originally been produced by an FM station in Santa Cruz, California. The road out of Kingston was free of trucks this Saturday morning, which made the climb over the Blue Mountains faster and much less brain-beating.

At one point our intrepid Toyota was pulled over by a speedtrap, where a Jamaican justice of the peace was holding roadside court. He gave me a pink summons for a court appearance in Kingston the following week. Back on the road, I wondered what Bob Marley would have done with this pink ticket. His spirit told me to crumple the evil document of Babylon and throw it out the window, which I did.

I'm always thirsty in Jamaica, and when I'm on the road I like to stop every half hour for water coconut, whose cool, invigorating juice is sipped through a hole chopped in the shell with a veteran machete. The coconut jelly is then eaten with a jagged slice of shell. Further on, we stop at the famous roadside shanties near Moneague where we buy buttered roast yam and salt fish, giant pineapples and papayas, exotic naseberries, blushy red Ethiopian apples and long strings of oranges and tangerines; the great bounty of the hills.

Turning off the main road, we drive towards Browns Town, deep in the heart of the garden parish, St. Ann. Cruising the tops and sides of inland ridges and vales, we can see the impossible deep azure of the ocean on the other side of the hills. The roads are rural, narrow and infrequently travelled except by flocks of goats and the intervillage vans that hurl passengers along these country lanes with breakneck abandon. Along the flat open spaces, steel poles have been erected at intervals along the roads to try to cut down on illicit ganja missions flown by Florida-based Cessnas and Beechcraft.

Deep in St. Ann, the land is heavenly and green. The ghostly great houses of the late sugar empire watch over the landscape from their promontories. A few people walk along the road. A man's machete gently slaps the side of his leg as he ambles slowly onward.

Through the teeming market town of Browns Town on a busy Saturday, a riot of dark stalls and bright fabric in primary colors, a sea of faces that recall Togo and Benin as much as the West Indies. A stop at a roadside shop for an ice-cold bottle of Ting, Jamaica's grapefruit soda, the best soft drink in the world. Standing in the shop, we watch Dennis Brown roar by with locks flying, at the wheel of his fancy new VW van, headed toward the party at Nine Miles.

Suddenly the road turns to gravel and we're winding on rutted rural *piste*. Jamaicans of all ages are heading up to Marley's hamlet on foot, carrying food and radios. Some shout for rides as we pass, but we're running full from Kingston.

Nine Miles, Rhoden Hall, Stepney District, Parish of St. Ann. We park, walk up a little hill past vendors of curry goat, roots tea and sinsemilla, and find seats next to the soundboard in front of a stage erected across the lane from Bob Marley's birthplace and tomb.

The landscape consists of rolling green hills, whose granite outcroppings are covered with people waiting for the show to begin. The afternoon is alternately radiant, then grey and cool as oceanic cumuli roll in from the sea. The sun sets behind the big hill in back of the stage late in the afternoon, and from then on the proceedings are illuminated by a single powerful bulb suspended over the stage.

The crowd is mostly Jamaican, but with a lot of youngish tourists who found their way inland from the north coast. People are building spliffs and waiting out the afternoon in good humor and expectation. In front of the stage is a sign that reads: "NO FILMING BY ORDER OF MANAGEMENT." The management here is strictly Rita Marley, Bob's widow and heir to the entire Tuff Gong empire. Back on Hope Road in Kingston, Rita is having a huge concrete wall built around the Tuff Gong studio compound, turning the one-time tropical mansion into a fortress. It seems that Mrs. Marley wishes to assert her control.

Bob Marley's simple cement tomb has been covered by a little chapel, grey-roofed and sided (perhaps temporarily) with sheetrock. Light pours in through stained-glass windows and flickers from the dozens of long candles and tapers that burn silently for the late reggae avatar. Outside, police stand guard with riot shotguns slung casually over their shoulders. On the roof of the tomb, a solitary white dove is perched.

The audience is full of dreads basking in the deep blue twilight, calling to new arrivals: "Sky is Clear!" "Pardon me, sir, would you give me a likkle sinsemilla thing?" "Just a likkle Junior Tucker?" Just as half a dozen dreads fire up their meticulously crafted spliffs, a uniformed colonel of the Jamaica Defense Force stalks through the crowd brandishing his swagger stick, making ostentatious sniffing noises, turning up his nose at the sweet aroma of St. Ann's finest draw. "Haarruummph!" The Rastas mock the colonel without mercy and dissolve into peals of derisive laughter as they puff happily away.

Peter and Mick at NBC, 1978

Saturday Night. Live. Backstage at Studio 8H, NBC, New York: a TV garden of earthly delights with the original, inspired *SNL* team, dozens of wandering, pondering Rastas, Peter Tosh, Robbie, Sly and the band, assorted professional hangers-on, Mick Jagger, Keith Richard. The occasion was the appearance of Tosh on the show, supported by his friend and record company executive, Mick Jagger.

In the dressing room: super-esoteric conversation between the Glimmers and the Sun of Reggae on the singing styles in Jamaican churches . . . Jagger speaks of wandering incognito around them, learning how to sing really high. Tosh very regal and totally lacking in nerves, Mick loose and at home, straddling Rasta reasoning and the vibes of the ultra-center of the '70s media zeitgeist backrooms of "Saturday Night Live."

The two madly different music masters eventually stroll out to the studio floor for the dress rehearsal, where they do the Temptations' "Walk and Don't Look Back" with great energy and humor, Mick jogging before he goes on, Peter slowly toking from his epic pipe, emitting an aura of "this is what the modern prophet should be doing." Mick looks a little grey before he hits the raised stage for the real show, but by the time of the midnight live performance, he is shining, funny and ready to rip and reggae. Tosh is as usual philosophical and unnerved.

The sight of these two characters standing quietly amidst the surreal, frantic costume changes going on all around them (Danny Ackroyd changing from a Jimmy Carter suit into a full Scottish outfit, kilt and all; Belushi anxious to remember his lines, while chatting soul-brother style with Keith, rock boffin, dark yet basically benevolent): this sight is a very special one, Magritte in the '70s, and brings a smile to my face, if only because of the absolute rightness of the whole thing, despite all odds.

Peter does "Bush Doctor" without Mick, and the live studio audience gets it and gives him a big hand, which Tosh aristocratically acknowledges and then disappears.

Reggae masters have a unique nervous system, sweetened by good herb, great music and the fulfillment of singing of spiritual dreams and futures to expectant Babylonian hordes. Mick and Keith slide into the New York night, stepping stones for Tosh's strange but superlative reggae career, obviously gaining satisfaction out of their catalytic role in bringing some exceptional roots music to the legions of *SNL* fans.

It has always pleased me a lot to see the Stones' very real connections with reggae music. Their deserved clichéd label as the world's greatest rock and roll band puts them in the right position to catalyze this music, as they have other black musics, for large audiences. Keith's uncompromised Zen musical accomplishment gives him the right and the innate knowledge to dally with reggae, give it a push, and give himself a rise at the same time.

Mick and Keith would deem a spiritual interest on their part as pretentious, but their visceral connection to the music makes a great deal of sense. Meanwhile, Peter Tosh continues to be relentless in every way, and it also served him well to find a friend in a Stone.

Rasta Irish Boy

At a cocktail party on Martha's Vineyard, July 1981 in honor of a family visiting from Ireland. Polite conversation: we compare our rather different Britishnesses. The Irish are the father, a country doctor, his sweet wife and their eleven-year-old son. My mind is there, but when they ask me what I do for a living, I momentarily consider saying something simpler than the truth just to keep the conversation from floundering in incompatible areas of lifestyle and occupation. I told the truth, however, and explained that I had just completed a videotape for Italian television about the recently passed-away Bob Marley. To my complete surprise, all three of these obscure Irish folks responded excitedly.

"Bob Marley, oh goodness, what a great man!" said the doctor.

"Oh, Bob. Bob Marley. Mr. Marley. A shame, isn't it? A big shame," said the wife.

"Marley and the Wailers? Bob Marley—he's my favorite. I have all his records. Did you actually know him? Did you meet him?" said the boy.

Bob had been big in Ireland. As he had in Italy. As he had in remote as well as central places all over the globe. The little Irish boy begged me to send him special, ungettable tapes I had.

I left the party shortly afterwards and realized that this had been the most spectacular epiphany of all. The pure unstoppable penetration of the music stunned me. The everlasting charisma of its sound and message suddenly resided full-blown in my being. Bob big in County Meath. Bob an idol in Zimbabwe. Bob brilliant in New Zealand. The man, he can't be stopped.

The music, well . . . it will play out our 1980s and '90s destinies. And maybe, if we are lucky, the unknown antennae of the dawn of the 21st century will receive it as the incorrigible holy anthem of a better future. —*D.S.*

Keith, Mick and Peter, backstage at "Saturday Night Live," 1978.

The view into the little hills from my back seat is *long*, surrounded by Jamaican mountain jungle. Giant turkey buzzards swoop low over the crowd, perhaps drawn by the spicy scent of stewing goat and I-tal food. Vendors are selling oranges. "See the orange man! Get your blood claat orange right here!"

The large painting of Bob holding his guitar that was displayed at his funeral is propped up against the stage, along with blown-up sepia portraits of Marcus Garvey and His Imperial Majesty Haile Selassie I. Red, green and gold bunting drapes the stage.

At 4:30 the sound system is switched on. Lui Lepke sings "Tribute to Bob Marley" on tape.

An hour later, after various members of the new Wailers set up their instruments on stage, Rita Marley, dressed in red and sporting tennis sneaks and a Tuff Gong eyeshade, appears on stage. She welcomes the throng, announces the program, and asks for good behavior with all the prim propriety of the lady schoolteacher on the skank of "One Draw." Then she introduces her priest, a handsome Ethiopian from the Ethiopian Orthodox Church who walks onstage in a black burnoose and prays, in heavily accented English, for the soul of Bob Marley. Then the priest holds his small black cross aloft in the St. Ann twilight and simply says "Our Father . . ."

It was like a dub version of the Lord's Prayer.

As night falls, a white-smocked Ethiopian reggae band takes the stage, but not before an intense Rastafarian woman announces that tape recorders and cameras are *dangerous diseases* and will be confiscated if discovered. Around this time, small groups of youths in mirror sunglasses and berets filter through the guests,

All I ever had
These songs of freedom
Redemption songs

threatening the various professional photographers trying to cover the event.

Dallol is basically an Ethiopian copy band, and they cover Wailers songs like "Who the Cap Fit" with little grace. They are followed by a Rasta dub poet who delivers a shining poetic rap/invocation that sets a sharp tone of spirit for the evening. As his staccato poetry jabs into the audience he is greeted with appreciative cries of "MURDER" and "BIM!"

Then the Wailers came on. I should say, the *new* Wailers came on. Seeco was absent, reportedly exiled for some transgression. Tyrone Downey, the band's avant-garde keyboard-man and Bob Marley's musical alter-ego, was touring with Grace Jones. Al Anderson was up in New York. Carlie and Family Man Barrett remain as one of reggae's greatest rhythm sections, and Earl "Wia" Lindo is on keyboards. Lead guitar Junior Marvin takes Bob's lead vocals, sometimes singing in partial phrases, so the Wailers now sound like Wailers-in-dub. Artman Neville Garrick is on percussion, and the band was filled out with veteran guitarist Gitzroy and Steven Stewart on keyboards.

From their sound it seemed that the Wailers were still trying to regain their automatic transmission while mourning their leader. Certainly, to almost everyone present, the old Wailers drive was absent that night.

But the musicians, obviously experimenting, still managed to mount a soulful and very satisfying show in tribute to Bob Marley, martyred by the epidemic scourge of our unhappy century. Cute Tuff Gong chanteuse Nadine Sutherland, not yet 14 years old, came out first, and did quick versions of her important single "Starvation"

and the last major Marley anthem, "Redemption Song."

Then, a dramatic moment. The I-Threes walked on.

Rita Marley. Judy Mowatt. Marcia Griffiths. The three reggae goddesses. Judy and Marcia wore scarves around their heads, long dresses and red, gold and green silk Wailers tour jackets. Onstage, the I-Threes don't smile much. They just look . . . awesome.

"It feels like a *party*," Rita exclaims. But it doesn't. It feels like something else. Rita tries to get the crowd to sing Happy Birthday to Bob, but the people seemed stunned, reminded again that Bob is in his box in that tomb over there with the candles and the incense. Rita tries again for a rousing Happy Birthday, but it's really not working. It feels like a wake.

But that's alright, too, and the I-Threes, arguably the best harmony singers in Jamaica when they stay on key, deliver a short set that begins with a subdued but beautiful rendition of "Nice Time," continues with an even more beautiful acappella harmony orgy on "That's How Strong My Love Is," and finishes with a long scatting skank with the Wailers on the theme: "Some like it hot/Some like it cold/Some like it in the pot/Nine days old." It sounds silly on the page, but that night in Nine Miles, it *burned*.

The I-Threes stepped off to great cheering, and Mother Booker, the great Cedella Booker, Bob Marley's mother, came on to sing. Mother Booker is a beautiful woman, robed in salmon-colored silk and golden Coptic crosses. Backed by hand-drummers, she improvised a chant based on Bob's last words to her in the Miami hospital from which he passed on. "Mother, don't cry. I'll be alright." It was an amazing performance, and by the end of it, she had the audience completely in her sway.

The night's entertainment was finished by her grandchildren, the Melody Makers, Bob's four children by Rita—Sharon, Cedella, Ziggy and Stevie. The kids did juvenile versions of their father's stately songs, and I decided to leave, feeling overcome with sentiment. Of all people, *of all people,* why did Bob Marley have to go? He was so important to so many, one of the very few truly planetary people. What a situation.

We drove back to Kingston in a three-car caravan, looping across the back roads of St. Ann, stopping at a lively roadside bar in Claremont for cold Heinekens and a taste of the jukebox. We stood outside, drinking and leaning on the dusty cars, excitedly exchanging views of the day, drinking in the beauty of the black night air of the garden parish, redolent of laughter, ginger lily and dew.

Later, on the road back to Kingston, with the JBC again playing Rick James and my friends asleep in the back seat and my bleary eyes trying to stay on the canyon road near the flat bridge at Raby's Corner, I thought to myself . . . *Goodbye Bob Marley. I love you.*

188

—*Stephen Davis*

People Speech

The "dub poets" of this chapter are often in tune with Jamaican popular music; some of their work—but not all—can, in one way or another, be heard to connect with reggae. They tend to acknowledge the influence of deejay artists such as U. Roy, I. Roy and Big Youth, and reggae lyricists such as Bob Marley, Peter Tosh and Bunny Wailer. Dub poets often speak in a language and articulate concerns shared with reggae masters; they seek to communicate with that enormous audience touched by the reggae performers.

The dub poets live on the cutting edge of poetry, an appropriate address for a new generation of reggae-inspired artists. In this chapter, Jamaican poet **Mervyn Morris** directs particular attention to five of the most talented: Linton Kwesi Johnson, Mutabaruka, Oku Onuora, Brian Meeks, and Mikey Smith.

Dub Poetry

The term "dub poetry" was promoted early in 1979 by Oku Onuora to identify work then being presented—often at the Jamaica School of Drama—by Oku himself, Mikey Smith and Noel Walcott. The dub poem, Oku has said, "is not merely putting a piece of poem pon a reggae rhythm; it is a poem that has a *built-in* reggae rhythm—hence when the poem is read without any reggae rhythm (so to speak) backing, one can distinctly hear the reggae rhythm coming out of the poem."

More recently, however, Oku has been arguing that any verse which refers to or incorporates music rhythms belongs in the family; poetry into which music rhythms have been dubbed, so to speak; dub poetry. He has begun to see Louise Bennett not only as a pathfinder in exploring Jamaican Creole, but as herself a dub poet behind whose verses we may hear Jamaican mento music and particular folksongs. He would claim Edward Kamau Brathwaite, who draws on jazz, Akan drumming, Caribbean rhythms; he would capture Langston Hughes, Sonia Sanchez and many other Black American poets influenced by Black American music. Fully extended, the Oku tendency would rope in writers such as Lorca, Nicolas Guillén and Edith Sitwell. While much may be learnt, no doubt, from a comparison of the ways in which divers poets dub music into their verse, it is probably more helpful to use the term more narrowly—as Oku originally did.

Sometimes the reggae connection is diffuse. But often we can distinctly hear reggae rhythms in or under the verse, as in:

night number one was in BRIXTON:
SOFRANO B sound system
was a beating out a rhythm with a fire,
coming doun his reggae-reggae wire . . .

Linton Kwesi Johnson, "Five Nights of Bleeding"

an de beat wel red
an de scene wel dred
an de man dem a loot an shoot
an de fia a bun
an de blud a run
an some people
doa kno
web fi tun . . .

Oku Onuora, "Reflections in Red"

The "dub poets" are not totally preoccupied with reggae rhythm. They are, of course, very much interested in Jamaican speech. They give thanks for Louise Bennett, the poet who from the 1940s has been demonstrating that Jamaican Creole, the unofficial language of the people, can be a medium of a subtle verbal art. "The mother of it all is Louise Bennett," says Mikey Smith. "I like to hear people talk, and listen to people speech," he says, and he tells of his fascination with the sounds of Jamaican language. He vividly remembers the impact on him of the oral advertising he first heard long ago outside a store on Orange Street in Kingston: "Come een, come een, come buy-up, buy-up; but no come een, come een, come tief-up, tief-up, for me wi beat-up, beat-up."

Like the deejay artists, the dub poets—Mutabaruka and Mikey Smith, for example—draw on patterned speech of that sort; on the routines of street peddlers; on the rhetoric of preachers and politicians; on proverbs, nursery rhymes, riddles, children's games; as in these lines by Mikey Smith:

waan good
nose baffi run
but me naw go sidung pan igb wall

189

like Humpty Dumpty
me a face me reality

one lickle bwoy come blow im orn
an me look pan im wid scorn . . .

or

bapsi kaisico she pregnant again
bapsi kaisico she pregnant again . . .

which alludes to a traditional rhythm sequence in a children's clapping game.

Dub poetry on the page is often little more than the script for a performer already familiar with his own material. Since the arrangement of lines does not often guide us into the rhythms, it is often difficult to receive the poem before one has heard it well delivered. In addition, some of the poets—no doubt constructing "eye Creole" to keep us constantly aware that what is being offered is not Standard English—write unfamiliar spelling such as "wel," "dred," "kno" in the Oku Onuora extract above, where the sounds represented are identical to standard pronunciation of "well" "dread," "blood"; "fia" (for "fire") to direct the reader towards one particular pronunciation of the word. In some cases —Linton Johnson's, for example—the spelling is approximately phonetic:

soh mek wi leggo mitalagy
dis is di age af science an' teknalagy . . .

The poems are meant to be *heard*; many lines yield little meaning until sounded.

Some of the poets write in Standard English some of the time. Linton Johnson and Mutabaruka, for example. One of the best of Oku Onuora's poems is in Standard English and hints no rhythmic connections with reggae:

You ask: Why do you write
so much about blood, sweat & tears?
Don't you write about trees, flowers,
birds, love?

Yes

I write about trees—
trees with withered branches
& severed roots

I write about flowers—
flowers on graves

I write about birds—
caged birds struggling

I write about love—
love for destruction
of oppression.

The need for an active response to oppression is a recurring theme in work by the dub poets as in reggae lyrics; though the degree and details of commitment vary from artist to artist. "Poetry can't win revolution; people win revolution," says Mikey Smith. But he believes his work may help make people more aware and may give them hope. Mutabaruka, for all his outcry against poverty and alienation, also remarks: "Me don't really feel seh de poetry gwine change de worl."

Whatever their reservations about the actual power of the word, the poets are critical of what

Peter Tosh has called "the colonial shitstem" and its legacies. They vividly describe underprivilege, neglect, police brutality, political warfare; the ghetto as a breeding ground of crime and violence. They expose cultural imperialism, the alien values of the schools; they re-enact the horrors of slavery and trace them into the present; they yearn to recover Africa. They distrust politicians and sometimes the present constitutional arrangements.

Their critical attitudes are not often aligned to any political party that has actually won electoral power. They tend to argue for "people power" with very general ideas on how this might ever be achieved. On foreign issues—Angola, Zimbabwe, apartheid—their positions are often more sharply defined.

Mutabaruka, a declared Rastafarian, is most often concerned about the inner life; and ultimately he seems to direct attention away from the material conditions noted in some of his work. "The man spiritual is above all"; in the end "all worldly/ things/ must go." Oku Onuora and Mikey Smith are steadily critical of what Edward Brathwaite has called the *status crow,* but—as to Jamaica, at least—in a manner largely consistent with liberal humanist responses.

Now I tun man
I sight up a revolutionary vision—
if we waan seh roots any at all
we haffi stop we muma from movin
from yard to yard

says Mikey Smith in a characteristic poem. Linton Johnson's are often militant contributions to political struggle, linked to specific events and naming names. The reality *there* is confrontation:

fashist an di attack
den we drive dem back

we gonna smash their brains in
cause they ain't got nofink in 'em . . .

Brian Meeks' published poems say yes to Marti, Angola, Garvey, Marx, Lenin, Bob Marley and the Wailers; no to Batista, Miami and the CIA. In "March 9 1976," for example, it is implied that a youth at a (socialist) dance has been murdered by agents of the US:

down Duke st.'s
closed bound-
aries crew cut
accountant
ticks off a
number/closes
the doors
on a stars and
stripes file.

Asserting their own commitment, the poets are, on the whole, alert for political fraud. Fashion-mongers of commitment are ridiculed in Oku Onuora's "Yesterday/Today/Tomorrow." Linton Johnson directly attacks the black petite bourgeoisie:

dem a seek posishan
aaf di backs af blacks
seek promoshan
aaf di backs of blacks

dem a black petty-booshwah
dem full a flaw
an' dem a black petty-booshwah
dem full a flaw . . .

Mutabaruka it is who turns a critical eye on the political pretensions of the poets themselves: "revolutionary poets/ 'ave become entertainers . . ."

One of the rhetorical devices shared by many of the dub poets is that they, somehow, are closer to "reality" than the sort of person previously called poet: "call me no poet/ or nothin like that . . ." says a Mutabaruka item. Oku Onuora's persona declares:

I am no poet   *laughter*
 no poet   *cry*
I am just a voice *sigh . . .*
I echo the people's *I am no poet*
 thought   *no poet*
      I am just a voice . . .

A voice that performs. The stage and the recording studio are, increasingly, essential contexts of the dub poet. Some of the poets are electrifying on stage: Mikey Smith, Oku Onuora, Mutabaruka use voice and movement with practiced care to hold their audiences and to point meaning. In contrast, the comparative stillness of Linton Johnson serves to focus attention on the word itself and the music in it or behind. Brian Meeks, when he performs in public, sometimes plays the flute and is nearer in style to Linton than to the more mobile three.

When they are making records, and sometimes on tour, the poets tend to include music. The combination is not always happy. The danger always is that the music will dominate, at some loss to our interest in the voice. The combination works best when the music complements or counterpoints the natural rhythms of the speaking voice, as in "Sonny's Letter," "The Black Petty Booshwah" (Linton Johnson), "Reflection in Red" (Oku Onuora), or Mutabaruka's "Everytime A Ear De Soun." It is good if, without dominating, the music can be of interest in itself; on Linton Johnson's records, the music is usually a pleasure, even when the combination hasn't worked.

In performing some of his poems unaccompanied, Mikey Smith makes us hear the music by his alteration of the natural rhythms of speech. In performance the lines
Say, Natty-Natty,
no bodder dash weh
yuh culture . . .

for example, become a heavily accented chant.

In two of the Jamaican 45s—Oku's "Reflection in Red" and Muta's "Everytime A Ear De Soun"—studio reverb is introduced. In both cases the technical effect has actually been written into the poem itself, so that when the poem is performed without music the reverb is nevertheless suggested: as in Oku's

dere can be
no peace
no peace
until/until
dere's equal rites
equal rites an
justice . . . tice . . . tice . . . tice . . .

"And black black black
the black birds clack
in the shak shak tree
but it black black black
from that mountain back
in yuh face, in yuh food
in yuh eye, in fac' . . .

—Masks, Edward Kamau
Brathwaite

Linton Kwesi Johnson

Mutabaruka

Oku Onuora

Brian Meeks

Michael Smith

Born 1952 in Chapleton, in the rural parish of Clarendon. Left Jamaica November 1963 to join his mother who had emigrated to England in 1961. Attended Tulse Hill Comprehensive School in Brixton from 1963 to 1970, and entered Goldsmith's College, University of London, 1973. Graduated in Sociology. In January 1977, he was awarded the Cecil Day-Lewis Fellowship and has since been a writer-in-residence in the Borough of Lambeth and Library Resources and Education Officer at the Keskidee Arts Centre.

Linton has been very active politically. After school he joined the Black Panther movement "to pursue the liberation of blacks from colonial oppression" and is now associated with the *Race Today* collective in Brixton. He has written extensively on Jamaican popular music for *Black Music* and *Melody Maker* and has performed to acclaim in Europe and the United States as well as England and Jamaica.

He now has a record label of his own (LKJ). Mikey Smith has appeared on that label, with "Me Cyaan Believe it" and "Roots."

Records:

Poet and the Roots (London: Virgin Records, 1977) VS 19012 /Disco 45/
Dread Beat an' Blood (London: Virgin Records, 1978) FL 1017 /LP/
Forces of Victory (London: Island Records, 1979) ILPS 9566 /LP/
Bass Culture (London: Island Records, 1980) ILPS 9605 /LP/

Books:

Voices of the Living and the Dead (London: Race Today, 1974)
Dread Beat and Blood (London: Bogle L'Ouverture, 1975)
Inglan Is A Bitch (London: Race Today, 1980)

(Formerly Allan Hope.) Born Kingston, 1952. Studied electronics at Kingston Technical High School. Brought up a Roman Catholic, he became Rastafarian in his late teens. Now resides in the parish of St. James with his family.

Muta had poems published in *Swing* magazine in the early 1970s, and was widely applauded at poetry readings some years before the emergence of Oku Onuora and Mikey Smith. Resists the label of "dub poet" because it refers to only one aspect of his work; had been a poet and performer for many years before people started talking about "dub poetry"—of which, however, his 45 rpm record, "Everytime A Ear De Soun," is very much an example.

With resonant baritone voice and Rastafarian locks, Muta is vivid on stage; well-received at Reggae Sunsplash 1981.

Records:

Everytime A Ear De Soun (Kingston: High Times, 1980) /45/

Books:

Outcry (Kingston: Swing Publishers, 1973)
Sun and Moon (with Faybiene) (Kingston: Stafford Harrison, 1976)
Mutabaruka: The First Poems (1970-1979) (Kingston: Paul Issa, 1980)

(Formerly Orlando Wong—father was half-Chinese.) Born Kingston, 1952. Attended various schools, including Camperdown High from which he was expelled. Associated with Walter Rodney, the Guyanese historian, who, in the late '60s, used to reason with Oku and others in Rollington Town. Oku helped to found a community school in the area.

Helped distribute the Black revolutionary paper *Abeng*, in spite of police harassment; arrested in March 1971, one week after his 19th birthday, and charged with robbery of the Rollington Town Post Office. During preliminary enquiry he escaped; was recaptured and convicted. Escaped again and recaptured again. He was shot. Sentence of 15 years was, on appeal, reduced to ten.

In spite of obstructive conditions, Oku began writing in prison. Poems were read on the Jamaica Broadcasting Corporation; and, under a liberalizing regime, he was allowed out of jail to take part in a few poetry readings, including one arranged by the Jamaica Centre of PEN International. *Echo*, his first collection of poems, published in 1977. Released on parole a few months later, Oku was admitted to the Jamaica School of Drama. Dropped out after a year.

An intense and compelling performer, Oku went to the 11th World Festival of Youth in Cuba in 1978. With the help of Linton Johnson, he went on tour in the UK and Europe in 1980-81.

Records:

Reflection in Red (Kingston: Prugresiv Aatis Muvmant, n.d.) /45/
What a Situation (Kingston, 1981) /45/

Books:

Echo (Kingston: Sangster's, 1977)

Born 1953 in Montreal to Trinidadian mother and Jamaican father and came to Jamaica, 1956. Educated at Jamaica College and on the Trinidad campus of the University of the West Indies. B.Sc. (Econ.) 1974. At the Jamaican campus of the U.W.I. he did an M.Sc. in Government (1974-76) on the development of the 1970 revolution in Trinidad and Tobago.

Brian worked in the Public Affairs Division of the Jamaica Broadcasting Corporation until, with other workers, he was declared redundant early in 1981. (The decision is being contested in the courts.) Brian presented a television programme called Sunday Report. Generally supportive of the People's National Party government from a position widely interpreted as left of it.

Like Linton Johnson, Brian is an expert on Jamaican popular music. In some of his talks he has analysed the political content of reggae. When he performs, he is careful to establish the rhythms of the work. On some readings he did for JBC radio, he also played the flute.

("Mikey.") Born Kingston, 1954. Educated "in the street" and at various schools including Kingston College Extension and St. George's College Extension. First big success was at a youth show in Golden Spring where he read a poem provoked by Ian Smith's rejection of black majority rule for Rhodesia. From a Social Development Commission workshop in Jones Town, he was selected for the Jamaica School of Drama; his early years were part-time. Graduated in 1980.

While at the Drama School, Mikey became well known in Jamaica for his rendition of "Me Cyaan Believe It." Like Oku Onuora, he performed at the 11th World Festival of Youth in Cuba in 1978.

Mikey is the most oral of the five. Characteristically, a Mikey Smith poem has a musical structure that needs to be received/perceived aurally. What is printed on the page is sometimes very misleading, even for Jamaicans.

An interesting visual performer, he put his Drama School training to subtle use, flexibly varying his effects according to the mood, the audience, the physical situation. He has a distinctive limp, the legacy of an accident when, in his early teens, he fell from a mango tree, breaking arms and legs.

Records:

Word (Kingston: Light of Saba 1978/002) /Disco 45/ (reissued London: LKJ, 1980)

Books:

ed. Edward Kamau Brathwaite, *Savacou 14/15: New Poets from Jamaica* (Kingston, 1979)

Photo Credits

Peter Simon: 2, 6, 7, 8, 11, 33 (top), 34 (margin), 35, 36, 37, 42 (margin), 43, 44 (left), 46 (top left), 47 (center right & bottom), 48, 51 (bottom), 52, 53 (center), 56, 59, 62, 63 (left), 64, 65, 67 (bottom), 68, 69 (right), 75, 79, 80 (top), 82, 84 (top right), 85 (bottom), 86 (center), 89 (right & bottom), 90 (center right & bottom left), 93, 94, 95 (left), 97 (top three), 98, 99, 102, 103, 104, 105, 106, 109, 110, 111, 113, 114, (bottom), 115, 117, 118, 119, 122, 124, (left & center), 125, 128, 129, (bottom), 130 (left), 131 (center), 132, 133, 134 (left), 135, 136, 137, 138, (center left), 139, 140, 141, 143, 144, 145, 146, 150 (left), 151, 159 (center), 160 (bottom), 168 (left), 169 (center), 170 (center), 172, 176 (top), 179, 180 182, (left & center), 183, 184 (center), 185 (right), 187, 188 (left), 192.

Adrian Boot: 1, 8 (top left), 11 (right), 29 (center), 31 (bottom), 34, (center), 44 (right), 48 (bottom left), 51 (top), 53 (right), 77 (left & bottom), 78 (right), 80 (left), 85 (top left & center), 86 (top right), 88 (bottom), 89 (left & center), 90 (center left & bottom right), 96 (center & bottom left), 147, 148, 149 (center), 152, 155, 156, 157, 158 (top), 159 (top), 160 (center), 163, 165, 168 (top), 170 (left & bottom), 171, 174 (left), 184 (left), 185 (left), 186, 188 (bottom).

Chuck Krall: 5, 47 (center left), 81 (right), 82 (left), 168 (bottom).

Brian J. Gill: 6 (inset), 64 (bottom).

Robin Farquharson: 8 (bottom middle), 13, 14, 30 (bottom), 50 (bottom), 58.

Alan Reininger/Contact: 8 (bottom right), 42 (bottom), 45, 77 (center & right), 173 (right), 174, 175, 176 (bottom), 177, 178 (center two).

David Burnett/Contact: 8 (top right), 88 top left), 96 (top), 126 (center), 129 (center left), 178.

Rand/McNally Inc: 10 (map).

Jamaica Information Service: 12, 17, 21 (left), 23, 29 (top & bottom right), 32 (top).

Bill Newlin: 15.

Stephen Davis: 16, 49 (bottom), 57.

Jon Goodchild: (maps) 18, 21, 68.

National Library of Jamaica: 18, 19, 20, 21, (right), 22, 23, 27, 32 (bottom), 38, 60 (left), 71 (left).

Jamaica Tourist Board: 24, 31 (top), 32 (center).

Peggy Haslam Collection: 26.

Daniel Lane/Gamma: 30 (top), 33 (center), 61, 67, (center).

L. Charlton/Kingston Star: 34.

Daily Gleaner, Kingston: 41 (center).

Michael Ochs Archives: 46 (right), 49 (bottom right).

Kate Simon: 46 (bottom), 63 (right), 66 (top center), 69 (center), 78 (left), 81, 85 (center & bottom), 90 (top), 91, 96 (Center right), 97 (right), 121, 123 (bottom), 129 (right), 132 (top far right), 139 (center), 166, 182 (top).

A. Gorson: 49 (top), 76.

Kim Gottlieb: 50 (center), 79 (bottom), 84 (bottom left), 151 (center right).

Deborah Feingold: 52 (top left), 92, 134 (right).

Luke Ehrlich: (diagrams) 54, 55.

Abbas/Gamma: (diagrams) 54, 55.

Chuck Fishman/Contact: 71 (bottom), 107, 130 (bottom).

Kwame Brathwaite: 72, 74, 150 (right).

"Land of Look Behind": 86 (left).

Stephen Gladstone: 87, 138 (top right), 142.

Johnny Black: 102 (left), 138 (bottom).

Dennis Morris/Virgin Records: 114 (top).

Brian Cooke/Front Line: 116.

Donna Cline: 96 (bottom), 124 (bottom).

Jeff Roth: 127.

Patrick Blackwood/Front Line: 126 (left).

Tony Owens: 144.

Annie Leibovitz/Contact: 149 (bottom).

Gerard Rancinar/Sygma: 154, 161.

Camera Press: 156 (left), 162.

Simon Fowler: 168 (left).

Donna Santisi: 167.

Michael Zagaris: 169 (right).

Chuck Pulin: 169 (left).